Fertility, Health and Reproductive Politics

Set in the context of the processes and practices of human reproduction and reproductive health in Northern India, this book examines the institutional exercise of power by the state, caste and kin groups.

Drawing on ethnographic research over the past eighteen years among poor Hindu and Muslim communities in Rajasthan and among development and health actors in the state, this book contributes to developing analytic perspectives on reproductive practice, agency and the body-self as particular and novel sites of a vital power and politic. Rajasthan has been among the poorest states in the country with high levels of maternal and infant mortality and morbidity. The author closely examines how social and economic inequalities are produced and sustained in discursive and on the ground contexts of family-making, how authoritative knowledge and power in the domain of childbirth is exercised across a landscape of development institutions, how maternal health becomes a category of citizenship, how health-seeking is socially and emotionally determined and political in nature, how the health sector operates as a biopolitical system, and how diverse moral claims over the fertile, infertile and reproductive body-self are asserted, contested and often realised.

A compelling analysis, this book offers both new empirical data and new theoretical insights. It draws together the practices, experiences and discourse on fertility and reproduction (childbirth, infertility, loss) in Northern India into an overarching analytical framework on power and gender politics. It will be of interest to academics in the fields of medical anthropology, medical sociology, public health, gender studies, human rights and sociolegal studies, and South Asian studies.

Maya Unnithan is Professor of Social and Medical Anthropology and Director of the Centre for Cultures of Reproduction, Technologies and Health (CORTH) in the School of Global Studies, University of Sussex, UK.

Routledge Contemporary South Asia Series

For the full list of titles in the series please visit: www.routledge.com/Routledge-Contemporary-South-Asia-Series/book-series/RCSA

Fertility, Health and Reproductive Politics

Re-imagining Rights in India

Maya Unnithan

Routledge
Taylor & Francis Group

LONDON AND NEW YORK

First published 2019
by Routledge
2 Park Square, Milton Park, Abingdon, Oxon OX14 4RN

and by Routledge
605 Third Avenue, New York, NY 10017

First issued in paperback 2021

Routledge is an imprint of the Taylor & Francis Group, an informa business

© 2019 Maya Unnithan

The right of Maya Unnithan to be identified as author of this work has
been asserted by her in accordance with sections 77 and 78 of the
Copyright, Designs and Patents Act 1988.

All rights reserved. No part of this book may be reprinted or reproduced or
utilised in any form or by any electronic, mechanical, or other means, now
known or hereafter invented, including photocopying and recording, or in
any information storage or retrieval system, without permission in writing
from the publishers.

Trademark notice: Product or corporate names may be trademarks or
registered trademarks, and are used only for identification and explanation
without intent to infringe.

British Library Cataloguing-in-Publication Data
A catalogue record for this book is available from the British Library

Library of Congress Cataloging-in-Publication Data
A catalog record has been requested for this book

ISBN 13: 978-0-367-78660-1 (pbk)
ISBN 13: 978-1-138-61096-5 (hbk)

Typeset in Times New Roman
by Wearset Ltd, Boldon, Tyne and Wear

Contents

Figures

Preface and acknowledgements

The ideas in the book have had a long gestation and have developed from research first undertaken in 1998 on childbearing and reproductive health. I was completing an application for funding from the Wellcome Trust on a sunny April afternoon in 1997, just minutes before I went into labour at the Royal Sussex County hospital in Brighton. The application for fieldwork funding was successful and six months later I was in India with baby Siddharth and two-year-old Arjun to work on women's perceptions and practices of childbirth and reproductive health in Rajasthan. I was excited to return to India to carry out research, this time in an urban context. The voluntary health centre on the outskirts of Jaipur, a city in which I grew up, provided a perfect 'peri-urban' setting between the rural and urban to begin a study on how ideas and practices around childbearing were changing. It was also an ideal context to study the politics of reproductive health, rights activism and policy-making as state government and NGO offices were located in the nearby capital city. Having spent my early childhood in Jaipur, I had a wide network of friends working in the field of development with whom I had collaborated on earlier work and whom I looked forward to involving in the research. Their support was crucial in gaining access to health planners and policymakers in the state, and their insights pertinent to understanding the wider politics of development and its changing trajectory.

In the following chapters of this book I develop an understanding of how reproductive power and control as diffuse and discursive becomes 'real' and knowable through people's experiences of childbirth, loss, death and infertility, and in their quest for well-being, health and social justice. I suggest that the exercise of reproductive power and control is central to the making of the modern state and citizenship at the same time as it is constitutive of 'indigenous' regulatory institutions (familial, gendered, kin and caste-based). It is the navigation, intentional and serendipitous, of these normative frameworks that forms the core thread of the following pages.

The book covers four longer periods (4–12 months) and several shorter periods of fieldwork (1–3 months) undertaken over the past twenty years. The work began with a focus on household decisions around family making and health-seeking. This entailed learning about how expertise in health was evaluated, and healers and health providers such as indigenous midwives, healers and gynaecologists were selected. It led to an inquiry about what 'reproductive health' meant outside development policy manuals and to insights into the cultural understandings and practices linked to the (gendered) body. The way women and men coped with and challenged the stigma of infertility as well as their complex engagement with technologies of procreation and contraception was another important area of investigation. The pervasiveness of the fear of infertility generated an inquiry into the kinds of support provided by the state which were not focused on fertility control alone and led to a reflection on what maternal health inequalities meant in practice. At the same time the declining work of established civil society organisations in delivering health services to poorer groups beyond the reach of the state became apparent as the state itself became an advocator of rights-based approaches. Civil society organisations, I found, were involved in 'rights work' not just in terms of promoting state health services but also in redefining how universal notions of rights were taken up within health-based development programmes. A focus on the role of civil society in translating and mediating health rights suggested discordant ways in which notions of rights were operationalised in sexual and reproductive health-care programmes. I thereby came to understand reproductive politics in terms of the opportunities and challenges faced by health and legislative activists.

Despite my familiarity with life, growing up in Jaipur and my earlier doctoral research in southern Rajasthan (Unnithan-Kumar, 1997), I could not have written about the issues in this book without 'being (back) there'. I found my discussions with women from different castes and religious backgrounds who visited the heath centre revealed very different motivations from what I had imagined underlay their search for biomedical, maternal and reproductive health interventions. Until then I had little understanding of the role of emotion (as trust linked to intimacy) in influencing women's choice of healers or in their decisions of contraceptive use or even in terms of inducing miscarriages (something not admitted openly by the women themselves). The fear of infertility among fertile women, something I had not imagined possible, led me to re-evaluate notions of 'efficacy' and the conceptual hold that healers have in the region. Similarly, without 'being-there' I would not have imagined how easily women and health providers spoke about sex selection or how they enabled each other to access such services. Exploring the reasons why sex selective abortions were sought by pregnant women have led me to re-think ideas of choice and reproductive agency.

The intricate connection between kinship and reproductive health rights which emerged from the discussions with men and women around expectations of work, including reproductive labour and linked entitlements in the family, has been a theoretically exciting avenue to investigate. For poor families in Rajasthan, kinship relations still form the primary means of social support and maternal care. Kinship ideologies (as a system of ideas governing social relationships) and the gendered expectations and obligations that accompany it powerfully shape, limit but also promote the realisation of reproductive and health rights. Reproductive health in such a context is a favoured aspect of women's health as it serves to continue the patriline, but women's 'individual right' not to bear children, for the same reason, becomes collectively sanctioned. In a context where sexual intercourse does not result in childbearing these very ideologies also serve to deny women their sexual rights. A simultaneous focus on the rights work of an array of differently positioned actors: state policymakers and planners, health providers, lawyers and sexual and reproductive health and legal rights activists and scholars made the meaning of human rights interventions in this context more tangible to me.

Caste politics in Rajasthan has been the backdrop to the research with the two main political parties; the Congress and the Bharatiya Janata Party (BJP) vying for electoral support especially from the Jat, Rajput and Gujjar dominant rural castes in the region. In exchange for their political support these castes have, in turn, sought caste-based reservations of jobs in educational, medical and legal institutions. The caste basis of politics and the fact that merit is not the primary criterion for the recruitment of doctors, health workers and judges, for example, has significant implications for the level of the quality of healthcare services and judicial standards. On my last trip in early 2018 I attended several meetings on the judicial crises (actual title of the meeting) in India, convened by lawyers and judges on corruption in the judiciary and fears of it becoming a 'self-perpetuating oligarchy' (Bangalore, 2 March 2018). To be able to attend such meetings and participate in discussions was a highlight of doing the field research in multiple urban settings as it situated the research in a 'thicker' institutional politics of development.

The accounts, lives and desires of the Muslim and Hindu families and especially the women and young girls I met: Zahida, Vimlesh, Jetoon, Samina, Rashida, Sunita, Anita, Samina and Rashida among others have critically shaped my ideas and thinking as set out in the following chapters in the book. I cannot feel fortunate enough to have been allowed to learn about their lives, loves and hardships. Through this book I hope to pay tribute in a small way to their incredible friendship and trust amid forbearance in times of ongoing physical, economic, social and emotional hardship.

In India I am in debt to a number of friends and colleagues, professionals, doctors, health practitioners, feminist scholars and health activists for sharing their work and thoughts with me as we debated and argued over the years about family planning, domestic violence, contraceptive choice, sex selective abortion, rights of infertile couples, surrogacy legislation, the universality of rights to healthcare and the relevance of human-rights paradigms in southern contexts. There was rarely an occasion where social, personal and academic discussions could be separated. The boundaries between academia and civil society are fluid in India, and many of my colleagues have creatively engaged in work across these fields. The insights of those who are living the intersection of the personal, academic, civil and political and are thus 'subject-near' have especially been an inspiration. The contributions of Kavita Srivastava, Narendra Gupta, Chhaya Pachauli, Ginny Srivastava, Jashodhara Das, Abhijit Dasgupta, Aruna Roy, Kirti Iyengar, Shobhita Rajagopal, Meeta Singh, Renuka Pamecha, Prem Krishen Sharma, Kanchen Mathur,

Dharmeshwari Sharma, Mohan Rao, Colin Gonsalves, N. Sarojini, Niraja Gopal Jayal, Amar Jesani, Sharad Iyengar, Tulsi Patel and Sunita Reddy, among others, have been critical in shaping ideas discussed in this book.

On the ground, the research could not have been carried out without the invaluable research assistance from 1998 onwards of Vipula Joshi, doctors Bannerjee, Aruna, Bajaj and Hanuman Singh, nurse Sreeja, Rajendran, Anil, Ramachandran, Lohit and other staff of the Khejri Health Centre, consultant gynaecologist and social worker Suman Mehendiratta, Auxiliary Nurse Midwife (ANM) Sushama and digital technology wizard Bhanwar Singh 'Pappu'. Research carried out eleven years later on the Economic and Social Science Research Council funded rights project was done in collaboration with Sumi Madhok and Carolyn Heitmeyer. I acknowledge their contribution in terms of the joint articles produced. Special thanks are due to Pradeep Kacchawa and Manju Sharma for research assistance during this period and to Surjit Singh, previous director of IDS, Jaipur for enabling access to the Institute's facilities. Neelabh Misra, Komal Srivastava, Ajay Mehta, Aditi Mehta, Ginny Srivastava, Nandini Khetan, Renuka Pamecha, Ladkumari Jain, Harveen Aluwalia, Jyotsna, Poornendu Kavoori and Indivar Kamtekar have all provided field research guidance, useful advice and support and refuge in India over the years, for which I am grateful.

The observations in this book have benefited from and been nourished and sustained by the inspirational work and guidance of some leading anthropologists, South Asian scholars, feminists and legal and health activist-researchers: Marilyn Strathern, Caroline Humphrey, Ursula Sharma, Jeanette Edwards, Sarah Franklin, Henriettta Moore, Stacy Pigg, Kalpana Ram, Ros Petchesky, Peter Aggleton, K.Sivaramakrishnan, Marcia Inhorn, Lynn Morgan, Ali Yamin, Siri Gloppen, Sally Sheldon and Ruth Fletcher in particular. At Sussex, colleagues, members of the CORTH research centre, and friends who have provided intellectual stimulation and crucial support have been Gillian Bendelow, Hayley Macgregor, Andrew Chitty, Jackie Cassell, Vinita Damodaran, Ralph Grillo, Priya Deshingkar, Janet Boddy, Rachel Thomson, Maria Moscati, Bobbie Farsides, Craig Lind, Alex Shankland, Paul Boyce, Rebecca Prentice, James Fairhead, Ann Whitehead, Margaret Sleeboom-Faulkner, Hilary Standing, Geert De Neve, Jane Cowan, Pamela Kea and other members of the anthropology department. Elsewhere in the UK and abroad: Soraya Tremayne, Paul Hunt, Kit Davis, Karina Kielman, Melissa Parker, Kate Hampshire, Sylvie Dubuc, Claudia Merli, Bob Simpson, Kaveri Qureshi, Sangeeta Chattoo, Liz Hallam, Karen Marie Moland, Josephine Reynell, Alison Shaw, Bregje De Kok, Jane Sandall, Perveez Mody and Ursula Rao have all generously shared their time for stimulating discussions around research in this book in different ways. I thank Sanjiv Kumar and Josephine Reynell for encouraging me to write about the 'doing' of the research, which I have included through the chapters and in the epilogue of the book.

Over the years, I taught at the University of Sussex where I have enjoyed discussions with my third year and graduate students who have never failed to challenge the basis of my politics and ethnographic experiences through their own experiences of embodied power and vulnerability, and their own positionality as compared to the lives of the women and men they have come to read about. They have held me accountable on a number of issues, including on how a focus on 'poor women' is justified when it can also result in their victimisation, or on what it means to view birth through the lens of suffering and deprivation rather than joy and fulfilment, and on how the discourse of rights in development can also be about the violence of representation. Rachel Olson, Catriona Shepard, Padmini Iyer, Martha Newson, Rebecca Ashley, Sajida Ally and Bronwen Gillespie have all during their graduate years at Sussex engaged with me in one or another of the finer aspects of the politics of reproduction. I have also had the pleasure to engage with and learn from graduates visiting CORTH from other universities: Liiri Oja, Sayani Mitra, Sveinn Goumundsson and Miranda Marks especially come to mind.

I am especially grateful for the funding I have received over the years, especially the first field research grant from the Wellcome Trust in 1998 which enabled me to begin the journey into the perceptions and practices of reproductive health. A number of small grants and periods of leave since then have been essential in nurturing the ideas in the book. The standard ESRC grant (RES-062–23–1609; 2009–11) to understand how 'rights' were perceived and mobilised in the context of sexual reproductive and maternal health, and further periods of work in Sexual Reproductive Health Rights with colleagues from Harvard and Bergen in Norway, and further funding from the Sussex Migration Centre, Research Development Fund, Wellcome Trust conference and workshop grants have been instrumental in facilitating international and UK-based engagement and discussion on matters central to this study.

I would like to thank the publishers of the following journals and books for permission to re-use material from my articles: *Berghahn publishers for the single and co-authored volumes in the series on Fertility; Routledge including the Taylor and Francis publishers of the two journals: Culture, Health and Sexuality and Global Public Health; Wiley-Blackwell for Development and Change; the Journal of the Royal Anthropological Institute; and from Contributions to Indian Sociology, 46 no. 3 Copyright © 2012 Institute of Economic Growth, New Delhi. All rights reserved. Reproduced with the permission of the copyright holder and the publisher, SAGE Publications India Pvt. Ltd, New Delhi and the Health and Human Rights Journal*, Harvard.

I would like to thank members of the production team at Routledge and especially Dorothea Schaefter for her encouraging support ever since I first sent her a book proposal in 2008! My friend Anne Marie Bur has been a star editing companion as we 'parallel lap-topped' our way through the joys and suffering of modern-day publishing.

As ever, without the unflagging support of the home team and from relatives near and far: Sanjiv, Arjun, Siddharth, Gerda and Narayanan Unnithan, the two Vikrams, and Nikki, Andrea, Sudha and Sherry Kumar, without whom I would not have stayed the course. Arjun's genius with open source maps and meeting book deadline strategies have been invaluable, as has Siddharth's help with the photos. Special gratitude to fellow traveller Sanjiv who first accompanied me to spend time with the Girasia all those years ago. I dedicate the book to the brave and amazing women and men I met in the villages and *basti*, at campaigns, in CSO offices, in research institutes in Rajasthan, as well as to my parents Gerda and Narayanan Unnithan whose own social activism has been sustaining and inspirational.

Acronyms

ANM	Auxiliary Nurse Midwife
ART	Assisted Reproductive Technology
ASHA	Accredited Social Health activist
AWW	Anganwadi Worker
CEDAW	Committee for the Elimination of Discrimination against Women
CHC	Community Health Centre
CSO	Civil Society Organisation
DLHS	District Level Health Survey
FGC	Female Genital Cutting
FSA	Female Selective Abortion
GNM	Gynaecology trained Nurse Midwife
GOI	Government of India
HRBA	Human Rights Based Approach e.g. to health
ICMR	Indian Council for Medical Research
IUD	Intra Uterine Device
JSSK	Janani Shishu Suraksha Yojana (safe mother and infant programme)
JSY	Janani Suraksha Yojana (safe motherhood programme)
LHV	Lady Health Visitor
MDG	Millenium Development Goals
NFHS	National Family Health Survey
NRI	Non-Resident Indian
NRHM	National Rural Health Mission
OCI	Overseas Citizen of India
ORS	Oral Rehydration Salts
PHC	Primary Health Centre
PIL	Public Interest Litigation
PNDT	Post Natal Diagnostic Testing
PWDVA	Protection of Women Against Domestic Violence Act
RCH	Reproductive Child Health
SRHR	Sexual and Reproductive Health Rights
SDG	Sustainable Development Goals
TBA	Traditional Birth Attendant
TFR	Total Fertility Rate
VHSC	Village Health and Sanitation Committee

1 Fertile subjects

Global reproductive politics at the intersections of caste, class and gender

It is 4 a.m. in one of the biggest *kacchi basti* (informal settlements) in Jaipur city and Sunila is in the last stages of labour. She is on a paper covered mat on the floor of her parent's single room tenement. It was over an hour ago that she had been rushed in a taxi to the house of a 'nurse' who works in the Jain hospital 2–3 kilometres away. She was ill and so, Vimlesh, Sunila's mother brought her back to the *basti* and hurried to get nurse Suman who lives down the *galli* (lane) from her. There is an urgency as mothers of pregnant women do not attend to any birth work themselves, as it is embarrassing and inappropriate. As Vimlesh explains, her main task as a mother is to let the nurse attending to her daughter have the things (*samaan*) she needs. Chhoti, a close friend from the *basti*, is also called to help out while Nila, Sunila's twin sister, is sent off to another friend's place with their younger brother Suraj, who is twelve years old. Sunila's father, Goga, is away as he works as a nightwatchman (*chowkidar*), but Nila keeps him informed by mobile phone.

This is Sunila's second child and it comes quickly, shortly after nurse Suman arrives. Vimlesh tells her daughter to *himmat rakh* (keep courage) and so she does not cry out (I am told no one in the *basti* came to know she had given birth that morning!). According to Vimlesh, the nurse takes her 'beepee' (blood pressure; English abbreviation used), administers a *dard vali sui* (injection of the labour enhancing drug, oxytocin) and massages Sunila's abdomen with mustard oil. Shortly afterwards she 'catches the child', while the placenta (*olnal*) comes out in a further contraction (*olnal dusri dard mein aa gayi*). It is a girl. The nurse cuts the cord (*nala*) with scissors she has brought in her box. She ties the cord with a sacred red and yellow thread provided by Vimlesh, cleans the baby with mustard oil, wraps her in 2–3 cloths, and gives her to Vimlesh to hold. The floor is wiped (by now Nila is back and helps clear everything up). The placenta is thrown in the rubbish heap (*kachra mein*), although if it had been a boy it would have been buried at the threshold. The nurse is paid Rs2,000/- for her *akeli mehnat* (handling the birthwork on her own). Sunila's husband (*admi*) is back in the village and is informed much later in the morning.

(Fieldnotes, Jaipur 2016)

The baby is Vimlesh's second grandchild. Her first grandchild (Sunila's son Ayush who is just over four years old) was born at the same private hospital where she had her son in 2003; she tells me that a number of women from the *basti* go there for the birth of their children. Although she adds, 'we had only gone there for a consultation but then her daughter Sunila's pains started and the nurse and doctor 'told them to stay'. We ended up paying Rs4,500/- … this was four years ago (although when we had Suraj, my son, there twelve years ago we were charged 2,500/-.)'

As we talk, I am reminded of the time that has passed since I first met Vimlesh over eighteen years ago, when I had two young children myself and her twin girls, Sunila and Nila, were nine-years-old. It was a time marked by her increasingly desperate attempts to conceive again, with visits to faith healers of different kinds and private biomedical practitioners. She gave birth to her son Suraj 3 years later and we had marked the occasion with celebrations. Ten years later I had the opportunity in 2013 to witness her shift in social status from becoming a mother (*jaccha*) to becoming a maternal grandmother *(nani)*.

I ask Vimlesh to help me reflect on the changes related to having babies over this time as I know her experiences embody the tremendous shifts that have taken place in the way the residents of informal settlements (a term I find preferable to 'slum'), villagers and migrants have experienced childbearing and birth in Rajasthan between 1998 and 2013. In this book I use her reflections as a migrant labourer and kacchi *basti* resident along with the accounts of other long-term respondents such as Zahida, who is a Sunni Nagori woman living in the peri-urban margins of Jaipur city in Rajasthan, to discuss how poor families negotiate shifting institutional control over their fertility and reproductive bodies.

The dominant experiences of change which emerge from the reproductive narratives of long-term informants such as Vimlesh and Zahida, and their husbands Goga and Rafique, highlight new forms of community (caste, class and religious) engagement with the state, the selective but increasing use of public health institutions, the continued resort to faith healers as well as permanent forms of contraception, and the rise in prosperity among the peri-urban poor as compared to the urban poor. I examine these issues in the following chapters in terms of the views and practices of different sets of actors who also inhabit their world: state and non-state development actors, medical and legal professionals and health and rights activists. The reproductive politics which emerges through all these accounts is framed by highly pluralistic as well as increasingly rights-based and global, market-oriented contexts in which healthcare is provided and health systems planned.

The aim of this book, overall, is to demonstrate in ethnographic detail the unique theoretical lens provided by the concept of reproductive politics to look at the diffusion of global norms such as reproductive rights and justice and what these mean for the poor in northern India. It moves us beyond an understanding of state effects to examine how changes in global ideas about reproductive health have led to changes in the functioning of the Indian State and the implications these have for institutional practices and related individual experiences of birth, health and social reproduction. In this book we consider how, through the 'fertile body', people experience, accommodate and challenge the simultaneous controls of caste, kin and state institutions. Equally, we learn about the changing practices of these institutions and the actors themselves. In an era of unprecedented economic and communication-based globalisation and increasingly pervasive rights-based development paradigms, the politics of the fertile, reproductive body in India provides critical insight into what concepts, such as modernity, development, equality, citizenship, health rights and social justice, come to mean in practice.

A sustained and grounded analysis of the politics of procreation, which is not just about family planning and population control in understanding social change, has been lacking in India where political theory on state-power has primarily focused on the building of modern institutions and processes in terms of political office, political parties and coalitions, elections and voting, and on development actors dis-embedded from reproductive politics. While the connection between formal political actors and the institutions of caste and kinship has been the subject of academic analyses, less focus has been placed on the gendered and sexed body as a subject of sustained political inquiry. In its focus on changing living and marriage patterns, the decoupling of marriage from childbearing and increasing acceptance of non-marital births, fertility postponement, increased voluntary childlessness and the refusal to have undesired children, the Second Demographic Transition (SDT) theory is of importance as it takes into account the shifting social, economic and technological landscape affecting fertility and family behaviour, unlike the classic demographic transition theory before it (Zaidi and Morgan, 2017).[1] This renewed demographic theorising has engendered a process of critical reflection on individual autonomy and self-actualisation as being neither gender, context (historical and social), nor power neutral concepts in the times we live in. Yet, like the previous demographic transition theory it continues to assume similar processes and patterns of change across time, places and cultures (Zaidi and Morgan, 2017, p. 484).

The core argument made through the chapters in this book is about how existing and emerging forms of regulation of the fertile and reproductive body (reproductive governance) is understood through an interpretive lens, notably through the experiences of childbearing, infertility, contraception and loss. An emic focus on the politics of fertility, conception and childbearing provides a 'thick' understanding of the gendered and class dimensions of power as biopower and agency (as reproductive agency). With its focus on human reproduction, the chapters in this book take us into the intimate, moral and experiential worlds where power is mediated and negotiated within and across the household, family, kin group, civil society, development planning and policy arenas, health, medical, and legal systems both within the state and transnationally. Reproductive politics, a concept I develop throughout this book, combines the gendered struggles over the body (as a physical, social and discursive entity) and wo/manhood in the interrelated worlds of families, policymakers, state bureaucrats, legal, medical and health professionals and practitioners, as well as in civil society contexts in India. I suggest that reproductive politics is understood through the ways in which it is embodied and negotiated, especially by women who find their identities deeply entangled with motherhood and, simultaneously, symbolic of family continuity and state development goals. Reproductive politics is equally about men but, in contrast, revolves around their *absence* in conceptions of the reproductive within familial and state policy discourse. In their mediation and 'translation' of health rights, development actors and health workers, whether as men or women, midwives or nurses, or as members of health-related civil society organisations are critical to the performance of reproductive politics in that they broker experiences of citizenship and of reproduction and health as interrelated domains of power.

As the ethnography of the everyday contexts of people's sexual and reproductive lives in the book makes clear, the boundary between localised, centralised and more transnational forms of power is not clear-cut: state and non-state (kin and civil society based) institutions are experienced as simultaneously benevolent and coercive, welfare oriented and regulatory. Here, power is conceptualised not only in a negative sense, as against individual freedom, but also as positive and supportive of individual freedom.[2] This dual aspect of power emerges in respondent accounts in this book in both a negative (class and gender, discriminatory and exclusionary) sense but also as a positive force of change at different levels and in different times (e.g. the beneficial aspects of state health sector restructuring, the widening provision of services, the access to 'free' diagnostics and drugs, the economic benefits of cash incentives attached to maternal healthcare schemes, or even as the individual freedom from reproductive and household labour entailed in the transition from motherhood to grandmotherhood).

Women's accounts of childbearing, as we learn in the following chapters, are not simply ones of birth and family planning (from the spacing of children to the termination of fertility) but, equally, those of infant loss and often about the anxieties and realities (physiological, emotional and social) of infertility. In Rajasthan, northwestern India, where the ethnography is situated, we find that the fear of infertility affects *all* childbearing women irrespective of the number of offspring they have born. A focus on the *infertile* body, in particular, makes visible a politics which remains absent in more general political theorisations on the state and political processes of citizenship, democracy and belonging in India. The absence of any official statistics on infertility reveals the unimportance of the issue in matters of health planning. Given that it is the poor who more frequently experience conditions of secondary sterility, widely prevalent in Rajasthan (aggravated by the lack of access to quality health services), suggests that health inequities are systemically embedded as well as reproduced within governance practice. Paying attention to infertility in the context of a state obsessed with fertility regulation provides critical insight into the processes of structural violence (Farmer, 1998; Das *et al.*, 2001), whereby forms of governance come to reproduce specific forms of reproductive stratification (Browner and Sargeant, 2011; Inhorn and Van Balen, 2002; Ginsburg and Rapp, 1995).

The trope of fertility-infertility also provides a distinctive lens by which to view the complex power dynamics *across* state and communities; wherein women experience their communities as coercive (with an attendant social pressure to bear children to propagate the kin line, especially sons) and the state as distant and uncaring, reflected in the almost non-existent provision of assisted procreative services offered in government health centres. That a large proportion of women and men resort to faith and religious healers to address child loss and infertility speaks to a subjecthood formed in the act of fulfilling community and family, rather than state, expectation of reproductive duties and obligations. It also suggests the significance of examining the self as constituted through reproductive success or failure, and what body-self connections come to mean and how they operate in practice.

Anthropological and feminist work on gender and the 'body' has provided a critical, intersectional understanding of reproductive politics as experiential, lived, enacted, and of the reproductive body as simultaneously subject and object, within and beyond the material body and as caught in diverse though interrelated flows of power.[3] Such a focus on the body, I find, has been particularly useful in conceptualising how 'rights' are differently configured in everyday contexts as claims and entitlements (Petchesky, 1998; Unnithan, 2003). The notion of the body as constituted and emblematic of a collective relationality, as in caste in India (but equally in Melanesia as argued by Strathern, 1984), gives rise to different senses of body 'ownership' and claim-making to do with the body, especially evident around childbearing, infertility and health. In this book I argue that these indigenous notions of body entitlement give rise to conceptualisations of reproductive rights that are distinctive from more universal ideas of rights, and of partible bodies not mapped onto partible selves.[4] These notions pose particular challenges, I suggest, to the project of the development state which increasingly seeks to instrumentalise rights in terms of notions of individual choice and entitlement in its gendered reproductive health programmes (as discussed in Chapter 2).

In this chapter and the next, I deliberate further on the conceptual significance of the reproductive body in making visible a politics which has been absent in more general political theorisations on the state and global political processes (an area of emerging theoretical concern within the anthropology of reproduction; Browner and Sargeant, 2011). By way of background on the dynamics of childbearing in the state of Rajasthan in India, I return to the insights of two key long-term respondents, Vimlesh and Zahida. Their similar and diverging experiences of the changing institutional dynamics of birth set the context for the more detailed discussion in the subsequent chapters. I then provide an overview of the theoretical underpinnings of this study focusing on how practices of power, gender and the body are intersectional when considered through the prism of caste and class in northern India, but also are more fluidly entwined than current theories of intersectionality acknowledge (see Brunson, 2016, for example).[5]

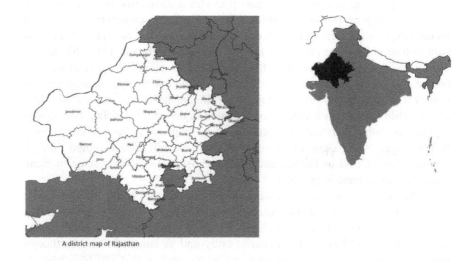

A district map of Rajasthan

Figure 1.1 Map showing State and Districts of Rajasthan.

Source: Arjun Unnithan Kumar, Python open source software, cartopy, accessed July 2018.

Note
This map may not represent the actual border of Kashmir, which is disputed.

Experiencing institutional change: birth as context in Rajasthan

> Not all the fruits that appear on a tree will grow
> > (Vimlesh referring to the loss of a baby in childbirth, summer 2013)

When Vimlesh gave birth to her twin daughters Sunila and Nila twenty-five years ago, she was at her mother's place in a *basti* in Delhi, where her parents had migrated for work from her father's village in the Tonk district of Rajasthan. At the time they had used the birth services of a *dai* (indigenous midwife). It was also a time when most births took place at home, in the village or *basti*, rather than in an institutional (hospital, clinic) context. Her experience corroborates the findings of the first National Family Health survey which documents that the numbers of institutional deliveries at the time were extremely low, accounting for 3 per cent of rural births and 7 per cent of urban births in Rajasthan (GOI NFHS, nd, p. 155). This was still the case when Vimlesh and her husband Goga came to find work (*mazdoori*) at the stone quarry in Jaipur in 1997 when they settled in Darana *basti*. Sunila and Nila were eight-years-old.

But by the time Vimlesh gave birth to her son Suraj in 2003, several women in the *basti* were going to private hospitals for the birth of their children; a time when the private institutions for birth were experiencing a boom in business. When Vimlesh and Goga had their son Suraj in 2003, they decided that he would be born in a private hospital (the Jain hospital, 'the one near *mama-ki-hotel*') for several reasons: the conception came after a long period of infertility (*banjhpan*); they were given to believe it was a boy (the sonographer had said they would get what they desired); and the girls were too small – there were no *sambhalne-vale* (people to provide care; a reason why women from the *basti* still go to the village for childbirth).

The early 2000s was a time when the central government was beginning to take steps to ensure that deliveries were attended by skilled (trained) birth attendants in hospital settings, marking a shift from previous maternal health policies which encouraged local midwives to train and attend births at home (Sheikh and George 2010). Following sweeping reforms brought in by the National Rural Health Mission in 2005, in eighteen states identified as having poor health and economic indicators in the country (including Rajasthan), in 2007 the *Janani Suraksha Yojana* (JSY; safe motherhood programme) was launched. The key idea behind the programme was to provide cash incentives to pregnant women as a means to encourage them to give birth in public[6] (and some privately accredited) hospitals in the state.

Implemented in Rajasthan over 2008 to 2009, the JSY programme was exceedingly effective in promoting institutional birth in the state, unlike previous attempts which focused on advocacy alone. Most of the interviews I carried out between 2010 and 2011 also reported childbirth in private institutions sanctioned by the government to provide cash payments. The district level health survey DLHS-3 survey (2007–08) for Rajasthan registered record breaking statistics for institutional births in the state, which were up by 40.7 per cent for rural areas and 67.7 per cent for urban locations – a truly remarkable feat given the fact that home births for rural and poor women had been the norm in the state since Indian independence seventy years ago. In 2011, the state government of Rajasthan won national acclaim for achieving the highest number of institutional births among all the states in the country as a whole.[7]

Members of Zahida's village in the peri-urban zone of Jaipur city routinely use public hospitals to give birth and more clearly represent the changing statistics around the shift toward giving birth in public institutions. Zahida, like Vimlesh, has been a long-term respondent since 1998 when we first met to discuss childbirth. Although she gave birth to her own children at home and in a private hospital, the younger women in her family and community of Sunni Muslims all now attend the JSY cash incentivised delivery programmes in the public hospital. Zahida suggests that it is because we are now in a time where '*pahele se sudhar ho gaya*' (things are better than before):

It is a time where treatment (*ilaj*) is free: 'SMS, Chandpol, Jaipuria, Sanganeri Gate, Satellite (all government hospitals and accredited centres) are providing free diagnoses (*jaanch*), x-ray and sonograph (English terms used). 'You just need to take your identity card (*pahchan patra*), especially if you are pregnant and need a sonograph…. My daughter-in-law got free check-ups and was paid Rs1,700/- (she had to show a copy of our ration card as proof)'.

(Fieldwork notes, 2015)

Goga, Vimlesh's husband also agrees it is a time of positive change, especially for men attending childbirth.

> In previous times I could not see the face of the baby or my wife for forty days. But now with women giving birth in hospitals, the nurse first gives the new-born to the father to hold and he can stand alongside and talk to them.
>
> (Fieldwork notes 2015)

Vimlesh is still wary of public institutions. She explains that government hospitals scare her because they find reasons to carry out operations immediately (*sarkari aspital mein jaane ka dar lagta hai kyon ki vahaan turant operation kar denge*). They put doubt and suspicion (*shuk, bhavna*) into you; they say the baby is *ulta* (breech) and then cut you and take the baby out (*cheera laga kar bacche ko nikaal dete hain*). I am surprised to learn of this new meaning for the word 'operation' (to mean caesarean section) rather than its pervasive association with tubectomies (female sterilisation procedures) carried out in the family planning drive in the late 1970s in northern India. For Vimlesh, the pain of the incision (*cheera*) of a C-section embodies the lack of any form of consultation by the health providers, a fact further reinforced by her own inability to decipher if the information provided is biased.

What is clear from Vimlesh's experience is that these new practices of 'safe motherhood' offered in public health institutions remain coercive and that although there is an increasing willingness to seek out biomedical intervention (and the nurse rather than the *dai*/indigenous midwife) these remain experiences of coercion and corruption (which makes a mockery of the rights-based policy shift to 'safe motherhood' as I discuss further in Chapter 2).

Despite more than six decades of the provision of medical services following Indian independence, most public doctors continue to assume that rural women are illiterate, ignorant of best health practices, and incapable of making informed decisions (similar observations have been made by Ram, 2004; Jeffery and Jeffery, 2010). Along with this kind of routine discrimination encountered in public contexts (hospitals, offices, educational institutions) the cash hand-outs provided, in reality, amount to little recompense as most of the money is used to cover payments to the hospital menials – sweepers, helpers and lower level nursing care, without whom it is difficult to have a clean bed or even access to drugs which need to be bought from the nearby medical stores. The charges are especially enforced on patients such as Vimlesh and her family, who are low caste Raigars. In fact, payments are implicitly acknowledged as compensation to the upper-caste care workers for providing services to those lower (more 'polluted') than them in the social hierarchy. Private clinics and hospitals, on the other hand, although costly, 'have no hidden expenses and are places where you are treated well'.

Attitudes on the ground to family planning have also shifted over the years in complex ways since the Indian state's strong drive to promote sterilisation in the 1970s. Sterilisation (especially laproscopic tubectomies) are increasingly being sought after by women who have achieved their desired family numbers and sex composition, a process which has become more marked in the period from 1998 to 2013. Zahida confirms this practice in her observation that women of her Muslim community now undertake the 'operation' as a matter of routine. While there had been fewer women of her generation who went in for a tubectomy, leaving this for when they were older and had 5–6 children, she says younger women are now taking the decision to limit their fertility after three or so children.

There is little resort to other contraceptive measures: 'In a hundred women in my community today you could say that 1–2 women go in for the copper T (intrauterine device) or use the *goli* (contraceptive pill)'. I ask Zahida whether the Imam has raised any religious objection to the increasing recourse to tubectomies. She suggests that the Imam disapproves, but that there is a widespread feeling that people do not want too large a family (*Imam sahib to mana karte hai par kya karen, jyada parivar nahi chahiye*). Young Reshma, the middle daughter-in-law of Jetoon (related to Zahida through marriage as her '*bua-sas*') confirms that she underwent sterilisation after her third child (a second son) – she had the 'double operation' (tubectomy done at the time of delivery by C-section) seven months ago. Although Reshma preferred to have the procedure at the private 'National' hospital (owned by a Muslim family) and paid for it, most of the Sunni women go to the government dispensary in the JG *kacchi basti*, 3–4 kilometres away. Zahida, who had by 2013 accompanied between fifteen to twenty women explained that the procedure is free, and the women were paid in cash (Rs700/-). As someone who 'brought' these women, she also received Rs150/- each time she went with them.

In my discussions on the desires for a changing size of the family, I am confronted by several paradoxical accounts showing that sterilisation has become popular at a time when there is an ostensible shift of state rhetoric away from family planning.[8] The Indian government, according to the perceptions of state health workers, has become more surreptitious in its support for a small family norm in its population agenda over the eighteen year period of my fieldwork.[9] This approach sits uneasily with the rights-based reproductive health approach taken at the International Conference on Population and Development (ICPD) in Cairo in 1994, to which the Indian state is a signatory.[10] The sterilisation focused population control approach had remained pervasive within even the rights-based health and population programmes from 2005 onwards. Despite the 'paradigm shift' brought in by the policy turn toward rights-based health programmes, for example in terms of having a choice of contraception, the state has continued to promote permanent contraceptive services at Primary Health Centres and sub-centres, and for the first time ever has also begun to involve the private sector in its family planning provision (as I discuss in detail in Chapter 2).

While the last decade has been marked by major rights-based provision and legislation with regard to work and employment, education and health (embodied in the Right to Information Act 2005; Right to Education Act; PWDVA, 2005), Zahida and Vimlesh, and residents in the poor, urban and peri-urban communities, do not really talk of 'reproductive rights' or even of the right to health when it comes to the state. It is in the cash benefits of an institutional delivery, rather than the access or 'right' to antenatal or delivery services provided by the state services, that women and their families perceive changes in the state provision. In turn, this has engendered a sense of their 'right to cash' rather than a right to health. *Huq*, or rights as Vimlesh tells me, is more a family/kin-land-property matter and very gendered. And when they do talk of rights, albeit in very singular circumstances, we find reference to *'huq'* cropping up in private clinics where doctors offer sex selection services to couples to meet the 'right' (as *huq*) of having a family of a specific gender balance. This suggests the complex entanglement of reproductive technologies with rights in the changing landscape of birth. While the advent of reproductive technologies provides access to medical technologies, which enable family-making according to gender preferences (sex-selective abortion), it also opens up ways of overcoming infertility, including through surrogacy (see Chapters 3 and 6).

Vimlesh and Zahida's childbearing accounts enable me to also get a sense of the skewed processes of rural and urban development, especially tangible in the peri-urban spaces where the research took place. Over the years of field-research, the households in the pockets immediately outside the city have prospered more than those in the urban *basti*. Samina, Rashida, Jetoon and Zahida, now in their late 40s and early 50s, all live in bigger houses. Jetoon's recently constructed house is a magnificent three-storey structure painted green with darkened glass windows and ceiling fans in all the verandas. In 1998 when I attended the birth of her son she lived in a two-room mud and concrete structure. Rashida's double-storey house boasts a washing machine. Samina and Jetoon have a car standing outside their house. All these women looked well and they say they now have daughters-in-law to do their work and can enjoy 'doing nothing' (no housework) and being grandmothers. Jameel, Zahida's brother-in-law, who used to work as a construction worker for 200/- a day in 1998, now runs an office as a property dealer (*dalal* – involved in the giving and taking of land, *zameen ka lena-dena*). The boom in land value and property prices in the peri-urban ring around Jaipur has made its agricultural residents, 'villagers' like Jameel, Rafiq, Salam and Asraf, spouses of the women I know, very prosperous. On the other hand, Vimlesh and her family and other 'urban' residents living in the *basti* have not had such dramatic improvements; they certainly have more gleaming pots and pans, a gas stove and mobile phones, but continue to live in the same house in a slightly improved economic condition than before. The disjunction in the livelihood trajectories and related prosperity of Zahida's relatives compared to those of Vimlesh and her family points to the skewed nature of 'development' in the region which has underpinned the prosperity but also reproductive well-being of their families.

Key concepts: power, emotion and agency

Situating power in the context of gender, caste and class in India

The understanding of power, followed in the book, is primarily Foucauldian and discursive because it enables a mode of conceiving power which is 'diffuse rather than concentrated, embodied and enacted rather than possessed, dispersed rather than coercive and as constitutive of agents rather than being deployed by them' (Gaventa, 2003). A key framing concept of the book is that of 'biopower' in the sense that it situates the operation of power in techniques of disciplining, ordering, ranking, making visible and subjecting to knowledge. I draw on Foucault's overall powerful framework which 'brings life and its mechanisms into the realm of explicit calculation' of the exercise of sovereign power (what he refers to as biopower; Foucault, 1976, p. 140), but follow Rose's closely related use of the term to refer to

> specific strategies involving contestations over the ways in which human vitality, morbidity and mortality should be problematised over the desirable form of intervention required, over the knowledges, regimes of authority and practices of intervention that are desirable, legitimate and efficacious.
>
> (Rose, 2007, p. 54)[11]

Conceptualised thus, biopower enables the exploration of power at several levels, across and not just within nation states (Hardt and Negri, 2000), as applied to 'development' (Ferguson, 1994; Gupta, 1995), in the context of health inequalities (Marmot, 2005; Popay *et al.*, 1998) and as interconnected with the practice of everyday life (De Certeau, 1984; Bourdieu, 1990; Fassin, 2004).

I use the material in this book to suggest that it is important to historically particularise and culturally situate Foucault's ideas. In India, the Hindu institution of caste functions as a mode of power which is discursive, diffuse, embodied and constitutive of subjectivity and subjecthood. Yet, and unlike the context of the emergent forms of state power in seventeenth and eighteenth century France that undergird Foucault's analysis, the institution of caste is not just 'pre-familiar' but also emergent (in the sense of being a product of colonial and post-colonial politics). As an ideology, caste, as constituted through the religious notions of Hinduism, suffuses everyday social and anatomo-political (in Foucault's sense) processes both of marriage, kinship, procreation and of the biopolitics of the state. Caste ideologies are particularly salient for the arguments in this book as they critically inform gendered, sexual, class and bodily subjectivities, and reproductive practice and agency; they serve to *routinise* inequality and legitimise as well as mobilise a hierarchically constituted social power.

A further note on caste at this juncture is to foreground the recognition of caste as a broader South Asian institution which has been constituted through colonial ideologies (Inden, 1990; Dirks, 2001) which in turn has pervaded the character of the modern Indian state and its political practices, including the control of women and men's reproductive and sexual bodies. Here it is Bourdieu's notion of habitus which is critical to understanding how different experiences of control accrete to shape individual dispositions over time and are transmitted through generations. The notion of 'habitus' provides a way of viewing caste and state ideologies as dynamically interwoven with class and embodied through an everyday social practice over time. Following Bourdieu's notion of 'practice' more generally, in this book 'reproductive practice' is taken as constituted by the interaction between the habitus and the setting of people's activities, or in Bourdieu's words as the relation between the habitus (as a socially constituted system of cognitive and motivating structures) and the socially structured situation in which agents' interests are defined along with the objective functions and subjective motivations of the practices (Bourdieu, 1977, p. 76). The notion of habitus, as Ram suggests, is particularly pertinent to locating class distinctions in Indian medical and healthcare practice (Ram, 2010, 2013) and, additionally, in illuminating the role that caste and gender play in such distinctions. While power works through specifically circumscribed sites: the body, the clinic – as Foucault demonstrates in his work on the 'medical gaze', the ways in which these sites are experienced depends on how the ideas and dispositions are carried over from other times and places (Bourdieu's notion of habitus is particularly apt, as Ram suggests, because it recognises the leakiness of both temporal and spatial boundaries.)

For Foucault, 'sex' (defined as a complex idea formed inside the deployment of sexuality (Foucault, 1976, p. 156) was a key arena which brought together the two forms of power related to the body (individual and social), and which enabled an entire micropower of control over the individual body to arise at the same time as it gave rise to comprehensive measures to regulate entire populations.[12] I suggest, however, that it is 'reproduction' (in the sense of procreation) that serves as a dominant trope of control, in ways that are distinctive from 'sex' in the exercise of biopower in the context of the development state in India (indeed reproduction is the means through which sex is hetero-normatised). For Foucault, on the other hand, reproduction only emerges as a salient focus of biopolitics in the context of the 'hysterisation' of women's sexuality. The chapters in this book suggest that there is an analytic dynamic salient in maintaining the distinction between sex and reproduction (much in the same way in which the case for a distinction between sex and gender was made previously by Moore (1988) among others). In the following chapters I discuss how the procreative/reproductive body (like the sexed body central to Foucault's theorisation) sits at the intersection of a distinctive kind of institutional politics (of state, kin and civil society organisations in India) operating within transnational fields of power, including the growing role of international organisations and trans/national/regional civil society working through mechanisms of development, legal aid and humanitarian medical services (Fuller and Benei, 2001; Kaviraj, 2010; Appadurai, 2002; Gupta and Sivaramakrishnan, 2011).

It is important here to note that privileging reproduction at the cost of sex is counter to a rising focus on sexuality following the influence of Foucault in the social sciences in the 1990s and through the 2000s (Herdt, 2010; Teunis and Herdt, 2007; Connell, 1995; Aggleton and Parker, 2010; Moore, 1988; Adams and Pigg, 2005; Cornwall and Lindisfarne, 1995) where less of an emphasis has been placed on reproduction as an analytic frame. The 'turn to sex' was particularly marked for radical feminists for whom a conceptual engagement with reproduction was regarded as participating in a project to essentialise the female body (by reducing it to its 'natural' state of reproductive function), leading to 'fixing' representations of women in ways which further patriarchal agendas of social reproduction.[13] To discuss women's sexual desires and practices, on the other hand, was considered by feminists and anthropologists, including those in India, as an exercise liberating women from the reductionism inherent in male-biased patriarchal views. If we track the conceptual work on reproduction on the other hand, I suggest that, compared to 'sex' which emerged as a powerful, political tool of analysis at the close of the twentieth century, 'reproduction' as a frame for analysis has been rendered a-political and conceptually less incisive. The resulting analytic hierarchy between sex and reproduction has not been without conceptual consequence with, for example, conditions such as fertility and infertility being disregarded by feminist analyses (Unnithan-Kumar, 2010; and Chapter 3 in this volume).

A critical body of anthropologists whose work has served as an inspiration for ideas in the book have situated reproduction at the centre, rather than at the margins, of social theory (Rapp, 2001; Strathern, 1992). Some of the 'big ideas' associated with ethnographies of reproduction in the 1980s and 1990s, as Taylor suggests, have been concerned with the constitution of cross-cultural and global inequalities, but equally have coalesced around ideas of relatedness in the context of an increasingly accessible and evolving array of reproductive, especially procreative technologies (see Taylor, 2004).[14] On the one hand, concepts such as 'stratified reproduction' (Colen, 1995; Ginsburg and Rapp, 1995; Rapp, 1999), 'pragmatism' (Lock and Kaufert, 1998) and 'reproductive margins and disruptions' (Inhorn, 2007), emerge during this period as critical contributions to anthropological and feminist theory. On the other hand, the increasing possibilities in Euro-American settings (at first) for people to engage in reproduction without sex, shifted the centrality of sexual deployment as a technology of power (in Foucault's sense) and prepared the ground for a new theorisation of the relations between power and the (fertile and reproductive) body.[15] Here, the theoretical concern has been driven by technologies which offer possibilities of reproducing without sex. While Strathern, 1992 and Edwards, 1993 chose to stress the role of the new procreative technologies in the production of difference with regard to moral regimes of relatedness (Strathern, 1993; Edwards *et al.*, 1993; Franklin, 1997; Carsten, 2000), others, such as Rapp, 1999; Lock, 2007; Inhorn, 2012, for example, used a focus on women's agency in the context of reproductive technologies as a way of rethinking notions of biopower and embodied agency. I draw on these concepts in this book and also more disparate scholarship on reproduction and social theory in South Asia (see for example, Das, 2015; Sarkar and Butalia, 1995; Jeffery and Jeffery, 1997; Van Hollen,

2003; Patel, 1994; Rozario and Samuels, 2002; Brunson, 2016)[16] to show how, for example, medical technologies are harnessed to socially reproduce caste-based kinship institutions and relations (Chapter 4), but are also repudiated and thus challenge modern understandings of reproductive health and biomedical efficacy (Chapter 3). The politics of procreative stratification developed in this book is informed by the broader turn in anthropological scholarship which investigates the social, political and ethical implications of the transnational flows of techniques and technologies, rights based discourses, and ideas of governance that coalesce as 'assemblages' (Ong and Collier, 2005; Browner and Sargeant, 2011; Jolly and Ram, 2004; Morgan and Roberts, 2012; Inhorn, 2012; Franklin, 1997), introduced further below.[17] Through the chapters I show how such 'assemblages' are also strung together over time and through shifting discursive and materialist frames.

Power, emotion and reproductive agency

An important dimension to situating reproductive power in India, which emerged during fieldwork, were the ways in which the exercise of power was constrained as well as facilitated by a range of emotional ties (of apathy, empathy or antipathy) between state officials and healthworkers and also between clinicians or community/family healers and patients. This leads me to suggest that emotion as socially constituted is simultaneously a technique of governmentality (as argued by Povinelli, 2006) as well as a mechanism for tempering power. As an analytic lens, I use emotion in this book in a social sense to examine how relations of intimacy constitute an ontological challenge to both gender-based expectations of the family and community as well as to the biomedical concept of reproductive health deployed by the state (especially Chapter 3).

Women's well-being is critically dependent on the kind of relationships they have with medical professionals, which is why most women in the *basti*, but also in the villages on the periphery of the city, choose their healthcare institutions according to one or two 'known' persons (a person who is trusted to take better care; Chapter 5). They fear bad treatment because of their class and caste. Their observation is not unfounded: a number of middle and upper-caste doctors in Rajasthan characterised lower caste rural women as 'dirty', full of bad odour (*budbou*) and lacking reproductive hygiene (and, more generally, as ignorant and illiterate). Lower-caste women, in turn, did not wish to go to hospitals unless in an emergency situation when all other options had run out, or unless they had pre-existing contacts with health professionals who respected them. Compared to private hospitals, public hospitals were regarded as uncaring, bureaucratic and inefficient compared to private clinics.[18]

Emotion as an analytical category provides an important framework to understand how and why clinics and hospitals are, above all, socially and politically constructed spaces (also van der Geest, 1998; Street, 2014). In her work on the subjectivities of lower class Tamil women, as shaped by their clinical encounters, Ram (2010, 2013) makes two important points which echo with women's experiences in Rajasthan: first, how class (and I would add caste) distinctions are re-established in medical encounters; and second, how the habitus (dispositions) of the classes are markedly variable, with the educated middle-classes being more attuned to biomedicine rather than indigenous medicine, even though a conviction in the efficacy of indigenous medicine exists across classes. The disdain for women based on their caste, poverty and associated 'ignorance' (illiteracy, including in matters of health and hygiene) has perpetuated a culture of callousness and lack of accountability in hospital settings.[19] Local myths and gossip among lower-caste communities, on the other hand, capture the extent to which childbirth is risky because of these provider attitudes (as I describe in Chapter 5). In childbirth, the story of the collective experience of 'having parts removed' without prior knowledge or consent was a major reason why women did not plan to give birth in public hospitals. At the same time, as we see in Chapter 4, patient-doctor alliances emerge around access to sex selective technologies, which are pitted both against the state and certain sections of civil society in the private health sector (providing an interesting example of what Rabinow (1996) has termed biosociality).

Emotion conceptualised in a social sense (Lutz and Abu-Lughod, 1990) also provides a critical lens with which to understand how the self is constructed beyond the individual body in contexts of child loss and infertility, where feelings of stigma, fear, intimacy, guilt and responsibility associated with childbearing pervade. In the various chapters of this book we see emotion being used as a political instrument such as in the form of spousal expectation and social pressure on women to bear children. On the other hand, its apparent absence (following women's acceptance of a divine cause of their infertility) helps them preserve a sense of dignity and self as defined through their childbearing. As Vimlesh explains more succinctly:

> of course we were sad when we lost Sunila's middle child despite all we did, but our luck was weak (*kismet kumzor thee*). As you know not all the fruits that appear on a tree will grow (*bel ke phal lagte hein tho sare nahi ugte*).'

In the accounts of both fertile and infertile women mentioned in this book, we see how the stigma women perceive, along with their intimacy with certain kin-persons, motivates them to undertake particular courses of action or inaction in meeting spousal and family expectations. The resort to healers in the context of their infertility, for example, provides some women with a sense of self-worth, as I argue in Chapter 3 but equally lends itself to inscribing patriarchal familial norms on the female body. Emotion as a displayed feeling is an especially powerful vehicle which infertile women deploy to deflect the force of the social and cultural pressure they face in terms of childbearing[20] and, in this sense, is critical to their agency in reproductive matters.

Emotion as linked to motivation (in Bourdieu's sense) is a powerful trope to understand how reproductive agency is imagined and exercised. The focus in this book on feelings of intimacy as a motivation for action in the domain of health enables a very different way of conceptualising agency from how demographers and development practitioners theorise agency, i.e. with regard to the 'autonomous' action of individuals as set apart from the collective of which they are a part (also see Townsend, 1997). When, in fact, especially in matters of reproduction, where collective decision-making is the norm, agency follows the senses of obligation, social pressures and advice received from kin as well as from one's spouse.

While I broadly draw on Giddens idea of human agency to mean, 'a reflexive monitoring and rationalisation of a continuous flow of conduct' (Giddens, 1984), I follow Latour's understanding of an *actor* as 'what is made to act by many others' (Latour, 2007, p. 46) and of *action* as something that 'is not done under the full control of consciousness; but rather as felt as a node, a knot and a conglomerate of many surprising sets of agencies that have to be slowly disentangled' (Latour, 2007, p. 44). Latour's understanding is useful as it suggests many others acting in one's own actions.[21] The acknowledgement of the role of the collective within individual action, especially relevant to the Indian context as we shall see in the following lines, also enables me to draw connections with the concept of relational autonomy (which reconciles agency with relationality); see for example, Manson and O'Neil, 2007; Thachuk, 2004; and Madhok, 2013).

In the following chapters, reproductive agency emerges as the expressions, desires, intentions and motivations, which underlie decisions to address issues of childbearing, which result in direct or indirect action or inaction (as a conscious as well as unconscious choice: Merleau-Ponty, 1986; Bourdieu, 1977; Ram and Houston, 2015). Reproductive agency in particular is seen to be reinforced by the emotions generated by social intimacy, affection, notions of reproductive responsibility, obligations, duties, desires to produce the appropriate sex and numbers of children, the need to allay anxieties about infertility, and the related loss of social standing and networks. Reproductive agency is dynamic and changes over the life course of the individual and in relation to changing social, physiological and economic circumstances – the thinking, feeling, decisions and actions which surround biological reproduction vary according to an individuals' shifting social position within the household, in relation to kin and associates, as well as with regard to economic conditions. Reproductive agency may be less in the early years of marriage for women, increasing as they gain social standing in their husband's caste and kin group.

A maternal-centric reproductive health and rights discourse

An important task of the book is to critically examine how ideas about the 'maternal' come to serve as a central framing device in state population, rights and development discourse in India. I use the term *maternalist frame* in a discursive sense, following Carreon and Moghadam's definition, to refer to 'elements of motherhood, mothering and maternal identities deployed to evoke meanings within a given context and elicit participation and/or support of collective action'

(Carreon and Moghadam, 2015, p. 19). The trope of motherhood has been much researched as an analytic device to describe women's role in the social and cultural reproduction of nations, the state, ethnic and religious groupings (notably Yuval-Davis, 1997; Kanaaneh, 2002; and others) as well as in the politics of social mobilisation and resistance (Carreon and Moghadam, 2015; Cornwall and Molyneux, 2008; Bernal and Grewal, 2014; and others). Here I use the concept to elucidate a singular kind of historically situated reproductive politics in India.

Women and maternity have been at the heart of the Indian state's development policy discourse on fertility and reproductive health from the time of national independence and, more particularly, from the new millennium onwards. The powerful deployment of regulatory maternalist frames in state and global development discourse (Grillo and Stirrat, 1997) is manifest at a number of levels: in its focus on reproductive health as primarily women's well-being through childbearing; in promoting reproductive rights as women's right to reproduce; in the policies and programmes of 'safe motherhood' as a means to stem maternal and infant mortality; as family planning policies focused on married women; and in surrogacy regulation which places value on the maternity of some women (wealthier intended mothers) compared to others (surrogates, Chapter 6). Even in the global Millenium Development Goals (MDG 2005–2015) the primary focus has been on maternal health (MDG5) rather than on the rights-based notion of reproductive health accepted previously at the Fourth Conference on Women in Beijing in 1995 (described by Yamin and Boulanger, 2013 as a drastic 'narrowing down' of the concept of reproductive health.

A notable effect of the prominence accorded to women's bodies in such southern modes of institutional governance has been 'the stabilisation of the category of 'women' within development discourse' (Menon, 2009, p. 94) driving ideas of 'gender sensitivity' and 'engendering development' to formatively shape development practice overall. One of the strands in this book is to examine how such frames are invoked by civil society actors and the intended and unintended consequences that result from an activism centred on women's maternal subjectivity. Moreover, as I suggest in the following chapters, ideas of 'gender as about women' and 'reproductive health as only about childbearing' endure alongside the ostensible shift in norms regulating institutional practice toward 'rights-based' development ideologies and practice.

Indian feminists and activists, especially from the 1970s onwards, have fought against the ideological hold that maternalist frames deployed by state development as well as caste-based institutions have over women's sexual and reproductive bodies. The prominence given in state development discourse to maternal health and women's rights has, instead, led to an appropriation of women's voices as well as their bodies in that, as Menon suggests, 'women are installed as victims and then spoken for' (Menon, 2004). The appropriation of women's bodies for furthering development agendas, as well as the need to mitigate the less visible forms of caste and family violence toward women, has been a theoretical and activist focus for Indian feminists. There is a significant level of physical violence, abuse and fear that is hidden within marital relationships, which emerges around reproductive decision-making and childbearing in particular. Everyday matters of contraception and the uptake of family planning measures may lead to family rifts and conflict. Fears of infertility, barrenness and the inability to produce male children all become focal points of domestic violence. The high levels of marriage payment in the forms of dowries that are demanded throughout the period of marriage, and despite the law against it, testify to the continuing devaluation of women and girls in Indian society.

Two specific and widely debated cases of rape, a most violent form of appropriation of (especially lower caste and class) procreative and sexed bodies marked important moments of feminist mobilisation framing the fieldwork: the gang rape of Bhanwari Devi, a state development worker in Rajasthan, who had been physically abused by upper caste men in her village in 1992 (Mathur, 2004); and that of the Delhi December 2013 rape of a medical student, who died following a violent rape carried out by young men from her lower middle-class neighbourhood. It has been clear in these cases, as well as in more everyday forms of domestic violence, that the trope of 'violence' has been an important means for civil society to mobilise support and solidarity. Equally such mobilisation has also lent itself to victimising the very women that need protection (Grewal, 2014; Menon, 2004; Mohanty *et al.*, 2001; Madhok, 2004; Madhok, Unnithan and Heitmeyer, 2014). Self-critical feminist activists, such as Flavia Agnes, 1999; Suneetha and Nagaraj, 2005 and others increasingly emphasise that 'violence' alone is inadequate in capturing the kinds of battles women face in the household and family which are located in the wider networks of caste, kinship and the community of elders. As a consequence, recent feminist thinking in India, with which findings in this book align, consider it imperative that historically rooted maternalist frames deployed by caste-based institutions are subject to interrogation.

The maternal and sexual in everyday social reproduction

In that caste ideologies, as internalised exert an everyday moral force to control gender relations, marriage, sex and birth, they become the most immediate form of maternal regulation. This is despite the fact that current forms of globalisation, economic progress, class dynamics and democratic politics in a liberalising India have challenged people's caste, kinship and religious dispositions. While there has been a delegitimisation of caste in political and legal arenas, particularly marked in the shifts in the language of political discourse and public institutions away from explicit references to caste (Beteille, 1991; Fuller, 1996), these 'modernising' processes have equally involved an essentialising of caste (increasingly rigidly defined by the scriptures).[22] And, as Beteille and Fuller suggest, while caste has gained a more egalitarian face in the public domain, including in terms of a reservation quota for women to stand for political office, it is the private, domestic domain which has become the main repository of hierarchic caste values and practices, with the community and family becoming the unit for the reproduction of inequalities (Beteille, Fuller, ibid.). Alongside these shifts are the different imaginings and practices of motherhood and kinship which have accompanied the global flows of technologies, bodies, ideas, policies and practices (Van Hollen, 2003; Ram, 2013; Das, 2015) making any general analysis of the relationship between caste, kinship, class, gender and power both singular as well as complex.[23]

Marriage and childbearing are key practices in the social reproduction of caste groups[24] (and in how sub-castes distinguish each other and maintain a hierarchy: Dumont, 1980; for example).[25] Women and men in Rajasthan, in lower caste and less wealthy lower-class households, especially in rural areas, continue to engage in and experience an unrelenting social pressure to marry and bear children. Young, urban, middle-class women and men who are in skilled employment inhabit a very different world in terms of dress, language, mobility, as well as their reproductive desires, imaginations and opportunities compared to rural (and often peri-urban) women. Nevertheless, structurally speaking, and across most everyday contexts, women gain social power through their reproductive capabilities and are at the same time subject to severe constraints (in mobility, dress, behaviour, for example) and social and cultural regulation as a result of their sexual maturation.[26] Certain social and moral norms remain axiomatic, as reflected in attitudes towards marriage. The young, urban, middle-class men I spoke with felt equally subject to pressures of marriage in the 'right social direction' and to bear children, predominantly leaving the choice of a spouse to their parents (personal interviews with Bhanwar, 2013–16).

This places women and men who seek to marry outside the caste group, whether through love or in same-sex marriages, under tremendous pressure to conform to the wishes of the family and community members.[27] While love or self-arranged marriages are prevalent in northern India, as Mody observes in her ethnographic study of love-marriages in Delhi, such marriages are regarded as aberrations, deemed to be based on lust but even more so because they are considered anti-social in that by ignoring the obligation to marry someone of their parents choosing, these couples challenge the cohesion of the social group and are disrespectful of the authority of wider kin, caste and community injunctions to respect caste boundaries (Mody, 2008, p. 18).[28] As Mody's work and other anthropological and sociological work on Indian marriage and kinship demonstrates, Hindu traditions with respect to marriage, as set out in religious texts such as the *Dharamashastra*, are more diverse than in popular discourse with regard to the form of marriage, e.g. by capture, persuasion, elopement (Vanita, 2009). In turn, individual choice and mutual attraction as the bases for marriage is also recognised and legitimised through reference to Hindu ideas of rebirth where attachments can be seen to be carried over from previous births, which are further legitimised through divine practice.[29] As Vanita discusses in her work on same-sex unions in India, it is Hindu ideas of love and rebirth which are drawn upon to support socially disapproved unions. For instance, the idea that couples may have been married in previous lives enables families to navigate the social disapproval, often conducting traditional ceremonies as a means to incorporate and 'adjust' bringing these couples into the familial fold (Vanita, 2009, p. 51). These adjustments are further taken into consideration within the Indian legal system where, for example, in the Hindu Marriage Act of 1955 there is provision for 'custom' to take precedence over written law which has implications for the way reproductive rights are legislated, as I discuss in Chapter 7.

Marriage as linked to childbearing in caste ideology is also primarily an important structurally determined route to social (kin-based) power for both men and women, through which they can expect to gain full ritual, social and legal status as adults. As individuals, men attain full ritual status before marriage (as in the thread ceremony among the upper castes) but it is through marriage that they are initiated into the important next step, as householders; the only means by which ordinary humans are able to perform virtuous actions and meet the *dharmic* striving for worldly goals (Madan, 1987).[30] A man's social status in society is derived from his ability to procreate, have children (to continue his lineage) and offer hospitality, all for which he is dependent on his wife.[31] For women, their devotion to their husbands, their sexual fidelity and their reproductive prowess gains them status and is intricately connected to a sense of self-worth.[32] Yet it is women, unlike men, who are morally and ritually circumscribed by the more 'visible' physical role they play in reproductive processes. They thus never attain an equal ritual or social status as the men they are so closely connected to, and whose importance they contribute so vitally toward.[33]

As fieldwork in Rajasthan made clear, childbearing and motherhood remain the dominant means through which a majority of women evaluate themselves as persons and, in turn, are valued by others. Motherhood remains a site for everyday negotiations, for choices to be made and agency imagined and practised. It suffuses the habitus, provides many dense points for socialisation, and forms the most potent form of social capital. It also provides distinctive and powerful ways of 'othering', for example, those who cannot bear children (those who are infertile), or of those who are beyond their capacities for childbearing.

Methods in entangled fields

The observations in the book are based on ethnographic field research on childbearing experiences, maternal health and reproductive rights carried out for different periods over eighteen years from 1998 onwards. Tracking reproductive experience over a long duration has facilitated a nuanced understanding of the working of power across time (following Scott, 1992)[34] and space, as women and men of lower classes and castes in northern India move through the life course and between rural, urban and peri-urban settlements.

A voluntary health clinic situated in the peri-urban area of Jagatpura, a railway town on the outskirts of Jaipur city, served as an excellent base to start the twelve month period of fieldwork in 1998 as it had patients from the villages bordering on the city as well as from the nearby *basti*.[35] Talking to patients, doctors and health providers at the clinic, I got to know of the diverse ways in which childbearing and health issues were approached and of the different bio-medical, social and discursive understandings of the body.

From then on began a long 'mapping' exercise of clinical terms and cat-egories, of local reproductive experiences and languages, and of how these were connected to the ideas of kinship, moral perspectives and the economic circum-stances of my respondents. I learned, for example, what the implications were of talking about menstruation as 'the cloth' (*kapda, latta*), of 'falling on the feet' (*pair padna*), or as the monthly emission of the blood of failed childbirth (*maha-wari*) or even as 'MC' (an abbreviated form of 'Menstrual Cycle', a popular ter-minology used by health workers). I learnt of how sex was talked about in the community, a shared, coded language operating among kin and friends often alluded to as 'bathing' (*nahaana)*, 'being happy' (*khushi hona*), and as 'meeting' (*milna*). I also learnt of reproductive conditions that were problematised and pri-oritised very differently by doctors and their patients. For example, even when the very common condition of smelly vaginal discharge (*safed pani*) was regarded as a 'normal' condition by the women, it was viewed by gynaecologists as requiring intervention for a reproductive tract infection.

Health professionals who were from the area and conversant with these local idioms were also the most effective in their treatment compared to those who were not (as I discuss in Chapter 5). The high number of nurses from Kerala, first observed during fieldwork, enabled me to understand why there was more scepticism among staff at healthcare sites about local caste aetiologies and rationalities in explaining illness.[36] But their own training and education also had a large part to play in dismissing local explanations of illness. In their contact with patients they often felt duty-bound to promote biomedical messages most forcefully (usually adopting a scolding tone).[37]

Caste and class hierarchies play an important role in clinical contexts; even though, officially, caste is not a factor in the recruitment of medical personnel. Most established doctors and consultants have upper caste and class backgrounds and have traditionally come from families who could afford to invest in medical education.[38] In Rajasthan, mainly the children of the Brahmin, Kshyatria and Kayastha families follow the route of medical education. Nurses, on the other hand, come from the lower/ lower middle-class and often from middle caste backgrounds.

That my main respondents in the slum and peri-urban settlements have been women from two religious communities – Muslim and Hindu – has been a ser-endipitous outcome of the initial fieldwork location, as the health centre was close to a large semi-rural settlement of Sunni Nagori Muslims as well as rural Hindu agricultural castes and later urban domestic workers. This spatial and social proximity enabled an insight into the extent that reproductive power and discourses of illness, body and health simultaneously work through the social and cultural categories of caste, class and religion. While Hindu and Muslim groups are portrayed in the health, development and demographic literature as having very different fertility patterns and reproductive health needs (where it is taken for granted that Muslim women have higher fertility rates and therefore require minimal contraceptive support, for example), field research revealed a more complex picture, including a shared culture of local aetiologies of body and illness, a shared knowledge of illness causation and health-seeking, as well as shared experiences of discrimination. Faith healers in particular symbolised religious syncretism on the ground: low caste indigenous birth specialists ('dai') would attend Hindu and Muslim births; cures from middle-caste healers and middle-class Muslim men and women were equally sought; and the Hindu *Nai* (barber caste) conducted circumcision for Sheikh boys *(sunnat)*. Local aetiologies of illness were also shared across caste and religion; miscarriages were attributed to *hawa ka jor*, the influence of powerful winds and infant death was seen to be the result of jealous women referred to as *dakan* (glossed as 'witch' by local English speakers). Religious differences were, nevertheless, also linked to socially distinctive practices which effected childbearing; for Muslim women the proximity and strength of their social networks *(sambhalne-vale)*, so critical to all poor women in the region, is a particularly distinctive feature of their social organisation which works in favour of childbearing women and their children (Unnithan-Kumar, 2001).

Field material used in the book is drawn from interviews, discussions, stories, narratives, life histories, surveys and focus group meetings undertaken in 1998, 2002, 2004, 2006, 2009–10, 2011, 2013, 2015 and 2016. The work on the childbearing practices of rural and peri-urban women, as well as men's attitudes to reproductive health, was conducted throughout 1998 with local research assistant, Vipula, an MA student in sociology. A high number of the over 100 women we spoke with consulted local healers, so I returned in 2002 for four months to work again with Vipula on the practices and attitudes of family and community-based faith healers. In 2004, an interest in examining how ideas of reproduction travel across the rural and urban contexts, and especially in how *basti* residents who were labour migrants experienced reproductive health, propelled me back. I worked with Vipula, as well as demographers Kirsty and Adriana, at the Sussex Migration Centre to write about the reproductive life course of the over 100 migrant *basti* women (and their children) we interviewed.[39]

The harsh economic and absent healthcare conditions in which childbearing took place led me to engage with civil society organisations (CSO) who were 'doing' something to support couples. Already familiar with a group of feminists working on the complexities of women's empowerment at the local research institute in the 1980s, I returned in 2009 for a year to engage with a broader set of CSOs working on health rights issues. Along with a small research team[40] I undertook work on the rights-based perspectives of members of thirty-four civil society health focused organisations, including medical and legal aid organisations. This was followed up by shorter periods of fieldwork on my own, with state accredited health workers and auxiliary nurse midwives (2015) and with local health centre staff on men's perceptions of their roles as fathers and husbands (2014–16).

The everyday field research took different forms and included accompanying women on their reproductive journeys from households to private clinics, government health centres and hospitals, to voluntary health counselling and legal aid centres. Vipula and I joined women on their visits to local midwives, family and community healers in their villages and towns, and to remoter shrines in the state. We interviewed male and female healers and health providers in clinical contexts and had countless conversations with gynaecologists, obstetricians, infertility specialists and general practitioners. The fieldwork with the research team in 2009 involved meeting with government health officers, health policy framers, human rights advocates and lawyers participating in civil society discussions and campaigns of the People's Health Movement on the right to health and for universal access to free generic medicine. This work brought me back in contact with previous colleagues and other scholar activists working transnationally and in international fora such as the World Health Organisation on global maternal health rights.

The fieldwork in these different, intertwined, locations produced observations not only linked to a specific place or group of people and ethnography in a conventional sense, but rather to what Merry has called 'de-territorialised ethnography' (Merry, 2006). The ethnography in the book goes beyond the 'multi-sited' to capture the transnational flow of ideas (as in the circulation of rights to health) at particular places and moments in time, therein 'grounding globalisation' (Burawoy, 2000; Nichter, 2008; Browner and Sargeant, 2011). Unlike previous anthropological research I carried out among farming communities in remote rural, southern Rajasthan (1986–87), the current work was

Figure 1.2 ASHA health workers completing the field research questionnaire.

co-produced and designed, especially where collaboration with health workers and activists had taken place. Work carried out by various research assistants that involved direct interactions with the women, health officials and public health workers, whose lives are documented here, has shaped the ideas presented in the following pages (as in Marcus, 2008). In some cases, especially with the research on the meaning of 'rights' with grassroots CSO workers, these entanglements have entailed the same individual as being both respondent and researcher.

Some facts and figures: the benefits and limits of databases

Health and demographic information collected through official surveys at the national and state level have provided a useful backdrop to understand the broader patterns and trajectories of childbearing, including the epidemiological conditions in which they occur. Surveys such as the National Family Health Survey (NFHS, see below) have also served as a comparative device in the extent to which the data resonates with or fails to capture the experience of the women and men I worked with. A survey of these surveys has further enabled me to gain some insight into how state officials think, perceive and selectively frame issues to do with maternal and reproductive health. These ideas formed the basis of subsequent interviews with state health and development personnel between 2010 and 2013.

The decade of the 1990s has been notable especially for the development of sophisticated health surveys by the Government of India, such as the National Family Health Surveys (NFHS, initiated in 1992) and District Level Household Surveys (DLHS, initiated in 1998), conducted by the countries' premier demographic research institute, the Indian Institute of Population Studies. The NFHS was an especially valuable resource when its initial findings were published in 1995, as it was the first population survey to include household level data on living conditions, food and health-seeking norms and practices based on actual field based interviews with the respondents. Although framed to focus mainly on fertility rates and fertility control issues, the survey generated important information relating to the more hidden aspects of health conditions, such as anaemia and child malnutrition (and related breast-feeding practices), which are the key factors driving maternal and infant deaths in the region. The more recent NFHS survey (NFHS 3, 2005–06), likewise, has contributed new data on domestic violence, HIV prevalence, male involvement in family welfare and attitudes to family life education for children in schools.

Data from these surveys also enable a comparative analysis of health and population trends across states and regions in India. For instance, Rajasthan is shown to have a decadal growth rate of 28.41 per cent (against 21.54 per cent for the country) which suggests that the population of the state continues to grow at a much faster rate than the national rate (with a fertility rate of 2.9 live births per married woman). Health indicators distinctive to the state are its overall higher infant and maternal mortality rates compared to other states (at 47 per 1,000 and

255 per 100,000 respectively at the time of research) as well as a poor sex ratio (926 girls to 1000 boys at the time of research. Further details on the trajectories of change and on child sex rations at birth are discussed in Chapter 4).

Rajasthan is among a handful of 'backward' or economically disadvantaged states in the Indian union (often referred to as part of a set of 'sick' states, BIMARU)[41] with the poorest gender indicators of development, i.e. literacy, employment, education and health. Three-quarters of the state's population of 68.5 million (Census of 2011) live in rural areas, the majority of whom are poor with little or no access to quality health services. Poverty and gender inequality combine with a lack of autonomy to underlie the high figures of maternal mortality still existing in the state. It is estimated that maternal mortality in Rajasthan is higher than the rest of India where one in every seventy girls who reach reproductive age will die from pregnancy, childbirth or abortion complications (compared to 1 in 8,200 in the UK (Kashyap, 2009)). Iyengar (2009, p. 273) suggest the trends in the Maternal Mortality Ratio (MMR) in Rajasthan varied from 627 per 100,000 live births from 1982 to 1986 to 445 during 2001 to 2003, with the major causes of death being from anaemia, unsafe abortion, haemorrhage, sepsis and tuberculosis, among others.[42]

Rajasthan, as Sinha (2005) so aptly describes for India more generally, is in a paradoxical situation where it has state of the art healthcare facilities at the same time as it has people dying of preventable causes (maternal and infant deaths being the primary among these). This is because the best services are concentrated in its urban and metropolitan centres and available through private finance rather than in the form of public services.

Health inequalities within each state are also significant and so the NFHS surveys carried out at the state and national levels were complemented by the tri-annual DLHS from 1998–1999 onwards with the specific aim of capturing variations across the districts *within* every state (the state being regarded as too large a unit to generate meaningful statistics to guide health interventions). In Rajasthan, for example, the DLHS 3 survey was undertaken in 2007–08 to collect data from over 40,000 households in the thirty-two districts of the state (with 80 per cent of these being rural households). Apart from data on the trends and provision of maternal and child health, family planning and reproductive health services (as in the previous two surveys), DLHS 3 covered the impact on beneficiaries of new programmes (especially the flagship safe mother and infant programmes, the Janani Suraksha Yojana (JSY) and the Janani Shishu Suraksha Yojana (JSSK) programmes), as well as the statistics of the new categories of health workers (the accredited health worker (ASHA) and members of the new health committees at the village level, such as the VHSC), which formed part of the State's National Rural Health Mission (NRHM 2005, operationalised in Rajasthan in 2007).

With regard to the quality of care during delivery, the statistics collected were not just on home versus institutional births as in previous surveys, but on additional categories, such as the joint category of 'home with skilled personnel' and the 'safe delivery' category (defined as a delivery attended by skilled health personnel such as a doctor, ANM/Nurse/Midwife, LHV/other). A significant addition in the recent survey is the category of 'other reproductive health problems', which, for the first time ever, includes statistics on infertility and obstetric fistula. The sensitivity of these surveys to respondents' lives can be attributed to the increasingly proactive engagement of civil society organisations in their planning and also to the socially sensitive training provided to researchers of the Indian Institute of Population Studies, Mumbai. However, even though the district level data has been more localised, it has been more difficult to interpret and synthesise, being increasingly regarded as 'unreliable' (Dreze and Sen, 2013).

At the national level, in 2012 the decision was taken to discontinue with the surveys as they existed. Neither the fourth round of the NFHS or the DLHS took place nor were the annual health surveys conducted, but instead an integrated National Health Survey (NHS) commenced in 2014 producing new data from 2015. While the rationale for the decision was given as a funding issue (the shift from a US Aid and UN agency reliant approach to wholly Indian health ministry funding) as well as one of integration, scholars and activists expressed concern that the decisions were politically motivated rather than based on welfare concerns. At a global level the push for data, especially in the form of maternal mortality indicators as part of the millennial and sustainable development goals (2005–15 and 2015–30 respectively), has had its own disciplining effects (Merry, 2011) as I discuss in the closing sections of the book

In terms of procuring information on caste groups, this has been difficult as no official databases exist – in line with the idea that the practice of caste is unconstitutional. This is despite the enduring social influence of caste in everyday contexts. Accordingly, information on the history, language and social divisions of caste in Rajasthan were gleaned from archival, district and other one-off social science surveys. In 1998, Jaipur district had over five million people inhabiting its 3,000 villages and twenty towns.[43] Sanganer Tehsil, where the field research took place, had 209 villages with residents mainly from Hindu castes, Jain and Muslim communities, but also small numbers of Sikh, Buddhist and Christian families. The majority of Hindus in the district are: Brahmin (especially Gaur, Bagia, Jagind, Khandelwal, Parasher, Pareek, Vyas and Joshi); Rajput (particularly from the Chauhan, Rajawat, Nathawat, Shekhawat, Chandela, Parmar, Bhati and Kacchhawa lineages); Baniya (Agarwal, Khandelwal and Maheshwari); Oswals (the majority of whom were Jains); Kayastha (Mathur, Bhatnagar and Srivastava); as well as Jat, Khati, Kumhar, Nai and Luhar. Lower castes, such as the Meghwal, Raigar and Dhanka, as well as Meena, were not enumerated in the available census information but were dominant in the peri-urban village context where the fieldwork took place and were officially recognised through caste registration documents (*jati pramaan patra*) necessary to gain Scheduled Caste quota privileges.[44]

A guide to the chapters in this book

The chapters in the book are not chronologically set out in terms of when the field research was conducted or in terms of the linear reproductive life course (i.e. from menarche to menopause) of the respondents. Rather, they work outwards and towards the material set out in the first two chapters, which provide the analytic framework and historical, social, political, institutional and methodological background to the study. Chapters 3–5 go on to challenge the institutional version of reproductive politics, health and rights set out in Chapter 2 from the perspective of those who are infertile (Chapter 3), those who choose to go in for female sex selection (Chapter 4), as well as from the perspective of midwives and health workers who mediate these rights in their work on the ground (Chapter 5). Chapter 6 discusses the commodification of reproductive labour by drawing on the recent legislation on surrogacy and the emerging discourse connected with this to demonstrate where and how state and societal control over reproduction coincide and where they remain apart. Chapter 7 focuses on the politics of civil society organisations who engage in 'rights translation', translating between universal and indigenous ideas of rights and as lawyers and legal activists working on domestic violence. Chapter 8 brings together the above themes in its discussion on the relations between gender and health rights and justice. Further information on these chapters is set out below.

The next chapter (Chapter 2) on State Empowerment and Reproductive Control develops the focus on gender and reproductive power set out in Chapter 1, in the context of state and non-state institutions, ideologies and development actors in India. The chapter is primarily an exploration of why the state in India has been especially interested in reproduction and how it has exercised a biopolitics focused on fertility control. We see how women's health is simultaneously caught in a web of institutional governance, politics and the workings of the development state, as well as by an international discourse on health system reform and rights-based discourse. We consider the means by which fertility and health come together in state policy and, along with education and employment, form a key site for development and the realisation of modernity. We also see how shifts in reproductive health policies (from those focused on fertility control to rights-based approaches to maternal health) become a way to understand the changing nature of the Indian State itself. The role of civil society organisations and actors in shaping state-civil society relationships especially in the arena of health further exemplifies this.

Chapter 3 on 'Infertility and Other Reproductive Anxieties: an ontological challenge to reproductive health' focuses on reproductive negotiation and claims-making in the context of infertility and child loss. Drawing on local aetiologies of the body and illness causation within faith healing, it examines the politics, dilemmas and moralities of kinship and gender at play in the context of reproductive decision-making in the family and household. This chapter discusses reproductive vulnerability in the context of economic uncertainty, including that faced by poor labour migrant families. It examines ways in which indigenous ideas of the body challenge biomedical understandings of reproductive health.

Chapter 4 on 'Sex selective abortion and reproductive morality: technology and the discourse on rights' uses the theme of reproductive technologies to discuss issues of surveillance and power in the domain of conception and contraception. Examining abortion and female selective abortion in particular, I argue that these technologies both reinforce patriarchal state power over women's bodies at the same time as they generate new modes of resistance and new alliances and subjectivities. The chapter shows how ideas of biopower are re-framed in the context of female selective abortion, where there is an alliance between patients and private practitioners *against* the state. Reproductive decision-making and outcomes are further examined in terms of the exercise and simultaneous erasure of choice and agency.

Chapter 5 on 'Maternal risk and its mediation: learning from health worker vulnerabilities' examines the practices and perceptions of health providers and public health workers in the context of a changing state and international discourse on 'safety' in childbirth and risk in the form of maternal and infant mortality. Based on ethnographic work with a diverse category of 'midwives' and health workers who belong to the communities they serve, the chapter considers what kinds of mediation take place between different (biomedical and indigenous) understandings of the body, health, risk and rights, and how this is shaped by the social and economic vulnerabilities of female public health workers.

Chapter 6 on 'Altruism and the Politics of Legislating Reproductive Labour: why surrogacy matters' discusses international surrogacy in terms of belonging, personhood as well as citizenship, and wider processes of reproductive stratification connected with the rise of reproductive travel. More locally and following a close reading of the surrogacy legislation-making process in India, it sets out to address questions about the nature of reproductive altruism, the commodification of reproductive labour, contemporary discourse on the meaning and exercise of choice and consent, and the possibilities opened up when reproductive rights are legally invoked through constitutional means.

Chapter 7 on 'Making Rights Real: legal activism and social accountability' examines the dynamic role of civil society organisations (CSOs) in translating, implementing and promoting rights-based approaches in India. In particular, it focuses on the language and legal discourse that has emerged in the wake of rights-based forms of development. It investigates why 'violence' has been an important, though limiting, legal and activist trope for claiming such rights. The chapter focuses on the practices of legal actors, lawyers and legal aid workers in a range of contexts; e.g. the high courts and family courts in 'traditional' as well as non-conventional settings, who are involved in 'translating' legal concepts of sexual and reproductive rights and the production of legal subjects.

In the concluding Chapter 8 on 'Reimagining rights: reproductive politics and the quest for justice', I draw on indigenous notions of reproductive rights and justice, introduced in the previous chapter, to reflect on what notions of plural forms of justice come to mean in practice. I combine Sen's work on realization-focused notion of justice with that of feminist and anthropological critiques of reproductive rights and justice to conceptually situate the idea of reproductive politics developed in this book. Focusing on institutional and community engagement with sexual and reproductive health rights frameworks in the global south, the chapter brings together the novel and critical insights of the book: on the relationship between justice and rights as locally mediated; on emergent forms of gendered politics of rights; on re-configured frameworks of citizen-state relations; on the collaboration and contestation between civil society organisations and the state as well as in relation to the communities they serve; and the place of health-related rights in the 'deepening' of justice and democracy in India.

We now turn, in the following chapters, to closely examine: how social inequalities are reflected and shaped through processes of human reproduction; how authoritative knowledge and power in the domain of childbirth is exercised across a landscape of institutions; how maternal health becomes a category of citizenship; how health-seeking is socially and emotionally determined and political in nature; how the health sector operates as a bio-political system; and how the diverse and trans-national languages and institutions through which moral claims over the body are asserted, contested and often realised.

Notes

1 As Zaidi and Morgan (2017) discuss the second demographic transition theory (SDT for short) offers individual value orientations as the principle determinants of a person's fertility and family behaviour.
2 My thanks to A. Chitty for alerting me to the implicitly negative connotations of power which dominate social science perspectives.
3 Anthropological contributions to thinking about the body as a conceptual framework have developed somewhat independently from kinship studies, and from the late 1960s onwards range from the idea of the body as template for social organisation and symbolic of societal classification and norms (Douglas, 1966) to increasingly consider the body as representative of the lived experience of the body-self, and as social agent (Csordas, 1994). Clearly in order to capture the kinds of experience we are talking about we need to go beyond the face to face and conscious aspects to include aspects of the unconscious, mental as well as in a bodily sense (and the phenomenological approach promoted by Merleau-Ponty (1986)). Bourdieu and Butler both have contributed vitally to scholarship on the body in terms of the *em*bodied and performed character of lived experience, body movements and practices or habitus (Bourdieu, 1977; Butler, 2011; among others).
4 This is not necessarily a Euro-American versus non-Euro-American distinction, as Greil, 1991 has so pertinently suggested.
5 Brunson's ethnographic work on family planning in Nepal shows how time, agency and feeling are aspects ignored by current understandings of intersectionality.
6 Cash incentives range between Rs1,100–1,500/- depending on whether women reside in an urban or rural area respectively.
7 This was given extensive media coverage and reported in local and national newspapers at the time with photos of trophies received by the state minister for health and family welfare.
8 State and district level health and family statistics also indicate that recourse to female sterilisation in Rajasthan went up to 41.3 per cent from 34 per cent in 1998–99 (GOI, 2007–08).

9 As is clear from the National Population Policy (see NPP 2000), an indication that the state's policies continue to be framed by a continuing fear of a 'population explosion' (Das and Uppal, 2012).

10 This is also the case as the public health sector is haunted by its past exercise of coercive family planning practices, especially in late 1970s when poor women in particular were identified as 'targets' to be sterilised. State coercion at the time resulted in a major mobilisation of civil society members against the coercive sterilisation programmes in the run up to Cairo and continues to this day as new programmes of 'safe motherhood' appear but continue to focus on contraception.

11 For Foucault the new form of state power (directed towards the processes of sustaining life rather than in promoting death, as previously was the case) was represented by two distinctive but combined 'poles' of political practice: bio-politics and anatomo-politics. Bio-politics was essentially about the regulation of populations by a sovereign power in the European context, combined with the exercise of power over individual bodies (their 'disciplining', which he labelled anatomo-politics; 1976). As Rose observes, the 'birth of biopolitics gave a vitalist character to the existence of individuals as political subjects' (Rose, 2007, p. 54).

12 Using ideas about sexuality as the bases for control, the state could achieve the dual objectives of regulating the social body and of disciplining the individual body.

13 See for example, Butler, 2011; Haraway, 1991.

14 As an independent theoretical concern for social scientists, human reproduction has emerged, disappeared and re-emerged over the past 4 decades. In anthropology it became a focus for social theorising in Schneider's seminal work on American kinship and the family (1968) but it is primarily in the 1970s with the rise of second wave feminism that a concern with explaining social reproduction in terms of gender and subordination in cross-cultural terms took place (McCormack and Strathern, 1980; Rosaldo, 1984, and others).

15 Morgan and Roberts (2012) make a similar point when they suggest that sex and reproduction can be analysed as distinctive domains in a context where, as Edwards *et al.* (1993) has previously demonstrated with regard to procreative technologies, sex and reproduction become separable.

16 Especially when compared with the more critical and challenging work on gender, sexuality and the body (Cohen, 2005; Pigg, 2001; Lamb, 2000; Srivastava, 2001; Boyce, 2007, 2014; Reddy, 2010 among others).

17 Ong and Collier refer to 'assemblages' as technologies that circulate across countries, people and cultures taking on specific forms as local ensembles and which 'define new, material, collective, discursive relationships, problematise existing relations and encourage new kinds of ethical reflection' (Ong and Collier, 2005: see also: Haker, 2006; Rabinow, 1996; Biehl and Petryna, 2013; Browner and Sargent, 2011; Cohen. 2005).

18 Often the same doctors who treat women in public hospitals, in a hurry and without due attention, become attentive and caring in the private clinics which they work in or own. General practitioners complain that in public hospitals they are deluged by patients but not so in private clinics enabling them to provide better care in the latter case.

19 This can be seen as prevalent in gender related development programmes more widely (Unnithan and Srivastava, 1997).

20 Ethnographic studies on emotion, where emotion connects body to self and is regarded as a manifestation of the embodied self (Rosaldo,1984; Jackson, 1989) as well as works on subjectivity and the somatisation of pain, violence and trauma (Das *et al.*, 2001) become key to defining reproductive politics as lived.

21 And through which actors are made to do things ('actants'). In other words, the question is not so much who is acting but what is acting and how (Latour, 2007, p. 60).

22 There has also been a comparatively recent emphasis on other kinds of 'substance' which constitute the material, tangible, visceral constitution of caste, such as 'on

bodies, blood, breastmilk, material goods, services, blessing' providing an alternative, non-Brahmanical and gendered register for understanding of caste (Raheja, 1988; Lamb, 2000).

23 As women gain reservation of 33 per cent of seats for political offices from the late 1990s, there is a de-coupling of public from private renderings of caste. As a social marker in the context of changing economic values and access to education, certain aspects of caste become less important (such as occupation) and others more prevalent (notably birth).

24 Most Hindu texts and oral traditions underscore the individual's duty (or *dharma*) or wider social responsibility to marry (Vanita, 2009).

25 While marriage and birth were seen as sites for the exercise of power in the earlier studies on caste (influenced by Dumont's 1980 work), the ways in which power was *experienced* in these domains and individually acted upon only became apparent through studies undertaken in later works (Sharma and Searle-Chatterjee, 1994; Raheja and Gold, 1994; Unnithan-Kumar, 1997) with a specific focus on the body and sexuality emerging in the 2000s (notably Cohen, 2005; Srivastava, 2001; Pigg, 2001; Adams and Pigg, 2005; Reddy, 2010). Similar practices exist among Muslim and Christian groups.

26 Their bodily movements reflect this control as in the covering of the breasts and of play with less abandon at menarche, and through marriage where the covering of one's face from relatives who are formed through marriage (and thus the shame of sexual union) is expected (habitus and bodily hexis; Bourdieu, 1977).

27 Most Hindu texts and oral traditions underscore the individual's duty (or *dharma*) or wider social responsibility to marry (Vanita, 2009).

28 Two important conclusions can be drawn from this analysis, that: i) love can neither be the criterion for marriage nor exist outside it; and that, ii) family making is not a matter for the individual.

29 The *Gandharva Vivah* based on attraction and mutual consent (rather than parental consent) is one such form of marriage sanctioned by Hindu divinities (myths and stories abound in the Mahabharata and Ramayana which celebrate this divine form of 'love' marriage). In Rajasthan, where most groups have historically claimed a social proximity to the feudal Rajput royal families, tales of love, war and conquest, and the bravery of women in upholding clan honour through *sati* and *jauhar* (individual and collective immolation of women) have shaped the social imaginary and discourse of caste and kinship in the region (Unnithan-Kumar, 1997). Similarly, in Pahansu in Uttar Pradesh, it is the Gujjar ownership of land affording them a ritual pre-eminence in gifting relationships that has determined the local social hierarchy (Raheja, 1988). Raheja's work follows in the footsteps of scholars such as Marriott and Hocart (see Quigley, 1993) for whom it was not purity and pollution but the maintenance of subordination through transactions which was the key to caste hierarchy.

30 The home, as Madan points out, is the prime location for ordered social conduct relating to life-cycle rituals, and I suggest, the means by which social relatedness and identity is conferred and experienced. For, 'it is here that the three fires of domestic life burn: ... the fire in the hearth, the fire lit periodically to perform rituals ... and the fire in one's body' (Madan, 1987, p. 34).

31 Hypergamous marriage in the right 'social direction' or marriage of the bride 'upwards' (*anuloma*) in the social hierarchy is perceived as enabling the father of the bride to ritually conclude his obligations toward his daughter (as guardian of her (sexual) purity and honour). In addition, in being able to 'gift' his pure (virginal) daughter without any thought of the return (*kanyadan*) the father in turn gains merit (*punya*) for his actions.

32 The female principle in Hinduism is accredited with both an autonomous and a destructive aspect which signals the power of mature women to act alone, at the same time pointing to the dangerous potential of such action. Unmarried Goddesses are

depicted as more violent and destructive than married Goddesses. In human society, this has been conceptualised in terms of the dangers surrounding the rampant sexuality of single, mature women reflecting the societal inability to harness their sexuality in the 'appropriate' manner. The co-significance of the male and female principles is also manifest in temples and shrines where icons of male deities are present alongside female deities. In southern Rajasthan male and female deities 'sit' alongside each other, as do the priests who serve them at public shrines (here the *mata* and *baosi* are regarded as brother and sister). The same is seen in household shrines where the *kuldevi* (literally, clan mother) and *baosi* (Bhairu) coexist to protect the interests of the family and lineage (Kakar, 1981; Kothari, 1982; Unnithan-Kumar, 1997). In certain cases, the co-presence and conjugality of the celestial couples is a central theme of daily ritual (for example in Saivite temples in Tamil Nadu and Kerala; Fuller, 1992) pointing toward the significance of regular sexual and ritual relationships between them as a means of preservation of the cosmos and by extension, of the social order.

33 The fact that wives are regarded as subordinate to their husbands (whom they must worship as gods) and yet without them their husband is not regarded as socially complete, reflects a wider principle within Hinduism where male divine authority is never regarded as complete without the complementary presence of a female principle. In religious as well as caste (especially Brahamanical) ideology and practice, male authority, sexuality and related patrilineal descent are regarded as primary and celebrated. In fact, male authority is seen to derive from female power (*shakti*) and thus while being regarded as supreme cannot stand alone from it.

34 I am mindful, following feminist historian Scott, that 'it is not individuals who have experience but subjects who are constituted through experience' (Scott, 1992, p. 26).

35 A fieldwork grant from the Wellcome Trust greatly facilitated the in-depth engagement I was able to have.

36 There has been a historical predominance of Malayali nurses in the health-sector in Rajasthan as elsewhere in the country (based on the preference for competent health personnel coming from the state of Kerala where education has been more widespread across classes and castes), although this is set to change as they take up jobs transnationally (in places such as the Middle East and the UK). This has led to more locally residing women being trained as nurses (further embedding caste hierarchies).

37 A fact observed especially in the context of midwifery and childbirth services across North and South India (for example, Jeffery and Jeffery, 1997; Van Hollen, 2003). In Rajasthan, the local nurses who were usually educated till class ten came from middle caste and class Hindu households. More recently, with rising immigration to the gulf countries, there has been an increase in the local recruitment of nurses (nurses from Punjab and Bihar as well as Rajasthan although government statistics show a deficit in numbers of health workers).

38 More recently, post-independence, with the quotas through the reservation policies for medical students since the 1970s, a rising number of medical students come from poorer and lower caste backgrounds. However, they are still in a minority and their recruitment remains mired in debates around positive discrimination and whether caste affiliation rather than merit underscores their abilities. The entry of students through reserved seats in medical colleges is the subject of debate as they are chosen for their caste background rather than their capability, knowledge and expertise. See Venkatesan's account of the 2006 agitation following the introduction of a 27 per cent reservation for Other Backward Castes in centrally funded institutions across the country, and the historical precedents to the medical students' and doctors' response to this measure (Venkatesan, in Sheikh and George eds, 2010).

39 Unnithan, M., McNay, K., and Castaldo, A., 2008. Women's Migration, Urban Poverty and Child health in Rajasthan. In *Migration DRC WP-T26, sussex.ac.uk/migrationdrc.org*

40 The team comprised of Pradeep Kacchawa an Indian doctoral research assistant and Carolyn Heitmeyer from the UK as a postdoctoral fellow on the project.
41 The term 'BIMARU' (*bimar* meaning 'sick' in Hindi) was coined by leading demographer Ashish Bose in the mid-1980s to refer to the states of Bihar, Madhya Pradesh, Rajasthan and Uttar Pradesh, whose development indicators were considerably lower than those of other states in India. (Written communication with Abhijit Das May 2011).
42 They also suggest that high fertility patterns (4.6 for rural women: Government of India DLHS 3, 2007–08) increase the lifetime risk of maternal death.
43 This is a significant albeit small proportion of the 40,000 villages in the state as a whole. The district was divided into seventeen tehsils each governed by a panchayat samiti (local administrative body) concerned with the jurisdiction of a specified number of villages.
44 The Meena have particularly been a historically dominant group in the Jaipur region and the district was until the early twelfth century partly held by Minas and partly by Rajputs of the Badgujar clan. The Minas were removed from power by the Kacchawa Rajputs who then gained ascendance over the Jaipur principality and ruled until independence in 1947.

Bibliography

Adams, V. and Pigg, S. eds., 2005. *Sex in Development: Science, Sexuality, and Morality in Global Perspective.* Durham: Duke University Press

Aggleton, P. and Parker, R. eds., 2010. *Routledge Handbook of Sexuality, Health and Rights.* London: Routledge

Agnes, F., 1999. *Law and Gender Inequality.* Oxford University Press: India

Appadurai, A. Deep democracy: Urban governmentality and the horizon of politics. *Public Culture* 14, no. 1 (2002): 21–47

Bernal, V. and Grewal, I., eds. 2014. *Theorising NGOs: States, Feminisms and Neoliberalism.* Durham: Duke University Press

Beteille, A., 1991. *Society and Politics in India: essays in a comparative perspective.* London: Athlone Press

Biehl, J., and Petryna, A. 2013. *When people come first: critical studies in global health.* Princeton: Princeton University Press

Bourdieu, P., 1977 *Outline of a Theory of Practice.* Cambridge University Press

Bourdieu, P., 1990. *The Logic of Practice.* Translated by Richard Nice. Stanford University Press

Boyce, P., 'Conceiving kothis': men who have sex with men in India and the cultural subject of HIV prevention. *Medical Anthropology: Cross-Cultural Studies in Health and Illness* 26, no. 2 (2007): 175–203

Boyce, P., Desirable rights: same sex sexual subjectivity, social transformation, global flows and boundaries – in India and beyond. In Unnithan, M., and Pigg, S. L., eds. *Justice, Sexual and Reproductive Health Rights – Tracking the Relationship.* Special symposium of the journal *Culture, Health and Sexuality* 16, no's 9–10 (2014): 1201–5

Browner, C. and Sargent, C., 2011. *Reproduction, Globalisation and the State: new theoretical and ethnographic perspectives.* Durham: Duke University Press

Brunson, J., 2016. *Planning Families in Nepal: global and local projects of reproduction.* Rutgers: New Brunswick

Burawoy, M., 2000. *Global Ethnography: Forces, connections and imaginations in a postmodern world.* Berkeley. University of California Press

Butler, J., 2011. *Bodies that Matter: On the discursive limits of sex*. London: Routledge

Carreon, M.E. and Moghadam, V.M., Resistance is fertile: Revisiting maternalist frames across cases of women's mobilisation. *Women's Studies International Forum* 51 (2015): 19–30

Carsten, J., 2000 *Cultures of relatedness: new approaches to the study of kinship*. Cambridge University Press

Cohen, L., 2005. The Kothi Wars: Aids cosmopolitanism and the morality of classification. In Adams, V. and Pigg, S., eds. *Sex in Development: Science, Sexuality and Morality in Global Perspective*. Durham: Duke University Press

Colen, S., 1995. 'Like a Mother to Them': Stratified Reproduction and West Indian Childcare Workers and Employers in New York. In Ginsburg, F. and Rapp, R., eds. *Conceiving the New World Order: The Global Politics of Reproduction*. Berkeley: University of California Press, 78–102

Connell, R.W., 1995. *Masculinities*. Cambridge: Polity Press

Cornwall, A. and Molyneux, M., eds. 2008. *The Politics of Rights: dilemmas for feminist practice*. London: Routledge

Cornwall, A., and Lindisfarne, N., eds. 1995. *Dislocating Masculinities: Comparative Ethnographies*. London: Routledge

Csordas, T. ed. 1994. *Embodiment and Experience: The existential ground of culture and self*. Cambridge University Press

Das, V., 2015. *Affliction: Health, Disease, Poverty*. New York: Fordham University Press

Das, V., Kleinman, A., Lock, M., Ramphele, M., Reynolds, P. 2001. *Remaking a World: Violence, Social Suffering, and Recovery*. Berkeley: University of California Press

De Certeau, M., 1984. *The Practice of Everyday Life*. Berkeley: University of California Press

Dirks, N., 2001. *Castes of Mind: colonialism and the making of modern India*. Princeton University Press

Douglas, M., 1966 *Purity and Danger: An Analysis of Concepts of Pollution and Taboo*. London: Routledge

Dreze, J and Sen, A., 2013. *An uncertain glory: India and its contradictions*. New Delhi: Allen Lane, Penguin Group

Dumont, L., 1980. *Homo hierarchicus: the caste system and its implications*. University of Chicago Press

Edwards, J., Franklin, S., Hirsch, E., Price, F. and Strathern, M. eds. 1993. *Technologies of Procreation: Kinship in the Age of Assisted Conception*. London and NY: Routledge

Farmer, P., 1998. *Infections and Inequalities*. Berkeley: University of California Press

Fassin, D., 2004. Social Illegitimacy as a Foundation of Health Inequality: how the political treatment of immigrants illuminates a French paradox. In Castro, A. and Singer, M. eds. *Unhealthy health policy: a critical anthropological examination*. Walnut Creek CA: Altamira Press, 203–14

Ferguson, J., 1994. *The Anti-Politics Machine: Development, De-politicisation and Bureaucratic Power in Lesotho*. University of Minnesota Press

Foucault, M. 1976 (1988). *The History of Sexuality Volume 1: The Will to Knowledge*. London: Penguin

Franklin, S., 1997. *Embodied Progress: A Cultural Account of Assisted Conception*. London: Routledge

Fuller, C. and Bénéï, V., eds. 2001. *The everyday state and society in modern India*. London: C. Hurst and Co.

Fuller, C., 1992. *The Camphor flame: popular Hinduism and society in India.* Princeton University Press.

Fuller, C., 1996. *Caste Today.* Delhi: Oxford University Press

Gaventa, J., 2003. *Power after Lukes: An overview of theories of power since Lukes and their application to development.* Accessed on 29th October 2012 at www.powercube. net/wp-content/uploads/n/power-after-lukes.pdf

Giddens, A., 1984. *The Constitution of Society: Outline of the Theory of Structuration.* Cambridge: Polity Press

Ginsburg, F and R. Rapp, 1995, *Conceiving the New World Order: The Global Politics of Reproduction.* Berkeley: University of California Press

Government of India, 2007–08. DLHS (District Level Household and Facility Survey) 3. Rajasthan. Ministry of Health and Family Welfare. http://rchiips.org/pdf/rch3/report/ RJ.pdf

Government of India, Ministry of Health and Family Welfare. NRHM, not dated. www. mohfw.nic.in/NRHM/Documents/Mission_Document.pdf (accessed 11 November 2010).

Grewal, I., 2014. Introduction. In Bernal, V. and Grewal, eds. I., 2014. *Theorising NGOs: States, Feminisms and Neoliberalism.* Durham: Duke University Press

Greil, A., 1991. *Not yet pregnant: Infertile couples in contemporary America.* New Brunswick NJ: Rutgers University Press

Grillo, R and Stirrat, R.L., 1997. *Discourses of Development: Anthropological Perspectives.* Oxford: Berg.

Gupta, A and Sivaramakrishnan, K., 2011. *The State in India after liberalisation: interdisciplinary perspectives.* London: Routledge

Gupta, A., Blurred boundaries: the discourse of corruption, the culture of politics and the imagined state. *American Ethnologist* 22, no. 2 (1995): 375–402

Haker, H., 2006. Reproductive autonomy in light of responsible parenthood: with new science comes the need for a new ethical discourse. Retrieved 14 May 2011, from www.hds.harvard.edu/news/bulletin_mag/articles/34-1_haker.html

Haraway, D., 1991. *Simian, Cyborgs and Women: The reinvention of nature.* London: Routledge

Hardt, M., and Negri, A., 2000. *Empire.* Harvard University Press

Herdt, G., 2010. Anthropological Foundations of Sexuality, Health and Rights. In Aggleton, P. and Parker, R. eds., *Routledge Handbook of Sexuality, Health and Rights.* London: Routledge

Inden, R., 1990. *Imagining India* Oxford: Blackwell

Inhorn, M., 2012. *The New Arab Man: Emergent Masculinities, Technologies and Islam in the Middle East.* Princeton University Press

Inhorn, M., ed. 2007. *Reproductive Disruptions.* Oxford: Berghahn

Inhorn, M., and Van Balen, F., 2002. *Infertility around the Globe: New thinking on childlessness, gender and reproductive technologies.* Berkeley: University of California Press

Iyengar, S., Iyengar K. and Gupta, V. Maternal Health: A Case Study of Rajasthan. *Journal of Health, Population and Nutrition* 2 (2009): 271–92.

Jackson, M., 1989. *Path toward a clearing: Radical Empiricism and Ethnographic Inquiry.* John Wiley and Sons

Jeffery, R., and Jeffery, P., eds., 1997. *Population, Gender and Politics: Demographic Change in Rural India.* Cambridge University Press

Jeffery, P., and Jeffery R. Only when the boat has started sinking: A maternal death in rural North India. *Social Science and Medicine* 71 (2010):1171–1718

Jolly, M. and Ram, K., eds. 2004. *Borders of Being: Citizenship, Fertility and Sexuality in Asia and the Pacific.* Ann Arbor: University of Michigan Press

Kakar, S., 1981. *The Inner world: A psychoanalytic study of childhood and society in India.* Delhi: Oxford University Press.

Kanaaneh, R., 2002. *Birthing the Nation: Strategies of Palestinian Women in Israel.* Berkeley: University of California Press

Kashyap, A., 2009. *No Tally of the Anguish: Accountability in maternal health care in India.* New York: Human Rights Watch

Kaviraj, S., 2010. *The trajectories of the Indian State: Politics and Ideas.* Bangalore: Permanent Black

Kothari, K., 1982. The Shrine: an expression of social needs. In Elliott, J. and Elliot, D., eds. *Gods of the Byways: Wayside shrines of Rajasthan.* Oxford: Museum of Modern Art.

Lamb, S., 2000. *White Saris and Sweet Mangoes: gender, aging and the body in India.* Berkeley: University of California Press

Latour, B., 2007. *Reassembling the Social: An introduction to actor-network-theory.* Oxford University Press

Lock, M., 2007. The final disruption? Biopolitics of Post Reproductive Life. In Inhorn, M. ed., *Reproductive Disruptions.* Oxford: Berghahn

Lock, M., and Kaufert, P., eds. 1998. *Pragmatic Women and Body Politics.* Cambridge University Press

Lutz, C. and Abu-Lughod, L., eds.1990. *Language and the politics of emotion.* Cambridge University Press

MacCormack, C., and Strathern, M., eds. 1980. *Nature, Culture and Gender.* Cambridge: Cambridge University Press

Madan, T. N., 1987. *Non-renunciation: themes and interpretations of Hindu culture.* Delhi: Oxford University Press

Madhok, S., 2004. Heteronomous Women? Hidden assumptions in the Demography of Women. In Unnithan-Kumar, M. ed., *Reproductive Agency, Medicine and the State.* Oxford: Berghahn, 223–45

Madhok, S., 2013. *Rethinking agency: Developmentalism, gender and rights.* New Delhi: Routledge

Madhok, S., Unnithan, M. and Heitmeyer, C. On Reproductive Justice: 'Domestic Violence', Rights and the Law in India. *Culture, Health and Sexuality.* 16, no. 10 (2014): 1231–44. See: http://dx.doi.org/10.1080/13691058.2

Manson, N. and O'Neil, O., 2007. *Re-thinking Informed Consent in Bioethics.* Cambridge University Press

Marcus, G. Ethnography in/of the World System: The Emergence of Multi-Sited Ethnography. *Annual Review of Anthropology* 24 (2008): 95–117

Marmot, M. The Social Determinants of Health. *The Lancet* Vol. 365 (19 March 2005): 1099–1104

Mathur, K., 2004. *Countering gender violence: initiatives towards collective action in Rajasthan.* New Delhi: Sage

Merleau-Ponty, M., 1986. *Phenomenology of Perception.* London: Routledge

Menon, N., 2004. *Recovering Subversion: Feminist Politics Beyond the Law.* Springfield: University of Illinois Press

Menon, N., Sexuality, caste, governmentality: contests over 'gender' in India. *Feminist Review* 91 (2009): 94–112

Merry, S., 2006. *Human Rights and Gender Violence: Translating International Law into Local Justice.* University of Chicago Press

Merry, S.E. Measuring the World: Indicators. Human Rights and Global Governance. *Current Anthropology*, Vol. 52 (S3) (2011): 83–95

Mody, P., 2008. *The Intimate State: love-marriage and the law in Delhi*. New Delhi: Routledge

Mohanty, C.T., Russo, A. and Torres, L., 1991. *Third World women and the politics of feminism*. Indiana University Press

Moore, H., 1988. *Feminism and Anthropology*. Minneapolis: University of Minnesota Press

Morgan, L. and Roberts, E. Reproductive governance in Latin America. *Anthropology and Medicine* 19, no. 2 (2012): 241–54

Nichter, M., 2008. *Global Health: why cultural perceptions, social representations and biopolitics matter*. University of Arizona Press

Ong, A and Collier, S., eds. 2005. *Global assemblages: Technology, Politics and Ethics as Anthropological Problems*. Oxford: Blackwell

Patel, T., 1994. *Fertility Behaviour: Population and Society in a Rajasthani Village*. Delhi: Oxford University Press

Petchesky, R., 1998. Introduction: Negotiating Reproductive Rights. In Petchesky, R. and Judd, K., eds. *Negotiating Reproductive Rights*. London and New York: Zed Books, 1–30

Pigg, S. Languages of Sex and Aids in Nepal: Notes on the Social Production of Commensurability. *Cultural Anthropology* 16, no. 4 (2001): 481–541

Popay, J., Williams, G., Thomas, C., and Gatrell, A. Theorising inequities in health: the place of lay knowledge. *Sociology of Health and Illness*, 20, no. 5 (1998): 619–44

Povinelli, E., 2006. *The empire of love: toward a theory of intimacy, genealogy and carnality*. Durham NC and London: Duke University Press

Quigley, D., 1993, *The interpretation of caste*. Oxford: Clarendon Press

Rabinow, P., 1996. *Essays in the anthropology of reason*. Princeton University Press

Raheja, G. and Gold, A., 1994. *Listen to the Heron's Words: Reimagining Gender and Kinship in North India*. Berkeley: University of California Press

Raheja, G., 1988. *The Poison in the Gift: Ritual, Prestation and the Dominant Caste in a North Indian Village*. University of Chicago Press

Ram, K., 2004. Rationalising Fecund Bodies: Family Planning Policy and the Modern Indian State. In Jolly, M. and Ram, K., eds. 2004. *Borders of Being: Citizenship, Fertility and Sexuality in Asia and the Pacific*. Ann Arbor: University of Michigan Press

Ram, K. Class and the clinic: the subject of medical pluralism and the transmission of inequality. In *Journal of South Asian History and Culture* 1, no. 2 (2010): 199–212

Ram, K., 2013. *Fertile Disorder: spirit possession and its provocation of the modern*. Hawaii University Press

Ram, K., and Houston, C., 2015. *Phenomenology in Anthropology: a sense of perspective*. Indiana University Press

Rapp, R., 1999. *Testing Women, Testing the Fetus: the social impact of amniocentesis in America*. New York: Routledge

Rapp, R. Gender, body, biomedicine: how some feminist concerns dragged reproduction to the center of social theory. In *Medical Anthropology Quarterly* 15, no. 4 (2001): Arlington: American Anthropological Association

Reddy, G. 2010 *With Respect to Sex: Negotiating Hijra Identity in South India*. University of Chicago Press

Rosaldo, M., 1984. Toward an anthropology of self and feeling. In Shweder, R. and Levine, R., eds. *Culture theory: Essays on mind, self and emotion*. Cambridge University Press

Rose, N., 2007. *The Politics of Life Itself: biomedicine, power and subjectivity in the twenty-first century*. Princeton University Press

Rozario, S. and Samuels, G., eds., 2002. *Daughters of Hariti: Birth and Female Healers in South and Southeast Asia. (Theory and Practice in Medical Anthropology and International Health Series)* London: Routledge

Sarkar, T. and Butalia, U., eds. 1995. *Women and the Hindu Right.* Kali for Women

Scott, J., 1992. Experience. In Butler, J. and Scott, J., eds. *Feminists Theorise the Political.* London: Routledge, 22–41

Sharma, U. and Searle–Chatterjee, M., 1994. *Contextualising Caste: Post-Dumontian Approaches* (Sociological Review Monographs). Oxford: Blackwell

Sheikh, K. and George, A., eds, 2010. *Health Providers in India: On the Frontlines of Change.* New Delhi: Routledge.

Sinha, A., 2005. *Indian Democracy and Well-being: an enquiry into the persistence of poverty in a dynamic democracy.* New Delhi: Rupa

Srivastava, S. Non-Gandhian sexuality, commodity cultures, and a 'happy married life': The cultures of masculinity and heterosexuality in India. *Journal of South Asian Studies* 24, no. 1 (2001): 225–49

Strathern, M., 1984. 'Subject or Object': Women and the circulation of valuables in Highland New Guinea. In Hirschon, R. ed. *Women and Property: Woman as property.* London: Croom Helm

Strathern, M., 1992. *Reproducing the Future: anthropology, kinship* and *the new reproductive technologies.* London: Routledge

Street, A., 2014. *Biomedicine in an unstable place: infrastructure and personhood in a Papua New Guinean Hospital.* London and Durham: Duke University Press

Suneetha, A and Nagaraj, V. Adjudicating (Un)domestic Battles. *Economic and Political Weekly* 40, no. 38 (2005): 4101–3

Taylor, J. Big Ideas: Feminist ethnographies of reproduction. Review article. *American Ethnologist* 31, no. 1 (2004): 123–30

Teunis, N. and Herdt, G., eds. 2007. *Sexual Inequalities and Social Justice.* Berkeley: University of California Press

Thachuk, A.K., 2004. *Midwifery, informed choice and reproductive autonomy: A relational approach.* Thesis (M.A.). Simon Fraser University, Canada.

Townsend, N., 1997. Reproduction in Anthropology and Demography. In D. Kertzer and T. Fricke eds., *Anthropological Demography: toward a new synthesis.* Chicago University Press

Unnithan (Unnithan-Kumar), M., 1997, *Identity, Gender and Poverty: New Perspectives on Caste and Tribe in Rajasthan.* Oxford: Berghahn

Unnithan, M., 2003. Reproduction, Health, Rights: Connections and Disconnections. In, Mitchell, J. and Wilson, R., eds. *Human Rights in Global Perspective: Anthropology of Rights, Claims and Entitlements.* London: Routledge, 183–209

Unnithan, M., McNay, K. and Castaldo, A., 2008. Women's Migration, Urban Poverty and Child Health in Rajasthan. In *Migration DRC WP-T26, sussex.ac.uk/migrationdrc.org*

Unnithan-Kumar, M. and Srivastava, K., 1997. Gender Politics, Development and Women's Agency in Rajasthan. In: Grillo, R. and Stirrat, R. eds., *Discourses of Development: Anthropological Perspectives.* Oxford: Berg, 157–83

Unnithan-Kumar, M., 1997. *Identity, Gender and Poverty: new perspectives on caste and tribe in Rajasthan.* Oxford: Berghahn

Unnithan-Kumar, M., 2001. Emotion, Agency and Access to Healthcare: Women's experiences of reproduction in Jaipur. In Tremayne, S., ed. *Managing Reproductive Life: Cross-cultural themes in fertility and sexuality.* Oxford: Berghahn, 25–52

Unnithan-Kumar, M. Learning from infertility: gender, health inequities and faith healers in women's experiences of disrupted reproduction in Rajasthan. *Journal of South Asian History and Culture* 1, no. 2 (2010): 315–27

Van der Geest, S. Special issue on hospital ethnography, *Social Science & Medicine* 47, no. 9 (1998)

Van Hollen, C., 2003. *Birth on the Threshold: Childbirth and Modernity in South India.* Berkeley: University of California Press

Vanita, R., Same-sex weddings, Hindu traditions and modern India. *Feminist Review* 91 (2009): 47–60

Venkatesan, V., 2010. The Dynamics of Medicos' Anti-reservation Protests of 2006. In K. Sheikh and A. George ed. *Health Providers in India: On the Frontlines of Change.* New Delhi: Routledge, 142–57

Yamin, A., and Boulanger, V., 2013. From Transforming Power to Counting Numbers: the evolution of sexual and reproductive health and rights in development and where we want to go from here. *Working Paper series* on the Power of Numbers

Yuval-Davis, N., 1997. *Gender and Nation.* London: Sage

2 State empowerment and reproductive control

Individual experiences of reproduction, selfhood and health in Rajasthan are caught up in much wider webs of power and control that exist at an all-India level and transnationally. This chapter explores how reproductive control (its language, techniques) is central to statecraft in modernising India despite an ostensible shift in state health policies from a focus on fertility control toward 'reproductive health', an explicitly global human rights-based, choice and participation-oriented approach.[1] It also moves beyond an understanding of the *effects* of the state to examine how changes in global ideas about reproductive health have led to changes in the functioning of the Indian State itself. Periods of my fieldwork from 1998 onwards have coincided with the most fervent implementation of universal, rights-based development programmes and policies in reproductive health. In this chapter I explore what the diffusion of global norms around reproductive rights and reproductive health has meant for the authority and functioning of the state in India, including in its relationship with civil society organisations.

A focus on the dynamics and discourse of reproductive health across state and non-state (civil society and community-based) institutions enables an examination of some of the less widely addressed issues in the existing literature on health and rights in India: How have rights-based and coercive population policies come to co-exist? Why does sterilisation, even if coercive, remain a popular choice in both state and community family planning practices? What is the impact of closer state-civil society working relationships for how reproductive health rights come to be framed and operationalised? What meanings of rights and empowerment are mobilised in the process? The work here, as in Chapter 1, sets out the grounds for an investigation in subsequent chapters into the role that institutional actors, such as public health workers (nurses, midwives), gynaecologists and civil society actors, play in the mediation, translation and 'vernacularisation' (following Merry, 2006) of universal reproductive rights. I return to these issues in greater ethnographic detail in Chapter 5 on health worker experiences with safe birth promotion and family planning, and in Chapter 7 on legal activism in the context of plural understandings of health, empowerment and reproductive rights.

Conceptualising the state as a 'dispersed ensemble of institutional practices and techniques of governance' (Hanson, Stepputat, *et al.* 2001, p. 14), I use reproductive health policies and programmatic practices to examine not only what the state *does* but, equally, what it *means* to development agents and recipients (Fuller and Benei, 2001; Mosse, 2004; Unnithan and Heitmeyer, 2012). I draw on ethnographic field research in 2004 and with a project team in 2009, where we conducted research with state officials and members of Civil Society Organisations (CSO)[2] involved in rights-based maternal health programmes and policy making. Through a focus on how the state comes into being in its everyday policy making and in its partnerships around rights work with CSOs (Bernal and Grewal, 2014), as well as in the perceptions and practices of its newly created category of reproductive health workers as discussed in Chapter 5, the work in this chapter contributes to recent anthropological scholarship on global perspectives on reproduction (Browner and Sargeant, 2011) and to anthropological theorising on the state in India (complementing the work of Gupta, 1995, 2001, 2012; Das, 1995, 2004, 2015; Shah, 2010; Sharma, 2014; Mathur, 2016; among others).

The focus of this chapter is on what can be regarded as the second phase of modern Indian statehood from the 1990s onwards, a period marked by economic liberalisation (Gupta and Sivaramakrishnan, 2011, Seetha Prabhu 1999).[3] The turn to liberalisation in 1991[4] embodied measures to boost economic growth but, along with processes of political decentralisation resulted in far more than a shift in the economy, it changed the nature of the Indian state itself (ibid.). This process is particularly striking when viewed from the perspective of its reproductive health rights discourse and policies. The 1990s was a decade noted for global campaigning against reproductive coercion and for international policy response to safeguard especially women's health and bodily rights (as discussed in later sections). For the Indian state it represented an undertaking in policy terms to engage with approaches to 'safe maternal and child-health' and to an explicit partnering with civil society in reproductive health programmes and planning, particularly in its National Rural Health Mission (NRHM) initiated in 2005.

From the late 1990s to the early 2000s the transition from a policy framework and language of rights into a programmatic implementation of rights emerged, on the ground, in the form of the restructuring of health delivery systems (from a population-based approach to a more people-centred healthcare approach). With the establishment of the National Rural Health Mission (NRHM) in 2005, the Indian government sought to restructure health services across the country with the specific remit of making them participatory, accountable and rights-based. The NRHM vision document placed particular emphasis on *community ownership* and decentralised planning through participatory processes 'in order to evolve transparent and responsive needs-based systems with a very clear pro-poor focus' (Gupta *et al.*, 2009; Unnithan and Heitmeyer, 2012, p. 292). The NRHM promised a more *holistic* approach to motherhood notably promoting institutional delivery along with attention to a choice of contraception (GOI, 2006),[5] an emphasis which had so far been absent in state policies driven by the demographic rationale of stemming high population numbers. However, rather than replace the earlier emphasis on population-based family planning, the

Figure 2.1 Government of India Ministry of Information and Broadcasting newspaper advertisement in 2018 announcing a new national nutritional programme.

language and approach of rights and people-centred policies has come to *co-exist* with the practice of population control and in the circles of health planning in the country (GOI, 2000).[6] Through a focus on the institutional processes and practices (state and non-state) of the rights-based programmes in Rajasthan, in this chapter I set out to explain why and how two contradictory approaches to health (population focused and people-centred) come to co-exist.

In a global setting, the simultaneous practice of contradictory strategies may, as Hanson and Stepputat (2001) suggest, be a hallmark of modern postcolonial states. Given the increasingly challenging conditions under which modern states function, where their authority is constantly being called into question through global markets, separatist movements and ethnic conflicts, on the one hand, but equally where the state is being framed as indispensable to global efforts (for instance, to deliver development programmes effectively or promote a human rights culture), new modalities of governance emerge which in turn necessitate, according to Hanson and Stepputat (2001) new ways to evaluate what states do and mean. It is in this context that I examine the perceptions of rights and policy-linked shifts in reproductive health practices of the Indian State. I discuss how 'choice' and 'participation' (key elements of a human rights-based approach to health: Gruskin and Tarantola, 2008) become imagined and performed by state development actors.

The ground-level implementation of rights-based reproductive health policies in India has mainly relied on the partnering of the State Health and Family Welfare department (and the central Ministry of Health and Family Welfare, MoHFW) with civil society organisations.[7] Indeed, as Bernal and Grewal note, NGOs have been normalised as key players when it comes to women's welfare and empowerment (Bernal and Grewal, 2014, p. 1). This is particularly the case in Rajasthan where there has been a long history of CSO work on empowerment to which I have been a witness.[8] CSOs engaged in the early experiments with empowerment as in the Women's Development Programme (WDP), (Kabeer, 1994; Unnithan and Srivastava, 1997; Mathur, 2005; Sharma, 2014), have since continued to build their knowledge and expertise on participatory forms of development, spawning some of the organisations and development programmes with whom work by the project team was carried out in 2009–2010 (further discussed below and in other states as in the Mahila Samakhya programme; Sharma, 2014). In the WDP, the objective of empowerment, as a processual means of enabling women and poorer communities to assert power (Kabeer, 1994), became a common ground for the meeting of feminist and development agendas at the time (Unnithan and Srivastava, 1997, p. 157). More broadly, from the 1990s onwards, as Cornwall and Molyneux note, development and human rights as fields of engagement came together through new connections forged by transnational (and especially feminist) activism (Cornwall and Molyneux, 2008, p. 3). It is in this context of activism in the closing decades of twentieth century that 'rights-talk' gain roots in global development.

The increasing centrality of 'rights talk' and 'rights work' in reproductive health policy implementation in India had, by the mid-2000s, further solidified state-civil society partnerships. Many of the new flagship 'pro-poor' initiatives introduced by the national United Progressive Alliance party after it came to power in 2004 drew heavily upon the expertise and technical skills of long-term established civil society organisations and members who had previously worked on women's development and empowerment programmes such as the Women's Development Programme in Rajasthan. At the same time, in working with the State on rights-based programmes, the organisational autonomy of CSOs vis-à-vis the state came to be challenged (Unnithan and Heitmeyer, 2012, 2014). Institutional collaboration on rights issues particularly highlighted the fact that the boundaries between state and civil society in India were more permeable than imagined, strengthening critiques of the idea that the state was distinct from civil society by scholars such as Chatterjee (1998).[9] Authors in Bernal and Grewal's collection, drawing on Foucauldian ideas of governmentality, similarly suggest a continuity between the state and civil society (Bernal and Grewal, 2014, p. 14).

Rights-based approaches to health, as proposed in this book, have reinvigorated the tired state narratives of progress and empowerment at the same time as they have generated critical public awareness of health service delivery. On the ground, an understanding of 'rights' (*adhikar* in Hindi) in a formal, legal sense became especially popular in Rajasthan following the success of the Right to Information (RTI) movement and the subsequent RTI Act of 2005.[10] *Soochna ka adhikar* (the Hindi phrase for the right to information) was widely experienced as the first collective manifestation of people power in post-independence Rajasthan to be successful in holding state officials to account (vis-à-vis the expenditure of development funds). The movement also provided a stronger sense of legitimacy to the rights work undertaken by CSOs, who were increasingly regarded as well placed to mediate on rights issues between the state and the people. But what members of CSOs themselves understood by rights and their own role in shaping new forms of empowerment in the context of rights legislation was less clear.

Field research between 2009 and 2010 on the lived experience of rights work among members of CSOs revealed positive attitudes of grassroots health activists toward state rights-based health interventions, insofar as the participation of community members was sought in health planning and in terms of enhancing access to public health services through an incentive-based safe motherhood programme such as the *Janani Suraksha Yojana* (JSY), further discussed in Chapter 5. CSO members were also engaged in rights campaigns which were in opposition to the state, such as to do with the right to generic medicine and, further, in contexts where a different language of claims framed by indigenous reproductive needs were being mobilised (as in the activism concerning rights to/against surrogacy and infertility services as I discuss in Chapters 3, 4 and 6). Alternative ground-up mobilisations which challenged the state and CSOs such as, for example, around the right to practice female sex selection also invoked the language of rights as I discuss in chapter 4. The concept of reproductive health rights as seen through the lens of the rights work of members of civil society organisations across the health and legal aid fields, invoked in a functionalist but also a strategic sense (following Petchesky, 2003; Unnithan and Pigg, 2014; Unnithan and Heitmeyer, 2012), has opened up new conceptual and practical spaces in which to challenge but also work with the state.

In this chapter, I suggest that the resulting fluid (and often uneasy) partnerships between the state and civil society organisations in their rights-based reproductive health work, can be regarded, as Gupta and Sivaramakrishnan (2011) suggest for India more generally, as creating a further set of conditions for the liberalisation process to reshape the public sphere in the name of economic development. For the various departments of the state, the alliances with CSOs on reproductive health rights issues has created further opportunities to present themselves as a dynamic force of rights-based development. As Biehl has noted in his work on state-civil society collaboration in promoting universal access to anti-retroviral treatments for AIDS sufferers in Brazil, 'such partnerships (have) become critical in shaping the perception of the state as transparent, ethical and actively pursuing social equity with regard to health' (Biehl, 2004, p. 118; Unnithan and Heitmeyer, 2012, p. 285; Biehl, 2007; also see GOI, 2006, p. 4). But such alliances are more complex in terms of how participation itself is envisaged (Cooke and Kothari, 2002). Underlying the very idea of participation and driving it, as Kothari argues, are 'morally invested oppositions of knowledge and authority resulting in the valorisation of 'local' knowledge and the continued belief in the empowerment of 'local' people through participation' (Kothari, 2002, p. 140; Cooke and Kothari, 2002). CSO organisations are diverse in terms of the ways in which they envisage 'choice' and 'participation', reflected in the fact that CSO workers often contest the very processes of which they are a part (also notably Sharma, 2011) as I discuss in the following lines.[11] It is worth noting here that CSO relationships with the state are also determined by the competition with multinational corporations who align with the State (Kothari, 2002).[12] Such critical perspectives add further depth to understanding the effects of globalisation on institutional collaboration between CSOs and the state (Appadurai, 2002; Fisher 2010; for example).[13] Local organisations in Rajasthan, up until the time of field research in 2009, drew on global rights discourse, transnational links and funding to both bypass the state, but also to work with it on rights-based health programmes (Unnithan and Heitmeyer, 2012). State regulation of NGOs since then (especially under the new government formed by the Bharatiya Janata Party, BJP, from 2014 onwards) have severely limited the ability of NGOS to receive foreign funds, threatening the survival and autonomy of such organisations as I discuss in the closing sections of this chapter.[14]

In the following lines, I begin by setting out a historical perspective on state approaches to reproduction, health and population growth which emerged in the late colonial period, especially in the early part of the twentieth century when India was moving toward its independence from British colonial rule. I then discuss how 'rights' emerge as a 'reproductive choice' in family planning policy from the 1980s onwards and the related critiques which emerge from within civil society. Analysing the language of policy in two significant government Reproductive and Child Health programmes, RCH-I and RCH-II, I emphasise the *return* to family planning in an era of rights-based governance, both at a policy level but also, ironically, in terms of individual practice among poorer women and couples. These observations lead me to reflect on the fact that the substitution of an existing biopolitics of population control with a biopolitics of the 'self' (Rose, 2007), aimed at enhancing individual choice and personal autonomy (de Zordo, 2012) is not as clear-cut as first imagined. The second half of this chapter provides ethnographic insights from a close examination of reproductive health-focused CSO work undertaken with a project team in Rajasthan to show how CSO work around rights issues creates new forms of institutional legitimacy and new forms of empowerment as a category of governance (Sharma, 2014).[15]

Population, fertility and health in colonial discourse in India

The concern in planning circles to limit India's population stems back to the colonial period. It was mainly in the late colonial period (1850–1947) in India that official administrative and medical attitudes toward population and health were most pronounced (Hodges, 2006; Arnold, 2006; Ramusack, 2006). Population issues were popularly connected to the use of birth control and contraceptives, although these ideas were less clearly articulated in policy terms. This was for a number of reasons, which ranged from the marginality of obstetrics and gynaecology within colonial medical practice to the few numbers of women medical doctors in the profession, their low status as well as their own contradictory positions on birth control (Ramusack, 2006).[16]

A significant point that arises from this historical literature and one which is of interest in understanding the making of the postcolonial state is the way in which the official discourse of societal reform was located within, and shaped by, Indian middle-class attitudes. It was upper- and middle-class women's inability to access medical care during childbearing, because of the purdah that they had to maintain, that prompted colonial intervention and resulted in the first steps to medicalise childbirth. The provision of facilities for the secluded upper caste and upper class women (who maintained purdah) was among the first priorities of medical aid projects and the new settings for childbearing, a key aspect in the colonial medicalisation of childbirth (Hodges, ibid.). The other key aspect was the training of indigenous midwives, who were considered dirty, unhygienic and unskilled in the practice of birthing.

It was not just middle-class bodies that were affected by colonial practices but, perhaps, even more significant was the way in which colonial attitudes and reform shaped middle-class thinking on the subject of population, health and reproduction, the implications of which are evident in the family planning and population policies in modern India. As Arnold suggests, the late colonial period saw a transfer of official ideas relating to the 'demonics' of population growth to members of the Indian middle class, ideas which became increasingly entrenched in the latter (Arnold, 2006). Equally, ideas of eugenics among educated Indians were reinforced through colonial contact, as reflected in the growth of Indian eugenics societies in the 1930s and 1940s (Hodges, 2006, p. 115).

   The concern of Indian eugenic societies for healthy children as the basis for a healthy nation fitted well with the debates of social reform to do with population growth and poverty which were taking place at the national level. However, as Hodges suggests, the Indian eugenicists addressed themselves to marriage reform (especially the custom of child marriage) as a means of bringing about positive social and demographic change. The connection of population quality to family planning and birth control only came about in the period around 1940s, when India moved toward independence. This shift also coincided with a decisive turn in national population policies to a focus on the poorer and lower classes.

   The emergence of birth control as a national policy toward the end of colonial governance is implied in Arnold's analysis of the different official views on population expressed in the census reports of 1921 and 1931. According to Arnold, there is a shift in the two census reports, as captured in the move to describe India's population as a 'problem' in J.H. Hutton's 1931 census report, as opposed to it being discussed as the population 'question' in the previous one (Megaw's 1921 report). The shift towards a Malthusian perspective in official thinking was primarily driven by the recent rise at the time in mortality through disease and famine, and the consequent increase in the population (well captured in the Demographic Transition Theory of the 1970s). Until the 1930s India's population was regarded as mainly controlled through climate and nature, disease and famine, and not as manageable through social practices such as birth control. In response to the sudden alarming increase in population, Hutton suggested that active measures such as birth control be put into place so as to curtail population growth. Arnold suggests that although Hutton made the first and until then unprecedented connection between population control, health and birth control, he nevertheless remained cautious in terms of advocating specific measures to achieve this control over population. His caution was in line with his administrative predecessors, who also felt wary of intervening in the *private* domain of native reproductive matters.

   The 'negative' (according to policymakers at the time) consequences of uncontrolled childbearing for women were only becoming evident in the data collected by the members of the colonial Women's Medical Service. Increasing documentation in the mid- to late-1930s showed that maternal mortality was a significant risk associated with childbirth, and much higher in India than in Europe at the time. The need to address maternal mortality emerged as a specific policy concern in the 1940s, particularly in the deliberations of the Bhore committee (1944–46) on the eve of Indian independence. The Bhore committee, progressive for its time, was instrumental in setting the agenda and framework for the public health services in an independent India, especially with regard to maternal and child welfare. Welfare was defined in terms of the provision of antenatal care for pregnant women, skilled attendance at childbirth and attention to postnatal care, the latter being neglected in the immediate post-independence health programmes which focused on family planning and fertility control and which, ironically, came to be embodied much later as a rights-based approach to

maternal health by the NRHM in 2005. It was fertility control that came to dominate the agenda of the newly formed Republic of India as it launched the world's
largest family planning programme after independence in 1950.

A strong rationale for family planning, since the start of official health planning in the 1950s, was in terms of the health benefits the spacing of children
conferred on married women. An entrenched idea within the colonial as well as
postcolonial state and medical establishments had been that the health of poor
women, who were most prone through malnutrition and anaemia to maternal
complications, improved substantially when their fertility was controlled. The
provision of contraceptives would empower them to practice spacing and would
bring them relief from constant childbearing and related physical exhaustion.

While it is undisputed that fertility control through contraceptive measures
can help women space children and regain their strength in their childbearing
years, in the following lines I suggest these interventions also have negative
health consequences which are often ignored by a government too heavily
focused on achieving its population targets. This observation has an empirical
basis – in Rajasthan, hospital staff openly admit that post-operative care following tubectomies is negligible, i.e. there is no care provided beyond the point of
family planning delivery.

It is also reflective of a population control approach 'that views women as
potential contraceptors or 'producers of too many babies' rather than as individuals whose health is of inherent …' value (Lane, 1994, p. 1303) as emphasised in the deliberations on the rights approach to reproductive health at the
Cairo Population and Development conference in 1994 (UNFPA, 2004, 2008).

New routes for thinking about 'fertility control as beneficial to women's
health' emerge within the wider culture of planning in the postcolonial state,
where the focus is on development and economic welfare as distinct from a colonial state – focused on management rather than the economic well-being of its
citizens (Ram, 2004; Chatterjee, 1998). Nevertheless, in terms of the logic and
state practices with regard to population and health, we see an overflow from the
colonial state into the liberalising postcolonial state, as discussed further in the
following section.

Providing choice, taking control: state family planning at the crossroads

The demographic rationale of family planning has been integral to India's population policy right from the start of the exercises in planning for development.

Family planning, as these population programs have come to be called, are
not, as Greenhalgh observes for China (2003, 2005), about decisions to do with
numbers of children or family size made by individuals, couples or families, but
rather a matter of governments deciding how many children are to be born to
each family. Modern Indian health-planning history from the 1950s onwards
tells us that it has been national governments that have held sway: population
control has been invested with an urgency and national importance that has

easily swept aside individual desires for childbearing. This was particularly the case in the mid- to late-1970s where the forced sterilisation practices of the then Congress Government, led by Indira Gandhi, disregarded the rights of individuals when they conflicted with the wider interests of the nation[17] (unlike in China where individual and state desires for population reduction seem to have coalesced more closely (Greenhalgh, 2003; Anagost, 1995).

Following the atrocities of the Emergency when the constitutional rights of its citizens were suspended, the mid- to late-1980s in India was a time of popular disillusionment especially in terms of the failure of the state to meet women's reproductive rights and related health needs.[18] Activists and feminist organisations in particular highlighted the malpractices and unethical conduct of health workers, who actively and routinely carried out coercive birth control strategies, albeit at the behest of their superior officers (Dhanraj, 1999).'Some of the most hard-hitting critiques of India's family planning programme emerged around this issue (see for example, Patel, 1994; Visaria, 2000; Jeejeebhoy, 2000; Ram, 2004; Rao, 1999; Qadeer and Vishwanathan, 2004). Their international lobbying brought global support against the reproductive coercion within the population control practiced by India and other nation states in the name of economic progress (Lane, 1994; Petchesky and Judd, 1998; Hartmann, 1995; Petchesky, 2003; Correa and Petchesky, 2008; among others).

The work of women's organisations and feminist population scholars drove the policy focus on rights and women's health at the International Population and Development conference in Cairo in 1994, where 'reproductive health' was defined as a 'comprehensive approach to women's health and well-being that included fertility and infertility, contraception, abortion, childbearing, maternal morbidity and mortality, sexuality, sexually transmitted diseases, menstruation and menopause' (Lane, 1994, p. 1303). For countries like India, the state was brought to book in that it became an international signatory to the Cairo agreement which clearly stated that citizens in highly populated countries had the right to choose whether and what kinds of birth control they wished to practice. But with international aid tied to demographic performance and the uptake of contraceptives, the Indian State, as scholar-activists suggest, preferred to mobilise targets to enforce reproductive control as a means of demonstrating accountability to its international donors rather than to its citizens (Rao, 1999; Visaria, 2000) and to practice population control even as it supported a policy of reproductive health rights. The compromised position of the state is epitomised in its policies toward sterilisation, in particular with reference to tubectomy procedures carried out on women.

Renewed emphases on sterilisation in rights-based reproductive and child health programmes (1997–2005)

In the following lines I examine the contradictory approach to family planning across the Reproductive and Child Health (RCH) programmes, RCHI (1997–2002) and RCH II (2003–05) (programmes which predated the National

Rural Health programmes of 2005). When the RCH programmes were rolled out it was stated that their 'strategic orientation' was to be consistent with the Millennium Development Goals, the National Population Policy (2000–10), the tenth five year plan (2002–07), the National Health Policy 2002 and the Vision 2020 document and would, therefore, promote a combined focus on reducing the maternal mortality rate, infant mortality rate and the total fertility rate.[19] At the same time, the programmes would promote couple protection (a term used for contraceptive uptake) through the provision of a range of contraceptive options from condoms and intrauterine devices (IUDs) to the pill. The provision of this range of contraceptives was referred to as the 'cafeteria approach' to family planning and was set out as offering reproductive choice to women and couples. According to principle 6 of the planning document, 'the programme would include voluntary and informed choices in administering family planning services (there will be) clear tasks for service providers to provide quality services to meet unmet needs of family planning and spacing methods in desirable quantities'.[20] In the same paragraph the document continues to state an overriding concern with population growth especially in the 'lagging' states (referring to the poor economic growth in the five states of Bihar, Madhya Pradesh, Orissa, Rajasthan and Uttar Pradesh),[21] where it was estimated it would take over twenty-six years to achieve the replacement level fertility rate of 2.1. Accordingly, in these states, financial incentives ('compensation') was to be provided to 'clients' (term used in the document) to enhance contraceptive uptake. Cash incentives ranged from approximately Rs600/- for tubectomies; Rs650/- for vasectomies; with a heftier sum of Rs5,000/- (including access to medical termination services) offered in case of failures. As a result of these policy measures, there was a return to state-promoted sterilisation in Rajasthan (an irreversible form of contraception) despite the contraceptive choice espoused in national policy documents.[22] In this sense, the RCH II plan was very much like the National Population Plan which reaffirmed the state's commitment to 'promote vigorously the small family norm to achieve replacement levels of TFR' (GOI MoHFW, 2000).

Female sterilisation or tubal ligation was described in the health plan documents on contraceptive choice as both popular and cost effective with little surgical time involved, as requiring inexpensive equipment especially with the recent mini laparotomy method employed, and where the client could be discharged two to four hours after the surgery (without need for post-operative hospital-based care) thus placing the least burden on institutional resources. Its popularity for planners was backed by evidence in the form of healthcare statistics which showed that sterilisation was the preferred option chosen by 34 per cent of currently married women at the time (in 1998–99)[23] compared in the same period with a low uptake of condoms (3 per cent of married couples), intrauterine devices such as the Copper T (2 per cent for currently married women) and male sterilisation (2 per cent of men). Accordingly, it was argued that sterilisation procedures were to be made available and provision was to be expanded in the future from the existing programme into 2005–10 to all the community health centres and primary health centres in the country (and not just the five 'lagging' states). Each location would be provided additional funds for an operation theatre and to hire a medical officer trained in sterilisation. Incentive packages were set up by the government to attract clinical organisations in the private sector to provide family planning services, especially sterilisation, (promising fixed payments for clients served by the private facility as well as access to public facilities on a fee sharing basis).

The renewed focus on sterilisation, despite being a surgical procedure subject to wide-spread and intense criticism in popular, health activist and scholarly arenas, not to mention the political risks involved in promoting sterilisation (as past experience of the Congress party in the late 1970s had made clear),[24] is reflected in its commanding position in the later, post-2005 version of the RCH programme during my field research. What this demonstrates is not just a continuing anxiety of the state around 'population explosion' but, more fundamentally, a lack of understanding, as Das and Uppal (2012) suggest, of the actual dynamics of population growth. India has an increasingly young population and recent observations of population growth suggest it to be youth-led reproduction and in the context of 'unmet (contraceptive) needs' rather than because of 'wanted fertility' (i.e. when couples simply desire to have an unspecified number of children). Young couples, as Das and Uppal, 2012 emphasise, require spacing rather than terminal methods of contraception as entailed in sterilisation. The predominance of sterilisation as a method provided by the state, as they point out, ironically leads to a greater spurt in population growth, precisely because younger couples rush to complete their families.

From a close reading of the state planning documents on the subject, I suggest that the continued emphasis on sterilisation signals a deeper neo-liberal rationale in operation. I suggest this is particularly evident in three senses. First, most other contraceptive methods are resource intensive and expensive to provide so are not regarded as cost effective. For instance, the copper T intrauterine device requires administering and counselling by a paramedic who has to be trained for this. It also requires monitoring over the period of its use. Sterilisation by comparison requires 'little surgical time, involves minimal discomfort and the client is discharged 2–4 hours after surgery' (GOI 2007, RCH I PIP, p. 87). Second, the use of reversible methods (IUDs, condoms and pills) is regarded as being a 'riskier' option for the state than sterilisation as it entails the possibility that women could 'change their minds' and discontinue use (RCH PIP, ibid.). Individual and couples' preferences and practices would also require monitoring and recording which would be difficult to resource. As a result, the very contraceptive methods over which women had most control were also those regarded as most 'unreliable' by health planners. As a result, even though the planning documents espoused a 'cafeteria' of contraceptive choice, in reality only one method (sterilisation) was available.[25]

State family planning policies reflect a state entangled within the desire to promote the liberal rights-based values of informed consent, choice and participation on the one hand, and the wish to be guided by economic principles and a demographic rationale based on fertility regulation and population management, on the other hand. The disjunction between provision and practice is a manifestation of policy ambivalences which Ram describes as a condition of the state being caught between two distinct guiding principles of liberalism and developmentalism. These principles become manifest in dual processes whereby they are both reiterated by the state and simultaneously subject to erosion (Ram, 2004, p. 85).[26] The disjunction between (the rhetoric of) state provision and the on the ground practice of its health workers has been the subject of concerted civil society activism to promote economic and health rights in India, as I discuss in the following section.

It is worth noting here that ethnographic insights on contraceptive practice in peri-urban Jaipur, which will be discussed in greater detail in Chapters 4 and 5, indicate, ironically, that sterilisation was by far the most popular form of contraception among the women interviewed. However, what was clear too was that there was a different popular rationale for the preference for sterilisation from that of policymakers. Among poorer families, the practice of sterilisation was favoured mainly because it required least intervention and follow-up by health workers ('safety' in user perceptions was conceptualised as protection from the inexperience of health workers). It was not so much that fears of sterilisation were not present, as indeed the many stories of botched operations confirmed, but, rather, it was more the case that tubectomies were regarded as the *least risky* option. Similarly, reversible forms of contraception on offer without the back up of appropriate counselling and paramedic support were perceived as 'unreliable' by the users themselves (also Iyengar and Iyengar, 2000).[27] This is further borne out by the greater response to the use of IUDs in voluntary health centres, I found, because of the sensitivity of care provided, unlike in public health contexts where service providers tend to be judgemental about the appropriateness of a woman's reasons for seeking IUD removal. Contraceptive pills were also less popular because they required both regularity and commitment, difficult to sustain by women who experienced heat and dizziness, which they perceived as dangerous side-effects of their contraceptive use.[28] Condoms were regarded as equally problematic and shameful in the context I worked in as they involved openly alluding to intercourse and talking about sex between spouses. The community-based preferences for sterilisation, alongside their resistance to using reversible methods, has, inadvertently, further strengthened the legitimacy of sterilisation as a state practice.

Activists and CSOs working with the communities and the state to help realise reproductive choice and health rights in Rajasthan have also faced some unforeseen challenges, both to their own independence and autonomy and also in terms of further promoting the authority of the state as I discuss below.

Diffusing and/or consolidating state authority? Civil society and the challenge of rights work

State implementation of reproductive health rights programmes has necessitated closer partnerships between state and civil society in ensuring community-based participation for a number of reasons, not least being the proximity (geographic and social) which grassroots organisations have with the families they work with. As Beja, a rural CSO health worker reflected, *Sarkar kanun, adesh aur kagazon ke beech hai*, the state sits amid the law, orders and papers (field interview, Jaipur, 23 October 2009). Beja, who was a member of the community he worked in, was referring to the limited reach of state officials and institutions compared to his own organisation.

In the following lines I discuss the changing forms of CSO work in health, including the shifting relationships between state and civil society organisations in the decade 2005 to 2015 when there was an intense focus on rights-based policies and legislation, such as the Right to Information Act (2005) and the Protection of Women from Domestic Violence Act (2005) in the country. In this section, I draw on field data collected with a research team between 2009–10 where material was obtained from interviews and discussions with members of thirty-four civil society organisations across the districts of Alwar, Bikaner, Chittorgarh, Ajmer and Jaipur in Rajasthan, and from subsequent papers published from this work (especially Unnithan and Heitmeyer, 2012 and Unnithan and Heitmeyer, 2014).[29] The section will also draw on observations based on my long-term interactions and field research (including from the early 1980s when I was a university student in Jaipur and Delhi) with members of the Institute of Development Studies (IDS), the Right to Information movement, People's Union for Civil Liberties (PUCL) – Rajasthan Branch, Rajasthan University Women's Association (RUWA), state health and family planning authorities, as well as the founders of women's counselling and shelter organisations (discussed in greater detail in Chapter 7).

Figure 2.2 Poster on 'Your Rights' depicting free and caring services at public hospitals.

Civil society in Rajasthan is highly dynamic and diverse, making overall categorisations difficult. (I was told there may be over 10,000 NGOs of different sizes operating in Rajasthan at the time of field work).[30] Nevertheless, a broad categorisation in terms of organisational structures and processes of CSOs in the state was undertaken during the research (Unnithan and Heitmeyer, 2012, 2014). As the field visits in 2009–10 revealed, there were health rights-based CSOs who were standalone organisations, such as Mutlub (pseudonym)[31] which tended to be relative newcomers compared with longer term health-based CSOs who had over time developed a number of ancillary networks constituted of smaller health related CSOs. Often, longer established organisations like Koshish, Jeevan, Seva and Bhedia (pseudonyms)[32] worked more broadly to alleviate poverty and economic discrimination in rural areas based on caste. Beja's organisation (which formed the basis of his reflections quoted above) had grown out of one such established CSO.

While a handful of established CSOs in Rajasthan worked directly with the state in policy-making, the smaller CSOs who were linked to them carried out intensive health rights advocacy work in the villages and districts in the state from the early- to mid-2000s onwards.[33] Their focus was on enhancing the quality of provision and equity in access to healthcare especially for poorer and more vulnerable communities and in bringing these communities into health planning processes as part of the state led NRHM programme for the first time. It is in this context that their participation was sought by the Government when it launched its large-scale National Rural Health Mission the NRHM in eighteen states of the country (GOI, 2006).[34] CSO participation was explicitly sought in Rajasthan to launch a core programme within the NRHM, which was the Community Monitoring Programme (CMP).[35] The CMP was initially run as a pilot scheme in 400 of the state's approximately 41,000 villages as a means to enable the community to monitor the state's provision of health services.[36]

This included a scrutiny by community committees of state health funds allocated to the primary health sub-centres and staff, and in planning the allocation of state health funds according to local health priorities. Under the NRHM, special provision was also made for rights-based sensitisation through the training of district and primary level health professionals, including the provision of instruction on the use of new rights-based techniques, instruments and protocols (such as the partograph, postpartum institutional care protocols and maternal death audit and review procedures). In the rest of the chapter I briefly review the experiences of some of these CSOs in carrying out state-related rights work to suggest that the new forms of collaboration around rights opened up not only spaces of democratic participation for community members and CSO members alike, but also affected their relationship and perception of the state, albeit in directly opposing ways (Unnithan and Heitmeyer, 2012). For the village-based communities involved in the CSO-led participatory processes of health rights, it was the power of the state rather than the community elders or civil society groups they worked with which emerged most forcefully. For the CSOs working to deliver rights-based programmes, the state continued to be an institution from whom rights had to be wrestled away from. 'Human rights are attained through struggle' was a common refrain among many activists in Rajasthan.[37]

Koshish

In 2009 Koshish worked closely with the state acting as a CSO 'hub' to coordinate the Community Monitoring Programme (CMP) in all districts in the state of Rajasthan. It had expanded from its base in southern Rajasthan to open an office in the capital city of Jaipur. In the 1970s Koshish had been mainly involved in the delivery of health services and health advocacy in the southern district of the state. Since then, Viraj (pseudonym), its founder, had left his practice of medicine to become a full-time committed advocate and practitioner of social and community medicine. I met him for the first time in 2008 when he came to London to participate in an international conference on health inequalities organised by Michael Marmot, pioneer of the social determinants of health model.

By 2009 Koshish had recruited extra staff (with better qualifications, who were younger, more urban and confident in their outlook) to its Jaipur office to undertake the work on the state NRHM programmes. Nirmala took over charge of the Jaipur office and ably assisted Viraj in meeting the demands of the CMP programme for Rajasthan. Within the overall programme, Koshish had been given the task to oversee the implementation and functioning of the new Village Health and Sanitation Committees (VHSC), a key component of the CMP. The VHSC committees were formed of a number of village representatives including a quota of 2–3 women, the designated government health workers (ASHA and ANM) and the CSO facilitators, who were tasked with formulating health plans with a focus on community health priorities. These plans and related decisions were then to be fed upwards through the CMP system. Field observations of these meetings in 2009 to 2010 revealed that the mixed gender constitution of the committee and the kind of participation (with the CSO facilitators prompting reflections and questions on funding and expenditure) was alien to most members, as was the focus on pregnancy and maternal health ('most people die of snake bites here', I was informed by a village elder). This was further evident in the lack of facilities for emergency obstetric care, with the primary sub-centre in a state of disrepair and being used at the time for the storage of pipes from the adjoining community well. While local CSO staff worked tirelessly to garner participation in the VHSC, there were a number of stumbling blocks they faced, not least the wider structural inequalities of caste and gender which prohibited men and married women from rural households to converse openly together in a committee or elsewhere.

Despite the evident apathy toward maternal health issues in the village VHSC meetings attended by local CSO staff, there was a keen interest in terms of community entitlements to do with water and property and in scrutinising the employment related development funds allocated by the state. The interest in particular (economic) forms of entitlement vis-a-vis the state owes its origins to the long-standing and effective campaigns of the right to information movement in the state.[38]

Throughout its work with the state and NRHM officials in Delhi and Jaipur, Koshish staff carried out a number of health related, rights-based advocacy activities and awareness raising work with members of its networks in southern Rajasthan where the organisation had first been established. Koshish staff in fact experienced greater success in their rights campaigning where they shared a common platform with other CSOs compared to their work on state commissioned programmes (as communicated by Nirmala, senior member of the organisation). The rights-based health campaigns which Koshish undertook were on a wide range of issues such as HIV, maternal entitlements in the right to food campaign and all issues taken up by the Indian chapter of the People's Health Movement, *the Jan Swasthya Abhiyan* (JSA).[39] Koshish was the Rajasthan hub for the JSA in India, and staff, especially members from the Jaipur office, were continually engaged in campaigning alongside other CSOs to mobilise the state to provide better healthcare services which, during the time of field research, was focused on promoting the access to affordable medicines.

Research undertaken by the Koshish staff had demonstrated that a large percentage of the income of a poor household was spent as 'out of pocket expenses' in procuring medicines. Their campaign on the universal right to access low cost and generic medicine was carried out over two years and brought together a number of other organisations, such as the pan-Indian organisation for the promotion of science education, along with local groups such as the domestic workers alliance and those fighting for the protection of women against domestic violence, on a common powerful platform. Following the significant and forceful mobilisation across the districts and country, the Rajasthan State Public Service Guarantee Act 2011 came into force, legalising the provision of free medicine in all state accredited hospitals (Unnithan and Heitmeyer, 2012).

While the collaboration at the level of the Rajasthan state ensured Koshish a central position to carry out health related development work within the state and procure significant funding to do so, it also generated a dependency on state funded resources. The time and resources for campaigning suffered as a result and, in turn, the reputation of Koshish as a legitimate organisation safeguarding people's health interests was questioned by other CSOs who claimed it to be a stooge of the government. The close collaboration that Koshish had with the state was reflected (and enabled) through the intimacies and friendship that the founding head of Koshish had with state officials at the state and district levels (such as the state director for health and family welfare at the time). The informal networks enabled the work of Koshish to be productive in delivering state development programmes. However, with the abrupt ending of the CMP at the national level and a consequent withdrawal of funding for the NRHM itself in 2014, which was disbanded in a favour of a much wider National Health Mission (NHM), Koshish faced a severe challenge to its survival.

The relationship between Koshish and the state health department and officials was very different from that of Mutlub, another important health based CSO, which also worked with the state and with various communities to bring

Figure 2.3 NGO poster on the 'Truth about Medicine' which accompanied the campaign on rights to low cost medicine. The poster depicts the similar effects of branded and low cost medicine in terms of health but not financially, with the former leaving you out of pocket (top left); an unnecessary injection when a pill would do (top right); the common prescription of excess medication (bottom left); the need to always request a prescription for generic drugs from your doctor (bottom right).

down the high figures of maternal and infant mortality in Rajasthan. It did so, however, in different ways from Koshish and with different long-term institutional goals, motivations and outcomes.

Mutlub

Based in southeastern Rajasthan, Mutlub was setup by a couple who between them had research qualifications in gynaecology, obstetrics and paediatrics, as well as a PhD in public health from a European university. Mutlub not only provided clinical services in the rural catchment area of southeastern Rajasthan but it was also a key provider of training for state health workers (nurse midwives, anaesthetists, gynaecological assistants) who worked at the district level. Set up as a CSO, it also had a research wing and both co-founders Mira and Suresh (pseudonyms) published their work in highly regarded clinical, medical and public health journals.

The ability to link clinical research to the social context in which the organisation worked was among its most impressive and distinctive aspects, which also lent it legitimacy in state health and planning circles. To take an example, Mira and Suresh led a survey of 216 couples expressing contraceptive preferences in their clinical field site in southern Rajasthan. The findings showed that the longer lasting ten-year copper T intrauterine device (CuT 380A) as compared with the three-year Copper T (200B) promoted by the government provided older women more choice and convenience compared to the permanent method of tubal ligation. (Iyengar and Iyenger, 2000). Their study found that the desire for the longer span of the ten-year Copper T also was more prevalent among older women who were less inclined to have children, while the three-year Copper T was more consonant with the reproductive preferences of younger couples. These reproductive preferences, they noted, were not completely straightforward in practice as there would always be some couples with 1–2 children who might wish to limit their families while others with more than two children might go in for different spacing methods. Their study set in its social context demonstrated how reproductive desires change with age and that contraceptive provision needs to be more nuanced accordingly.

With an emphasis on the biomedical aspects of maternal and infant health, as well as in their context-based reproductive and child health research, Mutlub had a distinctive contribution to make with regard to the implementation of the NRHM in Rajasthan. A major on the ground contribution by Mutlub in this context was in providing training to state health workers to improve practice around existing and new clinical guidelines in the provision of safe prenatal, antenatal and postpartum maternal care practices, on the techniques of working with new instruments such as the partograph as well as with regards to instilling an ethical rationale and sensitivity around rights-based safe birth work. Mutlub employed several medically trained staff alongside a cadre of graduates from social work and public health backgrounds. The organisation also trained local health workers and recruited staff assistance from among local communities in the region. In one session of a fifteen-day residential training course provided by Mutlub, which the project team observed, it was evident from the gynaecologist nurse midwives, labour room specialists and male nurse trainers attending that the sessions were keenly sought after, with participants finding themselves empowered through the ways the course had addressed the gaps in their skills and knowledge (Unnithan and Heitmeyer, 2012, p. 295).

While Mutlub did not draw on any rights-based language in its work or in its publications and research, and it did not present itself as a right-based organisation as such, it nevertheless addressed rights-based issues. As co-founder Suresh pointed out to the research team, the rights-based approach was embedded in the work of their organisation (ibid., 2012, p. 297). Whether this was in terms of enabling reproductive choice (through socially nuanced contraceptive provision or the trialling of socially adapted pregnancy testing kits) or improving the quality of care (through training of government and CSO staff) or in expanding the access to, and local participation in, reproductive health services (through their rural clinical outreach programmes), Mutlub's work was centrally situated within a rights paradigm.

In terms of working with state and national health officers, Mutlub had more policy success compared to Koshish, for example, in getting the state health department to adopt certain medical protocols, such as to do with post-partum care. This involved extending hospital stays to a forty-eight hour period to cover the most critical duration when maternal deaths could occur due to haemorrhage after birth; a small but highly significant intervention in reducing the chances of maternal deaths. Mutlub had less success in changing the contraceptive options provided by the state; this could be for a number of reasons to do with vested interests, including the cost, production and rollout of contraceptives. In terms of working with other CSOs, Mutlub maintained a distance from attendance at rights campaigns, although it did attend numerous workshops organised by Koshish and other CSOs across the country as well as by international funding agencies such as the UN, WHO and Centre for Reproductive Rights where its biomedical expertise was requested. Even though, as an organisation, Mutlub's technical expertise was highly respected in the wider CSO community, there were nevertheless points of friction. During the time of fieldwork during 2009 to 2010, Mutlub was critiqued for its support of the WHO policy which banned the recruitment and training of indigenous midwives (WHO, 2005; the broader effects of this policy are discussed in Chapter 5) and which was regarded by a majority of the other CSOs as a detrimental policy in that it marginalised critical, local knowledge around childbirth (CHSJ, 2008; Unnithan and Heitmeyer, 2012, p. 297).

Discussion

In this chapter I have used rights-based reproductive and maternal health policies and practices of the Indian state as an example of how an 'ensemble of institutional practices and techniques' can combine contradictory modes of reproductive

governance. In its simultaneous practice of contradictory approaches to reproductive health, i.e. 'choice-less', population-based family planning programmes
and people-focused (participatory) individual health prioritising initiatives, the
state has gained further reproductive control alongside popular perceptions of it
being a bearer of reproductive rights.[40]

Rather than practice a participatory and inclusive approach to contraception
and sexual reproductive health rights following the Cairo protocol, the Indian
state has ended up with a family planning programme where the contraceptive
choices provided are meaningless, and little has been done to provide an environment (in a structural and ideational sense) where reproductive choices are
enabled (in Petchesky's (2003) use of the term). Ironically, as I discuss in this
chapter, sterilisation continues to be regarded as the only viable option by both
state health officials and contraceptive users alike, albeit for differing considerations, illustrating how state officials and community members imagine 'choice'
differently.

At another level, in terms of the concept of participation, the ethnographic
observations in this chapter suggest that a more democratic and participatory
approach was adopted by the state in the matter of setting health-priorities in
rural contexts through a facilitation by CSOs under the Community Monitoring
Programme. However, this approach did little to shift wider patriarchal and hierarchic social norms underlying the existing gender-based practices and perceptions of health. There was apathy among members of the newly formed
committees, like the VHSC, who were neither able nor enabled to see how their
participation was relevant or beneficial to their health. In this context maternal
health and the related right to quality maternal health services remained of marginal concern.

What emerges is an instrumental use of 'choice' and 'participation' wherein
state health planners show little understanding that notions of self-realisation and
self-awareness at the heart of conceptions of empowerment are required for the
practice of rights (as feminist mobilising in development has so clearly shown:
Kabeer, 1994; Unnithan and Srivastava, 1997; Cornwall and Molyneux, 2008;
Bernal and Grewal, 2014; among others). Feminist paradigms of empowerment,
which addressed issues of dignity and respect critical to raising one's self and
social image (Cornwall and Molyneux, 2008) were lost sight of in the more
instrumental rights-based NRHM programmes. And similar to what Sharma
(2014) observed in her work on notions of empowerment in the Government-
NGO Mahila Samakhya programme, the 'mainstreaming of empowerment as a
category of governance ... carrie(d) with it the risk of an official subversion of
its radical possibilities' (p. 108).

As a powerful actor in the domain of reproductive health rights described in
this chapter, the state has been able to see off the challenge to its authority from
established CSOs with a long history of rights-based community work. While
the 'turn to rights' in policy-making in India in the opening decades of the
twenty-first century appears to have strengthened the legitimacy and capacity of
CSOs to inform state policies on reproductive health, with promising roles as

powerful mediators of development and critical brokers of citizen's entitlements to health care provision and benefits, in reality their mobilisation of rights-based frameworks, whether to change legal entitlements as in the case of Koshish or to re-frame technical guidelines of maternal care as in the case of Mutlub, has enabled the Indian State to become an even more powerful institution. CSOs remain important champions of reproductive health rights in India and are critical to the formulation and implementation of rights-based policies and to the performance of techniques of 'empowerment'. However, the contributions of CSOs co-opted within state-led processes remain invisible and submerged within state rhetoric and practice. They have, by contrast, enabled the state to fulfil its true role of being the 'mai-baap' (mother–father; i.e. paternalistic) bearer of rights.

In the next chapter, we shift away from a focus on the state to investigate the registers through which reproduction and health are invested with value 'on the ground'. How is authoritative discourse on population control subverted in everyday contexts? How are biomedical terms such as reproductive health which dominate state and public health perspectives reconceptualised through faith healing? How is the positive moral value placed on the fertility of women by families negotiated by women with state health workers in the everyday?

Notes

1 See Gruskin and Tarantola (2008) for an overview of human-rights based approaches to health.
2 There is a distinction made between the terms 'Civil Society Organisation' (CSO) and 'Non-Governmental Organisation' (NGO) as they have come into popular usage over the past three decades in India. Especially for members of CSOs it has been important to distinguish their work from what they regard as the profit-oriented strategies of the voluntary sector, as opposed to their own service-oriented public work (Tandon 1991; Das, A. personal communication, 2009). I use 'CSO' where organisations explicitly self-identified as such. I use the term 'NGO' in those instances where they are described in this manner in the secondary literature such as academic, government and media reports.
3 As Gupta and Sivaramakrishnan (2011) observe the pre-liberalisation state (1950s–1980s) or the 'developmental state' in India was increasingly characterised by its inability to deliver growth conceptualised on the basis of modernisation theories and Nehruvian ideals.
4 The main form of liberalisation was through currency devaluation and the de-control of trade and tariffs
5 Assistance to infertile couples was also mentioned at this time but never took shape in any provision on the ground.
6 This underlying logic of population control is clearly set out in the pages of the National Population Plan (or NPP; GOI 2000), which encourages planners to adopt a 'vigorous approach to family planning' in the new millennium.
7 The report of the state-led task group on public–private partnership under the NRHM explicitly recommended a partnership model as a key strategy for strengthening public health delivery across the different states in India and in the mutual interest of both partners (GOI 2006, p. 16).
8 My engagement with the Rajasthan's Women's Development Programme stems from the 1980s onwards (see Unnithan and Srivastava, 1997).

9 Chatterjee argues that the analytic dichotomy between state and civil society produced by western enlightenment-based theories of the state do not hold up in the post-colonial context in India.

10 As is well documented by feminist development activists Aruna Roy and others in civil liberty organisations who spearheaded the movement in Rajasthan through the 1990s.

11 Sharma's work on women's empowerment (2011) focuses on a government run NGO or GONGO and the relations between the organisations within such an institutional clustering. Her ethnography depicts the NGO as representing its relations with the state in a malleable and strategic manner depending on the audience and the desired outcome.

12 State-NGO partnerships are more recently under threat given the state's swing to align with multinational corporations. Kothari (2002) has documented this shift in terms of the losing battle of environmental NGOs to obtain state support to carry through legal cases of land and conservation related irregularities.

13 Both Appadurai (2002) and Fisher (2010) suggest in their work that transnational activism has enabled CSOs to bypass the control exerted on them by the State.

14 In 2016 the Ministry of Home Affairs under the BJP government issued notice to NGOs/associations in the country that they were required to submit mandatory annual returns for the past six years in compliance with the Foreign Contributions Regulatory Act, FCRA (2010) or face cancellation of their licenses to practice. Those that did not receive funding in this manner were also to submit a 'nil' return. NGOs wishing to receive funds would have to specially apply for a permit and for a unique identification number and card.
Chauhan, N. *Times of India*. 2018. https://timesofindia.indiatimes.com/india/3292-ngos-have-15-days-to-comply-with-fcra-rules-or-have-their-licences-cancelled/articleshow/63956761.cms Accessed on 20 September 2018.

15 Sharma regards empowerment 'as a novel mechanism of self-governance' in her work on Government-run NGOs in the women's development Mahila Samakhya programme (2014, p. 93).

16 Other important factors contributing to the relative in-action on reproductive matters in national planning and policy circles despite the advocacy of birth control on paper, was the sensitive nature as well as low priority accorded to the subject.

17 As Prime-Minister Indira Gandhi said in her 1970s public address on Indian's family planning programme, 'the rights of the nation come first and before the rights of its citizens'. *Something like a War* 1991.

18 Despite the very clear and positive start in the form of national plans to address women's health issues in the 1950s, the heavy handed and intensive emphasis on contraception alone led to increasing discontent. The dissatisfaction with the state peaked in the late 1970s with Congress Prime Minister Indira Gandhi's strong anti-poverty programmes of which the family planning programme was an important aspect.

19 In its Planning Implementation Programme (or PIP for short) document, the national Reproductive and Child Health II program has a chapter on 'Improving Health Outcomes' which starts with a concern with 'population stabilisation'.

20 In terms of 'rights' the PIP undertakes to ensure the provision of 'assured, equitable, responsive and quality health services. The word 'right' appears in three of the nine RCH II programme principles: principle 3, the poorest have the *right* (my emphasis) to get full value for the money being spent by the government or by themselves; principle 5, female children have an equal *right* to health, emergency medical aid and to live with human dignity; and principle 6, promoting contraceptive choice as alluded to above.

21 These states were also given the collective label of being an 'empowered action group' or EAG.

22 Other supportive measures included raising the levels of female literacy to 80 per cent from 40 per cent, realising a marriageable age at eighteen years rather than fifteen years, and increasing women's empowerment from low to high in the plan period.

23 The group of currently married women is not broken down by age which I have found to be an important factor in determining whether to go in for reversible or irreversible forms of contraception.

24 The renewed emphasis on sterilisation targets and camps have come back to haunt the current family planning program as public health provision is to be guided by 'expected levels of achievement' (or ELA) which is commonly perceived as the new phrase for 'targets' (Iyengar and Iyengar, 2000).

25 Additionally, even when the government promotes a single method such as the Copper T or condoms, sterilisation is continuously available and pushed as the most reliable method.

26 We see this unfolding in both the Indian and Chinese contexts but with different structures, engagement and outcomes. Ideas of modernity loom large in the success (in terms of bringing down the birth rate) of China's family planning programme. Anagost (1995) suggests this is because of the way the Chinese people have internalised and conflated being modern with having fewer children. Authors such as Greenhalgh have also remarked how the family planning programme was underscored by a national conscience which was convinced that to achieve prosperity and global eminence western birth control technologies had to be adopted (Greenhalgh, 2005). The scientific/medical bases of the contraceptive technologies further reinforced their acceptance as a sign of modernity.

The question here is why with the adoption of similar techniques of contraceptive sterilisation and the adoption of a similar rhetoric of family planning have the uptake of these programmes and demographic and social effects been so different in India and China? In both cases modernity and economic growth were the driving forces behind the population programmes. In both cases science and technology were invoked. And yet the policies have been more successful in China as compared with India. It is not that there has been no resistance to Chinese family planning measures (Anagost gives ethnographic instances of the different kinds of modes of resistance) but that overall there has been much more of an acceptance and positive valuation that at the same time emerges in people's own accounts as well. So even when there is suffering as a result of the decision to have fewer children, it is seen as a sacrifice for the good of the nation as a whole.

Greenhalgh (2005) argues that in China, it was the bringing together of three modes of thought and practice that resulted in the success of the family planning programme: the adoption of a specific version of western science and technology; a socialist state that focused on targets, and party led mobilisation. The effective mobilisation of party workers and socialist rhetoric combined with a general feeling of public shame associated with the 'abnormally' high level of population. The main anxiety with high population numbers was its negative impact on the quality of life and people themselves: too rural, backward and overly reproductive as opposed to the reproductively controlled bodies in modern Western Europe. The fact that China is now emerging as an economic power further reinforces in people's minds the benefits of controlling reproduction.

In India, by contrast, I would suggest there has been a different kind of national conscience, one that is marked by deep social and economic inequality. In this highly stratified context the majority of the people, especially the poor, see themselves as removed from, rather than as part of/ or contributing to the project of the modern nationhood. The state is conceptualised, socially and politically, as a far removed entity, to be suspicious of given past experience of reproductive coercion, to be resisted, an entity to be fought with to gain any kind of privileges. Thus, unlike in China, ordinary people in India, are unable to see themselves as contributing to the development of the state.

27 According to my own respondents in peri-urban Jaipur district, they get lost in the upper abdomen where they tend to 'stick' as well as hurt the husband during sex (fieldwork conversations with Samina, Zahida, 1998; also appear in Unnithan Kumar, 2002).
28 And as similar to other parts of the world where they have been introduced alongside different medical practices and are regarded powerful substances not just in a thera-peutic sense (Pool and Geissler, 2005).
29 The team comprised of two Indian Research Assistants Dr Pradeep Kacchawa and Ms. Manju Sharma, and a UK-based post-doctoral researcher Dr Carolyn Heitmeyer. All fieldwork interviews, discussions and comments which took place in Hindi were translated by myself, P. Kacchawa and M. Sharma. Pseudonyms used for CSOs in previous papers have been replaced by Hindi-linked pseudonyms in this chapter.
30 Interview with Viraj, head of an established CSO, July 2011.
31 The English pseudonyms used for the organisations in this chapter have been changed from how they appear in previous joint publications, to Hindi pseudonyms as requested by the respondents.
32 See previous endnote above.
33 While CSOs have been working with the state to deliver development programmes since the 1950s, it is only since the 1980s that their contribution has been actively recognised and funding allocated (Chandoke, 2005). From the early 2000s NGO parti-cipation in meeting development goals in health, environment and education began to be actively sought, with government NGO relationships in the health sector, for example, defined by a market-based economic rationale (Baru and Nandy, 2008).
34 In terms of financial outlay and personnel the NRHM was among the largest pro-grammes of its kind in the world; Lim *et al.*, 2010.
35 NRHM guidelines for Community Monitoring require that a 'Charter of Citizen's Health Rights' be prominently displayed in every district hospital, community health centre and primary health centre (Das and Bhatia, 2007, p. 21).
36 The first phase of funding for the Community Monitoring programme (2005–09) was provided by the central government. State governments were made responsible for providing the funds for the second phase (2009–12).
37 This trend is also unlike Bratton's observation that there is resistance from the state towards NGOs as the latter threaten to pluralise the hegemony of the state. A critical tension exists, as he suggests, between 'the government urge for order and control and the NGO quest for organisational autonomy' (1989, p. 570).
38 Jenkins and Goetz, 1999, for example.
39 The JSA is part of the world-wide movement which seeks to establish health and equitable development as key priorities through provision of comprehensive primary healthcare in line with action on the social determinants of health; Sarojini and Sen Gupta (2014).
40 The coexistence of population and rights-based approaches to maternal health can also be viewed from a different perspective: the fact that population control policies and the family planning programmes based on them did not work as planned (in stem-ming population numbers) to boost economic growth. The new emphasis on rights in development enables new links to be forged between the 'health of the nation' and women's health that population policies have relied on (Unnithan, 2003), wherein the rights of individual women are yet again subsumed within what is regarded as best for the nation (reminiscent of the excesses of the sterilisation campaign in 1977 where Prime Minister Indira Gandhi maintained that 'rights of the individual must remain in abeyance to rights of the nation'; Dhanraj, 1991).

Bibliography

Anagost, A., 1995. A Surfeit of Bodies: Population and the Rationality of the State in Post-Mao China. In Ginsburg, F. and Rapp, R., eds. *Conceiving the New World order: the global politics of reproduction.* Berkeley: University of California Press

Appadurai, A. Deep democracy: Urban governmentality and the horizon of politics. *Public Culture* 14, no. 1 (2002): 21–47

Arnold, D., 2006. Official attitudes to population, birth control and reproductive health in India, 1921–1946. In Hodges, S., ed. 2006. *Reproductive Health in India: History, Politics, Controversies (New Perspectives in South Asian History).* Hyderabad: Orient Longman, 22–51

Baru, R. and Nandy, M. Blurring of boundaries: Public-private partnerships in health services in India. *Economic and Political Weekly* 43, no. 4 (2008): 62–71

Bernal, V. and Grewal, I., eds. 2014. *Theorising NGOs: States, Feminisms and Neoliberalism.* Durham: Duke University Press

Biehl, J., 2004. The activist state: Global pharmaceuticals, AIDS and citizenship in Brazil. *Social Text* 80, no. 22 (2004): 105–32

Biehl, J., 2007. *Will to live: AIDS therapies and the politics of survival.* Princeton University Press

Bratton, M. The politics of government-NGO relations in Africa. *World Development* 17, no. 4 (1989): 569–87

Browner, C. and Sargent, C., 2011. *Reproduction, Globalisation and the State: new theoretical and ethnographic perspectives.* Durham: Duke University Press

Centre for Health and Social Justice Report on Traditional Birth Attendants, 2008. www.chsj.org/modules/download_gallery/dlc.php?file=441 (accessed 14 October 2011)

Chandhoke, N. 'Seeing' the State in India. *Economic and Political Weekly* 40 (11) (2005): 1033–9

Chatterjee, P. Beyond the nation? Or within? *Social Text* 16, no. 39 (1998): 57–69

Cooke, B., and Kothari, U., eds. 2002. *Participation: The New Tyranny.* London and New York: Zed Books

Cornwall, A., and Molyneux, M., (2008) *The politics of rights: dilemmas for feminist praxis. London,* Taylor & Francis

Das, A. and Bhatia Gitanjali, P.B., 2007. *NRHM: A summary of community entitlements and mechanisms for community participation and ownership for community leaders. Community Monitoring of NRHM: First Phase.* New Delhi: Centre for Health and Social Justice

Das, A. and Uppal, L., 2012. *Family Planning in India: A need to review our current approaches.* Publication of the National Coalition against the Two Child Norm and Coercive Population Policies

Das, V. and Poole, D., eds. 2004. *Anthropology at the margins of the state.* Santa Fe NM: Sar Press

Das, V., 1995. *Critical Events: An anthropological perspective on contemporary India.* Delhi: Oxford University Press

Das, V., 2015. *Affliction: Health, Disease and Poverty.* NY: Fordham University Press

De Zordo, S. Programing the body, planning reproduction, governing life: the (ir-)rationality of family planning and the embodiment of social inequalities in Salvador da Bahia (Brazil). *Anthropology and Medicine* 19, no. 2 (2012): 207–23

Dhanraj, D., 1991. *Something like a war.* Documentary film. London: Channel 4

Fisher, W., 2010. Civil Society and its Fragments. In Gellner, D., ed. *Varieties of Activist Experience: Civil Society in Asia.* New Delhi: Sage, 250–68

Fuller, C. and Bénéï, V., eds. 2001. *The everyday state and society in modern India.* London: C. Hurst and Co.

Gellner, D., ed. 2010. *Varieties of activist experience: Civil society in South Asia.* New Delhi: Sage

Government of India, 2000. *National Population Plan.* Ministry of Health and Family Welfare. www.nhp.gov.in/national-population-policy-2000_pg

Government of India, Ministry of Health and Family Welfare, 2006. *National Rural Health Mission: Draft Report of the Reconstituted Task Group on Public–Private Partnership under the NRHM*

Government of India, Ministry of Health and Family Welfare. NRHM, not dated. www.mohfw.nic.in/NRHM/Documents/Mission_Document.pdf (accessed 11 November 2010)

Government of India. 2007. *Document 2: The principles and evidence base for state RCH II Programme Implementation Plans* (PIPs). www.xiss.ac.in/RCH/Others/RCHII.pdf

Greenhalgh, S., Planned Births, Unplanned Persons: 'Population' in the Making. *American Ethnologist* 30, no. 2 (2003): 196–215

Greenhalgh, S., 2005. Population and Governance in China. In Ong, A. and Collier, S. eds. 2005. *Global assemblages: Technology, Politics and Ethics as Anthropological Problems.* Oxford: Blackwell, 354–72

Greenhalgh, S. Planned births, unplanned persons: 'Population' in the making of Chinese Modernity. *American Ethnologist* 30, no. 2 (2008): 196–215

Gruskin, S. and Tarantola, D., 2008. Health and Human Rights: Overview. In Heggenhougen, K. and Quah, S., eds. *International Encyclopedia of Public Health* (Vol. 3) San Diego: Academic Press, 137–46

Gupta, A. and Sivaramakrishnan, K., 2011. *The State in India after liberalisation: interdisciplinary perspectives.* London: Routledge

Gupta, A. Blurred boundaries: the discourse of corruption, the culture of politics and the imagined state. *American Ethnologist* 22, no. 2 (1995): 375–402

Gupta, A., 2001. Governing Population: The Integrated Child Development Services Program in India. In Hanson, T.B. and Stepputat, F., eds. *States of Imagination: ethnographic explorations of the postcolonial state.* Durham: Duke University Press, 65–97

Gupta, A., 2012. Red Tape: *Bureaucracy, Structural Violence and Poverty in India.* Durham: Duke University Press

Gupta, N., Chhaya, P., Ritesh, L. and Ford, R., 2009. *Community monitoring of health services under NRHM in Rajasthan: Report of the first phase.* Jaipur: Kumar and Co., Chittorgarh: Prayas

Hanson, T.B., Stepputat, H., Steinmetz, G. and Adams, J. eds. (2001) *States of Imagination: Ethnographic Explorations of the Postcolonial State.* Duke University Press, 14

Hartmann, B., 1995. *Reproductive Rights and Wrongs: The Global Politics of Population Control.* Boston, MA: South End Press

Hodges, S., 2006. *Reproductive Health in India: History, Politics, Controversies. New Perspectives in South Asian History* Vol. 13. Hyderabad: Orient Longman

Iyengar, K. and Iyengar, S. The Copper T 380A IUD: A ten-year alternative to female sterilisation. *Reproductive Health Matters* 18, no. 16 (2000): 125–33

Jejeebhoy, S.J., 2000. Safe Motherhood in India: Priorities for Social Science Research. In Ramasubban, R. and Jeejeebhoy, S., eds. *Women's Reproductive Health in India.* Jaipur: Rawat, 134–86

Jenkins, R., and Goetz, A. Accounts and Accountability: Theoretical Implications of the Right to Information Movement in India. *Third World Quarterly* 20, no. 3 (1999): 603–22

Kabeer, N. 1994. *Reversed Realities: Gender Hierarchies in Development.* London: Verso

Kothari, U., 2002. Power knowledge and social control in participatory development. In B. Cooke and Kothari, U., eds. *Participation: The New Tyranny.* London and New York: Zed Books, 139–52

Lane, S. From population control to reproductive health: an emerging policy agenda. *Social Science and Medicine* 39 (1994): 1303–14

Lim, S., Dandona, L., Hoisington, J. *et al.*, India's Janani Suraksha Yojana, a conditional cash transfer programme to increase births in health facilities: An impact evaluation. *Lancet* 375/9730 (2010): 2009–23

Lorgen, C.C. Dancing with the State: The Role of NGOs in Health Care and Health Policy. *Journal of International Development* 10, no. 3 (1998): 323–39

Mathur, N. 2016., *Paper Tiger: Law, Bureaucracy and the Developmental State in Himalayan India.* Cambridge University Press

Merry, S., 2006. *Human Rights and Gender Violence: Translating International Law into Local Justice.* University of Chicago Press

Mosse, D. and Lewis, D., eds. 2006. *Development brokers and translators: The ethnography of aid and agencies.* Bloomfield, CT: Kumarian Press

Mosse, D. Is Good Policy Unimplementable? Reflections on the Ethnography of Aid Policy and Practice. *Development and Change* 35, no. 4 (2004): 639–71

Nichter, M., 1996. Pharmaceuticals, the commodification of health and healthcare-medicine use transition. In Nichter, M. and Nichter, M., eds. *Anthropology and international health: Asian case studies.* London: Routledge, 265–326

Patel, T., 1994. Fertility Behaviour: Population and Society in a Rajasthani Village. Delhi: Oxford University Press

Petchesky, R. and Judd, K., 1998. *Negotiating Reproductive Rights: Women's perspectives across countries and cultures.* London: Zed Books

Petchesky, R., 2003. *Global Prescriptions: Gendering Health and Human Rights.* Zed Books

Pool, R and Geissler, W., 2005. *Medical Anthropology. (Understanding Public Health Series).* Maidenhead: Open University Press

Qadeer, I. and Vishwanathan, N., 2004. How healthy are health and population policies? The Indian experience. In Castro, A. and Singer, M., eds. *Unhealthy Health Policy: A critical anthropological examination.* Lanham MD: Alta Mira Press, 145–63

Ram, K., 2004. Rationalising Fecund Bodies. In Jolly, M. and Ram, K., eds. 2004. Borders of Being: Citizenship, Fertility and Sexuality in Asia and the Pacific. Ann Arbor: University of Michigan Press

Ramusack, B., 2006. Authority and Ambivalence: Medical women and birth control in India. In Hodges, S., 2006. Reproductive Health in India: History, Politics, Controversies. New Perspectives in South Asian History Vol. 13. Hyderabad: Orient Longman, 51–85

Rao, M., ed. 1999. Disinvesting in Health. Sage: New Delhi

Rose, N., 2007. *The Politics of Life Itself: biomedicine, power and subjectivity in the twenty-first century.* Princeton University Press

Sarojini, N., and A. Sen Gupta., 2014. *Realising the Right to Healthcare: A Policy Brief of the Jan Swasthya Abhiyan.* New Delhi: Sama Resource Group

Seetha Prabhu, 1999. Structural adjustment and the health sector in India. In Rao, M., ed. 1999. *Disinvesting in Health: The World Bank's Prescriptions for Health.* Sage: New Delhi

Shah, A., 2010. *In the shadows of the state: indigenous politics, environmentalism and insurgency in Jharkhand, India.* Durham: Duke University Press

Sharma, A., 2011. States of Empowerment. In A. Gupta and K. Sivaramakrisnan, eds. *The State in India after liberalisation: interdisciplinary perspectives.* London: Routledge

Sharma, A., 2014. The State and Women's Empowerment in India: Paradoxes and politics. In Bernal, V. and Grewal, I., eds. *Theorising NGOs: States, Feminisms and Neoliberalism.* Durham: Duke University Press, 93–115

Tandon, R., 1989. *NGO-government relations: A source of life or a kiss of death.* New Delhi: PRIA

Tandon, R., 1991. *Civil Society, the State and Roles of NGOs.* New Delhi: PRIA

UNFPA, 2004. *State of the World' Population. The Cairo Consensus at Ten: Population, Reproductive Health and the Global Efforts to End Poverty* Report NY: UNFPA

UNFPA, 2008. *State of the World's Population. Reaching Common Ground: Culture, Gender and Human Rights.* Report NY: UNFPA

Unnithan, M. and Heitmeyer, C. Global rights and state activism: Reflections on civil society: State partnerships in health in NW India. *Contributions to Indian Sociology* 46, no. 3 (2012): 283–309

Unnithan, M. and Heitmeyer, C. Challenges in 'translating' human rights: Perceptions and practices of civil society actors in Western India. *Development and Change* 45, no. 6 (2014): 1361–84

Unnithan, M. and Pigg, S.L., eds. Justice, Sexual and Reproductive Health Rights – Tracking the Relationship. *Special Symposium of the journal Culture, Health and Sexuality* 16, no. 10 (2014): 1181–8

Unnithan, M., 2003. Reproduction, Health, Rights: Connections and Disconnections. In Mitchell, J. and Wilson, R. eds., *Human Rights in Global Perspective: Anthropology of Rights, Claims and Entitlements.* London: Routledge ASA series, 183–209

Unnithan-Kumar, M. and Srivastava, K., 1997. Gender Politics, Development and Women's Agency in Rajasthan. In: Grillo, R. and Stirrat, R. eds., *Discourses of Development: Anthropological Perspectives.* Oxford: Berg, 157–83

Visaria, L., 2000. From Contraceptive Targets to Informed choice, in Ramasubban, R. and Jejeebhoy, S., eds. *Women's Reproductive Health in India.* Jaipur: Rawat, 331–83

World Health Organisation, 2005. WHO Traditional Medicine Strategy 2002–05. www.who.int/medicines/publications/med_strategy/en/

3 Infertility and other reproductive anxieties

An ontological challenge to 'reproductive health' and 'rights'[1]

As the exercise of biopower takes place at multiple sites and not just with reference to the state it is important to shift attention from the public institutions that regulate the reproductive body (the state, public hospitals, gynaecological clinics, policy contexts) to the sites at which these discourses are internalised, i.e. the lived body (Kielman, 1998; Sawicki, 1991). In this chapter the focus is on infertility, among the uppermost concerns of my respondents and yet notably absent from national health policies which have concentrated on population reduction, as we saw in the previous chapter.

In this chapter I describe how Hindu notions of pollution and inauspiciousness are central to understanding what the condition of sterility (*banjhpan*) means for the poor, childless Hindu and Muslim women in Rajasthan. A highly stigmatised and ritually polluting condition within Hinduism, infertility was equally stigmatised among Muslim women in the area of fieldwork. Given the centrality of women's fertility to their sense of personhood and ritual purity, infertility became experienced as an ontologically and ritually liminal condition for the women in the area of study. As a result, 'reproductive health' was, I argue in the chapter, primarily a quest to gain auspiciousness rather than to be free from reproductive infections per se.

Situated within culturally and historically specific understandings of reproduction and the body, indigenous conceptualisations of infertility spawned complex, plural trajectories of health-seeking, particularly burdensome for poorer women.[2] Biomedical cures were sought in combination with the intervention of faith healers,[3] although almost always the latter were considered more efficacious in the sense of 'having more force or hold (*pakad*)'. Healers provided women with opportunities to ritually negotiate the pollution of infertility at the same time as they helped them reduce the social and economic vulnerabilities associated with such a condition. They could also delay the quest for biomedical cures or work alongside them. In this chapter I argue that it is faith healers rather than biomedical professionals who have a conceptual hold over indigenous notions of reproductive well-being. Healers in Rajasthan recognised the body as constituted by social relations in a manner similar to Strathern's (1992) observations in her work on troubling the natural (taken for granted) basis of the body. The power of the healer rests precisely on their ability to re-make those social relationships 'disrupted' through infertility.

Indigenous concepts in Rajasthan, as I suggest in this chapter, not only serve as a framework to analyse health-seeking practice and the exercise of power on the ground, but, equally, in their authoritative position, provide a challenge to biomedical paradigms of reproductive health more generally. The focus on reproductive health as narrowly defined (in an epidemiological sense) is unable to capture the social, emotional, political and economic senses through which sexual and reproductive well-being is conceptualised in the region.[4]

In the following lines I set out how infertility is experienced and then consider the social and cultural processes through which the 'disruption' of infertility is managed through a variety of bodily healing techniques. I draw on anthropological studies carried out in Southern India (notably Ram, 2004; Riessman, 2000, 2002; and Kapadia, 1995) where most of the research on this topic has previously focused. Through empirical data on the health-seeking patterns of infertile women in Rajasthan and their routine recourse to faith healers, I examine the authoritative concepts at work through which healers help infertile individuals renegotiate social belonging and gendered identity, regaining the sense of well-being that flows from this.

More broadly, through a focus on infertility in this chapter I suggest a different kind of claim-making to do with the body and reproductive rights from that implied by the universal rights framework. The language and concepts of indigenous healing provide a differently embodied way of thinking about reproductive rights, away from the legal language of rights to one of moral claims embedded within and shaped through the force of cultural expectation, obligation and responsibility (Petchesky, 1998; Unnithan 2001, 2003). Rather than couched in individual entitlements to health or bodily autonomy, I found that poor women's claims to reproductive and sexual well-being and related health-seeking in peri-urban Jaipur were determined by notions of social obligation, spousal responsibility and loyalties which accompany social intimacy (Unnithan, 2001). This is not to suggest that legal notions of reproductive rights were not operative in the region, but rather that they were never invoked as such among the communities I worked with (this is discussed further in Chapters 6, 7 and 8 in the context of legal practices and activism around sexual and reproductive health rights). The connection between infertility and indigenous rights discourse on the body and reproductive rights provides a unique perspective on rights from the ground up, contributing anthropological insights to theoretical legal and political discourse on rights and fertility.

The fear of infertility in Rajasthan

Infertility was a condition feared by *all* the childbearing women I met; those women who were unable to bear children but, equally, by those who had given birth and 'proven' their fertility. The fact that this anxiety was widespread and ever-present for all women starting out in their reproductive life-course, and not just for those women who were infertile, also had a physiological basis reflected in the high levels of secondary sterility (i.e. when individuals and couples cannot conceive after their first child) that presented at the clinic I was based at. A number of my respondents, including Vimlesh and Zahida, had a long gap in conceiving after the birth of their first-born child and lived in a state of perpetual anxiety regarding their childbearing, even though their condition eventually turned out to be a transitional one. For women to be in a condition of *transitional infertility*, I suggest, is more pervasive than has been documented or acknowledged in the existing public health literature. It was also a condition that was routinised as most women lived constantly in reproductive uncertainty not knowing if they would produce more than one child. Stigma affected women in these conditions of secondary sterility as much as it did those who were permanently infertile (i.e. not being able to conceive at all and categorised as having primary infertility). The stigma of secondary sterility was further accentuated in the region for women whose first-born child was a girl (explored in the following chapter on female selective abortion).

Locally described as *banjhpan*, infertility in the area of fieldwork is a condition primarily associated with women. Infertile women were referred to as *banjhdi*, but there was no equivalent term for men. In fact, it was very common to find infertile women blaming themselves for their condition and for me to be told 'it is impossible for men to be infertile'. Gender ideologies in the region of fieldwork gave men primacy in procreation with them being regarded as the sole creators of children. Men were perceived to contribute a fully formed being through their 'seed/water' (*paani*) while women held the baby in their 'basket' (*dani* or *bacchadani*, literally baby basket). Women were perceived as contributing the 'basket' or 'vessel' to nurture what was created by men and were thus regarded as having a secondary, albeit supportive, role to men. Here we find that while certain ideas of the biological connectedness between women and their children (such as the significance of contributing the egg in procreation) are downplayed, other ideas of connectedness emerge (the significance of the womb and gestation). These notions further reinforce women's role as nurturers rather than procreators in local aetiologies and, in turn, gain them some privileges in the household. But, it is men, through the fact of their shared substance and in their role as creators, who gain 'rights' in their children.

Ideas about spousal responsibility were central to an understanding of the idioms in which reproductive claims were articulated. While women were expected to conform to marital obligations as wives and mothers, men were equally ideologically constrained in their role as providers to women who were their wives, sisters and mothers and children. Notions of duty associated with lower class men in Rajasthan rested on an expectation placed on them to 'provide' for their family, and this included money for food, shelter, clothes, education and healthcare.[5] In the conversations with women about the support they received from their husbands, what emerged was that often financial or economic provisioning was regarded as an index of the caring nature of the husband.

Hindu and Muslim men in the region, on the other hand, were expected to be assertive about their right to have sexual intercourse when they desired (considered a conjugal right), which is what made them men. As wives, by contrast, women could assert their conjugal entitlement to be made pregnant and to become mothers.[6] In this sense, women could and did question men's fertility if they failed to produce a child, as observed on the few occasions when a wife rather than the husband demanded a divorce. A man could not be held responsible for failing to provide sexual pleasure to his wife, but he could be held accountable for an inability to facilitate her childbearing (even though doubts regarding the inability to conceive were more likely to be aimed at women). A man's family could even be accused of failing to provide the appropriate, or conducive, atmosphere for conception (as we see in the account of Ghisi, below). Maternity in this case was a limited tool of power for women as wives.

Although the fear of infertility was one most expressed by women, it was an anxiety that was shared by all members of the husband's family. The anxiety was especially marked in the absence of a son to carry on the husband's line, or even in the case of there being only one son given the ever-present likelihood that he may succumb to disease or illness. A health consequence of this wider family interest in the birth of children is that women had the moral right to claim household finances for a consultation with reproductive health experts. This was in contrast to the negligible amounts of household money made available for the healthcare expenses of elderly women (even those who had produced a number of offspring) or for younger women before they bore children. Pregnant women, on the other hand, could claim financial support for any complications they faced during their antenatal period. They could demand to see a gynaecologist or insist that their husband take them to a faith healer and that he participate in the curing rituals prescribed by the healer.

Infertility was one of the most important of a set of reproductive and child health complaints for which women sought faith healers, which included menstrual disorders or *maheene ki pareshani* (the problems of the 'month') ranging from excessive bleeding to an absence of bleeding, the occurrence of frequent miscarriages, successive infant deaths, misdiagnosis by medical doctors or mishaps during medical treatment such as excessive bleeding after the sterility operation or in using the copper-T intra-uterine device. Menstruation itself was referred to as the 'blood of failed childbirth' providing a routine reminder of the connections between failed conception and pollution. Described to me by lower class couples and healers alike in Jaipur district, as we see below, infertility was perceived as the 'drying up/deficit of blood' (*khoon ki kami*) and of 'tied/blocked tubes' (*bandh nalli*) for which healers had the only cures.

In the following lines we learn from Vimlesh, Zahida, Miriam, Ghisi and Sharda about the ways in which infertility was conceptualised, the anxieties it generated, the health-seeking efforts it triggered and the social relations it affirmed and disrupted in this region of Rajasthan:

Vimlesh was unable to conceive after the birth of her twin girls. She strictly observed *chauth* to fast for the welfare of her husband and her own fertility which was seen as part of her concern for him. She travelled to Berwada during *chauth* with her upper caste neighbour in the *basti*. Vimlesh also fasted on a more regular basis every Tuesday (*mangal*) of the week. She visited several healers with her neighbour, including Sita the female faith healer (*mata mai*) in her slum who is possessed (*bhav aana*) by a spirit representing the 'seven sisters' (*sathu behna*). She also consulted with Khataram, another resident in her slum. A Hindu healer, he cured his patients by being possessed by a Muslim spirit (*the syyed baba*). Whenever Vimlesh returns to her husband's village for a wedding or funeral, or when someone is sick, she visits the site where her dead uncle-in-law is buried. He died childless and it is his spirit, she explains, which has caused her infertility. Vimlesh also undertook a course of drugs for her infertility at the voluntary health centre where I was based. She conceived a son shortly after.

(Unnithan-Kumar, 2010, p. 318)

Vimlesh talked about the effects of infertility as being physically visible on her body. She recounted how her body had become 'black' and how this was related to her heavy workload, which was the reason for the 'drying up' of the blood in her body. The inability to produce blood in enough quantity and quality is regarded by Vimlesh as underlying her condition of infertility and poor health more generally. She referred me to her poor eyesight, a direct consequence she pointed out of the lack of blood in her body. The physical effects of infertility, as described by Vimlesh, points to a master narrative which marks out 'weak' women as those who are poor whose bodies are ravaged by the hard, physical labour they engage in.

Infertility is part of a set of conditions which signified a 'weakness'. In physical terms, weakness or *kumzori* of the body is a common term used by men and women to describe any kind of bodily dysfunction and an overall physical weariness. Often the menstrual discomfort, pain and the inability to produce children was put down as being a symptom of *kumzori* or 'weakness'; see also Inhorn, M. (1994) for the use of weakness as a cultural idiom of male and female infertility in Egypt.[7] Other bodily dysfunctions connected with *kumzori* were white vaginal discharge (*safed pani*, white water) and to a lesser extent, the prolapse of the uterus (*shareer nikalna*, literally the body emerging).[8] The reference to 'weakness' in the accounts of poor women in Rajasthan has an epidemiological basis in that there are high levels of anaemia or haemoglobin deficiencies noted in the region (Government of India, NFHS 2006, 2016; Chattoo, 2018; Kauffman and Unnithan, 2015). What is less known is how pervasive this weakness is and how it is manifest in the form of infertility. The accounts of transitional infertility by women during fieldwork are especially revealing, as recounted by Zahida below:

Zahida was 35 years old and a mother of 6 children in 2000 when she recounted her experience of infertility and the resulting social castigation and hardship she had faced for over 7 years of her life (between the ages of 16 and 23 years). Zahida had been married at 14 years, a year after her menarche. She had a son in the first year of her marriage and then did not conceive for another seven years. In this intervening period, her marriage was precarious. Her in-laws had instructed their son to divorce her. Zahida was sent back to her parents' house for a trial period. The council of elders was summoned to consider her infertility in the wider context of her marital conduct. It was decided that because she had shown herself to be a 'good' (nurturing, diligent) woman her husband must be forced to take her back. During this time, Zahida constantly and desperately sought out interventions and advice from a range of healers. In one case a private infertility specialist diagnosed that she was pregnant but that the foetus was not developing. Her women companions advised her that her inability to carry a child to term was due to her being 'caught by an ill wind from above' (oonpar ki hawa). Accordingly, she sought out a jhadan ('sweeping', exorcism) from a faith healer of the Meena caste. She also procured a charmed necklace to wear as 'protection' from a 'bhangi' (untouchable) healer. She simultaneously undertook an ultrasound scan on the gynaecologist's advice and went on a course of drugs. She finally gave birth to a second child after seven years and went on to have 5 more children.

(Unnithan-Kumar, 2001, p. 319)

Zahida's account illustrates the fragile nature of her social relationships, which emerge as a result of her *transitional* infertility. Unlike Vimlesh, she was deemed to have had bad luck in being caught by an 'ill wind'. She also had little support from her husband and his family. Vimlesh, on the other hand, describes her husband as supportive and emphasises that the feelings of stigma are both self-imposed and come from the women she knows. Both women sought out cures from Hindu as well as Muslim healers and also from gynaecologists.

In the Hindu scriptures, infertility is portrayed as the 'other' of fertility which, by contrast, is associated with sacred female power (*sakti*).[9] In fact, the very of basis of female power is connected with the ability to bring forth human life. *Sakti* is a positive force only where it can be harnessed for social regeneration in morally appropriate ways. The tremendous power associated with *sakti* renders it dangerous in the sense that it can be 'all consuming' (men must guard against this female power) and 'uncontrolled' (in the potential for rampant sexual intercourse). Women at the onset of their fertile period (as in menarche) are subject to social regulation for precisely this reason. Among the Brahmin and non-Brahmin communities in Tamil Nadu, for example, this period is the subject of ritual cleansing in the form of elaborate puberty rituals (Kapadia, 1995); see also Ram (2013) for a similar association with inauspiciousness in Tamil Nadu.

Given the high value placed on social regeneration, infertility can be regarded as a form of social death. Infertility, like pregnancy loss and infant mortality, is associated with the rupture of social relations (and therefore a social rather than simply biological issue as Inhorn and Van Balen (2002) importantly point out). As Barrett (2008) observes in his study of Aghor healing practices in Benares, infertility, along with skin disorders such as leprosy and leukoderma within the family, represent not the end of a biological life but the loss of life lived among family and friends in a social world. According to Kapadia's ethnographic research in southern India, Tamil girls who do not menstruate and are unable to participate in these rituals are not considered to reach 'full' womanhood and continue to be perceived as 'unfinished' and un-gendered no matter what their age (Kapadia, 1995, p. 93). In Rajasthan as well, women who are childless are regarded as incomplete persons and inauspicious. Pregnant women are warned to stay away from infertile women (to avoid 'crossing their path') for fear of 'catching' this inauspiciousness. Explanations for pregnancy loss, subsequent barrenness, infant mortality (experienced by most women in the area of field-work) as well as maternal mortality were often put down to the contagion or spells cast through the gaze (*nazar*) of jealous, infertile women.

Only faith healers were regarded as having the ability to counter the effects and related stigma of *nazar*. More routinely, women such as Vimlesh as we saw above would undertake a weekly *vrat* or fast (especially on Tuesdays, considered to be the most auspicious) as well as participate in the many fertility related local and regional religious occasions such as Chauth, Holi, Gangaur, Shivratri and Teej. On these occasions married women of all castes undertake fasts to ensure their fertility and the health and the prosperity of their husbands. For infertile women these were auspicious occasions where they propitiated the deities through offerings of coconuts, red vermillion powder and rice/wheat seedlings, and requested divine intervention to make them fertile. To be seen to strive for motherhood and auspiciousness through ritual means, even though conception may remain elusive, was a necessary and strategic measure used by women of all social groups in the region.

Before I discuss how notions of infertility are mobilised by healers and com-munity members to address the stigma and disruption caused by the condition, and present a challenge to biomedical notions of reproductive health, I first move to explore in the next section how previous anthropological studies of infertility discuss the issues of anxiety, stigma and social disruption.

Disruptions: infertility in anthropology

As a theoretical concern within anthropology, infertility has provided critical insights into the 'disruptions' of personhood, kinship and of social reproduction more widely. As ethnographers such as Inhorn have noted, a breakdown in the linear biological narrative of conception-gestation-birth is at the same time a dis-ruption of the ways of being a person and of one's gender role (Inhorn, 1994; Van Balen and Inhorn, 2002; Becker, 2002; Ram, 2013; Riessman, 2000; Unnithan, 2010; Kielman, 1998; among others). The inability to procreate in many of these contexts, including in Rajasthan, has significant social, economic and political implications for individuals and for the social groups that infertile women and men belong to. A key anxiety associated with infertility for the family and kinship is that of the failure of social reproduction in a cultural, but also economic sense in terms of the transmission of property; foreclosing any possibility of the social perpetuity of those ageing without children (Bledsoe,

2002; Kreager and Schröder-Butterfill, 2005; Inhorn, 1994). For individual married women, infertility is connected with the real threat of losing their affinal attachment and with it the economic security of their household membership. To add to this, in their 'failure' to create a family 'naturally', infertile individuals and couples experience social disability where their physiological bodily failure becomes linked to a failure of the 'self' and a feeling of stigma (Becker, 2002; Greil, 1991; Rapp, 1999; among others).

Conditions of infertility and the stigma related to it are present in highly populated countries as well as less populated countries, though this may be manifest in diverse ways in terms of social power, status, security or perpetuity that having children confers (Inhorn, 2002). The greater the social value placed on childbearing (fertility), the greater the stigma attached to its disruption (infertility) is an observation well captured in Inhorn's phrase, 'the infertility-fertility dialectic' (Inhorn, 1994, p. 23). In each context infertility is seen to bring disruptions in the 'local moral worlds' of couples and families. As Gay Becker describes in her book, the Elusive Embryo (2000), the discovery of her own infertility led to the shocking experience of feeling stigmatised by her colleagues and others in America where she lived. Her experience brought home to her how motherhood and parenthood were defining features of what it meant to be a 'normal' woman and a 'normal' couple in the US. Drawing on Goffman's definition of stigma, Becker is also led to define stigma as 'a negative sense of social difference from others that is so far outside the socially defined norm that it discredits and devalues the individual' (Becker, 2002, p. 119).

Ethnographic studies undertaken in India (Patel, 1994; Riessman, 2000, 2002; Unnithan, 2010) and in Africa and the Middle East (Kielmann, 1998; Cornwall, 2001; Feldman-Savelsburg, 2002; Inhorn, 1994, 2003, 2012) emphasise the gendered and class aspects of stigma related to infertility, where the social, moral as well as economic burden of infertility is greatest for women in poor families.[10] The gendered burden of infertility is also heaviest for women, for whom childbearing and motherhood remains the key determinant of what it means to be an adult. In contexts such as Egypt and India, this is reinforced by local understandings of infertility as an inability to become pregnant a few months after marriage, and often as a woman's inability to give birth to a son (Inhorn, 1994; Patel, 1994; Riessman, 2000). This does not mean that male infertility is not acknowledged, nor that it is a condition devoid of humiliation. Indeed, the loss of virility which infertility represents is a condition which brings a high social cost in terms of social status for men. At the outset, however, men in the Egyptian, Indian or even East African contexts, as in the Pemba (Kielman, 1998) are rarely considered infertile and, as ethnographic work in the region suggests, are less burdened than women with the guilt of such a condition. (This is not the case in Euro-American contexts, as Becker describes, where technological intervention is more routinely sought). Part of the reason why men in the former context do not share the 'discredited' status associated with their infertility is because, as Inhorn suggests, in her study of male infertility and stigma in Lebanon and Egypt, their condition is not visible on the physical body.

The gendered nature of infertility is also evident in local discourses around reproductive responsibility. When combined with an increasing exposure to environmental toxins, men across the globe are becoming more at risk of infertility in terms of their low sperm count and impaired sperm motility (Daniels, 1999). Yet, as Daniels argues, there is no attendant shift in reproductive responsibility in the US, where she carried out her study, and women's consumption and life-styles continue to be regarded as posing potential threats to foetal well-being. When male infertility is recognised in contexts such as India and Egypt, women are not just blamed, they feel personally responsible for male infertility because it is regarded as something that could never happen to men. For women in these contexts, even more so than men, the failure (of their body) to produce children often leads to a sense of failure of the self (Greil, 2002; Martin, 1987) and other selves.

The body, as Greil argues, is not only something *one has* but also represents who *one is* and, hence, the extent to which body failure is perceived often determines the extent to which stigma is felt. One would expect stigma to be less in Euro-American, capitalist and bio-medically dominated societies where a mind/body distinction holds sway (Scheper-Hughes and Lock, 1987; for example) and the defective body when regarded as partible can be distanced from the sense of self. However, Greil (2002) documents the co-existence of both these ideas among the infertile American women he interviewed. In contexts where the body is perceived as distinct from the self (i.e. 'it is my ovaries/tubes that are at fault, and not me'), there the blame and shame associated with infertility can be displaced on to another agent. Where body-self connections are less clearly made ('my ovaries are me'), infertility will present a greater stigma.

The deeply hidden quality of male infertility makes it a particularly difficult health and social problem to address. However, with rising levels of medicalisation of male infertility and its recognition as a medical pathology, Muslim men in Egypt and Lebanon may also experience less stigma (effect on the self) associated with their infertility (Inhorn, 2004, 2012). Here we find that medical and technological processes work in favour of men compared to women. Contrary to this view, Becker notes that the disclosure of male infertility through the couple's resort to donor insemination practices in the US made infertile men more vulnerable to social stigma. She suggests, this is because semen donation is culturally associated with deviant sexuality compared to egg donation for infertile women, which is linked to altruistic practices (Becker, 2000).

The rise in the availability of assisted procreative technologies in the past decades, from the 1980s onwards, has primarily been in response to the plight of involuntary childlessness faced by individuals and couples in the Euro-American world. The contribution of reproductive technologies in enabling individuals to regain a strong sense of self in this context has been well documented in the anthropological work on infertility which emerged in the 1990s (Edwards *et al.,*1993; Franklin, 1997; Ragone, 1994) with some work also in non-Euro-American settings (notably Inhorn in Egypt, 1994). The rapid growth in clinical infertility services since then has contributed to a rising medicalisation (in the sense of an inevitable acceptance of medical authority) of infertility not only in technologically advanced countries but equally in rapidly globalising economies such as India. And yet, as Bharadwaj (2003) has shown for middle and upper-class families in the cities of Delhi, Mumbai and Jaipur, the processes of clinical in vitro fertilisation (IVF) procedures take place in secret to avoid the public knowledge of their infertility from spreading. The infertile couples of his study, however, prefer this intervention to adoption which they suggest would only exacerbate their association with the stigma of infertility (making their failure of kinship responsibilities more visible). Poorer couples in Rajasthan resorted to medical intervention for their infertility, but more routinely sought out faith healers.

The conviction that infertility requires *primarily* medical intervention is contested by lower-middle and lower-class couples and individuals in Rajasthan, as we see in this chapter, even as medical intervention is routinely sought for other conditions. The inability to conceive was an issue that frequently emerged in gynaecological consultations in public hospitals as well, although there were few technological means available for use by poor patients. Even the two newly established infertility clinics in Jaipur in 2002 had little to offer their patients apart from an ultrasound scan and a regime of drugs. Instead, women turned to healers to understand why and by whom they were 'caught', submitting to the 'hold' of a healer. Similar to Reynolds-Whyte's ethnography (1997) on healing rituals in eastern Uganda, there is the idea in Rajasthan that healing rituals are necessary to redress misfortunes of health, prosperity, marriage, reproduction and sexuality which are caused by the imbalances of 'relational power' (an imbalance in social relationships).[11] The ambiguities and uncertainties that the Bunyole in Whyte's study are trying to control, conceived of as failures ('misfortunes'), are not only to do with individual bodily disorders but also about kinship relations, agents, feelings and substances that affect them (Reynolds-Whyte, 1997, p. 33). Healing the self among the Bunyole, as for families in Rajasthan, is importantly linked to remaking ('adjusting') kinship relations and more than just about the individual body.

Focusing on the social meaning of infertility and its connection with multiple bodies and selves (Mol, 2002; Strathern, 2004) provides an important insight not only about how infertility is experienced but also how it is connected to agency in health matters. The widespread quest for infertility-related cures from faith healers in Rajasthan reflects a wider ethnographic fact, that people from across the different religions and communities not only shared a common aetiology of healing and a related universe of healers, but also shared an embodied ritual-based understanding of their inauspicious condition. Healers were efficacious precisely because they drew on this shared understanding of the social body-self. And, as Ram suggests in her work on spiritual healing in Tamil Nadu, the power of transformation located in the body[12] enabled mediums to 'turn people into new kinds of subjects (subjects of a goddess), and from a person whose troubles are insignificant, to one who matters because she matters to the goddess' (Ram, 2004, p. 169). It is in this sense that sessions with healers in Rajasthan enabled women to become legitimate members of their families, regaining their sense of personhood, at the same time as they challenged notions of citizenship and reproductive health as a medical concept.

Pakad: being caught by a spirit/healer

In Rajasthan, the 'weakness' entailed in being barren is often attributed to being 'caught' by a dissatisfied spirit or transmitted through social contact with other infertile women. Such conditions can only be addressed by a range of indigenous healers: specialist and informal providers. Faith healers rather than medical experts were overwhelmingly sought out by lower class infertile women and men as I came to realise following field research in 2002.[13] The sheer number of healers and networks operating in the area (over ninety-four healers were identified in a survey of seventy women living in the peri-urban village and *basti* settlements) came as a surprise as did the diversity in their healing services and practices.[14] Both male and female healers were consulted by poorer couples in the region and were of two broad categories: those who were established healers such as Gyarsi and Rehman (described below) to whom members of all religious communities and castes flocked. The other category was comprised of family and kin-based healers practising in Muslim as well as Hindu households, as the stories of Miriam and Ghisi respectively reveal in the following sections. Some of the most powerful healers were affinal relatives of the women seeking cures. The services offered and the power (*pakad*, literally meaning 'hold') exerted by these different healers varied. The greater the perceived *pakad* of the healer, the greater was the perception of their efficacy. It was the strength of the *pakad* which determined the choice of specific healers over others in individual quests for conception.

The route of consultations for infertility would start with an informal session with a kinswomen or women of other castes/groups who were considered knowledgeable about procreation and birth. Recognised as 'kin' midwives, (Unnithan-Kumar, 2002; and Chapter 5) these women healers would routinely advise a *safai* or cleansing of the uterus (through medical procedures such as a dilatation and curettage) as a way of ensuring a healthy conception in the future. The consultation with midwives would be accompanied by another routine quest for advice from elder men of the kin group (especially among the Sunni Muslim respondents) in family-based healing sessions. Thirty-four of the ninety-four healers identified during field work were such kin-based healers. Cures sought by poor Muslim and Hindu women in and around Jaipur showed a pattern whereby most women sought out family-based healers (referred to as *aouth* in the case of caste women and *syyed* among Muslim families) before visiting regionally renowned healers (*matamai, bhairu, hanuman*, as described below) or medical infertility specialists. The desire to move from healer to healer also depended on what was referred to as the *pakad* or hold of the healer. The *pakad* of family healers and some regional healers was considered particularly powerful.

In the following lines I examine the empowerment as well as the 'disciplining' (control) that women experience in their recourse to family and regional healers who practised across communities. The quest for healing begins with family-based healers and only then moves on to more established, non-family healers. For instance, regional healers such as Gyarsi and Rehman, described below, were usually consulted only after they had been either recommended or approved by family members and family healers.

The pakad ('hold') of the family healer

There were two types of family healers, affinal and natal, who provided advice on health matters to women in rural Jaipur. Male affines were the more dominant healers compared to men and women of the natal family. Research in 2002 on women's consultations with family members indicated a high prevalence of women's consultations with healers from the husband's family and through them a stricter control exerted by male affines. It was through these consultations that I learnt about how married women experienced reproductive power in their affinal homes and of the *pakad* or hold of the patrilineal group over them:

> Miriam was pregnant and Samina, her local midwife had diagnosed that the foetus was in a breech position. During her pregnancy as with her previous eight pregnancies, Miraim consulted with Pooran, the lower caste bhangi healer who became possessed by 'Baba' (which he claimed could be either Ramdeo Baba of the lower castes, Guru Nanak of the Sikhs, or a Muslim pir) transferring his power into saffron and red threads which he 'tied' the affliction with.[15] Then ten days before Miraim's baby was due she experienced pain and a dripping of fluid. She consulted with a gynaecologist at the government women's hospital in Jaipur city and was advised to seek admission immediately in the hospital. Miriam, however, returned home to seek advice from her father-in-law, who was a spiritual healer and who had treated her previously. Her father-in-law became possessed by the spirit of Shukker Baba and said she should not go to the hospital. The Baba (her father-in-law) said he would either kill her or the child would die if she went to the hospital. He explained her pains to be due to being possessed by the spirit of her husband's elder brother who had died shortly after being born. On the tenth day, the pains increased and childbirth was imminent. Her father-in-law/the spirit of Shukker Baba oversaw the process. Saira, a neighbour, and Farzan the kin midwife were also present. They helped deliver a baby girl.
>
> (Unnithan-Kumar, 2004, p. 69)

Miriam's example shows the strong influence affinal healers have over women's decisions to seek healthcare. Those faith healers and midwives who were most influential were likely to be relatives of the woman seeking assistance. But women from the same family may find their relatives effective to differing extents. Take the example of Ghisi and Sharda who are sisters-in-law in the Regar (lower caste Hindu, 'untouchable') community.

Ghisi the older sister-in-law complained of secondary infertility. At the time she had a daughter of five years, but said she had been unable to conceive after this child. She did become pregnant about five months before, but was unable to carry the baby to full term. Since she was married and in her husband's home, she was treated by her father-in-law's elder brother, Mangi Lal. He is possessed by the spirits of kali mata and bhairu (both malevolent, powerful spirits associated with protection of the lineage). When her miscarriage took place, he put it down to her falling prey to an ill wind caught at a crossing (intersecting paths are regarded as especially dangerous sites where bad spirits congregate). Ghisi says that after he said that, she began to have less faith in him. Sharda, married to Ghisi's younger brother, strongly believed in the powers of Mangi Lal, on the other hand. Two years after her marriage she had a miscarriage when she was four and a half months pregnant. Eight days before this she had been in pain and consulted with Mangi Lal who gave her sacred ashes, wheat grains and tied a thread around her waist. He cautioned her from going anywhere alone after 11 p.m. Eight days later Sharda went unaccompanied to the toilet at night, at around 12 p.m. Her husband was unwell and she did not bother to wake her mother-in-law. On her return she bled for three hours. She attributes her miscarriage to the fact that she did not adhere to Mangi Lal's instructions.

During my fieldwork in 2002, Sharda became pregnant again and did not go anywhere without Mangi Lal's consent. He had forbidden her to go to the doctors or to her natal home. Ghisi, on the other hand, had sought medical treatment for her secondary infertility from the voluntary health centre, where I met her. She had also returned to consulting the spiritual healer in her natal village. Ghisi became pregnant towards the end of my stay. She claimed her pregnancy was due to the intervention of the *matamai* spiritual healer in her village rather than as a result of the course of drugs she had taken from the health centre.

The stories of Ghisi and Sharda show differing views regarding the efficacy of a particular spiritual healer that exist among women, even within the same family.

Compared to Sharda, her younger-sister-in law, Ghisi, is able to resist her father-in-law's control over her body as a spiritual healer, partly because she has already had a child and thus proved her fertility. But, as the events unfolded, it became clear to me that Ghisi's confidence also stemmed from the fact that her relationship with her husband was deteriorating and thus her sense of responsibility towards him, and through him to his kin, had declined as a result. Sharda, on the other hand, got along well with her husband and was anxious to please him and produce her first child. In Ghisi's resort to the healer of her father's family, we see her negotiating an outcome which is emotionally directed towards those persons she feels more intimate with at the time. The failings of Mangi Lal, as broadcast by Ghisi, are used to provide her with a legitimate reason to travel back and forth to her natal home, giving her a mobility desired by most married women in the villages. Nevertheless, there is an agreement that faith healers are more effective than medical practitioners in general, as Ghisi's final explanation for her successful conception indicates.

The family healing sessions recounted here usually involved possession (*bhav aana*) of an elder male member of the woman's affinal group. The healers placed constraints on women in terms of visiting certain areas and moving about 'freely' (i.e. with no purpose of work). In these cases, the affliction was often attributed to the dissatisfied spirit of a family member who had experienced an unnatural death through an accident or illness as a child and was characterised as a dissatisfied and troubled spirit. It was often the case that when the advice of the family-based healer was regarded as ineffective (i.e. not yielding results after several consultations) women decided to consult with other healers and were often encouraged to do so by the family healers themselves. Through them, I was led to examine how 'pakad' was experienced *beyond* the family.

Pakad beyond the family: the multiple bodies of faith healing

Female Hindu healers called *mata-mai* were considered especially knowledge-able and efficacious and were known for providing actual 'solutions' beyond the 'advice' of the family healer. This was because, I was told, they drew on the intervention of a wider constellation of spirits 'seven sisters' (*sathu behna*) in identifying the causes and remedies for infertile women. In the following lines we consider the healing of Gyarsi, a *matamai* healer. We then examine the healing techniques employed by a male Muslim healer living in the same street as Gyarsi.

Gyarsi: Matamai and healing through bharna (the 'filled body')

'once mata arrives in me, like a doctor she asks, 'what is wrong'?
Gyarsi, Hindu female healer, fieldwork notes, August, 2005

Gyarsi Bai a female healer of the Hindu Banjara caste lived in the railway town of Jagatpura. Gyarsi was one of four *matamai* (who were all women of lower Hindus castes) operating within a radius of approximately eight kilometres, extending from the railway town into the nearby villages, with whom I had contact from 2005 till 2014. It was with great sadness that I learnt of her death in 2016.[16] Gyarsi has been performing healing sessions for over fifty years, she told me, when I met her in 2005 on the recommendation of women in the nearby Muslim village. In 2014, she continued to provide weekly healing sessions despite suffering from asthma and being eighty years of age. Gyarsi was possessed by the spirit of the *matamai* or *satu behna* (seven sisters) who she said entered (or 'filled'; *bharna*) her body every seventh and fourteenth day of the lunar cycle:

every *satam* (7th) and *chaudus* (14th), *mata-mai* fills my body (*bharna*). She asks questions and consults the *akha* (wheat grains) for solutions. She sweeps the afflicted with peacock feathers and tells them what they need to do to get better. She 'gives' them children (*bacchha deti hai*). She proscribes certain foods (*parej rakhti hai*), heals the shivering of hands and legs (*hath-panv ki bimari*; epilepsy); sorts out cases of the evil wind (*oonpar hawa ki bimari*), provides routes out of difficulties (*sangathan mein rasta bataati hai*).

(Fieldwork notes 2005)

It takes me a while to understand that the 'she' being referred to in Gyarsi's account refers both to herself and to the *mata-mai* spirit interchangeably, demonstrating an inter-corporeality between the human being and the spirit. This is also reflected in her speech; as Gyarsi talks, her tone suddenly changes for a short

Figure 3.1 Gyarsi (healer) standing in front of the *Mata Mai* Shrine.

Figure 3.2 Gyarsi arranging appointments with clients.

while and those seated around indicate it is *mata* speaking. Gyarsi explains *mata* is in her body (*shareer*) all the time but only attends to healing others at special times. Healing, she tells me, takes place through the possessed body of the healer. I learn how the body of the healer becomes a vessel through which healing is performed. As Gyarsi explains, 'I don't speak (act), it is *mata* who speaks (acts).'

What we find here is similar to other contexts of healing in southern India (Ram, 2013) and in Sri Lanka (Lawrence, 2000) where the spirit takes the body of the healer or medium to enact the healing: The medium becomes the healer only when their body is possessed, or as Gyarsi would say, 'filled'. In the case of the Amman healer whom Lawrence describes, a further mode of embodiment takes place; where the healer embodies (the pain and suffering of) the client, returning their bodies to a healed and thus fluent and articulate state of being. It is through this return of 'voice' that the petitioner, who has been silenced through the trauma of war and social disruption, is healed.

Mata mai is not the only spirit/healer in the region who cured sterility. Damodar was one such healer of the potter caste. He explained the *pakad* and 'filling' of indigenous healers in the following sense:

D: In my case, it is Ramdeo (his spirit) who does the 'work' (*kam*) of removing sterility. He empowers me to 'open' the 'mouth' of the uterus (*khoonk kholna*) and 'untie' the tubes (*bandh nalli kholna*).

(Fieldwork notes 2002; Unnithan, 2010, p. 322)

There are other bodily based forms of healing used by healers in the same area, but who subscribe to a different kind of bodily healing compared to *bharna* or filling. These healers use the techniques of *jhad-phoonk* (literally, shaking out-blowing).

Rehman: healing through Jhad-Phoonk ('the body extended')

There is a crowd of people in Jagatpura every morning outside the small tailoring shop of Rehman, a locally renowned Muslim healer. I get there at 7.30 a.m. to find a healing session in full swing with over thirty people sitting and standing around the patio of the shop. It is cold and many of the women and children are wrapped in thin shawls while men are smoking *beedis*. The crowd has a mix of labourers and workers, but there are also some middle-class couples. Toward the end of the session a middle-aged allopathic doctor arrives in his white Maruti car to enable his mother to consult with Rehman for her arthritic condition.

Rehman is sought after in the region as a specialist in curing jaundice (*peeliya*), typhoid, measles (*panijhara*), chicken pox *(motijhara)* and some chronic conditions. But most of all he is recognised for treating conditions created by the 'evil eye' (*nazar*) which especially effect young children (and which in local perceptions is strongly associated with child mortality). For this, he dispenses coloured threads (black for the evil eye and blue otherwise).

Rehman is continuously busy and, though squatting, moves with great dexterity waving his neem leaves as people present themselves before him. He is especially known for his practice of healing through administering the *jhada* (sweeping/ wiping/ dusting – associated with removing, emptying, cleaning) to the rhythm of a soft chanting of verses from the Koran. Often, his healing is accompanied by a gentle blowing of air over the afflicted parts. Patients with skin or jaundiced conditions are told to wash their hands and feet in chalky lime water provided at one end of the patio before the *jhada*.

Unlike Gyarsi, Rehman is emphatic that his healing does not involve *bharna* ('filling' of the body) either of himself as a healer or of his *grahak* (clients). Instead, his method was in extending the touch of his body through blowing and sweeping to the accompaniment of chants from verses in the Koran, thus distinguishing his technique from *matamai* healers such as Gyarsi. While Gyarsi and Rehman have two very different healing techniques involving the body, they are both known to have an equally valid 'pakad' (or force of healing). They share the strong, widespread belief that 'evil winds' are the root cause of illness (especially those conditions which have a sudden onset and are accompanied by a rise or fall in temperature).

'Each in their own place': healing and biomedical cures for sterility

I have a long discussion with Rehman after his clients leave and before he opens his shop for business. He kindly allows me, Vipula and Rohit (who helps with the translation of local terms) into the courtyard of his house. In terms of the efficacy of biomedicine, Rehman acknowledges clinical medicine as equally legitimate *within its own context* (reminding me of Evans-Pritchards (1976) explanation of Zande beliefs). For Rehman, 'the sweeping has its own place and biomedicine (*dawa*) its own (*jadha apni jagi hai, dawa apni*)', even acknowledging that in some conditions biomedicine would be mandatory (*sunnat*).

But it is Damodar who explains to me why sterility cannot be cured by biomedicine:

> M: You say that *angrezi dawai* (English Medicine) is so ineffective in treating the condition of sterility (*banjhpan*) – can you explain why?
>
> D: You see sterility is of a different making. It is a condition outside the 'control' of *angrezi dawai*. *Angrezi dawai* is good for coughs and colds – where there is no spiritual agency at work. It is also good for new illnesses which you get from eating foods grown through 'poisonous' (referring to chemical fertilisers) means. You must use injections *(teeke)* for these ailments because only one form of 'poison' can 'cut' (cancel) the other.
>
> (Unnithan, 2010, p. 322)

An insight into local aetiologies, as provided by the conversation with a well-respected faith healer such as Damodar, is especially important in understanding why biomedically based health programmes do not have any force (*pakad*) to them, even when they may be viewed as having some effect. Healers have the power to control the spirits, described as 'winds', which exert their own agency. These winds (*hava*) generally represent dissatisfied spirits of humans who have themselves had unfortunate or tragic ends to their lives and who come to inhabit marginal, ambivalent and impure sites (at crossroads or in the bodies of menstruating women) where there is danger and impurity. These winds are particularly dangerous for women, who due to their menstrual cycles are considered to be in *continually recurring states of impurity*.

A striking characteristic of the healing sessions with local healers was the manner in which the healers were able to deflect the blame associated with infertility away from the individual women themselves. The fact that there was a specific outside agent causing their infertility, as Damodar's explanation demonstrates, is a case in point. Nevertheless, according to these healers, individual women were to blame inasmuch as they created conditions of their own vulnerability, leading to their 'tubes' (fertility) being targeted by the spiritual agent in the first place. This was often explained to be a result of an act of 'disobedience' or deviance as we see in the case of Sharda, the young, lower caste Hindu woman recounted in the previous section.

There is little professional contact between the healers who practice in the local area. In general, they berate each other; this is especially the case among healers who provide similar services. There is, however, some degree of referral between the healers. The family based *aouth* often referred women to the more established healers such as the *matamai. Aouth* have also been observed to refer their family members to herbal healers if their own treatments have failed, or if they find themselves unable to establish control over the patient, especially in situations of family tension. The referral is made in very general terms and not to a specific healer but rather to a type of healer.

Spiritual healers such as the *matamai, bhairu and syyed,* whose sessions I attended, usually felt confident in their diagnosis of a patient's ailments. But if after repeated healing sessions they were unable to bring an improvement in the patients' condition or, more likely, when faced with a high-risk case, they would suggest that a bio-medical doctor be consulted. This suggestion was made in very general terms (*doctor ko dikhao*; go to a doctor), without reference to any specific doctor. If a woman complained of bleeding during pregnancy, the healer suggested she either get her uterus cleaned (*safai*) or get medicines for the growth of the foetus, leaving the choice of healer (midwife, private or govern-ment doctor) to the woman and her family. Faith healers, unlike midwives (as we shall see in Chapter 5), rarely suggest that an ultrasound scan be performed, either for bleeding problems or for determining the sex of the child. They usually determine the sex of the child themselves (often from the expression on the mother's face, which is then verified by recourse to ultra sound technology; see Chapter 4).

Concluding reflections: the challenge to notions of reproductive health and beyond

Ethnographic evidence in this chapter suggests that 'reproductive health' itself is conceptualised differently on the ground, as freedom from the fear of sterility, marking out the significance of healers in addressing anxieties to do with con-ception and social reproduction. While local health-seeking patterns suggest that biomedical and indigenous expertise combine in specific ways in the area of childbirth, as Ghisi's example illustrates, biomedical cures are inserted into a framework which privileges traditional healing, rather than replacing it. This tendency is also reinforced by the fact that infertility, unlike child and maternal mortality, is an issue that is ignored at the level of health policy and health pro-visioning. For instance, the Indian National Fertility and Health Survey, the leading health survey in the country does not contain any information on the pre-valence of infertility in the country or indeed on the extent of reproductive tract infections or other gynaecological morbidities. This is despite the fact that repro-ductive tract infections were the most common cause of secondary sterility (defined as the inability to conceive after the first child).

Infertility is not listed in national health documents as a 'health need', despite the evidence that a high proportion of women tend to be infertile because of reproductive tract infections often brought on by unsafe medical interventions and the sub-standard quality of healthcare on top of conditions of poverty (lack of access to water, nutrition or spaces for privacy in terms of conditions to wash). Infertility in poor rural women in India is often the outcome of a sequence of infections that originate in the vagina or cervix, ascend the tract to become Pelvic Inflammatory Disease (PID) which then result in infertility due to post inflammatory scarring (Oomen, 2001). Given the focus on contraception within reproductive health services provided to the poor, even a routine insertion of Intra-Uterine Devices could result in PID in that the insertion either pushes up lower tract infections or causes the infection if the insertor is not sterile, as Van Hollen documents in Tamil Nadu (Van Hollen, 2003). The frequent co-association of PID with reproductive tract infections in poor women makes infertility a serious health issue which needs to be recognised as such. Some writers, such as Inhorn and van Balen (2002) and Kielman (1998), argue that in highly populated countries the dominance of the myth of overpopulation is so strong that it obfuscates the prevalence of infertility, and the general public as well as policymakers are unable to 'see' or acknowledge its existence. Particularly in resource poor countries, the tendency to overlook infertility as a health concern may also be a convenient strategy to detract attention away from the state's interest in fertility control.

Infertility, as conceptualised by families, individuals and couples in Rajasthan, is a relational social condition which challenges the more clinically based ideas underlying the notion of reproductive health. Conditions of sterility or failed childbirth, infant deaths, miscarriage and menstrual complications are thought to be the result of being 'caught' by ill winds (*hava*) caused by the dissatisfied spirits of deceased men and women who have experienced misfortunes in their own lives. Women who are menstruating are especially prone to being prey to these spirits as menstruation is the bad, impure blood of failed childbirth and places women in recurring states of 'pollution'. Infant deaths on the other hand, are explained as resulting from the spells cast by jealous people through their evil glances (*nazar*; evil eye). They too are conditions that can only be resolved by faith healers. From observations of a number of healing sessions, I suggest that a key factor in the efficacy of faith healers such as the *mata mai*, for example, as described in this chapter, was their ability to draw on very different, social rather than physiological understandings of the body, as compared to that of anatomical medicine – providing a good illustration of anthropological concepts of the social body (Scheper-Hughes and Lock, 1987; Mol, 2002). In addition, I would suggest that faith healers are successful because they play a significant role in re-establishing conjugal relationships, aiding women accused of infertility to remake their connections with members of their family and the wider social group. In several healing sessions I found the Hindu *mata mai* had particular ritual tasks for the husband of the infertile woman to carry out as a pre-condition for her to become better. It is the ability to locate individual suffering in terms of a social disconnectedness which distinguishes the approach to the body in healing systems as compared with that of the partial body (viewed in terms of its parts) in biomedical systems (Good, 1993; Csordas *et al.*, 1994). As Susan Reynolds-Whyte (1997) and other anthropological scholars on healing have shown, healers are important because only they have the skills and competence to deal with disorders of the embodied self.

The health-seeking patterns and women's accounts of healing, especially in the context of infertility as discussed in this chapter, lead me to suggest that alternative conceptual framings of reproductive power as 'relational power' exist, as reflected in the concept of *pakad* or 'hold' of the family and of the healer. For married women especially, healers of the husband's family are powerful in enforcing the patriarchal ideals of social reproduction of the agnatic group, centred on the birth of children. The significance of family healers shows that matters to do with reproduction, in particular the need for regular conception in the early part of the reproductive life-course, is a routine matter of concern for women and for the entire family, affinal and natal. This both entails familial control over women's sexuality and procreation, but also means that family finances are available to facilitate women's reproductive health consultations. Women do get support from their families for seeking assistance when it comes to matters related to facilitating reproduction. The fact that women can contest the diagnoses and remedies of one healer with that of another affords them a sense of agency and participation in the reproductive decision making involving their own bodies. But to what extent is such agency symbolic of women's subordination to those very ideologies which discriminate against their sex? We discuss this further in the next chapter with regard to the practice of female selective abortion.

Notes

1 The terms reproductive health and rights are in single quotes to emphasise the contested nature of their definitions. The chapter draws on a previously published article on infertility in 2010 as well as subsequent conference presentations and field research in 2013 and 2014.

2 Poorer women carry a greater burden of 'structural violence' in terms of their poorer access to nutrition and water given the resource-scarce conditions in which they live which, in turn, makes them more vulnerable to reproductive tract infections, for example.

3 I use the term 'faith healers' following the suggestion of Indian scholars and local health activists who suggest a distinction needs to be made between such healers who draw on ideas of kinship and the social body as the basis for their healing rather than with reference to religious ideas per se.

4 Cornwall and Welbourn also critique the focus on health as a way of addressing rights relating to reproductive and sexual well-being (2001).

5 In reality, the actual support provided varied tremendously and was dependent on the individual predisposition of the men.

6 Publicly, there was little expectation my women respondents had from their husband to provide sexual pleasure and, in turn, there was the prevailing idea that women were not desirous of sexual pleasures. Equally, little importance was placed on an outward display of affection by spouses toward each other. This did not mean that women did not enjoy having sex, but, rather, that they did not have the moral right to exert any claims on their husband to fulfil their sexual desires.

7   Also see Unnithan-Kumar (2001).

8   Ramasubban and Rhishyaringa (2001) describe a similar notion captured in the term *ashakatapana* (literally without *sakti* or power) being used by Hindu as well as Muslim women in the slums of Mumbai to describe a whole range of reproductive, social and mental ailments.

9   *Caraka Samhita*, 2005; O'Flaherty, 1980; Wadley, 1980.

10   In her book, *Quest for Conception*, Marcia Inhorn (1994) recounts the devastating social consequences, but also debilitating economic implications, of infertility for poor Egyptian women for whom not producing children entails marital instability and financial insecurity.

11   In her study of the healing rituals in eastern Uganda, Reynolds-Whyte (1997) makes the important point that ritual is the therapy for afflictions of 'relational power' (an imbalance in social relationships). This is in contrast to afflictions treatable through the 'substantial power' of medical substances. In her work on the connections between uncertainty and affliction among the Bunyole in eastern Uganda, rituals are especially considered efficacious for afflictions seen to be caused by human agents (cursers, sorcerers) whose intentions are unclear. Alleviation involves making the sorcerer–victim relationship public, enabling negotiation and gift exchanges in appeasement.

12   Power is created in the body in this instance but not contained by it in that it extends to space, objects and groups as well.
     Ram suggests it is the body, rather than language per se through which possession itself must be examined (Ram, 2013, p. 164).

13   The high recourse to healers for infertility was especially intriguing given the increasing numbers of IVF clinics that were opening up in Jaipur (although given their costs these were in fact mostly available to wealthier, middle-class rural and urban families).

14   A result that emerged from the survey was that despite the eclectic and mixed providers from whom services were sought, over 74 per cent of the women mainly consulted with faith healers with a significant number of these healers (sixty of them) treating women for their infertility. Of the women who did consult with doctors, approximately half of them sought out doctors only after they had seen several healers and among these, approximately half of the women returned to spiritual healers for treatment after they had seen the doctor. Only 7 per cent of the women saw medical doctors in the first stages of their illness. There were only 6 women respondents out of a total of seventy women (approximately 9 per cent) who claimed not to believe in spiritual healers. Five of these women were Muslim and one belonged to the lowest Hindu caste. Two of the Muslim women were young, married women who had completed their schooling till class 5. One of them did not consult with spiritual healers for her own ailments, as her in-laws were orthodox Korani Muslims, who do not believe in spiritual healing and consider it to be a lower form of belief. She did, however, take her child to a spiritual healer (as well as to a herbal curer and also to an allopathic doctor) because she claimed only spiritual healers are effective in removing the bad effects of the evil eye on children. Another of the women said she was prevented from going to spiritual healers by her husband. She belongs to one of the wealthy households in the village. Yet another of the Muslim women claimed she had no suffering of the kind which spiritual healers could cure, otherwise she would go to them. The only Hindu woman who preferred not to go to spiritual healers was a Harijan woman who said she was treated badly by the spiritual healers because of her low social standing. She therefore only consulted with the government doctors for treatment.

15   The threads are wound around different parts of the body, but particularly around the waist for reproductive ailments. Pooran also prescribes that lemons and cloves be ingested or tied with the sacred thread at different places in the house or on furniture.

16   On my visit in 2014, I learn that Dakha, one of the other healers, is not receiving *mata* anymore, but rather it is her daughter-in-law (*bahu*) whose body is now being filled.

Bibliography

Barrett, R., 2008. *Aghor Medicine: Pollution, Death and Healing in North India.* Berkeley: University of California Press

Becker, G., 2000. *The Elusive Embryo: How Women and Men approach the New Reproductive Technologies.* Berkeley: University of California Press

Becker, G., 2002. Deciding whether to tell children about donor insemination: an unresolved question in the US. In Van Balen, F. and Inhorn, M., ed., *Infertility around the Globe: new thinking on childlessness, gender and reproductive technologies.* Berkeley: University of California Press, 119–34

Bharadwaj, A. Why adoption is not an option in India: The visibility of infertility, the secrecy of donor insemination and other cultural complexities. *Social Science and Medicine* 56, no. 9 (2003): 1867–80

Bledsoe, C., 2002. *Contingent Lives: Fertility, Time and Aging in West Africa.* Chicago University Press

Caraka Samhita 2005. R.K. Sharma and B. Dash (trans.) (Volume V Chikitsa Sthana Chap. XXVII–XXX) Varanasi: Kamba Sanskrit Services

Chattoo, S. Inherited blood disorders, genetic risk and global public health: framing 'birth defects' as preventable in India. *Anthropology and Medicine* 25, no. 1 (2018): 30–49

Cornwall, A. and Welbourn, A., eds, 2001. *Realising Rights: Transforming Approaches to Sexual and Reproductive Well-Being.* London and New York: Zed Books

Cornwall, A., 2001. Looking for a child: enduring and surviving infertility in Ado-Ado, SW Nigeria. In Tremayne, S., ed. *Managing Reproductive Life.* Oxford: Berghahn

Csordas, T. 1994. *Embodiment and Experience: The Existential Ground of Culture and Self.* Cambridge: Cambridge University Press

Daniels, C., 1999. Fathers, Mothers and Fetal Harm: rethinking gender difference and reproductive responsibility. In Morgan, L. and Michaels, M., eds., *Fetal Subjects and Feminist positions.* Philadelphia: University of Pennsylvania Press

Edwards, J., Franklin, S., Hirsch, E., Price, F., Strathern, M., eds., 1993. *Technologies of procreation: Kinship in the age of assisted conception.* London: Routledge

Evans-Pritchard, E., 1976. *Witchcraft, Oracles and Magic among the Azande.* Oxford University Press

Feldman-Savelsberg, P., 2002. Is Infertility an Unrecognised Public Health and Population Problem? In Inhorn, M. and Van Balen, F., eds. *Infertility around the Globe.* Berkeley: University of California Press

Franklin, S., 1997. *Embodied Progress: A Cultural Account of Assisted Conception.* London: Routledge

Good, B. 1993. *Medicine, rationality and experience: an anthropological perspective.* Cambridge University Press

Government of India. 2006. National Family Health Survey-3. Rajasthan http://rchiips.org/nfhs/pdf/Rajasthan.pdf

Government of India. 2016. National Family Health Survey-4. Rajasthan. www.rajras.in/index.php/national-family-health-survey-nfhs-4-rajasthan/

Greil, A.L., 2002. Infertile Bodies: Medicalisation, Metaphor and Agency. In Inhorn, M. and Van Balen, F., eds. *Infertility around the Globe.* Berkeley: University of California Press

Greil, A.L., 1991. *Not yet pregnant: Infertile couples in contemporary America.* New Brunswick NJ: Rutgers University Press

Inhorn, M. and Van Balen, F., 2002. *Infertility around the Globe*. Berkeley: University of California Press

Inhorn, M., 1994. *Quest for Conception*. Philadelphia: University of Pennsylvania Press

Inhorn, M., 2003. *Local babies, Global Science: Gender, Religion and IVF in Egypt*. London: Routledge

Inhorn, M. Middle Eastern Masculinities in the Age of New Reproductive Technologies: Male Infertility and Stigma in Egypt and Lebanon. *Medical Anthropology Quarterly* 18, no. 2 (2004): 162–82

Inhorn, M., 2012. *The New Arab Man: Emergent Masculinities, Technologies and Islam in the Middle East*. Princeton University Press

Kapadia, K., 1995. *Siva and her Sisters: gender, caste and class in Rural South India*. Boulder: Westview

Kauffman, G. and Unnithan, M., 2015. Perceptions and Impact of anaemia on women's health and work in rural and peri-urban households in Jaipur district, Rajasthan. Report, Khejri Sarvodaya Health Centre, Jaipur

Kielman, K., 1998. Barren Ground: contesting identities of infertile women in Pemba, Tanzania. In Lock, M. and Kaufert, P., eds. *Pragmatic Women and Body Politics*. Cambridge University Press, 127–64

Kreager, P. and Schröder-Butterfill, E., eds. 2005. *Ageing without children: European and Asian perspectives on Elderly Access to Support Networks*. Oxford: Berghahn

Lawrence, P., 2000. 'Violence, Suffering, Amman: The Work of Oracles in Sri Lanka's Eastern War Zone.' In Veena Das *et al.*, eds., Violence and Subjectivity. Berkeley and Los Angeles: University of California Press

Martin, E., 1987. *The Woman in the Body: a cultural analysis of reproduction*. Milton Keynes: Open University Press

Mol, A., 2002. *The Body Multiple: ontology in medical practice*. Durham NC: Duke University Press

O'Flaherty, W.D., 1980. *Women, Androgynes and other mythical beasts*. University of Chicago Press

Oomen, N., 2001. A decade of research on reproductive tract infections and gynaecological morbidity in India. In Ramasubban, R. and Jeejeebhoy, S. eds., *Women's Reproductive Health in India*. Jaipur: Rawat

Patel, T., 1994, *Fertility Behaviour: Population and Society in Rajasthan*. Oxford University Press

Petchesky, R., 1998. Introduction. In Petchesky, R. and Judd, K., eds. *Negotiating Reproductive Rights: Women's Perspectives Across Countries and Cultures*. New York, NY: Zed Books, 1–30

Ragone, H., 1994. *Surrogate Motherhood: Conception in the Heart*. Boulder: West View Press

Ram, K., 2004. Rationalising fecund bodies: Family planning policy and the modern Indian nation state. In Jolly, S. and Ram, K., eds. *Borders of being: Citizenship, fertility and sexuality in Asia and the Pacific*. Ann Arbor: University of Michigan Press, 82–117

Ram, K., 2013. *Fertile Disorder: spirit possession and its provocation of the modern*. Hawaii University Press

Ramasubban, R., and Rishyaringa, B. 2001. Weakness and Reproductive Health among Women in a Slum Population in Mumbai. In Obermeyer, C., ed, *Cultural Perspectives on Reproductive Health*. Oxford: Oxford University Press, 13–37

Rapp, R., 1999. *Testing Women, Testing the Fetus: the social impact of amniocentesis in America*. New York: Routledge

Reynolds-Whyte, S., 1997. *Questioning Misfortune: The pragmatics of uncertainty in Eastern Uganda.* Cambridge University Press

Riessman, C., 2000. 'Even if we don't have children we can live': Stigma and Infertility in South India. In Mattingly, C. and Garro, L., eds. *Narrative and the Cultural Construction of Illness and Healing.* Berkeley: University of California Press, 128–52

Riessman, C., 2002. Positioning Gender Identity in Narratives of Infertility. In Inhorn, M. and Van Balen, F., eds. *Infertility Around the Globe.* Berkeley: University of California Press

Sawicki, J., 1991. *Disciplining Foucault: Feminism, Power and the Body.* New York: Routledge

Scheper-Hughes, N. and Lock, M. 'The Mindful Body: A Prolegomenon to Future Work in Medical Anthropology' *Medical Anthropology Quarterly* 1, no. 1 (1987): 6–41

Strathern, M. The Whole Person and Its Artefacts. *Annual Review of Anthropology.* 33 (2004): 1–19

Strathern, M., 1992. *After Nature: English kinship in the late twentieth century.* Cambridge University Press

Unnithan, M., 2001. Emotion, Agency and Access to Healthcare: women's experiences of reproduction in Jaipur. In Tremayne, S., ed. *Managing Reproductive Life: Cross-cultural themes in fertility and sexuality.* Oxford series in Fertility, Reproduction and Sexuality, general editors: D. Parkin and S. Tremayne. Oxford: Berghahn, 27–52

Unnithan, M., 2003. Reproduction, Health, Rights: Connections and Disconnections. In Mitchell, J. and Wilson, R., eds. *Human Rights in Global Perspective: Anthropology of Rights, Claims and Entitlements.* London: Routledge, 183–209

Unnithan, M., 2010. Learning from Infertility: Gender, Health Inequities and Faith Healers in Women's Experiences of Disrupted Reproduction in Rajasthan. In Doron, A. and Broom, A., eds. *South Asian History and Culture, Special Issue on Health, Culture and Religion: Critical Perspectives.* London: Routledge, 315–28

Van Hollen, C., 2003. *Birth on the Threshold: Childbirth and Modernity in South India.* Berkeley: University of California Press

Wadley, S., ed. 1980. *The Powers of Tamil Women.* Syracuse NY: Maxwell School of Citizenship and Public Affairs

4 Sex selective abortion and reproductive agency
Technology and the discourse on rights

One should not 'take out' daughters, but the world wants sons – they say the line continues with them.... Daughters and sons are no different; they are both born through pain.

(Indira, 26 years, Hindu mother of four daughters and a son, Jaipur city, fieldwork notes)

Introduction

The period of my fieldwork from 1998 onwards coincided with a dramatic decline in the child sex ratio in India in favour of boys, with a notable increase in the practice of Female Selective Abortion (FSA) in Rajasthan, the adjoining states of Haryana and Punjab, and in the central Indian state of Maharashtra. The practice of female selective abortion, reflecting a strong preference for sons, has been statistically documented in India since the 1980s but also more widely in Asian countries such as China, Taiwan, Korea and Pakistan (Miller, 2001; UNFPA, 2004; Visaria, 2007). Son preference is itself widely prevalent in other Asian countries such as Nepal, Bangladesh and Vietnam (Kabeer *et al.*, 2013; Gammeltoft, 2014; for example). Its demographic implications have been a particular focus and it has been described as a practice underlying the demographic crisis of 'missing women' (Sen, 1990; Dreze and Sen, 2013).

Fieldwork on the subject in Rajasthan, between 2004 and 2010, revealed that sex selective abortion (termed *bhroon* or *jeev hatya*; literally, foetal killing/murder in Hindi) was openly practised and talked about by families who sought such services and by private practitioners who provided them. The *normalisation* of female sex selective abortion practice in Rajasthan was particularly intriguing for me given the widespread anxieties around infertility as discussed in the previous chapter, as well as the pervasive stigma against abortion among Muslim, middle-class as well as upper caste Hindu households. The co-occurrence of infertility and selective fertility practices, I suggest, points to the twin concerns with social reproduction as expressed by families in the area: to have children, but to ensure that at least one child is a boy. This did not mean that daughters were not valued, but that structurally after a certain birth order, usually the consecutive birth of two to three daughters, it was sons who were likely to be highly desired (an important distinction as examined further on in this chapter).

The invention and global circulation of 'Selective Reproductive Technologies' or SRTs,[1] a term Wahlberg and Gammeltoft (2018) use to refer to the practices and related technologies that aim to prevent or promote the birth of particular kinds of children, has especially enabled couples in India to have small families (and be modern) at the same time as conforming to the patriarchal demands of their families where the value of a son to carry on the 'family line' is openly expressed (Khanna, 1997, 2014; Patel 2007; Visaria, 2007). It is also a practice which has been punitively regulated by the Indian state (mainly through legislative reforms curbing the use by health providers of prenatal diagnostic technologies).

The failure of state and civil society organisations to control the practice, despite the promulgation of increasingly punitive legislation, can only be understood – as I elaborate upon below – in terms of the pervasive notion among doctors who provide such services as well as clients who seek their services, that FSA (female selective abortion) is morally acceptable. In this chapter I describe how the language of rights is invoked by these doctors (mainly gynaecologists) who see their service provision as meeting the rights of patients, and equally by pregnant women and couples for whom it is 'natural' and reasonable to want to abort female foetuses. In this chapter as in the previous chapter I suggest that the discourse on values of social reproduction at the level of the family stands in contrast to the 'modern' values of equality and progress held by the state and civil society (especially feminist) activists. And yet, in another sense, novel forms of 'cross class' solidarity have developed around the use of these technologies (such as between upper-class doctors and middle-class women who seek their assistance in terminating a female foetus) which both assist and resist the termination of pregnancy. This leads me to suggest that the technologies of termination examined in this chapter both re-enforce patriarchal state power over women's bodies at the same time as they generate new modes of resistance and new alliances and subjectivities across class (a kind of 'techno-sociality', building on Rabinow's ideas of biosociality (1996); see also: Gibbon and Novas, 2008; Gibbon and Reynolds-Whyte, 2009).

But, how have these technologies come to be embraced rapidly? How have they been made socially and culturally acceptable and meaningful in practice? And what kinds of moralities drive the divergent approaches to family decision-making in the region?[2] In this chapter I explore the social and cultural 'work' of reproduction that has enabled (or disabled) the use of technologies in aborting female foetuses. I also discuss the less visible, but equally political reproductive work, associated with it in the burgeoning statistics being collected on the subject.

Framed by a focus on the users and providers of FSA services, as well as state and non-state intervention practices to prevent sex selection in Rajasthan, this chapter suggests that gender inequality and anxieties to do with marriage and modernity drive especially middle-class use of technologies of termination, including those of sex selection, in their family building projects. To understand how these collective preferences work at an individual level I follow Latour's reasoning that 'an actor is what is made to act by others' (2007, p. 46).

Examining the processes through which son preference is practised especially enables me to discuss individual and family preferences for technological intervention in childbearing in the context of indigenous notions of reproductive rights and bodily autonomy to see how global concepts (of universal, reproductive rights) disappear and appear in local discourse on bodily autonomy, reproductive choice and control (Pigg, 2005; Franklin, 2005).[3] In line with other anthropological work on the social and cultural implications of reproductive technologies (notably Rapp, 2000; Lock and Nguyen, 2010; Ong and Collier, 2005; Gammeltoft, 2014; Wahlberg and Gammeltoft, 2018), I show how uneven the social response to technological intervention actually is (within families, but also across civil society and the state). A focus on FSA also enables me to bring forth a different perspective on reproductive agency than has been discussed in literature on the subject so far.

The emerging alliances between users and providers in their engagement with the selective reproductive techniques and practices have, for the childbearing women in question, served to modernise rather than limit their subservience to patriarchal reproductive norms as is evidenced in their own desires to undergo prenatal sex selection as discussed below. One of the striking findings of the in-depth interviews carried out in 2006,[4] and the reason which prompted the focus on women's agency in the context of selective reproductive technologies, was that the pregnant women I met themselves expressed desires to seek out sex selection practitioners. This was in contrast to my own expectations at the start of fieldwork that they might be subject to the coercion of kinsmen and affinal women and thereby victims of patriarchal ideologies wherein sons are highly valued. [It is important to note the role of birth parity in terms of son preference where it is often the case that abortion would likely be considered for a daughter conceived for the third time after the birth of two previous girls.]

The desire for FSA when acted upon could be interpreted in two ways. In one sense, women's resort to sex selective technologies could be viewed as symbolic of their further subordination to those very gender ideologies that discriminate against their sex. In this sense, their choice to undergo FSA is not an autonomous choice (as suggested by Euro-American feminist perspectives) at all. But, being mindful of context and heeding Petchesky's words of caution, it is important to examine the environment as enabling or disabling of such choice to fully understand the meaning of reproductive choice (Corrêa and Petchesky, 1994). In a second and different sense, pregnant women's resort to FSA can be taken as an example of their reproductive agency in the face of patriarchal control, where their actions represent an attempt to protect themselves and their daughters from future social discrimination. In this context women's decisions to undertake FSA could be characterised as pragmatic (Lock and Kaufert, 1998) or even as making them 'moral pioneers' in Rapp's terms (where they are forced to judge the value of their offspring; Rapp, 2000, p. 4).

Reproductive choice, as I suggest in this chapter, emerges in this part of India as consequent upon an assemblage of factors, ranging from the structural conditions which enable choice and systemic inequalities which frame the wider backdrop of this choice to more individual drivers linked to sociality such as emotion (partner intimacy; sense of responsibility), pragmatism (cultural and material), altruism (ideas of sacrifice and or selfishness related to parental roles), and concerns with social and physiological risk associated with reproductive technologies.

In the following lines I first provide a background on FSA in India setting out the changing patterns of occurrence, regional variation, and legislative and civil society interventions. The next section, based on fieldwork findings with regard to marriage anxieties suggests that wives' attitudes toward female children and FSA, are shaped by two critical social processes relating to marriage: first, the economic transactions engendered through marriage in the form of dowry payments which consolidate family standing, caste, gender and class hierarchies; and second, the obligations, expectations and moral force of marital ties which underlie and critically shape women's engagement with reproductive technologies, including those of sex-selection. I then explore the emerging discourse on rights and entitlements that has accompanied the easy access to reproductive technologies in general in India. Finally, I discuss agency in the context of new forms of bio-sociality (in the same sense as used by Rabinow, 1996; Gibbon and Novas, 2008), and bio-alliances that arise in the context of civil society and state attempts at the regulation of access to reproductive technologies. It is in the emerging forms of activism of civil society organisations and especially of feminist groups on the issue of FSA, wherein they partner with the state, that we see new everyday forms of bio-sociality emerging especially around such technologies of termination. Feminist activism around FSA has been substantive (SAMA 2010) but stands in stark contrast to an absence of activism around abortion more generally.[5]

Background: pre-natal sex selection in India from the 1980s onwards

The changing pattern of the Child Sex Ratio (CSR, 0–6 years) in favour of boys over the past thirty years in India, between the 1980s to 2010s, can be best understood in terms of the availability of ultrasound and abortion technologies, the social, geographical and economic propensity to undertake sex selection, and in terms of state policies on family planning and legislative controls. In Rajasthan, I suggest that the state's response to FSA can be regarded as taking place in two distinct phases – to do with weaker and stronger (more punitive) state interventions during the 1980s to 2000s and 2000 to 2010s respectively.

The initial rise of FSA saw it as an urban, largely middle-class phenomenon which emerged in the northern and western states of the country. Demographers in particular demonstrated the significance of correlating the practice of FSA with economic growth and urbanisation (Dasgupta, 1987; Khanna, 1997; Miller,

2001; Visaria, 2002; Bhat and Zavier, 2003; Sudha and Rajan, 2003). In some states, Punjab and Haryana for example, which experienced the highest levels of agricultural-based economic growth, capitalist development and urbanisation since the 1960s, the sex ratio was as low as 874 and 861 girls to every 1,000 boys born, respectively, compared to an all-India average of 933 females for every 1,000 males (Visaria, 2007; 2001 census figures). FSA is regarded in these studies as primarily an urban phenomenon (although already rapidly spreading to the rural areas) and associated with middle and upper caste families, rising levels of household income and with the education and employment of mothers in these locales (Patel, T., 2007). Other studies suggest that with the decline in the size of families there is also an extent to which there is a decline of son preference (Bhat and Zavier, 2003; Khanna, 2003), but this is not accompanied by an increase in daughter preference or son aversion (Khanna, 2014).

The state response to this first phase of FSA was primarily legislative, consisting of the promulgation of the Pre-Natal Diagnostic Testing Act (PNDT Act 1994) which prohibited the use of diagnostic sex selective procedures. At this stage state officials did not seek to actively intervene to regulate the delivery of ultrasound services by medical practitioners. The census in 2001 indicated a continuing increase in FSA and alarming declines in the figures of Sex Ratio at Birth (or SRB, which is a better indicator of FSA than the Child Sex Ratio but is less reliably measured (Dubuc and Coleman, 2007). Accordingly, the PNDT Act of 1994 was reformulated to include a prohibition on 'Pre-Conception' testing. The resulting PC-PNDT Act of 2003 came into effect which made FSA a jailable offence with imprisonment up to three years and a fine of Rs10,000/-.

From 2001 onwards there has been a spread of the practice to rural areas and in social terms to lower down the class and caste hierarchy, as borne out by my fieldwork as well as studies elsewhere in Rajasthan which suggest these FSA trends are indicative of a stated daughter aversion rather than simply a manifestation of son preference alone (Palriwala, 2008; for example). Despite the new legislation, in the decade from 2001 and 2011 the most recent census of India trends (2011) showed a continued rise in FSA across the districts in the state. Jaipur district, where fieldwork was conducted, witnessed a decline from 899 girls to 1,000 boys in 2001, to 861 girls to 1000 boys in 2011, a drop of 2.8 per cent over ten years representing a highly statistically significant decline in the birth of female children. The overall Child Sex Ratio in the state during this period was 909 girls for every 1,000 boys (or 909/1,000) in 2001, this declined to 888/1,000 in the 2011 census (as compared to an overall India figure of 933/1,000 in 2011).

One of the challenges for policymakers and civil society groups has been the great variation of FSA not just across the country but *within* each state and over time. In Rajasthan, for example, there is tremendous variation in each of its thirty-three districts. The district variation in FSA during the period of fieldwork, as noted in the census figures, has been highly statistically significant. For example, we see higher CSR figures (i.e. comparatively less skewed) in the 2001 census in the southern districts of Rajasthan such as Banswara (964/1,000) and

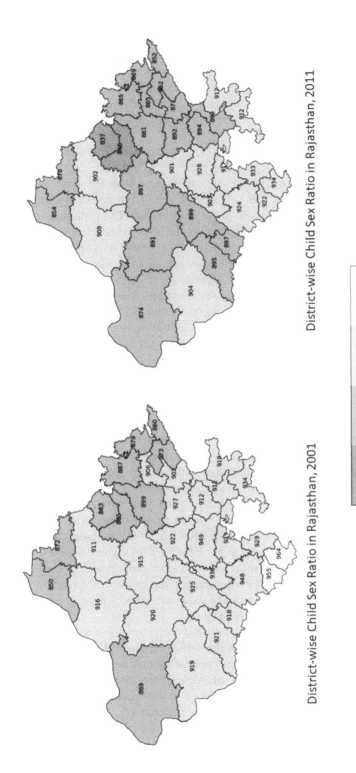

Figure 4.1 District-wise Child Sex Ratio in Rajasthan 2001–2011.

Source: Arjun Unmithan Kumar, Python open source software, cartopy, accessed July 2018.

Dungarpur (955/1,000) compared to the north (Ganganagar 850/1,000), west (Jaisalmer 869/1,000) and parts of the eastern region of the state (the districts of Jhunjhunu, Karoli and Dholpur). In the 2011 census, the districts of Jhunjunu and Sikar in the eastern region of the state showed the most skewed figures with CSRs of under 850 girls per 1,000 boys (i.e. a downward trend in these districts) along with a decline in the two southern districts of Dungarpur and Banswara to 922/1,000 and 934/1,000 respectively.

The figures of these 'missing girls' in the last census of 2011 clearly demonstrates the inability of existing legislation, and especially the Pre-Conception and Pre-Natal diagnostics Act (PC-PNDT Act) of 2003, to stem the resort to ultrasound diagnostics. Despite the 2003 Act, which resulted in few convictions, the figures continued to rise as reflected in the 2011 census. The continuing rise in figures of 'missing women' as evidenced in the 2011 census led to rigorous, punitive state intervention, this time in partnership with CSOs. It included the setting up of PCPNDT 'cells' and a cadre of surveillance officers deployed on the ground to actively carry out 'sting' operations on both service providers as well as middle-men involved in offering sex selection services (fieldwork attendance at a state level meeting of CSOs and government district level functionaries in Jaipur 2010; see also Singh and Srivastava, 2008). Given the development of even more refined sex-related diagnostics (through blood samples) offered through the internet in recent years, FSA practices have at the same time become more difficult to evidence and prosecute. The practice has thus disappeared from public view more recently and gone 'underground' as a result of state surveillance.

It is important to note that in the face of this 'growing tide of daughter aversion' (Palriwala, 2008), positive and not just punitive measures have also been undertaken by civil society organisations, often in partnership with the state. In the last decade these have included community-based incentive schemes to celebrate the girl-child through the *badhai patra* or letters of congratulation on the occasion of *balika janmotsav* (the birth of girls), state provision of monetary support toward girls' education, and the *prastav patra* (where issues relating to the girl child are presented as items to be discussed in village-based *panchayat* committees as in the initiative of the organisation C-FAR). These measures have had an effect in certain districts (most notably in Ganganagar in northern Rajasthan) primarily due to sustained civil society intervention but have had little ripple effect across to other districts in the state (interim SRS figures, September 2015; personal communication Meeta Singh).

However small-scale these community-led interventions may be, they are critically significant as we will see in the following lines. We now turn to an understanding of how FSA practices are normalised, embedded in local biopolitical worlds through the language of 'rights' and reproduced within the everyday. As Indira suggests in her reference to the 'continuation of the line' through the birth of a son (quote at the start of the chapter), it is the significance of social reproduction that shapes and drives attitudes and practices on gender preferences, including to do with FSA. At the heart of my conversations with women about reproducing a certain kind of family was the importance of marriage as an institution and its relation to the reproduction of the household economy (in the form of labour contributions, money and goods in dowry and cash through employment) and its related social value for family members. It is economics rather than religion which is a critical factor in the continuing recourse to FSA as fieldwork across Hindu and Muslim communities in Rajasthan suggested.[6] While *in some contexts middle class women's increasing access to employment is being* valued and a reason cited for the decline in FSA in Bangladesh by Kabeer *et al.* (2013) , this is not the case in India where the quest for bigger dowries remains an important factor in marriage, as we now examine in more detail.

The desire for FSA: marriage anxieties and son preference in the context of modernisation

> Tomorrow my daughters will be sad [as they know they can't get married]. Then as a mother I can't take that. I will be sad. Who knows what kind of a man she will marry? How much of goods (*saman*) will we have to give them (the in-laws)? We have to give them a complete set of goods (*poora saman*). Even then there may be no happiness
>
> (Zahida, Muslim mother of five sons and one daughter, Sanganer district, fieldwork interview, 2009)[7]

Zahida's observation is especially instructive as it highlights the centrality of marriage in structuring the quality of life for mother and children, including for those who are unborn. The overwhelming anxiety linked to a family's inability to secure an appropriate reproductive future (through the right marriage) for their daughter indicates that girls are being valued (in the sense that their welfare is focused upon) at the same time as they are being discriminated against in certain middle-class families (through the practice of FSA). To understand the impact of FSA in terms of the shifts in the way children are valued, it is the anxieties (of status, inheritance, securing the future) that are generated by changing social institutions such as marriage which require critical scrutiny.

A focus on marriage is central to understanding how the gender hierarchy and reproductive politics operate in India and how girls come to be less valued, in a structural sense, than boys, in the social reproduction of kin, family and community. Notions of biological difference play a key role in legitimising gender and familial (sub-caste) hierarchies upon which marriage exchange is based. The biological basis to gender hierarchy is set out in classical texts on the Hindu religion as well as in Ayurvedic ideas of procreation (Bock and Rao, 2000; Unnithan-Kumar, 2008a) as referred to in Chapter 1. In caste ideology, blood is seen to be associated closely with the male sex and semen (or life force) is regarded as its purest and most concentrated form. 'Blood' (rather than 'genes') is regarded as the central substance of relatedness. And, in turn, it is marriage which is considered the primary institutional mechanism that regulates the transmission of blood.

The emphasis on regulating marriage within the same, though widespread, caste group (referred to as endogamy) stems from the social concern of ensuring that children, especially boys, are able to carry on the 'purity' of their patrilineal heritage (Dumont, 1980). Marriage to those outside the appropriate sub-caste leads to pollution (from the 'mixing of blood'). The concern for purity within a set of marriageable castes, in Rajasthan as elsewhere in northern India, operates alongside a gender norm for marriages to be hypergamous, in the sense that women of lower status families should marry men of upper status so that 'wife-taking' families always remain socially superior to 'wife-giving' ones (Parry, 1979; Unnithan-Kumar, 1997; Chapter 1 in this volume). Very similar notions of bodily pollution, lineage purity and caste-type hierarchies operate among lower-class Muslims in India (Shaikh, 2007). In Islam as well, the tie by *nasb* (lineage) or relation by blood is considered to be one of God's great gifts to his worshippers (Inhorn, 2003, p. 107).

Marriage payments such as dowry (where cash and goods are gifted by the bride's family to the groom's family) continue to be an important factor in determining the way families' think and act in relation to marriage in India,[8] including the more upwardly mobile Muslim families (Sharma, 1984; Unnithan-Kumar, 1997; Shaikh, 2007). This is despite the educational and occupational changes that middle-class families are undergoing. Anxieties around marrying the socially appropriate partner and possessing the requisite amount for the marriage payment of one's daughter are manifest across castes and the middle- and lower-class in Rajasthan.

The idea that dowry payments are a prerequisite to be undertaken by the bride's family is also supported by an implicit notion of the bride as a 'burden' (particularly in an economic sense) to her husband's family. This idea continues to dominate marriage practices despite the fact that significant numbers of middle and lower middle class women are now in waged employment. But even when women make financial contributions to the household, their contribution remains ideologically devalued – an observation noted from the 1980s (Sharma, 1984; Standing, 1990), which still holds today. This is unlike in Bangladesh, for example, where a decline in son preference has been noted due to an increase in women's employment levels (see Kabeer *et al.*, 2013). On the contrary, in India dowry payments have become an important source of household goods among the middle class and are soaring in line with inflation (another trend noted by Sharma in the 1980s).

The expectation of dowry-related gifts carries on well into married life. Indira told me:

> They (the in-law family) have been troubling my sister to get her husband a motorbike. They beat her and ridicule her. Finally, my father borrowed Rs10,000 and got his son-in-law a motorbike. They have stopped bothering her now, but who knows for how long.
>
> (Unnithan, 2010, p. 157)

The prospect of a heavy financial expenditure at the marriage of daughters is a key factor driving people to resort to sex selective abortion in India. Urban living and wanting 'to be modern' (in lifestyle and consumption choices) are more recent reasons given for son preference. Private clinics in the mid-2000s openly advertised their sex-selection services as inducing couples to 'spend now' (on procuring the services) to 'save later' on a hefty marriage and dowry expenditure in case a girl is born (Patel, T., 2007). These trends are not mitigated by women's increased earning capacity as we saw in the case of Bangladesh and therein pose a dilemma for those who advocate that the way to redress gender inequalities against women is primarily by increasing women's access to economic resources (Dagar, 2007).

The social trends noted above suggest that whatever positive cultural and familial constructions of daughters exist, in particular the mother-daughter emotional bonds highly valued by all the women I spoke to, get overlaid by a discourse increasingly dominated by market-determined values, as in dowry payments. Here, gender inequality and hierarchy is reinforced and reconstituted in a form which is ever more difficult to contest. It is this powerlessness that mothers such as Zahida, Indira and others, who come from poorer families, refer to as their inability to stem the 'sadness' of the future their daughters will face, an irrevocable reality of their lives. Female selective abortion allows mothers to take limited pragmatic steps to prevent discrimination against their daughters at the same time as it continues to support and reinforce the gender hierarchy as 'natural'.

The practice of pregnant women who resort to FSA is informed not only by their experience of gender discrimination in marriage and their notions of son preference, but also by their specific understandings of the role of abortion technologies more generally, a discussion we return to in the final section of the chapter. We first examine some of the enabling conditions underlying the recourse to sex selective procedures.

'Normalising' FSA: 'rights', moralities and new networks of medical authority

The dramatic growth in FSA in India in the past two decades has, to a significant extent, been attributed to the increasing availability and easy access to the foetal ultrasound scan. As elsewhere in the world, scanning technologies have been heralded by the medical profession as a scientific breakthrough enabling accurate diagnoses and increased biomedical efficacy. Dr M., a gynaecologist at the city's public hospital, informs me of the professional use of the scan in her practice since the 1980s, at almost the same time when its regular use within gynaecological consultations was taking place in Europe and America. Dr M. in particular mentions the breakthrough the use of ultrasound technology has enabled her to make in her own research. The more routine use of the scan in India has emerged only in the last decade and is connected with its local manufacture and related low cost. In 2003 it was already estimated that there were over 100,000 machines in use in the country (Bose and Shiva, 2003).

The use of the scan is associated with modernity and progress by doctors and their clients alike. Especially in the private health sector in the early 2000s it was the latest 'must have' medical technology which conferred modern status on the clinics which offered scanning services. The ease with which the scanning equipment could be obtained and transported enabled a range of local practitioners (qualified and spuriously qualified) to offer sex detection sonographic services (Patel, T., 2007; Khanna, 1997, 2003; Bose and Shiva, 2003). This was despite the ban placed on such practices by the Pre-Natal Diagnostic Testing Acts (the PNDT Act of 1994 and the 2003 PC-PNDT Act). Although the strict directives of this act, which mandate the registration of clinics and doctors owning and using the machines, it is an aspect of the new regulations which has been especially difficult to monitor and enforce. Consequently, the large number of private clinics and doctors offering this service who openly flouted the ban has been the subject of considerable feminist and civil society concern within India in the past decade (Singh and Srivastava, 2008; Palriwala, 2008; Bose and Shiva, 2003; Dagar, 2007; Patel, V., 2007; Patel, T., 2007; among others).

The increased circulation and 'consumption' of scanning machines has led to a diffusion of the medical authority related to the use of this technology, away from medical hospitals and gynaecologists to private practitioners offering services in small clinics and temporary locations. New networks of medical authority have arisen which consist of local midwives, informal and formal private practitioners and even at times the more formal and trained public hospital personnel. Zahida, as a provider of 'cases' (women who seek FSA) was in such a network in the mid-2000s herself. She would receive around Rs200/- for her role while the doctor would earn Rs500/- with the remainder of Rs1,500–1,600/- going to the clinic where the abortion service was provided. I was able to speak with the doctor (referred to as Doctor B. here) for whom Zahida was the conduit. Unable to understand the reason for Doctor B. to undertake such a risky procedure, especially in the face of state legislation outlawing such practice and the vocal opposition from health activists and the media, I sought out her views on the subject.

DOCTOR B. (DB): If a woman who has four daughters comes to me and says she wants a son, then this is her right (*huq*) and I have to help her. She is oppressed by her in-laws, so I have to help her.

MU: But what about the fact that the population of girls overall is declining in India?

DB: See, I believe boys and girls are equally good. But very few people are satisfied if they don't have a boy. Doctors have to judge what is right and what is wrong in each individual case. Let us take Anokhi Ram's case. Anokhi came to me saying she wanted to know if her fifth child was going to be a girl or boy. I persuaded her to have the child anyway. It was a girl and she died in 6–8 months as they did not feed her well. They are very poor. They didn't give her any treatment or care. Then she came back at the time of her sixth pregnancy. Now they have a son – they are so happy as a family. They bring him here for every cough that he has.

MU: But is this not gender discrimination? Should it be allowed?

DB: Women will always be different from men and there will never be equality. Even now, we are both earning, men and women both work, but we are still not valued equally. There are greater expectations from women. Women themselves believe this. Women patients who come here for sterilisation or infertility tests said we should test them and leave their husbands alone in case they become disabled (unable to earn). If the man becomes weak how will they eat (*admi kumzor ho jaye ga tho khana kaise khayenge*)?

MU: But isn't there any sin (*paap*) attached to killing the foetus (*jeev hathya*)?

DB: Patients are not worried about *paap*. In fact, they are most concerned and in 'tension' about having the right conception.

(Unnithan, 2010, p. 161)

The conversation with Doctor B. illustrates the underlying ethic of social service that frames the way in which doctors think about their work, including the provision of FSA services. To understand the basis of the divergence between the activists' and doctors' views on FSA, it is necessary to examine the notion of social service that is deployed by doctors in their discourse of FSA. Doctor B. firmly believes that doctors should help patients achieve what is in the patients' best interests (*hith*) and that this is a case-by-case decision. In her interview, she highlights the reality of gender discrimination in the everyday practices in the household where female neglect is manifest through a denial of food and care. Such neglect takes place more in connection with an ideology of discrimination and irrespective of the actual amounts of food available (as the early studies of Sen and Sengupta (1983), and others have also shown). A recent study of the shifting child sex ratios in five districts across four northern states, including Rajasthan (Palriwala, 2008) concludes that 'deliberate and unavoidable neglect' of girls is an important factor in their mortality. Doctor B's pertinent observation also brings her views close to those of the feminists themselves, although she herself opposes the increased surveillance of doctors. For her, state control over doctors would only drive the practice 'underground' (to be offered in secret) and at the same time as it would violate the rights of women who seek their services. For those seeking FSA doctors rather than the state are seen as best serving their reproductive interests.

At the same time a number of health activists as well as patients regard the medical provision of FSA as primarily profit oriented. Zahida informed us that, 'Doctors do it to keep their hospital and practice going. To get more clients they will do anything.' The use of FSA for profit has been marked in the private health sector. In the last two decades, India has seen a tremendous growth of private health services (Nandraj, 1994; Baru, 1998) and a related surge in health consumerism (Nichter, 1996). Private medical and health practitioners follow the market logic in offering the kinds of services unavailable in public hospitals and clinics. Sex-determining ultrasound consultations, abortions beyond the safe period of the first trimester (and as late as five months) and infertility-related medical interventions are among the most popular of the reproductive services provided.

The role of medical professionals in contributing to the widespread practice of FSA has been critically focused upon by the media and is an issue that has generated major concern among women's groups and voluntary health organisations working to limit the powers of doctors through appropriate legislation and its enforcement. It is not so much the formulation of laws that is at stake, but why is it that the laws are ineffective. The people's campaign, led by women's groups and health-related civil society groups (including the People's Union of Civil Liberties in Rajasthan), have in the past years been successful in securing convictions of those doctors who flout the PNDT ban. Although there had been only one conviction of a doctor during fieldwork, despite the fact that approximately 100 doctors were reported to be violating the law in twenty-two districts in the state (Singh and Srivastava, 2008), the message that doctors are not above the law is getting through. A key insight to emerge from recent activist reflections on the protests against FSA has been that the actions undertaken by the Indian Medical Council and its Rajasthan counterpart, the RMC, have been more effective in restraining doctors than any legal action taken under the PC and PNDT Act (Singh and Srivastava, 2008).

Ever-expanding technologies of termination in the age of the global biological (Franklin, 2005) have promoted new forms of biosociality as we see in the alliances and solidarities between practitioners and clients of FSA. The practitioner-client connections set them against other relationships being forged between state and civil society actors, as we saw in Chapter 2. Feminist influenced CSOs, including the PUCL in Rajasthan have organised 'sting' operations and allied with the state to convict doctors who provide sex selection services (Singh and Srivastava, 2008). This suggests that forms of therapeutic citizenship (Nguyen, 2005) are emerging, which are fractured and supporting as well as contesting the use of selective reproductive technologies.

Maternal bonding and ways of 'seeing'

For rural and peri-urban middle class married women in Rajasthan, the sex of the foetus establishes the vulnerability of their position within the affinal family. For a pregnant woman, the fear for her future security became complexly intertwined with her emotions for the child, as was abundantly clear in the accounts of women I heard. The scan, because it could ascertain the sex of the foetus, was perceived as a technology which alleviated the physiological, social and emotional trauma following the birth of a female child to a woman with no sons. In this sense, I would suggest the ultrasound scan was locally regarded by the women I spoke to as primarily an instrument to detect the 'deviant' or debilitating sex of the foetus. In much the same way as Gammeltoft has observed in her ethnography in Vietnam scanning technology has 'fixed' the label of abnormality to the conception of girls (Gammeltoft, 2007; Dagar, 2007).

Another key social consequence of the increased use of ultrasound scans in antenatal health checks has been the growth of the social knowledge related to 'seeing' or knowing what is inside the womb. The ways in which scans have spatialised and localised knowledge of reproduction has played a vital role in shaping people's responses to reproductive technologies, as has been extensively documented by scholars working on abortion related decisions in the 'Northern' countries (Stanworth, 1987; Petchesky, 1987; Rapp, 2000; Georges, 1997; Taylor, 1998; for example). Their analyses especially points to the role of the scan in forging new social ties, where the mother along with her wider family group relate to and engage with the foetus as a person (Taylor, 1998). Such images have reinforced those who are pro-life and against abortion. As a consequence, pregnant women's rights are viewed as opposed to those of the foetus, a view which reinforces the idea of women who seek abortion as heartless and self-oriented (Petchesky, 1987; Martin, 1987).

In Rajasthan, I have argued to the contrary, that maternal-foetal bonding at the time of the ultrasound is less likely because of the functional ways in which the scan is interpreted (Unnithan-Kumar, 2004). Because of a lack of communication between the sonologist and pregnant woman during the scanning procedure, lower class women especially do not 'see' or interpret the foetal image in the same way as their northern counterparts. In most cases the monitor is not turned towards them so they do not get to view the image or if they do, they fail to recognise or understand what it is they are meant to be seeing (Vimlesh's account in Unnithan-Kumar, 2004). The only two pieces of information provided by the sonologist are: whether everything is okay (*sab theek hai*) and, less directly, whether they are getting what they wished for (in terms of a boy).

The actual practices that constitute the scanning procedure do nothing to encourage the 'pleasure' involved in seeing the forthcoming baby (as Georges recounts for Greek women) or the opportunity to 'socialise' with it as is common among American women (Taylor, 1998; Rapp, 2000). Gammeltoft (2007), in her study of pregnant women's resort to foetal scans in Hanoi, makes a similar observation regarding the functional use of the scan. She suggests that Hanoi women's constant recourse to the foetal scan is more to 'check-up' for the absence of foetal disability in their desire to produce quality children, than it is to derive pleasure or bond with their offspring.

It is important to understand what women 'see' (know) when they view the image of the foetus. Different ways of 'seeing'/knowing underlie the different kinds of emotions which are generated through such a gaze (of pleasure, affection, relief, connection, and anxiety and fear, for example) and which, in turn, influence subsequent reproductive decisions and actions. I have shown how the scan is an important site to understand how social values related to childbearing and gender difference are articulated, constituted and contested. The rise in its popularity is linked to its potential for medical research within reproductive medicine, its conferral of a scientific and modern status to medical entrepreneurs, and the demands its satisfies in terms of meeting the reproductive anxieties of married women within aspiring middle and lower class families in Rajasthan.

FSA in the broader context of the use of contraceptive technologies

An understanding of gender selective abortion practices in Rajasthan needs to take into account local ideas about pregnancy termination and related technologies. Medical intervention to terminate women's fertility has been popular in Rajasthan since the 1950s onwards, and reproductive technologies to do with sterilisation (popularly referred to as the 'operation') or even induced abortion *(safai or bacchha kadna)*, for example, are not 'new' in this sense. In some cases voluntary abortion was regarded positively by some women. Even female sterilisation in some cases was regarded as highly desirable by a number of rural and urban lower class women I worked with in the 2000s. This was in marked contrast to the widespread suspicion and fear of sterilisation which accompanied coercive state family planning practices in the late 1970s and 1990s (see *'Something Like a War'* 1991, for example). I found instead that the lower caste Hindu and poorer Muslim women I worked with embraced these technologies of termination in two senses: first, in their idea of the positive role induced abortion played in fertility enhancement and, second, in enabling them to meet the moral expectations of giving birth to the appropriate number and sex of children as a means of fulfilling their marital obligations and becoming good wives.

The greatest demand for contraceptive services among Hindu and Sunni women I met was for the tubectomy (locally referred to as the 'operation') at a particular point in their reproductive life course. Qualitative as well as demographic studies of contraceptive behaviour in India show that women are most likely to go in for an irreversible tubectomy *after* they have achieved the desired sex and number of children rather than seek it as a measure to space children across their reproductive life span (Visaria, 2007; Patel, T., 1994, 2007). According to Indira:

> Mummy-ji (referring to her mother-in-law) wanted another grandson so I could not get operated (undergo sterilisation). It was so difficult. I wanted just one son and daughter. Even if there was no son, I would have gone in for the operation after 2 daughters. I had the operation two years back when my daughter was 5 years old. This was after Mummy-ji died. I have 5 children: the oldest is a boy who is 15 years old. The other four are girls. The youngest is 7 years old. The older daughter is mature (i.e. menstruating) now. I will have a problem (i.e. marrying her off). The *dahej* (dowry) nowadays requires *saman* (goods) in the range of Rs21,000/-.
>
> (Fieldnotes 2008)

Indira's views stand in contrast to the perceptions of the public health authorities that there was no demand for tubectomies due to the coercive practice of female sterilisation under the family planning programme between the late 1970s to the 1990s (as discussed in Chapter 2). In fact, sterilisation was regarded by especially middle-aged rural and peri-urban women (in their late 30s and 40s) as an effective means of coping with an otherwise unregulated fertility given the social conditions under which they lived. It is important to note that sterilisations of younger women were not considered and routinely resisted by both communities demonstrating the point that contraceptive preferences shift depending on where women are in their reproductive cycle. It is also important to note that sterilisations were equally sought by both Muslims and Hindus, belying the popular conception among local health workers that the Muslim community in the area had no use for reproductive services.

Few women used reversible contraceptives although several expressed an interest in them. The low resort to modern contraceptives was perhaps well placed as the prevailing contraceptive options presented to women were, in general, neither proven to be safe (especially the Nirodh condom distributed through the public health system) nor physically tolerable by weak-bodied women since intrauterine devices, such as the Copper-T, and hormonal pills were known to cause excessive bleeding in weak and anaemic women. When it came to contraceptives such as IUDs and condoms, midwives and married women generally had similar ideas. According to Samina, the kin midwife, the Copper-T sticks right up in the women's vagina and gets full of 'meat' or it comes right down to the mouth of the vagina and causes discomfort during sex.

Zahida, the only woman among fifty-five Sunni women interviewed who used the Copper-T, which had been fitted for her during her last birth, claimed her husband complained of physical irritation during intercourse. She said, however, she was afraid to remove the Copper-T as she knew she would become pregnant again and she did not want any more children as she had conceived six times already (her last pregnancy had resulted in twins). In a more recent communication with her, I learned that she had removed the IUD and was pregnant again. Zahida preferred to undergo yet another pregnancy to meet the sexual satisfaction demanded by her husband. At the same time, she was convinced by her conversations with other women such as Samina, the kin midwife, that the Copper-T was undesirable.

Shahnaz, in her early twenties, was among the younger Sunni mothers I got to know. Unlike Zahida, Samina, Jetoon and scores of other women in their thirties in the village, Shahnaz had had a secondary education. She was also the only woman I met who used condoms. Yet, she was as ignorant of them as Samina. She and Samina asked me if condoms (Nirodh) were safe, saying that they had heard that they were unreliable and could fill up and burst (*phatna*) inside the woman. Shahnaz also asked me if it was true that men and women stuck to each other during intercourse if they used condoms. I said I also used condoms and thought that with correct use they are effective. Shahnaz said I probably bought the expensive ones rather than using the government ones which were free of cost. I said yes, this was indeed the case and I did not have any experience of the safety of Nirodh condoms. Shahnaz said she used condoms only because her husband, who worked in the export factory nearby, had got all kinds of progressive ideas from his work place. They had to hide them from his parents whom they stayed with and who would have disapproved. They had only recently started using condoms and Shahnaz wanted to continue, at least until her young daughter was 2–3 years old. Shahnaz's use of condoms and Zahida's use of the Copper-T can best be explained in terms of the influence of kinswomen and men on them as well as their own initiatives and predisposition, rather than in terms of the effects of education (in Shahnaz's case) or effective outreach of health services (for Zahida).

None of the Sunni women consulted with the Auxilliary Nurse Midwife (ANM, the primary public health worker in the area) on the issue of contraception. This is despite the fact that among the ANMs' main duties is the promotion of contraceptives as a means of spacing children. (The ANMs are provided with hormonal pills, condoms and IUDs to distribute (Unnithan, 1998)).

Most Sunni Muslim and Hindu caste women in the fieldwork area were severely anaemic or physically exhausted from previous pregnancies or hard physical labour, with little nutritious food that they usually suffered tremendous weakness during their pregnancy. With any sign of bleeding during pregnancy all women immediately sought the services of private women doctors, for whom there was a hefty fee. The outcome of such bleeding was routinely to carry out a *safai* (literally, cleansing, referring to a medical termination of pregnancy or MTP, as differentiated from *girna* literally to fall; referring to miscarriage) and 'sonography' (or the ultrasound scan) – with fees ranging from around Rs400/- for women who were 2–3 months pregnant, to Rs800/- for later pregnancies.[9] Including transportation, medicines and bed charges women spend between Rs500/- to 1,500/- for a medical termination of pregnancy.

There was a general feeling that while some midwives provided medicines to abort the foetus, previous experiences of women showed this to be a risky procedure. Samina, the Sunni kin midwife, said it was relatively easy to abort a foetus as all that was needed was to pierce the sac (*bachhadani*) with a cloth-tipped stick dipped in a particular solution. Usually the foetus aborted between half an hour and two hours after the piercing. In some cases it could take up to twelve hours. She said she never performed abortions as they were dangerous and there would be retribution from the community. However, Zarina, a Muslim midwife who lived in the city, had performed abortions for Gathro and Zahida's sister. Both Zahida and Gathro warned me of the suffering (*pareshani*) and great heat of the medicine (*garmi*) which entered the head to cause dizziness (*chukker*) and nausea (*ulti*). Such medicine was dangerous (*khatarnak*) and it was best to get *safai* (MTP) performed in a hospital. I found that Nagori women, having assessed the risks attached to undergoing abortions from local healers were, in fact, resorting to the medical termination of pregnancy (MTP) in high numbers. The religious sanctions against 'unnatural' interference in childbirth did little to stop Nagori Sunni women from undergoing an MTP. In fact, both Nagori and indeed Hindu women in the area resorted to the MTP almost as a means of spacing children in lieu of using contraceptive devices.

The high incidence of *safai* leads me to suggest that it is regarded as the easiest means of spacing children over which women have control and is unlike the pill or intra-uterine devices which are considered physically risky and culturally unacceptable. Moreover, women were able to effectively mobilise their networks of kin, natal and affinal, to lend them money for the MTP procedures. For their MTP, Zahida and most other women from the Nagori village would visit 'Neetu', a woman gynaecologist who worked in a privately funded hospital. There are a growing number of such private hospitals because of the inability of state run hospitals to cater to the demands of their women patients both because of the sheer numbers, as well as in their reputation for providing shoddy, albeit free, services.

Ethnographic studies on contraceptive behaviour in India as in several other parts of the world (Paxson, 2005; Johnson-Hanks, 2006), have also documented the preference for pregnancy termination over the use of contraception as a means through which women exercise birth control. Early stage induced abortion was used by a large number of younger, fertile, rural and urban lower class women to space their children in Rajasthan (Patel, 1994; Unnithan-Kumar, 2004). It remains a popular choice for these women compared to the use of reversible contraceptives such as condoms, Copper-T, hormonal tablets and contraceptive injections. Paxson (2005) notes reproductive preferences which are similar to those of poorer Rajasthani women, operating among middle class Greek women. The popularity of abortion as a means of contraception in Greece, despite a Family Planning programme promoting individual and choice oriented fertility control, can be explained, according to Paxson, in terms of its 'fit' with Greek moralities to do with appropriate reproductive behaviour. Abortions in this context are seen as allowing women to fulfil their patriarchal obligations (to have children) at the same time as they meet their individual aspirations to be good mothers (who give up their children if they know they cannot provide for them).

As in the Greek example, described by Paxson, women's technological preferences in Rajasthan have to be seen in terms of how they 'fit' with what is considered appropriate sexual and reproductive practice. The shame associated in talking about sex, men's (and often women's) taken for granted attitude about women's lack of sexual rights or sexual needs, and women's 'naturalised' connection to constant childbearing (and related lack of use for reversible contraceptives) are all conditions which make it difficult for women to resist becoming pregnant. This in turn contributes to their view of induced abortion (*safai*) as a means which enables them to show both wifely compliance in being available for sexual intercourse at the same time as providing a temporary relief from constant childbearing. In this context it is not difficult to understand why abortions may be used by women as a method of child spacing compared to a resort to reversible contraceptives (such as condoms) which involve negotiation and 'sex-talk' between husbands and wives.

Safai, which involved abortion followed by dilatation and curettage procedures, was regarded by the childbearing mother and local midwife alike as a beneficial intervention as it was through the 'cleaning' of the womb (*bachhadani*) that a healthy conception in the future was ensured. The cleaning ensured the removal of any traces of 'bad blood' (mothers' fluid which had nurtured foetal tissue from previous pregnancies) which could 'spoil' the next child. *Safai* was particularly advised by the local midwives when foetal growth was seen to be impaired, such as found in the condition called *chhod*. Chhod was described to me as the sticking of the foetus to the womb of the mother (or possibly an ectopic pregnancy) which resulted in the 'drying up' (*sookhna*) of the baby. In such cases, the midwife would be unable to detect any signs of foetal growth and a 'cleaning' of the womb was regarded as the only possible solution to prevent the birth of a 'weak' child.

Embedded in these practices is the notion that pregnancy termination through technological means secures a better quality of one's fertility in the future and ensures better quality children (conceptualised in terms of physical strength). Technological intervention is thus an investment in one's own reproductive future and in the health of the children that are produced. The power of techno-logical intervention is further reinforced in that it is seen as a cure for infertility. In a context like Rajasthan, where fertility is highly valued and infertility greatly feared, contraceptive technologies are seen to be both highly resisted, in the case of state enforced sterilization imposed on women with more than two children, as well as embraced in the form of *safai* or cleaning of the womb as desired by women at particular moments in their reproductive cycle.

The seemingly contradictory association between the use of contraceptives and the preservation of reproductive potential has also been noted by anthropolo-gist Caroline Bledsoe in her study on Gambian women's fertility behaviour. The connection between reproduction and contraceptive use is even starker in con-texts such as the Gambia where, contrary to expectation, it is *infertile* Gambian women who most use western contraception. This is due to the strong associ-ation made between contraceptive devices and the preservation of reproductive potential, otherwise 'spent' during childbearing (Bledsoe, 1998, 2002). Bled-soe's research is based on the findings of the contraceptive behaviour of women like Kaddy Sisay, a thirty year old Gambian woman who failed to produce chil-dren although she carried at least four pregnancies. Following her reproductive mishaps, Kaddy embarks on a long course of Depo-Provera, otherwise used as a means to control fertility. In order to understand Kaddy's resort to methods of spacing children, 'where there are no children to space' (1998, p. 16), Bledsoe turns to the wider connections made between reproduction and health by the Gambian women in her area of study. Here, childbearing is regarded as a trau-matic assault on the health of women, whose bodies age as a result. In order to halt this ageing associated with reproduction, women require a 'recovery period'. Contraceptives are popular because they enable women to procure periods of recovery and halt the body ageing associated with childbearing.

What emerged from the local discourse around induced abortion in Rajasthan was the positive light with which it was regarded. The absence of a negative moral discourse surrounding abortion appeared to be paradoxical given the high value placed on fertility and childbearing in Rajasthan. It is because the two are connected in local discourse, where abortions are seen as birth enhancing, that I suggest they are accepted as part of the patrilineal discourse on social reproduction. For women, they provide an opportunity to control their pregnancies at the same time as they prove their fertility and their men's virility. Regarded alongside the advent of new technologies of diagnosis and termination, the local value placed on abortion has led to new opportunities of family-building for communities as well as for medical practitioners.

Concluding reflections on agency

Lower middle class Rajasthani women's increasing resort to FSA presents a paradox for social scientists, feminists and policymakers. Does it represent women's desires and practices to control and better their conditions or does it symbolise their subordination to gender ideologies that discriminate against their sex? In India, medical intervention in reproduction is seen to increase the collective social control over women's bodies at the same time as women exercise reproductive autonomy, as feminists writing in the North in particular have argued (Martin, 1987; Petchesky, 1987; Stanworth, 1987; Petchesky and Judd, 1998; Morgan and Michaels, 1999; among others). But what of the desires expressed by individual women for FSA and their agency?

What is suggested in the chapter is that paying close attention to how women understand their reproductive options and the role that contraceptive technologies can play in them provides a clearer insight into how they will act in relation to providers and in the face of state regulation and activist interventions. Taking Latour's notion of agency as not being about individual action alone but rather as a number of agencies which drive the actant (person who is acted upon), we can begin to understand why women seek FSAs as a pragmatic response to the gender unequal conditions in which they live.

In women's embrace of abortion technologies and FSA in Rajasthan, we see that it is precisely in the social space between their own desires (including for a safer future for their children) and wider familial and class-based expectations (for a better standard of life) that a preference for sex-determining reproductive interventions exist. It is a combination of individual as well as collective interests that merge in their reproductive decisions to abort babies, including those of the female sex.

The salience of this perspective is clear when we consider the wider social, marital and, especially, conjugal context where notions of self and control over one's body are both collectively constituted as they are individually desired, crafted and experienced. The responses of lower and middle class women to technological intervention in Rajasthan reflect a wider interactive social process in which these women continually participate, which serves their own interests as well as those of wider social groups to which they belong (also noted by anthropologists for other parts of the world: De-Bessa, 2006; Kielman, 1998; Lock and Kaufert, 1998; Bledsoe, 2002; Paxson, 2005; Johnson-Hanks, 2006;

Cornwall, 2007). This kind of participation is captured in Lock and Kaufert's (1998) concept of 'pragmatic' agency, whereby individuals do not necessarily either comply with, or resist, the 'disciplining' that accompanies technological interventions, but often act in accordance with pragmatic considerations. Such pragmatic actions may be tactical (Cornwall, 2007) but could equally well be strategic.

But what pragmatism means, and how it is shaped by particular understandings of reproductive duty and obligation and how these change over time, is critical to furthering an understanding of the processes of social reproduction. Lower and middle class women in Rajasthan undertake pragmatic decisions to undergo abortions to prove fertility as a conferral of motherhood, but they also undergo FSA to comply with son preference for the increased social acceptability it confers on them. The resort to sex selection in childbearing becomes pragmatic in a context where social institutions and values continue to favour men and, by extension, their sons (for example, a son is required to light his father's funeral pyre and to conduct the last rites: Bock and Rao, 2000). In the absence of sons, mothers of only daughters are often thought to be infertile (Patel, V., 2007; Unnithan-Kumar, 2008b), a perception prevalent in other patriarchal contexts such as Egypt (Van Balen and Inhorn, 2002).

Given the continued ideological and structural significance of male children in the social reproduction of the family and community, the social cost of not bearing sons is great and falls heavily upon the couple, but more so on women. By meeting the 'quota' of sons in the family, women are less likely to be the subject of ridicule and stigma. The 'work' of childbearing is less for women if, after bearing two to three children who are female, the sex of the next child can be determined. The decision to undergo FSA can also be viewed as pragmatic in the long run due to the real economic benefits and security it provides mothers in their old age, especially when widowed and living in the households of their sons. These are concerns that are not reduced by rising household incomes and urbanisation. The pragmatic aspects of women's reproductive decisions become even more salient in a context where modern living, in smaller spaces with an ever greater dependency on the market, necessitates a small family. It also enables couples to be both 'modern' (have fewer children) and 'traditional' (have sons) at the same time.

The increasing resort to sex selection among middle class families over the past two decades is a clear demonstration of the convergence of aspirations for modern living alongside a continued participation in familiar and established trajectories of social reproduction. Reproductive technologies, such as those that allow sex selection, are regarded as actually helping couples 'plan' their smaller families (Khanna, 2003, 2014; Patel, 2003, 2007). Sex selection strategies may also be conceived as optimising the health and well-being of existing children (Patel, 2003; Palriwala, 2008) in that more resources are available to be spent on fewer children.

The anti FSA messages and work being carried out by the state with the help of CSOs is being interpreted on the ground to mean that all abortion is bad. This represents a retrogressive step in the face of previous work undertaken by health activists and feminists to promote women's access to contraceptives from the 1990s onwards. Further, the heavy and punitive regulation of the use of ultra sound machines, especially from 2011 onwards, means they are not even being used by practitioners to carry out regular detection of foetal and gynaecological abnormalities (personal field observations). These two trends indicate that, overall, the situation for women's health has deteriorated with no real availability or choice to undergo abortion services and no provision of ultrasound technologies for detection of routine foetal and maternal anomalies. (Most clinicians I found were frustrated by the lengthy administrative procedures required by the government for procuring and maintaining ultrasound machines, and anxious of the bribes they may have to pay). What has also been striking to observe has been the convergence of state and feminist campaigning for stricter and punitive legislation to monitor and control FSA, a trend regarded by feminist activists in the UK, for example, as denying women control over their bodies (Unnithan and Dubuc, 2017). Overall, the lack of a mainstream feminist mobilisation on abortion in India further feeds into the closing down of contraceptive choices for women in the country.

The study of FSA in this chapter has shown that technologies in themselves do not bring about social transformation, but it is in how they are made socially meaningful that their power lies. The preference for using non-reversible termination technologies, such as abortions and sterilisation, as contraceptives in Rajasthan, for example, is in striking contrast to the northern Euro-American contexts, where it is reversible technologies (the pill, condoms) which have enabled the separation of reproduction from sexual intercourse that are popular. These very different reproductive technologies are desired precisely because, taken together, they allow women to have more freedom and choice in relation to their childbearing. Female selective abortion is used by individual Hindu as well as Muslim lower middle class women to better the 'quality' of their contribution to the patriarchal family and gain prestige in a context where gender inequality remains a social reality.

Notes

1 The term has developed as a means to differentiate these technologies from 'Assisted Reproductive Technologies' or ARTs and the more general category of 'New Reproductive Technologies' under which all such practices were initially categorised in the early social science studies on the subject (Wahlberg and Gammeltoft, 2018, p. 1).

2 As far as I am aware, there are no studies on FSA that take this approach to the practice in India and none on the subject at all as it is practiced among Muslim families. Sex selection is a difficult subject to gain accurate and reliable ethnographic information on without relationships of trust borne out of long term fieldwork and continuing ties with respondents.

3 Pigg discusses a very similar process in terms of the globalisation of ideas of 'nature' with regard to sex (Pigg, 2005), while Franklin (2005) raises the issue in her concept of the 'Global Biological'.

4 The chapter draws on in-depth ethnographic work which forms part of a paper published previously (Unnithan, 2010). This includes interviews with four Muslim and six lower middle class Hindu women living in the peri-urban outskirts of Jaipur city and in one slum area in the city. Interviews and discussions were also held with health providers, including five gynaecologists (two based in private and three working in public hospitals), two community health workers (one Hindu and one Muslim) and three prominent health activists (two feminist upper middle class, urban women and one middle class male, all Hindu).
5 Personal observation and discussion with activists including legal scholar activist Jayna Kothari.
6 Kabeer makes a similar observation on the practice in Bangladesh (Kabeer, 2013).
7 Unnithan-Kumar, 2010.
8 The importance of marriage in determining the quality of offspring and, ultimately, of society in India is also reflected in the distinctive nature of eugenics discourse in colonial India where it was marriage reform rather than genetic manipulation which was regarded as the primary means of ensuring the quality of descendant populations (Hodges, 2006).
9 These refer to MTP prices in 2002.

Bibliography

Baru, R., 1998. *Private Healthcare in India: social characteristics and trends.* New Delhi: Sage

Bhat, M. and Zavier, F., Fertility decline and gender bias in northern India. *Demography* 40, no. 4 (2003): 637–57

Bledsoe, C., Reproductive Mishaps and Western Contraception: An African Challenge to Fertility Theory. *Population and Development Review* 24, no. 1 (1998): 15–57

Bledsoe, C., 2002. *Contingent Lives: Fertility, Time and Aging in West Africa.* Chicago University Press

Bock, M. and Rao, A., 2000. Indigenous Models and Kinship Theories: an introduction to a South Asian perspective In Bock, M and Rao, A., eds. *Culture, Creation and procreation: Concepts of South Asian Kinship in Practice.* Oxford: Berghahn

Bock, M. and Rao, A., eds., 2000. *Culture, Creation and procreation: Concepts of South Asian Kinship in Practice.* Oxford: Berghahn

Bose, A. and Shiva, M., 2003. *Darkness at Noon: Female Foeticide in India.* Survey of project report on Child Sex Ratio and Gender Imbalance with reference to Punjab, Haryana and Himachal Pradesh. New Delhi: Voluntary Health Association of India

Corrêa, S., and Petchesky, R., 1994. Reproductive and sexual rights: a feminist perspective. In Sen, G., Germain, A. and Chen, L.C., eds. *Population policies reconsidered: health, empowerment, and rights.* Boston MA: Harvard University Press, 107–23. (Harvard Series on Population and International Health)

Cornwall, A. Taking Chances, Making Choices: The Tactical Dimensions of 'Reproductive Strategies' in Southwestern Nigeria. *Medical Anthropology* 26, no. 3 (2007): 229–54

Dagar, 2007. Re-thinking female feticide: Perspectives and issues. In Patel, T., ed., *Sex Selective Abortion in India.* New Delhi: Sage, 91–135

Dasgupta, M.D. Selective discrimination against female children in rural Punjab, India. In *Population and Development Review* 13, no. 1 (1987): 77–100

De-Bessa, G.H. Medicalization, Reproductive agency and the desire for surgical sterilisation among low-income women in urban Brazil. *Medical Anthropology* 25, no. 3 (2006): 221–64

Dreze, J. and Sen, A., 2013. *An uncertain glory: India and its contradictions*. London: Penguin. Allen Lane

Dubuc S. and Coleman, D. An increase in the sex ratio of births to Indian-born mothers in England and Wales: evidence for sex-selective abortion. *Population and Development Review* 32, no. 2 (2007): 328–32

Dumont, L., 1980. *Homo-hierachicus: The caste system and its implications*. University of Chicago Press

Franklin, S., 2005. Stem Cells R Us: Emergent Life Forms and the Global Biological. In Ong, A., and Collier, S., eds. *Global Assemblages: Technology, Politics and Ethics as Anthropological Problems*, 59–78

Gammeltoft, T., 2007. Sonography and Sociality: Obstetrical Ultrasound Imaging in Urban Vietnam. *Medical Anthropology Quarterly* 21, no. 2 (2007): 133–53

Gammeltoft, T., 2014. *Haunting Images: A cultural account of selective reproduction in Vietnam*. Berkeley: California University Press

Georges, E., 1997. Fetal ultrasound imaging and the production of authoritative knowledge in Greece. In Davis-Floyd, R.E., and Sargeant, C., eds. *Childbirth and Authoritative Knowledge: cross-cultural perspectives*. Berkeley: California University Press

Gibbon, S and Novas, C., eds. 2008. *Biosocialities, Genetics and the Social Sciences*. London: Routledge

Gibbon, S. and Reynolds-Whyte, S., eds. Introduction, Biomedical Technology and Health Inequities in the Global North and South. Special edition for *Anthropology and Medicine* 1, no. 2 (2009): 97–103

Hodges, S., ed. 2006. *Reproductive Health in India: History, Politics, Controversies. New Perspectives in South Asian History 13*. Hyderabad: Orient Longman

Inhorn, M., 2003. *Local babies and Global Science: Gender, Religion and In Vitro Fertilisation in Egypt*. New York NY: Routledge

Inhorn, M., and Van Balen, F, 2002. Interpreting Infertility: a view from the social sciences. In Inhorn, M. and Van Balen, F. eds., *Infertility Around the Globe: new thinking on childlessness, gender and reproductive technologies*. Berkeley: University of California Press, 3–33

Johnson-Hanks, J., 2006. *Uncertain Honour: Modern Motherhood in an African Crisis*. University of Chicago Press

Kabeer, N. Diverging stories of 'missing women' in South Asia: is son preference weakening in Bangladesh? *Feminist Economics* 20, no. 4 (2013): 1–26

Kabeer, N., Huq, L. and Mahmud, S., 2013. Diverging Stories of 'Missing Women' in South Asia: Is son preference weakening in Bangladesh? *Feminist Economics*, 138–63 online doi: 10.1080/13545701.857423

Khanna, S. Traditions and reproductive technology in an urbanising north Indian village. *Social Science and Medicine* 44, no. 2 (1997): 171–80

Khanna, S., 2003. Fatal/Fetal knowledge: Women and NRTs in urbanising North India. Paper presented at the AAA Meeting in the panel on *Reproductive and Genetic Technologies and Kinship Ideologies in South Asia*, 19–23 November, in Chicago, US

Khanna, S., 2014. 'A 'City-Walla' prefers a Small Family': Son Preference and Sex Selection among Punjabi Migrant Families in Urban India. In Unnithan-Kumar, M. and Khanna, S. eds. *The Cultural Politics of Reproduction: Migration, Health and Family Making*. Oxford: Berghahn, 152–67

Kielman, K., 1998. Barren Ground: contesting identities of infertile women in Pemba, Tanzania. In Lock, M. and Kaufert, P., eds. *Pragmatic Women and Body Politics* Cambridge University Press, 127–64

Latour, B., 2007. *Reassembling the Social: An introduction to actor-network-theory.* Oxford University Press

Lock, M and Nguyen, V-K., 2010. *An Anthropology of Biomedicine.* Hoboken NJ: Wiley-Blackwell

Lock, M. and Kaufert, P., eds. 1998. *Pragmatic Women and Body Politics (Cambridge Studies in Medical Anthropology) no. 5.* Cambridge: Cambridge University Press

Martin, E., 1987. *The woman in the body: A cultural analysis of reproduction.* Milton Keynes: Open University Press

Miller, B. Female-Selective Abortion in Asia: Patterns, Policies and Debates. *American Anthropologist* 103, no. 4 (2001): 1083–95

Morgan, L. and Michaels, M., eds. 1999. *Fetal Subjects and Feminist positions.* Philadelphia: University of Pennsylvania Press

Nandraj, S. Beyond the Law and the Lord: quality of private healthcare. *Economic and Political Weekly* 29, no. 27 (1994): 1680–5

Nguyen, V.K., 2005. Antiretroviral Globalism, Biopolitics and Therapeutic Citizenship. In Ong, A. and Collier, S., eds. *Global Assemblages: Technology, Politics and Ethics as Anthropological Problems.* Malden: Blackwell Publishing, 124–44

Nichter, Mark, 1996. Pharmaceuticals, the commodification of health and healthcare-medicine use transition. In: Nichter, M. and Nichter, M., eds. *Anthropology and international health: Asian case studies.* London: Routledge, 265–326

Ong, A. and Collier, S., eds. 2005. *Global Assemblages: Technology, Politics and Ethics as Anthropological Problems.* Malden: Blackwell Publishing

Palriwala, R., 2008. Aversion to Daughters: A study of declining sex-ratios. In *Women's Equality*, a journal of the All India Women's Democratic Association 1, 15–18

Parry, J., 1979. *Caste and Kinship in Kangra.* London: Routledge

Patel, T., 1994. *Fertility Behaviour: Population and Society in Rajasthan.* Delhi: Oxford University Press

Patel, T., 2003. Partisanship and Science: Prenatal Diagnostic techniques in India. Paper presented at the *Decennial Conference of the Association of Social Anthropologists of the UK and Northern Ireland.* Manchester

Patel, T., ed. 2007. *Sex Selective Abortion in India: Gender, Society and New Reproductive Technologies.* New Delhi: Sage

Patel, V., 2007. The Political Economy of Missing Girls in India. In Patel, T., ed. *Sex Selective Abortion in India.* New Delhi: Sage, 286–316

Paxson, H., 2005. Family Planning, Human Nature and the Ethical Subject of Sex in Urban Greece. In Adams, V. and Pigg, S., eds. *Sex in Development: Science, Sexuality and Morality in Global Perspective.* Durham: Duke University Press, 95–125

Petchesky, R., 1987. Foetal images: The power of visual culture in the politics of reproduction. In Stanworth, M., ed. *Reproductive technologies: Gender, motherhood and medicine.* Minneapolis: University of Minnesota Press, 87–102

Petchesky, R., and Judd, K., 1998, *Negotiating Reproductive Rights: Women's perspectives across countries and cultures.* London: Zed

Pigg, S., 2005. Globalising the Facts of Life. In Pigg, S. and Adams, V., eds. *Sex in Development: Science, Sexuality and Morality in Global Perspective.* Durham and London: Duke University Press, 39–67

Rabinow, P., 1996. Artificiality and Enlightenment: from sociobiology to biosociality. In Rabinow, P., ed. *Essays in the Anthropology of Reason.* Princeton University Press, 91–112

Rapp, R., 2000. *Testing Women, Testing the Fetus: the Social Impact of Amniocentesis in America.* New York: Routledge

Sen, A. and Sengupta, A., 1983. Malnutrition of rural children and sex biases. *Economic and Political Weekly of India.* 28, 855–62 (Mumbai: Sameeksha Trust)

Sen, A., 1990. More than 100 million women are missing. NY Review of Books. 20 December issue

Shaikh, N., 2007. *Negotiating divorce in multiple legal forums: Sunni Muslim women in Mumbai.* D.Phil. Thesis, University of Sussex

Sharma, U., 1984. Dowry in India. In Hirschon, R., ed. *Women and Property – Women as Property.* London: Croom Helm

Singh, M., and Srivastava, K., 2008. *Saving the Girl Child.* Seminar 583. March, New Delhi: Malvika Singh

Something Like a War. Film. 1991. Directed by Deepa Dhanraj. D&N Productions

Standing, H., 1990. *Dependence and Autonomy: Women's employment and the family in Calcutta.* London: Routledge

Stanworth, M., 1987. *Reproductive Technologies: gender, motherhood and medicine.* Minneapolis: University of Minnesota Press

Sudha, S. and Rajan. I. Persistent daughter disadvantage in India: what do estimated sex ratios at birth and sex ratios of child mortality risk reveal? *Economic and Political Weekly* 38, no. 41 (2003): 115–36

Taylor, J., 1998. Image of contradiction: Obstetrical ultrasound in American culture. In Franklin, S. and Ragone, H., eds. *Reproducing Reproduction.* Philadelphia: University of Pennsylvania Press, 15–46

UNFPA (United Nations Population Fund), 2004. The Cairo Consensus at Ten: Population, Reproductive Health and the Global Effort to End Poverty. *Report on State of the World Population.* New York: UNFPA

Unnithan (Unnithan-Kumar), M., 1997. *Identity, Gender and Poverty: New Perspectives on Caste and Tribe in Rajasthan.* Oxford: Berghahn

Unnithan (Unnithan-Kumar), M., 1998. '*Women's Reproductive Health in Rajasthan: policies, perceptions and strategies*', unpublished report to Wellcome Trust

Unnithan, M. Female Selective Abortion beyond 'Culture': gender inequality and family making in a globalising India. In *Culture, Health and Sexuality Special Issue on 'Quality of Offspring – the impact of new reproductive technologies in Asia'*, ed. M. Sleeboom-Faulkner 12, no. 2 (2010): 153–66

Unnithan-Kumar, M., 2008a. Kinship. In Mittal, S. and Thursby, G., eds., *Studying Hinduism: key concepts and methods.* London: Routledge

Unnithan-Kumar, M., 2008b. Reproductive Rights, Health and Culture. Background chapter for UNFPA *State of the World Population Report 2008.* New York: UNFPA

Unnithan, M., Dubuc, S. 2017. Reflections on the recent controversy around gender selective abortion in the UK. Published online in *Global Public Health*, at: www.tandfonline.com/doi/full/10.1080/17441692.2017.1346694 and in Unnithan, M. and S. de Zordo, Re-situating Abortion: Bio-politics, Global Health and Rights in Neo-liberal Times. *Global Public Health* 13, no. 6 (2013)

Unnithan-Kumar, M., ed. 2004. *Reproductive Agency, Medicine and the State.* Oxford: Berghahn

Visaria, L. Deficit of Women in India: magnitude, trends, regional variations and determinants. *The National Medical Journal of India* 15, no. 1 (2002): 19–25

Visaria, L., 2007. Deficit of Girls in India: can it be attributed to Female Selective Abortion? In Patel, T., ed. *Sex Selective Abortion in India*. Delhi: Sage, 61–80

Wahlberg, A. and Gammeltoft, T., eds. 2018. *Selective Reproduction in the 21st Century*.
London: Palgrave Macmillan

5 Maternal risk and its mediation

Learning from health worker vulnerabilities

That birth is fraught with uncertainty is a key premise underlying biomedical as well as development and indigenous discourse on childbearing. The growing medicalisation of birth has been accompanied by a rise in biomedical theorisations of risk. The clinical management of midwifery, for instance, has notably become saturated with the language of risk and protocols especially in highly medicalised, low mortality settings such as in the US, Britain and Europe (Bryers and van Tiejlingen, 2010; Coxon *et al.*, 2016). Considered as part of wider processes of reflexive modernity (Beck, 1992; Giddens, 1984; Lupton 2013), objective, epidemiological measures and standards of safety have come to set the gold standard of medical assessment and practice (Lambert, 2013; Adams, 2013) including in human rights based approaches to health (Unnithan, 2015). In a context of health provision which is increasingly rights-based, a close association is made between risk and rights in that women are entitled to childbirth that is *free of risk* (see, for example, The NICE-National Institute for Clinical Excellence, UK guidelines on delivery protocols for midwives).[1] Such notions of maternal risk and safety, in turn, shape the work and value of health workers such as birth attendants and contraceptive promoters. In terms of the implications for midwifery in the UK for example, as Scamell and Stewart (2014) note, there has been a shift in clinical governance away from any individual, autonomous forms of midwifery practice (those based on personal experience and intuition; what they call embodied knowledge) toward adherence to a clinical protocol which is systematically formulated and evidence-based.[2]

Indian health policies cast public health workers such as Auxiliary Nurse Midwives (ANM) and the more recent community-based Accredited Social Health Activist (ASHA) as responsible for mitigating the biomedical risks associated with childbearing and for achieving the national and global, maternal health goals of 'safe motherhood'. Yet, as observations in this chapter suggest, the nature of 'risk' associated with childbirth and family planning is social as much as it is biomedical. Health worker care accordingly needs to be defined and acknowledged in a broader context of 'social risk', a term I use to refer to the risk posed *to* social and kin relationships (following Reynolds-Whyte, 1997; Kaufert and O'Neil, 1993) which intersects with, rather than opposes, biomedical forms of risk. Risk in this wider sense is considered in the following lines as both 'a reflection of the realities of childbirth as well as constitutive of these realities' (Kaufert and O'Neil, 1993, p. 33).

In this chapter I discuss how maternal risk is constituted and mediated in the era of rights-based development through the embodied work practices of women health workers trained by the state (ASHA and ANM) as well as indigenous midwives (glossed as '*dai*'). A key argument in this chapter is how the 'risk' to women's health is intimately linked to the vulnerabilities and constraints faced by the midwives and health workers often chosen from within the communities they work in. In their practice of mediating birth and the provision of maternal, infant and contraceptive care, health workers as the ASHA and ANM are at once the agents and the subjects of state maternal health policies. Their practices are simultaneously shaped by indigenous and biomedical discourse of risk and safety in childbirth. If the state consolidates power by drawing on biomedically based notions of risk (Fordyce and Maraesa, 2012), then wider, socially based and subject near understandings of risk, I suggest, provide an insight into the processes through which such power is challenged. Paying attention to the inter-subjective, relational (Strathern, 1992; Reynolds-Whyte, 1997) and structural contexts which shape notions of 'risk' in birth, family planning work and the social relations of care, this chapter, as with other chapters in the book, opens up new routes of inquiry into the exercise and production of reproductive power in India.

When I began field research in 1998, the available statistics recorded that only 7 per cent of urban births and 3 per cent of rural births in Rajasthan took place in an institutionalised (public or private) setting (GOI NFHS, nd p. 155). Despite a major investment by the state in midwifery and health worker training services since Indian independence (Jeffery *et al.*, 2002), the majority of rural women in Rajasthan gave birth at home in the care of indigenous midwives, seeking 'outside' (unknown) assistance only in emergencies.[3] Over the past decade, with the introduction of cash incentivised institutional deliveries under the JSY national maternal health programme of the NRHM and with the introduction of the new category of the ASHA worker, there has been a phenomenal rise in the numbers of hospital births. In 2012–2013, toward the end of my field research, the number of institutional deliveries had risen considerably to a staggering 78 per cent across rural (75.2 per cent) and urban (88.3 per cent) areas of the state (GOI, AHS-Rajasthan, 2012–2013).[4] In promoting institutional delivery through cash incentives for women and for health worker performance, the NRHM national health policy has led, as argued in this chapter, to new forms of vulnera-bilities and risks (social and biomedical) both for women who give birth to chil-dren and for the health workers who assist them. It has further reinforced the observations in Chapter 2 of the state as an active and powerful mediator of health and well-being, promoting a market in healthcare services (Dasgupta, 2011).

The impetus for institutional delivery in India's national health programme stems from a development rationale often applied in high mortality settings in the global south, which echoes northern models in equating medicalised birth with biomedical safety (i.e. a lower risk of mortality). Anthropological studies on midwifery and childbirth in a number of such settings suggest that in fact there is a process of selection at work here where particular understandings of risk are privileged and not others, revealing conflicts over power and meaning (Obermeyer, 2000, p. 175; Pigg, 1997). Such work suggests that ideas about midwifery and maternal risk are politically and morally framed, with especially significant implications for categories of practitioners such as indigenous midwives who become symbols of outdated and harmful maternal health practice (Pigg, 1997; Van Hollen, 2002; Pinto, 2008; Berry, 2010). As anthropological work on the framing of midwifery within development discourse has shown, the 'indigenous midwife' appears in contradictory ways: either as a symbol of harmful practices and 'risk' (Cosminsky, 2012) or as a symbol of a culturally sensitive and inclusive (participatory) means of development through an engagement with the community (Pigg, 1997). A review of Indian maternal health policies in the following sections demonstrates how these two contradictory views on indigenous midwives (referred to as Traditional Birth Attendants or TBAs) have simultaneously shaped their participation and subsequent exclusion from the state's safe motherhood programmes. I also discuss the apathy affected practices of new categories of health workers (the ASHA) in the context of caste-based and bureaucratic working conditions to show the complex ways in which the neglect of patients becomes routinised (also see Varley, 2015).

In the following lines I first describe the labour and concerns of indigenous midwives, who until very recently were the dominant providers of assistance during birth, working alongside faith healers (as discussed in Chapter 3) as well as biomedical practitioners to promote a distinctively indigenous continuum of care. Following on from this I discuss the life and 'work-worlds' of ANM and ASHA maternal healthcare providers and consider their efforts to mitigate the combined effects of social, biomedical and bureaucratic risks entailed in their work.

Precarity in the work of indigenous midwives: managing blood, kinship and household labour

A significant proportion of the early period of research captured in this book involved spending time with indigenous midwives referred to as *dai*, a generic term used for local women who contributed valued and expert assistance over the course of childbearing leading up to and at birth. As a category, *dai* referred to a range of women, rather than a single person, who were vested with authority based on their knowledge of childbirth and the reproductive body (Unnithan-Kumar, 2002; Rozario, 1998; Pinto 2008). In Rajasthan, *dai* were known to recognise the dangers and risks associated with births and took decisions on whether to address them or to refer these women to other experts.

Each birth in the fieldwork context was 'plural' in the sense that it represented a conjunction of different forms of medical and religious expertise considered efficacious in the context of a constellation of recognised dangers ('risk') that a woman was thought to face (similar to Jordan's observations in the

Yucatan; Jordan 1997). In the villages around Jaipur, it was often the case that several *dai* would be chosen by the pregnant mother and her mother-in-law to attend the delivery. The decision about the number and combination of dai attending the birth was made in terms of the estimated difficulty of birth (*keda jaapa*) and in this sense represented a first assessment of 'risk' as we see in the case of Jetoon's birth which I attended in 1998.

In March 1998, Jetoon, who was thirty-five years old, delivered her ninth child (she had six live children, one previous miscarriage, and a child who died at a year-and-a-half). The women present at her delivery were Samina, the kin midwife (she was Jetoon's father's brother's son's wife), Mehmuda, the well-regarded elderly Pathan midwife of the minority Muslim community in the village and Dhanni, the Raigarin ('untouchable' caste) midwife and myself. I arrived to find Jetoon in the designated 'delivery hut' (*japa ghar*) having contractions every three to five minutes. In one corner was a rope bed (*charpai*) with some thin cotton covers in a heap. The ground was covered in loose sand and in the middle lay a jute sac (*bori).* At the other end there were a few bricks. Jetoon had her *kurta* (shirt) on but had removed her *salwar* (pant). She was holding on to Dhanni. As the contractions increased she lay on the jute sac clasping her legs to her sides. She would get up every five minutes, usually for a contraction and get onto two bricks, one set under each foot, facing Dhanni. She kept moaning '*bai, bai, baiyon*' (literally, woman, woman, women). After every couple of contractions, Dhanni would pour a teaspoonful of sesame seed oil in her hand and vigorously massage the opening of Jetoon's womb. At one point Jetoon asked to be 'cut' but Mehmuda, the Pathan midwife said they never do that and that it was up to Allah to make the opening big enough.

Samina and Mehmud, on the other hand, massaged Jetoon's back at intervals and during a contraction they vigorously pushed her stomach downwards (unaware of the risk of rupture to the uterus that this may entail). Dhanni, on the other hand, sat all the time watching with intermittent attempts to further widen Jetoon's cervix using both hands. Before she inserted her fingers she would wipe them with a scrap of cloth taken from a small bundle placed next to the jute sac. Mehmuda helped with lifting Jetoon and easing her down, and along with Dhanni and Samina inserted her fingers into Jetoon's cervix at regular intervals to check the position of the baby's head. Mehmuda proclaimed the baby's head was a whole finger away from the opening and it was only when it came to the top third of the finger (*choodi)* should any injection be used to speed the delivery. We had all been told that Maulana, the Unani doctor from the nearby village, had been summoned by Jetoon's husband. Despite Mehmuda's request to delay the injection, Maulana immediately entered the hut, eyes cast on the ground, and injected Jetoon with Oxytocin in her thigh.

Few other women entered the hut. Jetoon's mother did not come into the hut, although she prepared the hot water, provided the bucket and all else that was requested. This was, I was told, because of embarrassment (sharam) and also because mothers could not watch their daughters undergoing any pain and suffering. Jetoon's nanad (husband's younger brother's wife) went to and fro, bringing whatever the midwives requested and bearing advice and information to people on both sides of the door of the hut.

Mehmuda requested a small iron stool which was brought from Samina's house. Mehmuda circulated this seven times over Jaitoon. She then asked for a Rs5/- coin which she also swept around Jaitoon seven times saying 'Respected old man of the valley, give us your favour for a child is to be born in your neighbourhood' (*ghati vale baba, ahsaan karo, aapke mohalle mein bacchha hone vala hai*). Mehmuda said she needed to placate the spirit of the Baba as Jetoon was in such pain, as she was at the time of each of her births. She said they should have given Jetoon castor oil to drink with her milk and the baby would not have had such difficulty turning (*arundi ke tel se bachha ghoom jaata hai).*

Samina spoke less than Mehmuda and it was usually to confer with her and Dhanni about the passage of time. Dhanni only ever said anything when she inquired about the time. The rest of the time she either stretched Jetoon's cervical opening, provided physical support when Jetoon was helped onto the bricks by Mehmuda and Samina or lit herself a local cigarette (*bidi*). She said the cigarette helped her mark time.

Both Mehmuda and Samina were anxious to leave as soon as possible. Mehmuda said her husband was unwell and Samina complained her household chores were left undone. Maulana re-entered hurriedly to give Jetoon a second injection. Approximately two-and-a-half hours after I arrived, Jetoon proclaimed, 'a big one is coming', and two contractions later a large part of the head of the baby emerged. Dhanni put her hand in and removed the cord (*bachhe ki nalli*) from around the emerging baby's neck and then helped him out but did not touch the baby once it lay on the sandy floor of the hut. The baby was covered in white skin and both Mehmuda and Samina said this was because of the buttermilk that Jetoon had probably drunk. Dhanni then slowly pulled at the umbilical cord and brought the placenta (*olnaal*) out. Both the baby and the placenta were very small (the latter fitted in the palm of the hand and the baby could not have been more than a kilogram). Dhanni then rolled the remaining scraps of cloth into a ball and inserted this into Jetoon's cervix after which Dhanni got up to wash her hands … everyone agreed her work was over. Mehmuda left to go back to her husband.

Samina took over where Dhanni had left off, and massaged the umbilical cord (with attached placenta) towards the baby. Jetoon was made to sit up. A reed and thread were passed in through the door. Samina tied the yellow and deep orange thread tightly around the cord and then Jetoon cut it with the sharpened reed. Jetoon was then helped onto the rope bed and Samina took hold of the baby. She asked for hot water. When this was brought a couple of minutes later she asked me to add this to the existing bucket of cold water. Both the bucket and the *parat* (slightly deepened iron vessel used for agricultural and domestic tasks) were brought to her. Samina then balanced the baby on her feet in the *parat* and vigorously washed it with soap and water and then wrapped in a clean old shirt. Samina *held* the baby for a short while and massaged the bridge of his nose. He was then further wrapped in another small piece of cloth and placed on the left side of Jetoon.

Jetoon's mother and sister-in-law brought some mud to cover the placenta, excreta and blood which lay in the hut and removed these in the *parat*. They returned after throwing the placenta in the nearest rubbish heap to put fresh sand on the floor and recoat it. They then gave Jetoon a cup of tea. Samina had a quick cup of tea and rushed back home to tend her buffalos. Jetoon's children then came in and surrounded their mother. Several other women neighbours also entered and joked with the children about the qualities of the newborn. Samina said the baby should be named Akib. After this, Akib was brought outside to an elderly Maulavi (knowledgeable about the Koran) who had arrived to give him the *ajaan* (blessing of Allah in his ears) only after which he was allowed to ingest food/drink (the ritual is called *roza kholna*).

(Extract from Unnithan-Kumar, 2002, pp. 112–14)

Several key issues emerge from the account of Jetoon's delivery. One of the most striking aspects at the time for me was that that there was no single authoritative midwife (the *dai*) but, rather, a range of women who pooled their expertise and shared the risks presented by the pollution of childbirth. The women present at Jetoon's birth worked together to carry out a number of tasks, such as: i) to absorb pollution (mainly undertaken by Dhanni, the lower caste midwife); ii) to address pain (mainly by women who are kin such as Samina who massages Jetoon, and Mehmooda who invokes the spirit of the old man of the valley); iii) to maintain a balance of body humours between hot and cold (Samina, Mahmuda); iv) to assist in the practicalities (Jetoon's mother and sister – in-law); v) to check progress of the baby through the birth canal (Dhanni, Mahmuda); and vi) to take postpartum care of the baby (Samina). This also had to do with the ways in which risk was conceptualised and managed on a case-by-case basis. The number and combination of midwives present at a birth is not automatically a function of the number of previous children (i.e. fewer midwives the more births a woman has had), but more to do with the relative difficulty and danger associated with birth. I was told that Jetoon is known to experience a 'difficult' labour and birth (*keda jaapa*) which is why she had so many *dai* in attendance. For 'normal' delivery only two women are required who are *aage-peeche*: one who sits at the back (*peeche*) of the woman in labour (to massage/provide pain relief) and one in front (*aage*) to receive the baby.

Although the women *dai* worked collectively, this did not mean that they were regarded as equally authoritative. As I have suggested elsewhere,[5] in the case of rural Sunni women such as Jetoon, as compared with rural Hindu caste women, birth is usually attended by two kinds of indigenous midwives: those who are kin, and those who are lower caste Hindu midwives (Dhanni is more widely known in terms of her caste, as a lower caste, *raigarin, dai*). While both kinds of midwives have experience of delivering children, there is usually a division of labour between them when both are co-present. The 'kin-midwife' usually provides emotional and physical support to the mother and supervises the lower caste midwife when checking for the dilation of the cervix and for progress of the baby in the birth canal. The lower caste midwife, when present, usually assists the mother in the descent and delivery of the baby (sometimes the whole process is carried out by the kin-midwife herself especially if the birth is predicted to be without complications). This entails assisting the baby out of the birth canal, handling the umbilical cord and delivering (though not disposing of) the placenta (*olnaal*). Once the placenta has been expelled, the lower caste midwife is free to take her small remuneration and leave. The payment she gets is variable depending on the sex of the child and whether it is the first born. It can be up to several hundred rupees (Dhanni received Rs51/- for delivering Jetoon's eighth baby).

Those women who were socially proximate to the mother such as Samina had the most authority. Childbirth expertise is more socially distributed when compared to biomedical practice. This also holds true for reproductive complaints and the management of menstrual blood. Menstrual blood was considered 'dangerous' because once expelled by the body it became highly susceptible ('attractive') to 'ill winds' (*hawa*) and with it to the social manipulation of 'jealous' women (sometimes glossed as witches or *dakan*). Infertile women in particular, as we saw in Chapter 3, could cast spells on menstrual blood to reproduce their infertility in others. It was this imminent danger that was considered the key underlying cause of women's reproductive ailments and mishaps and for which midwives and healers were routinely consulted. When conditions were identified which included weakness (*kumzori*) and fevers, menstrual problems (*mahawari ki pareshani*), breech conditions as well as loss and death as in infertility and infant mortality, the *dai* would work in conjunction with, and share the same therapeutic space with faith healers. For the *dai*, menstrual complaints were part of a set of other reproductive complaints such as, 'pain in the stomach, pain in the tubes (*nalli*), bleeding during pregnancy, 'cleansing' (*safai*) or dilatation and curettage, miscarriage (*bacha girna*; literally baby dropping), abortion (*bacha girana*; making the baby drop), ante-natal and postpartum complications such as *bacha sookhna* (drying of the baby) as well as vaginal discharge (*safed pani*) and complications with breastfeeding (*boba dena*; giving the breast).

It is important to note here that while the negative discourse of menstrual blood as 'the flow of dirt' and its association with pollution is predominant, the disorders are not associated with a lack of hygiene or the need to be clean. This observation ties in with much of the ethnographic writing around menstrual blood as symbolic more of danger than 'dirt' the world over (Buckley and Gottlieb, 1988; Douglas, 1966) even though more polyvalent cultural constructions are missing in this literature (Kapadia, 1995). In South Asia and India in particular, work on menstrual perceptions and practices have been linked to differences between Brahmanic and non-Brahmanic kinship ideologies as discussed in Kapadia's work in Tamil Nadu. Compared to the 'hidden' nature of menstrual discourse in North India, menstruation in the southern states with matri-lateral kinship practices such as in Tamil Nadu is publicly celebrated with feasting and gifting to the pubescent girl (also Van Hollen, 2003). Menstrual horoscopes are used by non-Brahmanical communities to match daughters with prospective grooms. It is believed that 'it is through women's body, now (in menarche) linked to the celestial bodies in their orbits around the earth and through her blood, blood that will nourish and create progeny that the next generation is born' (Kapadia, 1995, p. 71).

The discourse around menstrual blood in turn has implications for the way indigenous midwives are perceived, whose role is more positively associated with birth in South India (Van Hollen, 2003) compared to the north (Rozario, 1998, 2006, p. 15; Patel, 1994; Jeffery, Jeffery and Lyon, 1989, 2002). These contrasts are, however, mediated by dynamic conditions presented on the ground such as the changing opportunities presented by biomedical technologies and when *dai* work is in conjunction not just with local healers, but with biomedical practitioners. For example, if bleeding arises during pregnancy then it is very often the case that a cleansing (*safai*) is recommended by the *dai* for which a private gynaecologist will be consulted.

Indigenous midwives address risks such as removing the umbilical cord from the neck but also acknowledge conditions beyond their competence – a reason why for instance the cord is cut only after the placenta is delivered is to allow the baby to be taken to the hospital attached to the placenta to ensure blood supply. The inability to address the dangers posed by a 'difficult' birth may also result in summoning private doctors to administer oxytocin injections to speed up the labour. In other cases, indigenous midwives frequently consulted 'nurses' (women who worked as birth assistants in clinics who may not always be biomedically trained). Samina said she often called nurse Parvati from Ramganj (a Muslim dominated area in the inner city) when she faced birth complications in her work. The nurse charged Rs500/- for her services (which included drug, injection and transport costs).

The significance of addressing childbirth through the combined expertise of the *dai* and state auxiliary nurse midwives, however, is on the decline and driven, first, by the policy trajectories on birth attendance in India which have stopped *dai* training programmes (in line with the WHO Directive 2005), and second, in the neo-liberal resistance to pluralism which regards only biomedical and commoditised forms of intervention as appropriate to meeting people's health rights. Such notions are emerging in health policy circles and, equally, among public health workers themselves. Locally too, no one wants to do *dai ka kaam* (work of the dai) anymore and increasingly birth is associated with institutional delivery. In addition, financial incentives are provided to women to give birth in hospitals, which includes small sums for health workers who do *motivation ka kaam* (the work of motivation). As a result, over the last decade hospitals have been flooded by deliveries even though they continue to have a low health system capacity (personal observation by a gynaecologist at the main women's zenana hospital in Jaipur), poor facilities and a related poor quality of services (Ravindran 2009, for example).

From birth work to 'multi-purpose' work: the declining relevance of midwives

In the early state midwifery programmes in India, only indigenous midwives (traditional birth attendants or TBA) who had undergone biomedical training were allowed to assist in delivery. The inclusion of TBAs in a systematic way in public health programmes was sought in the late 1950s shortly after India embarked upon its Family Planning programme in 1952 (the first and largest in the world). Initially, once trained their employment justified two kinds of development rationalities: i) that of empowerment, where the thinking was that having women of the community learn midwifery skills 'empowered' local women to take better (biomedical) control of their own birth needs and contexts, and ii) that of cost efficiency where having a larger number of partially skilled women in the health force was considered more financially rewarding than to invest in fewer highly trained specialists. (More recently the benefits of this approach emerge in the context of policies of 'task shifting' (Cataldo *et al.*, 2015; Standing and Chowdhury, 2008)).[6]

The everyday delivery of public maternal health services from the 1960s onwards rested on the shoulders of a vast and variously skilled cadre of health workers in India. Between the 1970s and the 1980s, TBAs joined the ranks of front line health workers and, along with the auxiliary nurse midwives (ANM), were regarded as important recipients of 'training' through specifically designed training programmes. Although *dai* training programmes existed from the 1860s in colonial India, they were sporadic and urban biased, and indigenous midwives were regarded as dirty and ignorant and blamed for obstetric mishaps (Jeffery *et al.*, 2002). Post-independence TBA training programmes were driven by international recommendations based on the universal Primary Health Care (PHC) model developed in 1978 which stressed the role of indigenous practitioners as allies in improving the health of the community (Alma Ata Declaration, 1978).

TBAs were subordinate in qualifications and roles to auxiliary nurse midwives (ANM) who received midwifery training for 1–2 years and, unlike the TBAs, were qualified to conduct deliveries at the primary health centre (set up to provide basic services to 5,000 people and which were run by ANMs). The role of TBAs declined in the 1980s as the numbers and responsibilities of auxiliary field health workers grew. While TBA training continued to be supported, it was reduced from a period of three months to six days in the early 1990s and then further to one day every month for twelve months from 1997 onwards: levels which were regarded as too low to comply with WHO standards for skilled attendance at birth.

In 2005 in the new NRHM programme and following WHO guidelines, it was decreed that indigenous midwives would not be recipients of training and were dropped altogether as health workers in the new maternal health programmes. Training programmes were slowly wound up and made obsolete in 2005 when a major shift in the rationale and focus of health programmes toward institutional birth meant that TBAs were completely bypassed as health workers in the local context. The emphasis on skilled birth attendance by the ANM slowly declined as well from the 1990s onwards and to the period leading up to the NRHM in 2005. As the brief of the ANMs expanded to becoming multi-purpose workers and referral agents, they were themselves to focus less on providing skilled birthing services (Mavlankar *et al.*, 2010). Consequently, we find there is no rise in the number of deliveries conducted by the ANM whose focus is diverted toward antenatal care and, in particular, to the provision of iron-folic acid tablets and immunisation injections (Mavlankar *et al.*, 2010). The shift in focus from midwifery skills to antenatal provision was accompanied by a decline in the necessary equipment for delivering babies and a rise, instead, in family planning promotion material, technologies and devices. Contraceptives such as condoms, pills and IUDs become available at the sub-centre along with posters and leaflets which spread the virtues of family planning. The ANMs increasingly became regarded as health workers whose primary aim was to motivate cases for sterilisation and whose birthing skills became redundant and secondary to their acting as a conduit for emergency birth referrals.

In March 1998 I met Sushma, the Malayali ANM who had been posted to work in the regional primary health sub-centre in the Goner area of fieldwork. Sushma was in Khatipura, one of eleven villages she toured as part of her work. She had come to top-up the supply of drugs (iron-folic acid tablets, ORS packets and quinine tablets) and contraception (Cu-T intra-uterine device, Mala-N hormonal pills and condoms) at the AWW centre there. She only talked to me about the significance of the family planning work she was assigned to undertake. She told me that she has been trained to insert the Cu-T, but could also assist the doctors in the referral centres with DNC and MTP (cleaning and medical termination of pregnancies), and was called upon to perform these operations. As an ANM, we see that Sushma was 'reduced to the role of a paramedic whose activities were limited to family planning, immunisation and superficial healthcare' (Mavlankar *et al.*, 2010). With the narrow focus on family planning, the provision of public services at the village and block level deteriorated, in turn, rendering rural women vulnerable to the vagaries of a market in maternal health services. This is borne out by the huge boom of birth services offered by the private sector at this time. I was informed that normal deliveries in Jaipur at that time cost as much as Rs2,000–10,000/- (£25 to £125 at the time) with C-section deliveries of up to Rs30,000/- (£400).

As we saw in chapter 2, between 1997 and 2003, the Ministry of Health and Family Welfare (MoHFW) launched its new RCH-I programme in which a comprehensive and integrated reproductive service approach was devised to act as a corrective to the overly family planning (i.e. contraception orientated) character of primary healthcare services. However, on the ground ANMs continued to push family planning in their work. Sushma told me that her target for 1998 was fifty-three cases of women who accepted family planning methods. The previous year it had been thirty-five cases, which she had exceeded. When I pointed out that there was a huge push for expunging family planning targets, she said the only change she had experienced was that *'cases don't get money anymore'* (i.e. no cash incentives were attached to this kind of work anymore).

As ANMs came to have a minimal role in providing childbirth assistance on the ground they were required to join forces with a new agent, the ASHA (Accredited Social Health Activist). As I argue in the final section of the chapter, it is the perceptions, work vulnerabilities and the nature of working conditions (caste-based, hierarchic, bureaucratic, apathetic, non-consultative) that determine the quality of the services the ANM and ASHA can offer, which effect their desire and motivation to do so. Functioning in a work environment where expectations are to complete multiple tasks at the same time as having to compete for remuneration has led to a reproduction of apathy and blame (see George, 2007 for examples of poor maternal health worker accountability in Karnataka) which characterises much of the public health provision in India.

Being an ASHA: managing the risks of 'not enough skill', 'too much work' and material deprivation

Asha apne saas ka virodh jub nahi kar sakti to kis ghar mein ja ke ladegi?

> In which house can the ASHA fight when she can't oppose her own mother-in-law?
>
> (Senior NGO worker, Jaipur, fieldwork notes, September 2016)

In 2005, the NRHM framework incorporated a new category of health worker, the ASHA, in its *Janani Suraksha Yojana* (JSY) or safe motherhood programme. The primary work assigned to the ASHA was 'to act as motivator and educator for women in the villages' and to identify and accompany pregnant women to the hospital. The NRHM guidelines defined the role of the ASHA in the JSY as that of an 'honorary volunteer' who was to 'escort' women for institutional deliveries (though not undertake the role of birth companion per se (GOI NHSRC, 2011, p. 2)). The ASHA, selected by community leaders from among the residents of a village, must have passed their eighth class to be eligible to apply for this honorary position. In Rajasthan, an ASHA worked as a *sahayogini* (helper) in the JSY programme and was responsible to two government departments: the health department and the Women and Child Development department (her remuneration came from the latter division and from the programme funds allocated to the Integrated Child Development Scheme or ICDS which oversaw the *anganwadi* crèches and attendants). By the time of fieldwork in 2009, over 300,000 ASHA had been selected and this was further advanced to approximately 825,000 women working as ASHA nationally (GOI NHSRC, 2011).

The category of the ASHA, designated as a 'multi-purpose' health worker, reflects the shift towards an integrated development approach. ASHA were appointed 'to ensure the health status of a community through: i) securing people's access to health services; ii) improving health practices and behaviours, and iii) providing essential and feasible healthcare provision' (GOI NHSRC, 2011, p. 3). Aside from accompanying women to give birth in hospitals, a key activity which she undertook along with the ANM was to promote family planning, in particular the use of reversible methods of contraception (IUD, condoms and hormonal pills). This promotion work would take place as part of a whole host of other activities which were part of her everyday schedule of: home visits to pregnant women and children under five years, referral to government facilities for a pregnancy complication, sharing knowledge of best breastfeeding practices, prevention of diarrhoea, promoting immunisation for infants and contraceptive choices available and undertaking sputum tests for the identification of TB. The government JSY (and more recently JSSY infant focused) programmes cover the costs of paying honoraria to the ASHA and providing them with relevant training over a period of twenty-three days to ensure knowledge of key practices for maternal and infant survival. Each ASHA is provided with an identity card, bag, badge and drug kits (filled monthly and containing a range of items from ORS and paracetamol to contraceptives and betadine).

While there have been large numbers of ASHA recruited and a substantial cash investment, little is known about their work experiences and the extent to which they are able to realise what they are tasked to do. Recent government statistics suggest great regional variations in maternal health outcomes, despite a significant overall increase in numbers of institutional deliveries in the state.

Figure 5.1 ASHA workers watch a government documentary on the role of State health workers.

Fieldwork observations suggest the need to go beneath the statistics to understand the effectiveness of the ASHA in terms of the kinds of vulnerabilities (social, economic and political) that being an ASHA entail, their effects on her disposition (in Bourdieu's sense, 1977) and her own perceptions of the barriers to maternal health.

As the ASHA and ANM are at the interface of the community and the state it is especially important to see how they deploy their power in the field of maternal health. Rather than view them simply through the lens of their work as government health functionaries, we need to see them as inhabiting different fields of power: social, medical and occupational; as mothers and daughters-in-laws; as earning members of their households; but, equally, as women who may have the same social conditions as the women they care for. Adopting such a lens enables us to see how health work is affected by social processes outside the world of health per se. These are also perspectives not captured in public health surveys and biomedical research which are rarely designed to raise questions about health workers' intimate lives and work experiences as they are shaped by the shifting day-to-day anxieties of material poverty and poor access to health services.

In 2015, I had arranged to meet with twelve ASHA who were attached to the *anganwadi* centres of nine villages in the Sanganer sub-division (*tehsil*) of Jaipur district. These were women who were aged between twenty-three and forty-five years old and had educational qualifications that ranged from eighth class to an MA and BEd. They mainly belonged to middle and lower income families of the Kumawat, Meena, Raigar, Goswami, Berwa, Mahawar and Rajput castes. The group of ASHA included Anju, Govindi, Deepa and Mamta who were ASHA for nine years (from the very beginning of the programme in 2006), Chhoti and Savita who had been working for five years as well as relative newcomers Sonia, Renu, Rekha, Sheela and Sunita who had been ASHA for between one and three years.

In our group discussion on 'what is the work involved in being an ASHA', several key themes emerged from among those present. These were: i) that as an ASHA one was primarily engaged in *motivation ka kaam* (the work of motivating women and children to participate in the antenatal visits, immunisation schemes and in using contraception); ii) that it involved a tremendous amount of field based work (*field ka kaam jyada rehta hai*) which involved walking long distances to cover a number of villages which was physically exhausting and, as it was combined with the motivation work, also emotionally draining; and iii) that the pay involved was not commensurate with the work expected.

The 'motivation work' (*motivation ka kaam*) carried out by the Asha involved regular visits to all the village households (typically 200 in number), which involved discussions with pregnant, lactating and young mothers identified and the use of persuasive arguments and convincing tactics to ensure these women would go through with their children's immunisation plans and follow this through by bringing their children to the AW centre. The work of motivation is itself based on a lot of preparatory 'field based' work (*field ka kaam*) which included monthly household surveys (an average of ten households per day) as part of providing a detailed socio-economic and maternal health related profile of the village (*gaon ki bhumika*). As one ASHA said, 'the whole burden of maternal health work has come to rest on us'. This was an observation made especially in comparison with the work of the ANM a permanent member of the safe motherhood programme with a salary of 30,000 to 40,000 rupees a month in 2015. As one ASHA explained to me, the work carried out by the ANM was 'merely one of injecting women and children' (referring to the immunisation programme) which could be carried out at the *anganwadi* crèche centre itself. There was an overall sense among the ASHA I spoke to, of a highly imbalanced and unjust remuneration system accompanied by a lack of recognition (*pehchan*) of their work. As one ASHA said:

> We get only Rs1,600/- as a fixed sum. Over the past nine years since I first started working as an ASHA, the money we get has only risen marginally, from Rs500/- in 2006 to 1,100/- and then to 1,600/- in the past five years. And it is not just, there does not seem to be any recognition of our work (*pehchan nahi*) or even of our presence. We have to accompany women to give birth in hospitals but we are not recognised there – we have to stand in line (queue) like everyone else (regular patients). The doctors and staff do not even bother to inform us of what has happened to the woman we have accompanied to the hospital.
>
> (ASHA Focus group, fieldnotes, 2015)

There was a chorus of agreement from other ASHA in the group. It was clear that their work was accorded low value and status in both medical spaces and in their communities. Two other key issues emerged from within the group: first, that while a number of ASHA had opted for the job from a sense of *seva* (service), money was the key incentive for them to undertake the work; and second, it was clear that they had all faced difficulties navigating the power of their co-workers, especially the ANM, and of powerful members in the house-hold – the husband and in-laws.

Let us examine these issues in further depth as they each provide important insights into the intersection between government policy and the habitus of the ASHA, the state's lowest paid and yet most significant maternal health worker.

Incentives and sentiment

Conflicts around the pay that village level functionaries received for their work in development projects and programmes is not a new phenomenon – either in Rajasthan or elsewhere in India. As the experiences of Rajasthan's flagship Women's Development Programme (WDP) in the late 1980s and 1990s demonstrated, the *sathin* (female village level companions) were motivated to join the programme for the honorarium they received for their 'voluntary' work in promoting women's empowerment, the status that government employment afforded them and because of their desire and expectation that they would eventually gain permanent government positions with a fixed income (Mathur, 2004; Kabeer, 1994; Unnithan and Srivastava, 1997).[7]

Under the JSY safe motherhood programme, cash amounts ranging from Rs1,400 (approximately US$31) in rural areas to Rs1,000 (approximately US$22) in urban locations were deposited into bank accounts of women who gave birth in hospitals (Lim *et al.*, 2010). Apart from a small salary, ASHA who accompanied pregnant women for their delivery would only get cash linked to their performance and would be compensated for their time in specific circumstances, such as attendance at training sessions and monthly work review meetings. As Renu explained:

> Apart from my salary of 1,600/- (paid by the Women and Child development department into my bank account online), I receive Rs300/- online for registration of women and 3 antenatal check-ups. I then get 300/- whenever I accompany a pregnant mother to a government hospital (this too online). I also receive 100/- for every child vaccinated against measles and 50/- for a DPT booster administered. If I get a woman to undertake sterilisation after 2 children I will get 1,200/-, other wise 200/- for women who go in for sterilisation after 3 children.

Financial incentive schemes as described above are promoted by states and international agencies globally as they drive rapid improvements in health provider performance, and this is especially the case in weak health infrastructure and information systems (Magrath and Nichter, 2012, among others). While the idea of rewarding better performance can be a positive step toward keeping up worker morale and motivation, the policy must be realised, as Magrath and Nichter as well as the ASHA example suggests, in the context of the underlying values and social processes that affect workplace motivation, to capture the impact of such policies beyond the health system. Conceptualising health worker motivations in terms of Bourdieu's concept of *disposition* (a frame which orients actors towards actions, rooted in a system of dispositions, i.e. the *habitus*), they argue that pay for performance programmes (P4P) bring about changes to health worker motivations by increasing their access to different forms of 'capital' (economic, social, symbolic), which can effect significant changes in the quality of social relationships and wider social change. At the same time P4P can *undermine* motivation and performance by increasing competition between workers, mistrust among patients (who clearly see that the nature of their healthcare is financially motivated) and, crucially, by encouraging the use of 'gaming' strategies among health workers (Magrath and Nichter, 2012, p. 1780). Referred to as a deployment of 'strategies of maximising performance in relation to rewarded behaviours', 'gaming' can include any number of actions such as the falsification of data, oversupply of services, neglect of less rewarded patients or aspects of healthcare. Rita Kanwar, a slightly older ASHA who had a disabled husband, provided insights into how such gaming strategies might naturally suggest themselves and lead the ASHA to lean toward work in the private health sector to the neglect of her public sector work. She said she was very often contacted by private nursing homes who requested her to bring them clients (*grahak*) for their delivery services. Their pay rates were high and Rita would get almost Rs1,000/- for a delivery (the pregnant woman would pay about Rs5,000/-) which was double the amount she hoped to receive at the public health centre. The amount would be even more if a C-section delivery was advised. Besides she preferred the private providers as they treated her well and, furthermore, she noted, '*you don't have to stand in line'* (referring to a queue to be attended to by the hospital staff). Rita's frank disclosure of other sources of income was made with the justification that she had to support a family, given that her husband was disabled and could not work. She had no concerns about the unethical aspects of supporting private providers who charged much higher rates for delivery services. I would suggest that it is the JSY with its focus on cash incentives that has legitimised such a commodified approach to birth.

Returning to Rita's comment above about being noticed in clinical spaces, I found this echoed the sentiments of the wider group of ASHA in their experiences of working with other health workers. Renu, who had arrived a bit early, gave me the chance to talk at length with her about her work as an Asha since 2013. She said ASHA were in competition with the ANM around the 'targets' they had to fulfil. The women whom she motivates in the village cannot be registered by her, even if they decide to undergo immunisation or give birth in hospitals, because the ANM says, unless they go to her at the centre, she will not register them as part of Renu's cases. This is a problem for Renu and she says, 'the big madam (supervisor) at Goner asks me what is the reason my *target* is so low', and 'what can I say to her'? Renu explains the ASHA are set a target of motivating twelve to thirteen pregnant women a month for antenatal care (vaccines and tablets) and hospital delivery. (I am surprised by the use of the word 'targets' given its association with the coercive family planning goals set for health workers and realise that there remains a culture of targets in birth and family planning work, as discussed in the next section.)

When asked how the relationship with the ANM be rectified, another ASHA suggested that the ASHA be given 'training' to do the injections themselves and that they could take over the role of the ANM who seemed superfluous to them as they had now acquired the skills of making 'slides' (for malaria and TB detection). A number of ASHA agreed that they should be provided with further skills training. Although a number of ASHA present said they received support from their ANM, and this was especially in the context of negotiations with community leaders (at the panchayat or village councils), they felt it was incommensurate with the gatekeeping role they were subject to.

Cash incentives have contributed to the culture of reproach and competitiveness between this set of health workers who need to work as a team for 'integrated services' to be realised (Mishra, 2014; my single quotes). As an ASHA health worker in Mishra's Udaipur study suggested, although they valued trust and teamwork they faced institutional obstacles such as differential incentives, evidencing a system focused on reporting and differential rewards.

Here health worker management takes place in a context of reproach and apathy rather than empathy (as documented for health care workers in Kenya (Brown, 2016) which results in disruptive social ties rather than solidarities around work.

Another crucial element in understanding what drives, motivates or pulls the ASHA back in her work is the social context of her life as a junior and dependent member living in a joint household with her in-law family in a village of affines. For most ASHA healthworkers the support of their families had motivated them to apply for the job in the first place. As Renu described, *'it was my husband (a teacher in a private school) who brought home the form. He filled it out for me.'* Without daily support from affinal family members, the job would be impossible. Renu recounted that her youngest son was only four months when she went for training. Her mother-in-law (*saas*) accompanied her and looked after the infant, bringing him to her to breastfeed at regular intervals during the meeting. In terms of her daily work as an ASHA, Renu had an agreement with her elder sister-in law (*jethani*) to share the cooking and making of tea for the eight members of their household.

There was a general consensus, among the ASHA I met, of the critical support of kin, especially that of husbands. There was also agreement about the lack of power that the ASHA wielded with older women as well as with men from her husband's village, severely restricting her ability to be effective at the household level in her *motivation ka kaam*. I witnessed the powerlessness of the ASHA at an NRHM village committee meeting in Alwar in 2010 where the ASHA were sitting with their heads covered in the presence of their male 'in-laws' (all village members of the husband's village are regarded as 'in-laws'; Unnithan and Heitmeyer, 2012). With regard to the ineffectiveness of the ASHA in the households she visits, a senior NGO worker captured this in her comments to me about the misplaced expectation of health planners about the effectiveness of the ASHA when 'she cannot even contest the authority of her mother-in-law': *'asha apne saas ka virodh jub nahi kar sakti to kis ghar mein ja ke ladegi?'*

The ineffectiveness of the ASHA has begun to emerge as a key concern in recent health planning and development literature (GOI NHSRC, 2011; Mishra, 2014; Magrath and Nichter, 2012). We now turn to the other important aspect of her work as a motivator for contraception, to understand her situation more fully.

The other side of birth work: sterilisation and the culture of 'targets'

Family planning has been a focus throughout maternal health policy since the beginning of the planning process, but its character has changed from a focus on compulsory sterilisation (*non-reversible*) to a more voluntary approach. Following the 'turn to rights' (Chapter 2) and India's pledge to promote informed choice and comprehensive counselling with regard to contraceptive methods, there has been a policy swing toward *reversible* methods. As we saw in Chapter 2, under the NRHM the Government of India (GOI) has simultaneously promoted incentivised institutional birth as well as financially rewarded *voluntary* family planning programmes as a means of meeting women's rights.[8&9] The

ASHA and ANM category of trained workers are emblematic of this twin policy of the state in their dual role in promoting 'safe delivery' as well as 'voluntary' family planning. On the ground, these health workers are expected to deliver a 'package of services' which promote child immunisation, institutional delivery as well as contraceptive choice.

The post of the ASHA was created in 2005 with an eye to advancing community awareness of especially the *reversible* methods that women could use. The performance of the ASHA and ANM, both tasked with family planning work alongside promoting institutional birth and child immunisation, continues to be monitored by indicators in terms of targets (numbers signalling the uptake of contraception). The underlying policy rationale of promoting family planning in high population, high mortality settings is powerfully driven by the public health perspective where the risk in reproductive events are weighted toward the risk to life and a related set of statistics which demonstrate that contraceptive use has the potential to reduce maternal deaths (Obermeyer, 2000). The WHO, for example, suggests that contraceptive use prevented 218 million unintended pregnancies in developing countries in 2012 and averted fifty-five million unplanned births, 138 million abortions (of which forty million are unsafe), twenty-five million miscarriages and 118,000 maternal deaths (WHO, 2014). Public health literature underscores the significance of using reversible methods in contexts where birth intervals (spacing) between children is less than three years as this predisposes mothers and infants to a higher risk of death.

Rajasthan is one such context where over 80 per cent of women with one child do not use any form of contraception (NFHS 3). Among the women who do go in for contraception there is an overall preference for the terminal method of sterilisation with over 42 per cent of women being on record in seeking out sterilisation (DLHS, 2007–08). My own observations support this popularity of non-reversible methods (for the group of women who have achieved their desired family size; Unnithan-Kumar 2001, 2003). To what extent is the ASHA able to promote a different form of contraceptive behaviour from that which is popular?

A close look at the actual work practices and perceptions of the ASHA on family planning reveals structural, economic, affective, and local and health system limitations which negatively impact on her ability to promote contraceptive choice. For instance, ASHA health workers may have contraceptive biases (toward reproductive age-determined voluntary sterilisation) similar to others in her community (a fact little recognised in various ASHA training literature) as Donnelly (2013) has also found in her study of thirty-nine ASHA in Udaipur district in Rajasthan. The bias toward sterilisation is also strongly driven by a pressure to fulfil 'targets' set by the state (observed by Donnelly). In addition, I would suggest that the ASHA's inclination to reinforce the benefits of sterilisation rather than other forms of reversible methods is also largely because she, herself, is convinced of the harmful nature of the copper-T (intra-uterine device) and Mala N (contraceptive device) based on her own experiences (most ASHA have undergone sterilisation or use condoms). I was repeatedly reminded by the ASHA about the safety of sterilisation procedures compared to IUD insertions or hormonal pill regimes. A combination of ASHA experience and state directives to fulfil targets thus combines to influence their health promotion practices on the ground.

As the coercive health programs of the 1970s taught us, contraceptive targets are a particularly powerful regulatory device which ensured that public health workers and gynaecologists were in constant cycles of an ever increasing production of sterilised bodies. Public health workers were caught in a bind as their job security was linked to the achievement of a certain 'target' number of family planning cases (for example thirty-five per annum or even fifty cases or more as Sushma (an ANM) suggested above (and Dhanraj, *Something Like a War*, film 1991; Visaria, 2002). Given their own modest earnings, health workers become hostage to the state's family planning agendas making them among its most coercive agents. The need to fulfil their quota of sterilised cases led health workers to use a number of incentives (both monetary and in kind) in most cases, including outright threats and coercion, to make couples agree to undertake the 'operation'. The groundswell of popular opposition to such strategies as well as active political support from feminist and health activist groups (1990s to early 2000s) resulted in the official removal of such targets as indicators of health workers efficiency and motivation. There was a shift, instead, to a Community Needs Assessment Approach in 1996, which focused on drawing up contraceptive needs in consultation with the community. Health worker performance in this domain would be measured by 'Expected Levels of Achievement' (ELA targets) in conjunction with the family planning indicators. Prominent activists and researchers in India, K. Iyengar, A. Das and others such as V. Ramachandran have noted a target approach has continued to dominate the outlook of health workers even as health provision takes on a new form and language (personal communication, 2010; also see Visaria, 2002). This continued prevalence of targets points to the lasting effects of the disciplining practices of health workers. The continued focus on targets and the poor institutional support for reversible forms of contraception comes at a cost – the need to raise awareness of *informed* and voluntary contraceptive choice (e.g. of reversible contraceptives).

As a tool of the state, 'targets' wield authority and in the context of family planning decisions show a resilience in the minds of healthcare workers since the coercive campaigns of the Indira Gandhi government from the late 1970s. Targets speak the language of science and are thus conceived as being able to provide a factual depiction of reality. What is clear from the ASHA and ANM experiences is that the authority of the state, and its language of numbers and targets, exerts power over its workers as it is does upon the women whose reproductive bodies it seeks to control. As several scholars have noted, for instance in relation to the emerging discourse around HIV and Aids (Treichler, 1998), the language of numbers may also be an authoritative way of representing data which not only obscures the realities, but seeks to provide an illusion of control (also Greenhalgh 2005).[10]

Gynaecologists in public hospitals in Rajasthan also promote the message of contraception and reduction in family size often more zealously than health workers and also seem more self-disciplined in Foucault's sense of the term, about the benefits of family planning. This is reflected in the popular fear of utilising hospitals for childbirth as demonstrated by poorer couples in Rajasthan. There is a strong belief that, as one woman said to me, 'you go in to have a child and they do your tubes at the same time' (referring to a tubectomy) or put more succinctly by another respondent: 'they do two jobs in one bout of anaesthesia (*do bihoshi mein ek kaam*)' referring to the simultaneous procedures of birth and sterilisation carried out in the public hospitals.[11]

Concluding discussion

Through a detailed consideration of the changing labour and lives of a set of village level health care and government functionaries, this chapter has demonstrated that the risks and vulnerabilities to women's health are connected with social, economic and moral worlds of the healthcare workers beyond a biomedical discourse on risk. The discussion of risk presented in this chapter is not a critique about medicalisation or technocratic birth procedures, but rather it makes a case against 'over-medicalisation' where biomedical approaches to risk which stem from a physiological concern with individual mortality are the only consideration in a context of other, social forms of risk. The answer to what constitutes over-medicalisation is revealed through attention to the singularities of health work vulnerabilities. Risk approaches, which are dominant within development discourses of maternal health, are yet to reflect this. As I argue in this book and elsewhere (Unnithan-Kumar, 2001), public health policy and provision do not recognise the significance of emotion, attachments and desire in people's orientation toward certain kinds of healthcare choices and provision. Indeed, very little of the public health literature about maternal mortality pays attention to the complex ways in which poor women and men (as users or providers of healthcare) – in contexts where maternal mortality is high, such as in India or West Africa, for example – negotiate social and emotional risk in their access to maternal healthcare or engage with plural forms of knowledge to mitigate social and biomedical risk (Bledsoe, 2002; Bledsoe *et al.*, 1988, 1998; Unnithan-Kumar, 1998, 2001; Cornwall, 2007). Medical anthropologists suggest that the global health community has over emphasised individual risk factors at the cost of an integrated, cross-cultural, subjective and historical approach to health care (Biehl and Petryna, 2013; Lock and Nguyen, 2010; Das and Das, 2007; Das 2015).

Anthropological studies of reproductive risk in lower- and middle-income countries (LMIC), where maternal mortality is high, indicate a more complex on the ground understanding of maternal health risks where biomedicine may inform in part, whole, or not at all, community notions and experiences of maternal vulnerability and related health-seeking (Reynolds-Whyte, 1997; Pigg, 2005; Fordyce and Maraesa, 2012; Obermeyer, 2000; for example). In highly medically plural societies such as those operating in India, there are competing forms of childbearing expertise and treatment efficacy (Jordan, 1997; Davis-Floyd and Sargent, 1997) as people participate in mixed economies of care. As described previously in Chapter 3, relatives and healers play a significant role in authorising recourse to specific treatments and health providers (Kielman, 1998;

Bledsoe, 2002; Unnithan, 1998, 2001; Pinto, 2008) and mediate the relation women have with both indigenous and skilled birth attendants.

With institutionalised birth fast becoming the norm in Rajasthan we see new practices emerge in the handling of social risk. The umbilical cord is cut at the hospital by a nurse who is not a kinsperson, where previously it used to be the birth mother who did this as kin-midwives would not wish to undertake the responsibility of severance. The placenta (*olnaal*) of a boy is brought back to be buried near the home, whereas the placenta of baby girls lands up in the hospital rubbish bin (*kachra patra*), as they would do in the village rubbish heap. And yet there is very little information and interrogation of bio-medical risk by mothers and accompanying family members at a birth. When I ask about bio-medical procedures, I am told the delivery is done in the horizontal position and women are not kept long in the hospital. Zaida's *bhanji* (first cousin from the mother's side) had terrible bleeding in 2016 when she got back home after child-birth in hospital. They rushed her back to hospital, but she died on the way. And yet Zaida and other women were happy with giving birth in hospitals. Their evaluation of it being a 'good place' to give birth now (*pahle se acchha*) was because 'the birth mother gets Rs1,400/- and free food (dal, rice and curd)', a very significant reason for low-income families to participate.

Maternal precarity, including at birth, is equally grounded in wider economies and legacies of deprivation effecting both those who receive healthcare and those who provide it. Development interventions that focus only on subsidizing *individual* women's access to institutional care through providing incentives for them and for the 'voluntary' health workers who accompany them, reproduce a set of neo-liberal assumptions underpinning much contemporary gender and development discourse: that for poor users or providers of health care to become empowered they must necessarily participate in the market economy [and seek freedom from traditional social institutions (Hickel, 2014). In addition, schemes such as the JSY have been seen to promote a sense of entitlement to cash rather than promote empowerment in terms of reproductive choice (Dasgupta, 2014).

Even where there is clear evidence, as described in this chapter, that the JSY has been highly successful in encouraging women to deliver at hospitals rather than at homes, we cannot presume that delivery in institutions will automatically guarantee maternal and infant safety (i.e. avert deaths; Ravindaran, 2009). As we saw in the large-scale statistical survey of district level data, the introduction of the JSY led to a substantial increase in 'in-facility' coverage (that is, of women giving birth in public health facilities), but less of an increase in coverage in terms of antenatal and postpartum care (Lim *et al.*, 2010). While the study by Lim *et al.* attributed the 'probable reduction in peri-natal and neo-natal deaths' to the increased institutionalization of birth, the researchers were unable to detect an effect on the number of maternal deaths (pp. 2009–23).

State healthcare training programmes which transform local people into health workers have had another less well-documented effect in that they have dismantled the socio-cultural basis of indigenous birthing expertise, much as Pigg has so aptly observed with regard to TBA training programmes in Nepal

(1997). Biomedical skills themselves were partially, but also incomprehensibly, transferred in the short period of the training with little emphasis on actual practice: the focus being on instructions to do with hygiene, messages on safety and nutrition, family planning education and a theoretical emphasis on referral. The training programmes before and within the JSY have been carried out in a similar vein. However, what they have taught women like Samina, Dhanni, Rita and Renu, indigenous midwives and health workers whose experiences are recounted above, have, instead, been the skills of what information on health and healing practices to communicate and what to withhold from their medical superiors (such as to do with the agency of spirits, healing rituals; also see Mishra, 2014), and how to 'game' the system.

The gaming of the system is encouraged by a culture of 'targets' and discourse on 'motivation' on the one hand and cash incentives which drive competitiveness rather than teamwork and trust among the ANM, ASHA and AWW. And yet in terms of their own motivation, ASHA workers are sustained through their emotionally supportive engagement with their co-workers, family and community members. Given the realities of their limited economic circumstances and social powerlessness, we also get a sense of why their approach to health on the ground is neither empathetic nor 'rights-based' (in terms of facilitating the empowerment of the women they serve) but rather self-seeking and money oriented. Due consideration needs to be given in policy discourse to sentiment and the financial security of health workers as a way of ensuring maternal safety.[12] Overall, there needs to be deeper policy engagement with embodied constructions of gender, social power and politics among health workers in analysing what maternal risk is and where it 'sits', to address maternal vulnerabilities on the ground.

Notes

1 Here the idea of risk is used to frame time based delivery protocols for midwives. It is precisely this 'time management' that Scamell and Stewart (2014) find to be the most 'disciplining' aspect of risk-related protocols that midwives conducting vaginal examinations, in their study, experience. When labour is 'too slow' and does not conform to the anticipated timetable then it becomes high risk and subject to medical intervention. Midwives, on the other hand, were particularly concerned about 'starting the clock' of fully established labour and the cascade of medical intervention this entailed. And, indeed, their ethnographic findings suggested that maternity care was best provided when midwives creatively found spaces to practice their embodied as well as encoded knowledge, balancing the divergent concerns with risk and time.

2 What they refer to as encoded knowledge; Scamell and Stewart, 2014, p. 84.

3 The figure on TBA presence is ambiguously recorded in government records: according to NFHS 1995 figures, in rural Rajasthan 42 per cent of all births are attended to by traditional birth attendants (TBA) and 38.9 per cent by only 'relatives and others', accounting for over 80 per cent of the births. The NFHS-2 fails to define either TBAs or give further details about the category 'relatives and others', presuming the two as a distinct set of health service providers.

4 There are significant variations across the thirty-two districts of the state with low rates of institutional delivery especially in Barmer and Jaisalmer, the western, outlying and extremely arid districts.

5 Unnithan-Kumar, 2002.
6 Standing and Chowdhury, 2008: community health workers are of four types: generic (plugging the gaps/ least valued/ secure); specialist workers (for tuberculosis, malaria; face less market competition); mediators (support users to negotiate pluralism and the market); and the expert patients (who use IT and are well informed).
7 As we argue in our chapter, the expectation to gain permanent employment was contrary to the voluntary approach promoted by feminist activists who had conceived the programme in the first place (Unnithan and Srivastava, 1997).
8 The National family planning policy, NPP 2000, aligns with the government's pledge to promote informal choice and comprehensive counselling with regard to contraceptive methods.
9 This mix of birth and contraceptive service is part of a new *comprehensive* and *integrated* service delivery approach to provide a *continuum* of care in the context of childbearing (GOI NHSRC, 2011). The approach is in line with global principles (WHO guidelines, 2002) to deliver care which is preventive and curative, provided over time and across different previously vertical, health sector programmes (Mishra, 2014).
10 Greenhalgh (2005) notes a similar effectiveness of state planning which focuses on targets in China's promotion of its one child policy, although in the Chinese case it was also political, party led mobilisation at the local level which monitored people's participation.
11 Clinicians and medical doctors play a critical role in promoting certain family planning methods, i.e. in terms of their focus on contraceptive research in reproductive medicine. As with IVF research in the UK, doctors in the Indian context are propelled to find more novel and 'quicker' methods of achieving contraception. The stated aim is to provide methods which require least intervention, such as surgery. Contraceptive research over the past two decades has been a fertile area of research as seen in the numbers of pills and injectables (Depoprovera, Norplant) that have been developed in the past few decades. Such research is well known for its lack of regard of side-effects, often leading to less publicised, devastating reproductive outcomes for women (Chayanika *et al.*, 1999). One such example is provided by the investigation around the clinical trials to do with quinacrine sterilisation in India and elsewhere in the developing world (George, 2004). Here the anti-malarial drug quinacrine was found to be an effective way of causing sterility through the burning and resultant scarring of the tissue in the fallopian tubes. Despite inconclusive clinical trials as to the safety of this method, the drug has been administered to over 100,000 women in twenty countries over the past thirty years. As George suggests, Indian doctors have led the way and have been able to bypass the legal and other regulations effectively through their money and research eminence within the scientific community.
12 There has been some recognition in a recent government evaluation report of the sheer amount of responsibility placed on the ASHA, and where the recommendation is to consider what skills to limit her to (GOI NHSRC, 2011, p. 32). The report also provides a word of caution on ASHA evaluation procedures, suggesting that if ASHA are considered to be link workers (rather than direct providers of care) then their efficacy should not be measured in terms of the drop in maternal or child mortality but rather less ambitiously in terms of the overall, not individual, *increase* (emphasis in original) in institutional delivery and immunisation coverage (2011, p. 32).

Bibliography

Adams, V., 2013. Evidence-based Global Public Health: subjects, profits, erasures. In Biehl, J. and Petryna, A., eds. *When People Come First: Critical Studies in Global Health.* Princeton University Press, 54–91
Beck, U., 1992. *Risk Society: towards a new modernity.* London: Sage

Berry, N., 2010. *Unsafe Motherhood: Mayan Maternal Mortality and Subjectivity in Post-War Guatemala.* Oxford: Berghahn

Biehl, J. and Petryna, A., eds. 2013. *When People Come First. Critical studies in global health.* Princeton University Press

Bledsoe, C., 2002. *Contingent Lives: Fertility, Time and Aging in West Africa.* Chicago University Press

Bledsoe, C., Banja, F., and Hill, A. Reproductive mishaps and western contraception: an African challenge to fertility theory. *Population and Development Review* 24, no. 1 (1998): 15–57

Bledsoe C., Ewbank, D. and Isiugo-Abanihe, U. The effect of child fostering on feeding practices and access to health services in rural Sierra Leone. *Social Science and Medicine.* 27, no. 6 (1988): 627–36

Bourdieu, P., 1977. *Outline of a Theory of Practice.* Cambridge University Press

Brown, H., Managerial Relations in Kenyan Healthcare: empathy and the limits of governmentality. *Journal of the Royal Anthropological Institute* 22, no. 3 (2016): 591–610

Bryers, H. and van Tiejlingen, E. Risk, theory, social and medical models: a critical analysis of the concept of risk in maternity care. *Midwifery* 26, no. 5 (2010): 488–96

Buckley, T. and Gottlieb, A., eds. 1988. *Blood Magic: The anthropology of menstruation.* Berkeley: California University Press

Cataldo, F., Kielmann, K. and Kielmann, T. Deep down in their heart they wish they could be given some incentives: a qualitative study on the changing roles and relations of care among home-based caregivers in Zambia. *BMC Health Services Research* 15, no. 36 (2015): 1–10

Chayanika, Kamxi and Swatija, 1999. *We and Our Fertility: the politics of technological control.* Mumbai: Comet Media Foundation

Cornwall, A. Taking Chances, Making Choices: The Tactical Dimensions of 'Reproductive Strategies' in Southwestern Nigeria. Medical Anthropology 26, no. 3 (2007): 229–54

Cosminsky, S., 2012. Birth and Blame: Guatemalan Midwives and Reproductive Risk. In Fordyce, L. and Maraesa, A., eds. *Risk, Reproduction and Narratives of Experience.* Nashville: Vanderbilt University Press, 81–101

Coxon, K., Homer, C., Bisits, A., Sandall, J. and Bick, D. Reconceptualising risk in childbirth. *Midwifery* 38 (2016): 1–5

Das, V., 2015. *Affliction: Health, Disease, Poverty.* New York: University of Fordham Press

Das, V. and Das, R., 2007. How the Body Speaks: Illness and the life-world among the urban poor. In Biehl, J., Good, B. and Kleinman, A., eds. *Subjectivity.* Berkeley: University of California Press, 66–98

Dasgupta, J., 2011. Ten years of negotiating rights around maternal health in Uttar Pradesh, India. *BMC International Health and Human Rights* 11, Suppl 3, S4

Dasgupta, J., 2014. *A Framework for applying human rights based approaches to prevent maternal mortality and morbidity.* Lucknow: Sahayog

Davis-Floyd, R., and Sargent, C. 1997, eds, *Childbirth and Authoritative Knowledge.* Berkeley: California University Press

Donnelly, K., 2013. *Accredited Social Heath Activists' Knowledge, Attitudes and Practices regarding Family Planning in Southern Rajasthan.* ARTH, Udaipur: Draft report

Douglas, M., 1966. *Purity and danger: an analysis of concepts of pollution and taboo.* London: Routledge

Fordyce, L. and Maraesa, A., eds. 2012. *Risk, Reproduction and Narratives of Experience.* Vanderbilt University Press

George, A., 2004. In Search of Closure for Quinacrine: Science and Politics in Contexts of Uncertainty and Inequality. In Unnithan-Kumar, M., ed. *Reproductive Agency, Medicine and the State: Cultural Transformations in Childbearing.* New York: Berghahn Books, 137–60

George, A. Systemic bias in the routine delivery of primary care. *Reproductive Health Matters* 15, no. 30 (2007): 91–102

Giddens, A., 1984. *The Constitution of Society: Outline of a theory of structuration.* Cambridge: Polity Press

Government of India (GOI), Annual Health Survey, Rajasthan 2012–13, nd

Government of India, District Level Household and Facility Survey, 2007–08 (DLHS-3).

Government of India, National Health Systems Resource Centre, 2011. *ASHA: Which way forward? Evaluation of the ASHA programme.* Delhi, NHSRC publication

Greenhalgh, S. 2005. Globalisation and population governance in China. In Ong, A. and Collier, S. eds., *Global Assemblages.* Wiley-Blackwell, 354–73

Hickel, J. The 'girl effect': liberalism, empowerment and the contradictions of development. *Third World Quarterly* 35, no. 8 (2014): 1355–73

Jeffery, P., Jeffery R. and Lyon, A., 1989. *Labour pains and labour power: women and childbearing in India.* London: Zed Books

Jeffery, P., Jeffery R. and Lyon, A., 2002. Contaminating states: Midwifery, childbearing and the state in rural North India. In Rozario, S. and Samuel, G. eds. *The Daughters of Hāritī: Birth and Female Healers in South and Southeast Asia.* London and New York: Routledge, 90–108

Jordan, B., 1997. Authoritative Knowledge and its Construction. In Davis-Floyd, R.E. and C.F. Sargent eds., *Childbirth and Authoritative Knowledge: Cross cultural Perspectives.* Berkeley: University of California Press, 55–79

Kabeer, N., 1994. *Reversed realities: Gender hierarchies in Development.* London: Verso

Kapadia, K., 1995. *Siva and her Sisters: gender, caste and class in Rural South India.* Boulder: Westview

Kaufert, P. and O'Neil, J., 1993. Analysis of a dialogue on risks in childbirth: clinicians, epidemiologists and Inuit women. In Lindebaum, S. and Lock, M., eds. *Knowledge, power and practice: anthropology of medicine in everyday life*, 32–54

Kielman, K., 1998. Barren Ground: contesting identities of infertile women in Pemba, Tanzania. In Lock, M. and Kaufert, P., eds. *Pragmatic Women and Body Politics.* Cambridge University Press, 127–64

Lambert, H. Plural forms of evidence in public health: tolerating epistemological and methodological diversity. *Evidence and Policy* 9, no. 1 (2013): 43–8

Lim, S., Dandona, L., Hoisington, J., Spencer, L.J., Hogan, M.C., and Gakidou, E. 'India's Janani Suraksha Yojana, a conditional cash transfer programme to increase births in health facilities: An impact evaluation', *Lancet* 375, no. 9730 (2010): 2009–23

Lock, M and Nguyen, V.-K., 2010. *An Anthropology of Biomedicine.* Hoboken NJ: Wiley-Blackwell

Lupton, D. Risk and emotion: Toward an alternative theoretical perspective. *Health, Risk and Society* 15, no. 8 (2013): 634–47

Magrath, P. and Nichter, M. Paying for performance and the social relations of healthcare provision: an anthropological perspective. *Social Science and Medicine* 75, no. 10 (2012): 1778–85

Mathur, K., 2004. *Countering gender violence: initiatives towards collective action in Rajasthan.* New Delhi: Sage

Mavalankar, D., Vora, K., and Sharma, B. The Midwifery Role of the Auxiliary Nurse Midwife. In Sheikh, K., and George, A. eds, *Health Providers in India: On the front-lines of change.* Delhi: Routledge, 38–57

Mishra, A. Trust and teamwork matter: Community healthworkers' experience in integrated service delivery in India. *Global Public Health.* 9, no. 8 (2014): 960–74

Obermeyer, C. Risk, Uncertainty and Agency: culture and safe motherhood in Morocco. *Medical Anthropology.* 19, no. 2 (2000): 173–201

Patel. T., 1994. *Fertility Behaviour in Rajasthan.* Oxford: Oxford University Press

Pigg, S., 1997. Authority in Translation: Finding, Knowing, Naming and Training 'Traditional Birth Attendants' in Nepal. In Davis-Floyd, R and Sargent, C., eds. *Childbirth and Authoritative Knowledge,* 233–62

Pigg, S.L., 2005. Globalising the Facts of Life. In *Sex in Development: Science, Sexuality and Morality in Global Perspective.* Durham and London: Duke University Press, 35–66

Pinto, S., 2008. *Where There is No Midwife.* Oxford: Berghahn

Ravindran, T.K.S., 2009. *Equity in maternal health policies.* Presentation at Wellcome School of Bioethics, Mumbai, November

Ravindran, T.K.S. and Khanna, R., 2012. Many a slip between the cup and the lip: Universal access to safe abortion services in India. Dahod, Gugarat: Sahaj- Commonhealth

Ravindran, T.K.S. and Mishra, U. Unmet Need for Reproductive Health in India. *Reproductive Health Matters* 9, no. 18 (2001): 105–13

Reynolds-Whyte, S., 1997. *Questioning Misfortune: The pragmatics of uncertainty in Eastern Uganda.* Cambridge University Press

Rozario, S., 1998. The dai and the doctor: discourses on women's reproductive health in rural Bangladesh. In Ram, K. and Jolly, M., eds. *Modernities and Maternities: Colonial and postcolonial experiences in Asia and the Pacific.* Cambridge University Press: 144–76

Scamell, M. and Stewart, M. Time, Risk and Midwife Practice: the vaginal examination. *Health, Risk and Society* 16, no. 1 (2014): 84–100

Something Like a War. 1991 Documentary film. Director: Deepa Dhanraj. D&N Productions

Standing, H., and Chowdhury, M. Producing effective knowledge agents in a pluralistic environment: what future for community health workers? *Social Science and Medicine* 66, no. 10 (2008): 2096–107

Strathern, M., 1992. *Reproducing the future: anthropology, kinship and the new reproductive technologies.* Manchester University Press

Treichler, Paula A., 1999. AIDS and HIV Infection in the Third World: A First World Chronicle. In Treichler, P., *How to Have Theory in an Epidemic: Cultural Chronicles of AIDS.* Durham and London: Duke University Press, 99–126

Unnithan, M. and Heitmeyer, C. Global Rights and State Activism: Reflections on Civil Society-State Partnerships in Health in NW India. *Contributions to Indian Sociology.* Delhi: Institute of Economic Growth 46, no. 3 (2012): 283–309

Unnithan, M., 1998. '*Women's Reproductive Health in Rajasthan: policies, perceptions and strategies*', unpublished report to Wellcome Trust

Unnithan, M. What Constitutes Evidence in Human Rights Based Approaches to Health? Learning from lived experiences of maternal and sexual reproductive health. *Harvard Journal of Health and Human Rights* 17, no. 2 (2015): 45–57

Unnithan-Kumar, M. and Srivastava, K., 1997. Gender Politics, Development and Women's Agency in Rajasthan. In: Grillo, R. and Stirrat, R. eds., *Discourses of Development: Anthropological Perspectives.* Oxford: Berg, 157–83

Unnithan-Kumar, M., 2001. Emotion, Agency and Access to Healthcare: women's experiences of reproduction in Jaipur, In Tremayne, S., ed. *Managing Reproductive Life: Cross-cultural themes in fertility and sexuality.* Oxford: Berghahn

Unnithan-Kumar, M., 2002. Midwives among Others: Knowledges of Healing and the Politics of Emotions in Rajasthan, Northwest India. In Rozario, S. and Samuel, G. eds. *The Daughters of Hāritī: Birth and Female Healers in South and Southeast Asia.* London and New York: Routledge, 109–29

Unnithan-Kumar, M., 2003. Reproduction, Health, Rights: Connections and Disconnections. In Mitchell, J. and Wilson, R., eds. 2003. Human Rights in Global Perspective: Anthropology of Rights, Claims and Entitlements. London: Routledge, 183–209

Van Hollen, C., 2002. 'Baby Friendly' Hospitals and Bad Mothers: Manoeuvring Development in the Postpartum Period in Tamil Nadu. In Rozario, S. and Samuels, G., eds. *The Daughters of Hāritī: Birth and Female Healers in South and Southeast Asia.* London and New York: Routledge, 163–82

Van Hollen, C., 2003. *Birth on the Threshold: Childbirth and Modernity in South India.* Berkeley and Los Angeles: University of California Press

Varley, E., 2015. Abandonments, Solidarities and Logics of Care: Hospitals as sites of sectarian conflict in Gilgit-Balistan. *Cult Med Psychiatry* doi: 10.11007/s11013-015-9456-5 (accessed July 2018)

Visaria, L. 2002. Deficit of women in India: Magnitude, trends, regional variations and determinants. *The national medical journal of India* 15, no. 1 (2002): 19–25

WHO, 2014. Contraception: fact sheet. Geneva: World Health Organisation

6 Altruism and the politics of legislating reproductive labour

Why surrogacy matters

Introduction

Global flows of reproductive technologies, reproductive tissue, as well as infertile couples over the past two decades as part of the wider phenomenon of 'medical tourism' (Inhorn, 2011) have been accompanied by a significant rise in state legislative and regulatory protocols as instruments and practices to do with Assisted Reproductive Technologies (ARTs) became more accessible in countries such as India. Transnational surrogacy arrangements began to take place in India in 2002 following efforts by the Indian Council of Medical Research (ICMR) to legalise and regulate commercial surrogacy in the country (Smerdon, 2008; Unnithan-Kumar, 2013).[1] The Ministry of Health and Family Welfare has since brought out a slew of state guidelines in the form of the Assisted Reproductive Technology draft bills (2008, 2010, 2014). Surrogacy was, until 2016, a key component of the ART draft bills and, though not passed as an Act by the Indian parliament, there were guidelines invoked to adjudicate in specific child custody court cases (e.g. PUCL file, 2008). In August 2016, a separate Surrogacy Bill was drafted and approved by the Union cabinet, to the surprise of campaigners and legal experts given that the previous bill of 2014 was much more comprehensive in its regulation of ART procedures, providing checks on a range of technological and clinical practices in which surrogacy procedures are embedded. In this chapter I track the shifts in surrogacy legislation, especially the debates around the progressive and retrogressive elements of each bill to understand the new kinds of socio-legal, feminist and ethical discourse on reproductive labour and maternal altruism emerging around fertility and childbearing in India.

The legal interventions and state policies on ART, especially surrogacy, have been subject to intense debate and contestation by feminists, activists and scholars across the global south and north. Of particular contention is the extent to which the legislation promotes a market in reproductive labour and the exploitation of the maternities and bodies of poor women in low- and middle-income countries such as India, until recently a growing global hub of commercial surrogacy (Yasin, 2011; Twine, 2011; Pande, 2014; Rudrappa, 2012; Reddy and Qadeer, 2010). A focus on transnational surrogacy arrangements reveals new social, ethical and political challenges for law and policymakers, but equally provides unique insight into how global processes of reproductive stratification work on the ground and their implications for embodied experiences of citizenship.

Feminist scholarship outside the Euro-American context on the political, social-cultural and moral meanings of surrogacy (Kahn, 2000; Teman, 2003; Smerdon, 2008; Qadeer, 2009; Pande, 2009a, 2009b, 2010a, 2010b; SAMA 2010; Bailey, 2011; Rudrappa, 2012; Twine, 2011; Rao, 2012; Tanderup *et al.*, 2015) rightly focuses on how surrogates and transnational couples negotiate the complex moral, clinical and social processes involved in surrogacy and kinds of 'culture-work' that is undertaken in the process. The chapter extends this work by approaching the issue of surrogacy from the perspective of poor infertile Indian women living in the same social and moral world as the surrogate and for whom private sector infertility services are inaccessible due to the high costs involved.[2] It draws upon ethnographic research that intersects with, rather than overlaps with, the research on women who are or have been gestational surrogates, to bring attention to the social implications of a commerce in reproductive labour driven by recourse to technologies of assisted procreation and their effects on global processes of stratification and inequality.

The legislative deliberations on surrogacy in India are used in this chapter as a means to reflect on three conceptual issues to do with power and women's bodies within feminist anthropology: reproductive stratification, relational autonomy and the commodification of reproduction.[3] Toward this end it draws on anthropological studies of surrogacy as *lived experience* (Teman, 2003, 2010; Kahn, 2000; Pande, 2009a, 2000b, 2010a; Ragoné, 1994, 1999), the feminist notion of *relational autonomy*, which recognises that individuals are situated within an array of relations and ways of experiencing and expressing choices that constitute their lives (Meyers, 2001; Mackenzie and Stoljar, 2000; Thachuk, 2004; Madhok, 2004) and the idea of *informed consent* as a primarily 'communicative transaction' (where it is the quality of information that is provided and how it is received that is critical in ensuring the process as ethical (Manson and O'Neill, 2007).

The analysis presented in the chapter is limited in that it draws on field research with infertile women but relies on secondary sources for the experiences of surrogates in India. Private infertility clinics in Indian cities such as Anand, Delhi, Mumbai and Bangalore have been pioneering in the domain of surrogacy in the country and a focus of social science analyses, including ethnographic investigation (Smerdon, 2008; Pande, 2009a, 2009b; Gupta, 2012; Rudrappa, 2012; Bharadwaj, 2003; Tanderup *et al.*, 2015). I also draw on interviews and discussions with fertility specialists, gynaecologists, feminist activists, academics and members of voluntary organisations over a six-month period in 2010 and during shorter visits to India in 2015 and 2016.[4] My views on surrogacy have also been shaped by discussion on and with British surrogates at public meetings and workshops on surrogacy in the UK in 2016.[5] Secondary source material on surrogacy used in this chapter is drawn from scholarly texts, field based work and media reports primarily from Gujarat, the neighbouring state to Rajasthan with a similar social and cultural composition of low-income Hindu caste and Muslim communities.

An analysis of these texts, as well as field based material, leads me to suggest that despite an explicit framing which acknowledges the rights of the infertile to bear children, Indian ART legislation promotes this right selectively for those who have the resources to pay for assisted reproductive services. This is particularly notable, as I argue in this chapter, given the absence of assisted reproductive services for poorer women in India. Even though surrogacy may be experienced as positive by the women who undertake it (Pande, 2009a; Rudrappa, 2012; for example) and by the Indian State which considers itself progressive with legislation which ostensibly focuses on the welfare of Indian surrogates, legal guarantees are not deep enough to ensure surrogate women's reproductive autonomy and well-being. Surrogacy in India remains symbolic of much wider stratified systems (such as caste and class) and processes of inequality and reproductive injustice (Bailey, 2011; for instance).[6]

When viewed in terms of the rights of infertile couples overall, the 2010 and 2016 bills can be regarded as promoting what Colen (1995) has termed 'stratified reproduction', a concept developed further by other anthropologists (notably Ginsburg and Rapp, 1995; Rapp, 1999; Browner and Sargeant, 2011; Twine, 2011). The concept is specifically used to refer to contexts where 'reproductive labour is differentially valued and rewarded according to the inequalities of access to material and social resources in particular historical and cultural contexts' (Colen, 1995, p. 78). In this chapter I use the notion of stratified reproduction in a wider sense, following Rapp, to mean, 'A lens through which we can see how representations of pregnancy and parenting, gender relations, socioeconomic futures and collective as well as familial aspirations for the next generation are also being reproduced' (1999, p. 311). I also suggest that as an 'assemblage' (in Ong and Colliers (2005) sense)[7] surrogacy in India is not only an example of what Franklin has called the *global biological* i.e. where the global comes into being as a biocultural condition (2005, p. 61) but as a form of the *stratified* global biological. Ethical inconsistencies relating to surrogacy appear to co-exist with structural violence in a manner similar to what Sunder Rajan has observed in the context of the growth of clinical trials in India, and with the growth of global bio-capital more generally (2007).[8] When seen from the perspective of poor Indian women and men who are infertile, the access to ART becomes a privilege: the rights of some individuals and couples to reproduce and exercise procreative agency is valued, others are not.

State legislation and policies to do with conception in India demonstrate a long history of, and stubborn focus on, drastic measures to limit the population birth rate (for example, through the two-child norm to gain political office, as well as the promotion of tubectomy despite the rhetoric of contraceptive choice, as acknowledged in the National Population Policy (GOI, 2000; SAMA, 2010). However, in contrast to state population policies thus far, which have emphasised family planning programmes to restrict fertility, the law and policies to do with surrogacy promote and celebrate fertility, representing a watershed shift in state population perspectives. But in a context where the state and the law have been regarded suspiciously and circumvented, to what extent will the policies supposedly promoting surrogate welfare make a difference with regard to women's autonomy on the ground?[9]

By way of background I first describe why surrogacy has provided fertile ground to think through and understand some of the conceptual challenges to kinship raised by the technologies of assisted procreation and their regulation.

Why surrogacy matters (as an academic concern)

Made possible through the advent of technologies of assisted procreation such as in-vitro fertilisation (IVF), surrogacy has disrupted the idea that families are biological, 'natural' entities, but shows them instead to be socially and culturally constituted. Surrogacy has been a specific focus for anthropologists working in the area of kinship because of the questions it raises about the 'natural' basis of two fundamental human institutions: the family and motherhood. The fact that kinship connections with offspring are forged through means other than 'blood' has particularly destabilised notions of a kinship based in 'biology', as Ragoné (1994, 1999); Strathern (1992, 2003); Franklin (2005); Edwards *et al.*, (1993); and others have so powerfully argued.

Ragoné's pioneering work on surrogacy in the US demonstrates that soon after surrogacy was made possible, there was an overwhelming preference for gestational forms of surrogacy (where the surrogate gestates the fertilised embryo but does not contribute any of her own reproductive material) over more 'traditional' surrogacy arrangements (where the eggs of the surrogate are used). Gestational surrogacy is preferred by commissioning parents as well as surrogates in the USA, for instance, as it removes the surrogate as a contender for having any 'real' (i.e. genetic) ties with the baby she gestates. It is a preference driven by strong genetically based Euro-American ideas of relatedness. Gestational surrogacy is popular, Ragoné argues, precisely because it removes the genetic or biological bases of relatedness enabling a denial of any 'real' kinship between the surrogate and the baby she brings to term (1999). In gestational surrogacy, the recourse made by all parties to the genetic bases of relatedness allows the intended couple as well as the surrogate to disengage from any potential claims to motherhood that the surrogate may make or be obliged to undertake with regard to the baby. The denial of kinship in gestational surrogacy has also enabled the practice to be undertaken by women and couples across race and ethnic groups, as Ragoné suggests in her work with black women in the US who served as surrogates for white couples (1999).

The advent of ARTs has not only enabled infertile women unable to bear children themselves to become mothers but has also opened up the possibilities of parenthood for those unable to legally adopt children (people who are single, elderly or in same-sex relationships). At the same time, surrogacy has fragmented or multiplied the notion of parenthood from one rooted in the biological contributions of a heterosexual couple to acknowledge the bodily, genetic as well as non-genetic contribution of a third party, namely the surrogate and/or donor of gametes. Parenthood emerges as fragmented[10] across persons who contribute biogenetically, socially and financially to the making of a child. Of particular interest has been the way that surrogacy has dislocated the notion of motherhood as situated within a single person. As Almeling (2011) among others suggests, women can separate maternity into several parts: one woman can provide the egg; another can carry the embryo; and a third can raise the child – all three can lay claim to motherhood. Surrogate babies have the possibility of having three potential mothers: the genetic (donor); the gestational (surrogate); and the social (intended mother). This has necessitated a complex negotiation of personal and kinship based identities between people who may not have been otherwise related.

Popular notions of what constitutes motherhood are further challenged by surrogate arrangements which clearly demarcate women who bear children for others (surrogates) from women and men who will eventually nurture them (intended parents). Cultural ideals in many parts of the world stipulate that women especially should be altruistic and selfless when it comes to reproduction, the family and in their roles as mothers. Reproductive choice when expressed differently from these ideals pits women against this altruistic image and here the exercise of choice is regarded as a subversion of the very existence of kinship and family ideals.

Paid surrogacy services challenge the idea of motherly altruism (and question whether the surrogate will willingly relinquish the baby upon birth) and also raise the spectre of the commodification of reproductive labour, a key issue within feminist debate as I discuss further below. The legal and governmental deliberations around surrogacy in the UK have centred on limiting surrogacy to voluntary participation, based on altruism as a means of maintaining a clear separation between the processes of human reproduction and the market. Regulations of such kind reinforce the notion that it is 'unnatural' to expect monetary recompense for reproductive services as embodied in surrogacy.

Altruistic surrogacy arrangements revolve around relationships based on the idea of the 'gift' whereby the surrogate is motivated by love or altruistic inclinations for the infertile couple, who are often close friends or relatives. Within anthropology, close attention has been paid to the practice and language, especially that of the 'gift', adopted by surrogates and other key parties as a means to counter the commercial aspects which shroud the 'natural' process of becoming a mother. Surrogacy is often referred to as a 'gift of life', a 'gift of love' (Ragoné, 1999; for example) or even the 'gift of motherhood' (Teman, 2010; for example). As these studies show, recourse by surrogates to the language of the gift, one as precious as that of life, situates the practice beyond the realm of the monetary to within that of the (gendered) gift economy. Ragoné suggests that there is less use of gifting language in gestational surrogacy compared with traditional surrogacy because, in the latter case, surrogates literally 'give a part of themselves'. This in turn speaks to the stronger genetic tie perceived in traditional surrogacy in Euro-American kinship.

However, the language of gifting and sense of altruism persists in other contexts where gestational surrogacy is the norm and surrogates are paid for their services, as in India. In Gujarat, western India, for example, ethnographic work describes how surrogates talk about the 'sacrifice' (entailed in the notion of the gift) of their duties as mothers to their own children that their surrogacy entails (Pande, 2009a). Clinicians who provide surrogacy services are also observed to draw on the language of gifting and sacrifice in their depiction of surrogates as saviours (Pande; for example). In their emphasis on the 'helping hand' of clinics and surrogates to commissioning couples, clinicians further reinforce the idea that the recourse to technology is 'natural' and inevitable (as observed when IVF first emerged in the UK (Edwards *et al.*, 1993).

Pande's work is instructive in demonstrating how the gift itself is imagined and articulated in very differently commoditised economies and across cultural frameworks. The popular western dichotomy made between gifts (not determined by the market) and commodities (to which market value is attached) is itself being challenged by several social theorists (Strathern, 2011; Spar, 2006; Zelizer, 2000). Strathern, for example, suggests that even within highly commoditised economies gifts may not be diminished by payment. In reality, the dichotomy between gifts and commodities is less clear-cut as anthropologists (Sharp, 2000; Scheper-Hughes, 2000; and Strathern, 2011) have found. In the case of organ donation, for example, there is a link between donation (gift) and procurement (market) in that the language of the gift serves the interests of the market in enabling more bodies and body parts to be rendered bio-available for circulation and transaction (Sharp, 2000; Scheper-Hughes, 2000).

The commodification and especially monetary value ascribed to procreation by the sale of reproductive tissue (eggs, sperm and gamete) and reproductive labour (hiring the services of the surrogate) has been a contentious issue of debate among feminist, ethicist and legal scholars as well as anthropologists. The question as to whether women should be paid to bear children other than their own (and receive monetary compensation) raises the point of whether reproductive labour has itself been 'naturalised' (taken for granted). While scholars have gathered evidence which suggests that surrogates support some form of payment (Rudrappa, 2012; Surrogacy UK, 2015), there has been a tendency to side with feminist ethicist interpretations of the hidden exploitation that is entailed in contracting for surrogacy services.

It is worth noting that there are two main strands to feminist thinking on surrogacy which have influenced anthropological perspectives: one set of feminist arguments work to support surrogacy payments and argue that women have the right or freedom to enter into surrogacy contracts underscoring their entitlement to exert control over their own bodies and labour; other feminists argue that commercial surrogacy commodifies women and their bodies and that surrogacy is a form of cheap labour which exploits poor women (Twine, 2011). Further on in this chapter we examine how these two positions are entangled in the context of surrogacy legislation and practices on the ground in India.

The increasing over-representation of Blacks, Hispanics and Latinos as gestational surrogates in the US in the past decade has raised concerns about how race and class inequalities structure the surrogacy industry in the US (Twine, 2011). The increasing traffic in reproductive technologies, tissues and bodies across the global north and south further highlight the class, ethnic and gender stratification of reproductive labour across and within national boundaries. When viewed through a wider 'cross-class' lens, state regulation in India can be seen to reinforce stratification among women based on their procreative abilities. The health of Indian surrogates who bear children for wealthy infertile couples is rewarded through state assured high-quality medical care while poor, infertile Indian women have virtually no services of assisted procreation. As an institution, surrogacy like other assisted reproductive practices has, at the widest level, become a tool in the exercise of state power: surrogacy tourism brings the Indian economy major revenues, even though it sits uneasily alongside population policies (Reddy and Qadeer, 2010) which promote contraceptive technologies to restrict poorer women's fertility. Most recently, surrogacy legislation has been used in India to promote an exclusionary, patriarchal, biologically determined and heteronormative approach to parenthood and the family (the parliamentary bill of 2016 as discussed below).

While these trends have been accompanied by a rise in the use of ethical tools and instruments by state governments, as we see further below, their ability to facilitate informed consent and uphold reproductive autonomy and informed choice is questionable as argued by feminist scholars and anthropologists. Like other anthropologists working elsewhere on these issues, I have found that the increased regulation, whether to ensure informed consent or value reproductive labour, has remained disconnected from local moral worlds.

To understand how the surrogacy regulation impinges upon the lives and bodies of surrogate women as well as the infertile women they live among, and the ways in which it shapes how procreative value and decision-making takes on the ground, we first turn to situate surrogacy in the context of the experiences of the poor infertile women who come from the same region and cultural background of western India as the surrogates themselves.

Surrogate decision-making in context

In rural western India where women's role in reproduction is taken so much for granted that there is little overt value associated with it (Patel, 1994; Unnithan-Kumar, 2001) the arrival of paid surrogacy arrangements has the potential to lead to a significant reassessment of women's childbearing by the family, community and the state. As one surrogate notes, '*With my first surrogacy (fee), I could get my husband's kidney operation done, admit my son in an English medium school, and buy a small flat ...*' (DG, twenty-seven-year-old mother of two, as quoted in the *Sunday Hindustan Times*, 13 March 2011).[11] The really important question that emerges from this perspective is whether surrogacy as a means of economic empowerment bestows greater reproductive autonomy and status on the women who act as surrogates? What does consent actually mean or represent in these conditions? And what does this tell us about the role of the bill in legitimising new reproductive arrangements between those related through surrogacy and those unable to participate in social reproduction? As discussed below, aside from the legislative domain, there are two more immediate sites where the dilemmas posed by the commercialisation of childbearing are mediated and reproductive autonomy and subordination experienced: the community (as the repository of ideologies of reproduction: Meyers, 2001)[12] and the family (as the site where gendered difference is experienced and negotiated)[13] on the one hand and the clinic on the other.

Women in poor economic circumstances find they have little choice but to take up surrogacy when the opportunity is raised by their affinal family. As one surrogate in an ethnographic study of the fertility clinics in Anand, Gujarat, told the researcher, 'it is our *majboori* (compulsion) to undertake surrogacy' (Pande, 2009a) The choice (or lack thereof) to undertake surrogacy in this sense reflects systemic inequities associated with poverty and structural violence, wherein large-scale economic and political inequities predispose the vulnerable to suffering (Farmer, 1997), where 'compulsion' makes visible the moral dilemma posed by the choice of 'surrogacy-or-poverty' (Bailey, 2011, p. 736).

In rural western India the lack of choice exists in another sense: reproductive decision-making on when and how many children to have; when to have sexual intercourse; and whether to use contraceptives, for example, are less the decision of the woman than of her husband and his family. This is not to imply that women have no decision-making capacity but, rather, that reproduction is considered more a matter for the patrilineal group and particular kinspersons within them rather than for any one individual (Unnithan-Kumar, 2001). A married woman's reproduction and sexuality are closely monitored by her affinal family, so despite the collective decision-making entailed in matters of childbearing, she usually has the sole responsibility for ensuring that reproductive outcomes, conception and birth, are successful. In Rajasthan, the social cost of the inability to conceive at all (due to infertility) or to conceive disabled or dysfunctional children, or even in some cases only girls, is great (Chapter 3, also Patel, 2007).

As we saw in Chapter 3, women suffer economic hardship and social death as a consequence of being (even potentially) infertile. They also suffer economic hardship as a result of their infertility (also see Inhorn, 1994). The quest for cures drives them to undertake expensive interventions at private clinics driving them further into debt.[14] Both Vimlesh and Zahida, who suffered from secondary sterility (as described in Chapter 3), went on to have children subsequently through the medical interventions at the voluntary health centre which treated them for reproductive tract infections. Like a high percentage of women, their inability to reproduce had been the result of reproductive tract infections (causing secondary sterility) connected with their poverty and the lack of access to basic amenities such as water, food and timely care.[15] Their example is indicative of the anxiety even women who have produced children have, of becoming infertile. Their worry is well-founded for two key reasons: i) due to the high incidence of reproductive tract infections which underlie sterility in the region; and ii) their poor economic conditions which prevent easy access to private sector infertility specialists. Given the social conditions that make childbearing imperative and autonomy limited, where women's bodies are regarded (even by themselves) as in the service of the wider kin group, it is not surprising that surrogate women are also regarded as serving the collective (in terms of the economic benefits their surrogacy brings) and yet find themselves as *majboor* or lacking in choice.

The patriarchal right to think about and use women's bodies for tangible benefits has a longer history in practices, such as in dowry where women who are unable to generate a sustained or substantial flow of resources from their natal homes to the affinal home are subject to abuse (Sharma, 1984). However, in the case of dowry payments (which flow from the girl's family to her husband's family), it is women's work value, including her reproductive labour that is ideologically dismissed. Rather, it is the social status that her family connection will bring her spouse's family that is highly regarded. The lack of choice in dowry practices flowing from kin-based control of women's bodies is a logic also demonstrated in surrogacy. So while more overtly market-oriented transactions are involved in surrogacy services which challenge the devaluing (and erasure) of women's reproductive labour that occurs in dowry arrangements, nevertheless there is a similar lack of choice flowing from kin-based control over women's bodies.

Surrogate arrangements remain devalued by community members when measured in terms of the responsibilities associated with successful and appropriate childbearing (that is, within marriage). Adultery is a serious social offence across caste and class, especially for women, who are often subject to physical, sexual and domestic violence (as documented in the PUCL reports following implementation of the Protection of Women from Domestic Violence Act 2005). While their immediate families support them, surrogates face ostracism and stigma from the wider caste community, often being called 'prostitutes' for bearing the child of a man other than their husband. This is the case even when no sexual intercourse is entailed in surrogacy (Pande, 2009b). A male gynaecologist working in the health centre for government employees in Jaipur told me he thought surrogacy was disgusting as it is adulterous to carry another man's (i.e. not the husband's) child to term (Doctor M, interview, March 2010).[16] Surrogates take on the shame of 'adultery' and hide their pregnancy from members of the community. Yet, despite facing moral disapprobation from the wider kin and community, surrogates themselves talk about their surrogacy as an act of 'sacrifice' to secure the welfare of their family.[17]

Another striking feature of the way surrogates recover value from what they do is in their recourse to a language of selflessness and of viewing their 'baby-work' as undertaken for securing the future of their own children. This is in contrast to the language of gifting per se (Pande, 2010a).[18] In fact, dowry payments in themselves challenge ideas of the gift as altruistic. Indian surrogates blur the boundaries between gifts and commodities through recourse to the ideology of dowry (see Pande, 2011). My own ethnography on dowry payments also suggests that while viewed ideologically through the lens of the 'gift', in practice such transactions come to be seen as payments associated with a woman's labour, including her reproductive labour (Unnithan-Kumar, 1997, p. 193; Goody, 1990).

Gifts (or *dan*) including that of dowry (*kanya-dan*) procure the well-being and auspiciousness of the donor, placing them in a higher social status than the receiver (Raheja, 1988; Goody, 1990; Unnithan-Kumar, 1997). Tangible reference to this emerges when the surrogates Pande interviewed describe their contribution in terms of substance (blood, breast milk) and the effort/labour of gestation in creating the child, factors which they refer to as creating a relationship with the child which is equal to if not stronger than the genetic tie.[19] As Pande suggests, surrogates are recovering reproductive value in what they do through the idea they are making babies for others through a mixture of self and others' substance. Through the sharing of their bodily fluids surrogates create relationships of obligation and duty which bind them to the surrogate child and commissioning couples. Thus, rather than the absence of notions of parental responsibility, as Haker (2006) suggests for those participating in embryonic stem cell regeneration, the perception of surrogates demonstrates instead a selective reformulation of existing ideas of relatedness. It is in these accounts that we also see reproductive autonomy and agency expressed, not simply a lack of choice and submission to family diktat.

The discussion so far has situated the experiences of surrogates in the context of marriage, marriage payments and the social reproduction of the family, challenging the control that others (the state, commissioning couple, medical establishment) have over their fertility and reproduction. In the final section of this chapter, I push these ideas further to examine what the singularities of surrogacy as seen through the eyes of infertile women in Rajasthan and of Indian feminists mean for conceptualising reproductive autonomy. As a background to this I first consider the nature of legal regulation of surrogacy in India.

Lessons from the legal regulation of surrogacy

State concern with the need to regulate the growing private market in assisted reproductive services, including surrogacy, led to the drafting of the first ART Regulation Bill in 2008 following consultation with a number of state and non-state institutions including civil society organisations. Private clinics in India had begun to offer immediate- and low-cost services (relative to their western counterparts), two of the key reasons underlying the increase in the choice of India as a destination for foreign infertile couples.[20] In addition, until 2016 private clinics were able to provide a regular supply of surrogates and were free from the service exclusions operative in other countries on the basis of age, sexual orientation,[21] marital status and perception of success rates (Palattiyil *et al.*, 2010).

The Indian state has, over the past three decades, invested heavily in the development of medical tourism, including assisted reproductive technologies, to boost a modern and competent healthcare structure in the private sector (Reddy and Qadeer, 2010). As noted by Reddy and Qadeer, the state promoted medical tourism in the private sector in the 1990s to combat the sluggishness of the public health system. In order to build up a competitive health service infra-structure, the Indian government provided a number of incentives (including financial), particularly to private hospitals. It reduced import tariffs for medical equipment and set in place procedures to expedite medical visas and promote joint health insurance collaborations (Mukherjee and Nadimipally, 2006; Smerdon, 2008; Anchayil and Raheem, 2009). The development of world-class healthcare facilities offering competitive costs was regarded as critical to India's ability to participate as a major global player in the world economy, and also to its ability to harvest foreign exchange reserves, estimated to be in the range of US$445 million in 2009 (SAMA 2010; Thomas, 2009; Anchayil and Raheem, 2009) and up to two billion dollars in 2016 with over 25,000 surrogate babies being born annually in India (Parthasarthy, 2016). The demand for the ethical regulation of private, surrogacy services in India came from foreign nationals and governments as well as from feminist activists worldwide.

The ART Regulation Bill [2008, 2010 2014]

The ART Regulation Bill and Rules, as drafted by the Indian Council of Medical Research in 2008 (and its modified versions in 2010, 2014; GOI, 2005, 2008, 2010) set out guidelines ranging from the duties of clinics to the rights and duties of patients, donors, surrogates and children.[22] *Surrogacy* was defined in the bill as

> an arrangement in which a woman agrees to a pregnancy, achieved through assisted reproductive technology, in which neither of the gametes belong to her or her husband, with the intention to carry it to term and hand over the child to the person or persons for whom she is acting as a surrogate.[23]

Surrogacy was considered as legal in the regulations if undertaken by a woman who was: (1) between twenty-one and forty-five years of age, who had consent from her spouse, if married, and provided she acted as surrogate for no more than three live births for any couple;[24] (2) consented to giving up the baby, relin-quishing all parental rights to the commissioning individual or couple; and (3) consented to undergo medical tests relating to sexually transmitted diseases and other communicable diseases which may endanger the health of the child (see Form J, Agreement for Surrogacy, appended to the bill).

As a legal document, the ART Bill was commendable for its detail and clarity about the procedures involved, responsibilities, terms and conditions under which processes such as surrogacy were to be undertaken. The bill was pro-gressive in the sense that it recognised the debilitating social, economic and stig-matising effects of involuntary childlessness. It also upheld the right of the infertile to bear, and to try for, children and, more radically, acknowledged the responsibility of the state to fulfil this need through the provision of appropriate services, technology and regulation.[25]

More controversially, it acknowledged the rights of surrogates to be paid for their reproductive labour (fuelling concerns related to the commercialisation of women's reproduction) as well as the expenses they incurred during pregnancy. The specific amount of expenses to be paid was left as a matter for negotiation between the surrogate and the commissioning couple. The issue of payment has been a cause for concern among feminists in the south and scholars who rightly suggested that financially poor victims of structural violence have less choice or bargaining power in such situations (Sunder Rajan, 2007; SAMA, 2010; Bailey, 2011).[26]

In terms of the surrogate, the bill safeguarded her rights in the case of a child born with birth defects. It also stated that she could terminate her pregnancy at will (see Appendix 1 for Form J, Agreement for Surrogacy, pp. 91–94). The clause on the termination of the pregnancy at will was not, however, considered in relation to a further requirement which was that all payments received by the surrogate were to be refunded in such an event, except in cases of medical complications. Given the extreme poverty and indebtedness which most often drives surrogacy in the first place, as critics argue, it was unrealistic to believe that the surrogate could exercise choice to terminate her pregnancy or that she would have any real bargaining power when it came to negotiating the terms and amount of money to be refunded.[27]

More directly interventionist, the bill subjected surrogates to invasive procedures such as foetal reduction in the event of multiple pregnancies, if desired by the commissioning couple, and Caesarean sections if recommended by the doctors, as Tanderup and colleagues document in their study of clinics offering surrogacy services in Delhi (2015). More routinely, the surrogate's consent was written into the initial agreement rather than sought for a continuous medical regimen of injections, blood tests, screening and diagnostic procedures. Less explicit, but of major implication, was the discrimination against the surrogate which arose from the language (English) in which the agreement and consent form were written. Given that English is not the first language of most surrogates and that a majority are indeed illiterate rural women, the understanding of what consent entailed was left to the vagaries of a conscientious translator, as discussed further below. It is worth noting as well that the surrogate was not provided with any legal support by the state with the clinic acting as their legal representative, including as the representative with the banks.[28] Given that the clinics also acted as providers of counselling services, it would be apt to regard the surrogate as a 'captive of the clinic' (Qadeer, 2010, p. 209).

Feminist and civil society organisations in India particularly criticised the bill for predominantly upholding the research and promotion of ART services and the interests of the providers, especially private clinics and the commissioning couple, over that of the surrogate or the baby (Qadeer, 2009, 2010; Shah, 2009; Sarojini and Sharma, 2009; Tanderup *et al.*, 2015). Other important criticisms of the bill raised by these scholar-activists included: i) the fact that in denying the surrogate the possibility to register as the birthing mother, the bill protected the rights of the intended patients; ii) in ensuring that the surrogate underwrote all the major risks of the procedures, including her own death, natal and postnatal complications, foetal reduction and any risk of HIV transmission, the bill clearly protected the interests of the clinics and sperm banks; iii) the health risks to the surrogate were further disregarded in the clause that enabled her to have three surrogate births and three cycles of ova transfer (increased to five live births with no specification of the number of IVF cycles, in the 2010 version of the bill) nor any decision-making power with regard to C-section delivery; and iv) in favouring a quick transfer of baby from surrogate to commissioning parents, the bill downplayed the developmental needs of the baby (even as it claimed to ameliorate the bonding related anxieties of the commissioning parents as well as the commercial surrogate). The rights of the new born baby were further undermined in terms of its survival, right to a safe home and the automatic right to know its identity (only if sought out and not before eighteen years, unless for medical purposes). The rights of the child to citizenship were addressed in 2008 (see below).

The few instances in which the surrogacy guidelines have been invoked are particularly revealing in respect of what and for whom recourse to the law is possible and effective. Of the two cases known so far, both were in 2008 and concerned the custodial rights of the intended parents (in one case a Japanese father and in the other a German couple) and their difficulty in securing travel documents, visas and citizenship from their own countries for the surrogate children; Baby Manji in the first case and German twins in the other (PUCL correspondence, 2008; Bromfield, 2010).[29] In both instances, the social parents were eventually able to adopt these children in their respective countries. The surrogacy bill was tightened, especially as a response to the experience of the German couple, permitting surrogacy arrangements to take place only if proof of citizenship for the child was presented by the intended parents. In both cases, the guidelines revealed lacunae regarding the ability of the surrogacy legislation to protect the rights of the new born baby to an assured and safe home (as identified by the Eighteenth Law Commission Review in 2009). One of the few modifications in the 2010 version of the bill was the mandatory requirement for foreign couples to produce a certificate from their countries ensuring the child will be considered a legal citizen of that country (SAMA, 2011).

The long-pending, recently aborted Indian ART Bill (2008, 2010) was progressive in that it recognised the rights of the infertile to bear children as well as, more controversially, the rights of the surrogates to be paid for their reproductive labour and expenses incurred during pregnancy. And yet, while having the virtue of instituting and clarifying clinical procedures (to do with consent, for example) and supporting the rights of infertile couples to access ARTs, the bill, as Indian feminists (Qadeer, 2009, 2010; Shah, 2009; Sarojini and Sharma, 2009; among others) argued, primarily focused on the clinics and commissioning couples[30] and promoted ARTs without being concerned with surrogate welfare beyond the provision of standard ethical instruments used in clinics (SAMA, 2011; Tanderup *et al.*, 2015). The limitations of the 2010 Bill also stemmed, first, from its attempts to introduce Euro-American notions of autonomy (with an emphasis on the distinctiveness and separateness of the subject)[31] and informed consent into a setting with very different cultural values. A second limitation with what it proposed was that it offered quality medical healthcare services for those who could afford ART intervention in a context of significant class and gender-based inequalities in access to reproductive healthcare, thus determining who could fully participate in reproduction and enjoy the rewards of their labour (Reddy and Qadeer, 2010).

Surrogacy (Regulation) Bill 2016

At the end of August 2016 as I was finalising this chapter, the Union Cabinet approved the draft of a new Surrogacy (Regulation) Bill. The bill sought to ban commercial surrogacy completely. Surrogacy in India was from now on only to take the form of *altruistic* surrogacy, defined as undertaken by surrogates who were close relatives and immediate family members of the intended parents.

> Persons who are eligible to seek surrogacy services are required to engage a close female relative, not necessarily related by blood, in a transaction where no money changes hands between the commissioning couple and surrogate mother, except to meet medical expenses.

Further to this, the bill states that surrogacy services would be available only to those who were childless and heterosexual couples who had been married for at least five years and were Indian citizens (excluding Non-Resident Indians and Overseas Citizens of India, NRI and OCI respectively).

The proposal to permit some categories of people to access surrogacy services (a further example of reproductive stratification promoted by the state) has been labelled as unconstitutional by legal activists such as S. Parthasarthy. For Parthasarthy, an advocate of the Madras High Court: '*If parliament were to pass the Surrogacy Bill in its current form, the law would certainly violate the constitutional pledge of equal treatment*' (Suhrith Parthasarthy, *The Hindu*, 1 September 2016). According to the view of legal activists such as Parthasarthy, the proposed bill was unconstitutional as it set itself up against two fundamental rights. First, in denying homosexual, gay, single women and live-in couples to become intended parents and only permitting those who live in heterosexual marriage relationships, it violates the right that everyone enjoys to procreation. Second, it violates women's right to their personal liberty to use their bodies as they please. In its clause of only allowing those who are childless to access surrogacy services, I would argue that the bill has also promoted stratified inequality among those who experience secondary infertility within the country. A majority of poor women and couples in Rajasthan, as we saw in Chapter 3, experienced conditions of secondary sterility as socially and economically debilitating. The bill in its stipulation of childlessness would disqualify such women and men from their right to procreate.

Feminist and women's health organisations have also questioned the bill on a number of fronts, although their focus has been on the other controversial aspect of the bill where the emphasis has been on altruism rather than commerce. While most of these groups had argued for more stringent regulation of the commercial aspects of the previous ART Bill,[32] they were not in favour of a complete ban but, rather, advocated a ceiling on the amount of money paid and the number of times a woman could act as a surrogate. As such organisations rightly point out, the assumption that if a woman is not paid to be a surrogate she will not be exploited in any other manner is flawed (Nadimpally *et al.*, 2011; SAMA, 2011). It also raises the question as to whether a complete ban on commercial surrogacy is justified and made from a position of privatising what is best for the woman. Along with legal activists, these groups rightly see the new bill as a reflection of what a patriarchal state conceives of as 'natural' and 'unnatural' reproduction and its disgust at practices it regards as depraved (Parthasarthy, 2016).

The rules regarding the surrogate's marital status, determining who can participate in surrogacy and who cannot, is important in understanding how the bill works to maintain, as well as to shift, widely prevalent ideas of appropriate parenthood. The bill, as in previous bills, upholds heteronormative ideals of parenthood in its reference to married couples. Same-sex couples living in India and other places where such alliances are regarded as illegal continue to be excluded from seeking surrogacy by the 2016 Bill. While previous bills have acknowledged that women who were single could both commission and undertake surrogacy, in the 2016 Bill neither unmarried nor single women are considered as surrogates or for surrogacy services.[33]

From the perspective of the surrogates, as elaborated upon in the section above, the legislation is clearly not cognisant of their notions of kinship or the pecuniary realities which drive the women to undertake surrogacy or the attendant 'culture-work' that is required to alleviate the stigma they face. In only recognising gestational surrogacy,[34] but not traditional surrogacy where the eggs of the surrogate (rather than those of a donor or of the commissioning woman) are used, the bill reinforces biologically deterministic models of motherhood when it emphasises that it is the genetic substance of the commissioning couple rather than the gestation by the surrogate which defines motherhood.[35] However, the biogenetic model of kinship that is thus reinforced is at odds with the ways in which surrogates and poor infertile women themselves construct relatedness.

Reproductive autonomy, consent and choice in context

The advent of assisted reproductive technologies, Haker argues, has resulted in a shift in the concept of reproductive autonomy, from being regarded as a negative right (in terms of women's rights to non-violation of their bodily integrity as experienced in the Indian sterilisation campaigns, for example) to being a positive right in terms of the right to access ARTs. Reproductive autonomy, as she suggests:

is not synonymous with liberty in the sense of mere individual autonomy …
rather it takes women seriously as moral agents who must decide what kind
of life they want to live, together with others, in particular social contexts
and given institutional constraints

(Haker, 2006, p. 1)

Ethically, it situates every woman as a moral agent, accountable for the decisions she makes.

Feminist and cross-cultural studies of autonomy (Mackenzie and Stoljar,
2000; Meyers, 2001; Thachuk, 2004; Sherwin, 1998; Madhok, 2004; for example)
have been especially important in challenging the assumption of autonomy as
equated solely with the individual, even as they have been pivotal in securing
women's autonomy over their reproductive choices (including the right to
oppose forced methods of curbing fertility, as well as the right to choose *not* to
procreate (Meyers, 2001). In developing the notion of 'relational autonomy',
these scholars bring recognition to the fact that individuals are situated within a
wide number of relationships which influence, directly or indirectly, the capacity
for decision-making. But, as Meyers suggests, and the examples of infertile and
surrogate women in the chapters in the book demonstrate, the scope of socially
condoned autonomy with regard to mothering is far less extensive than it initially appears to be. The significance of the concept of relational autonomy is
that it enables an analysis of power as framing the contexts in which decisions
are taken.

The focus on power in reproductive decision-making is especially salient in
India where patrilineal ideologies and institutions (sites of 'matrigynist idolatry',
Meyers, 2001, p. 737) still determine procreative practices. It is important to
note here that I am not suggesting that women cannot be individual decision-
makers with regard to reproduction in these contexts but, rather, that they cannot
emerge as autonomous in the manner conceptualised by feminists in terms of
having a 'well co-ordinated repertoire(s) of agentic skills which they can call
upon routinely to inform their decision about how best to go on' (Meyers, 2001,
p. 742). In contexts where reproductive decisions regarding the timing and
nature of sex, the number and spacing of children, the use and type of contraceptives, for example, are collectively, though not necessarily unanimously, determined by the family and community, consent, as an ethical principle that upholds
individual autonomy, becomes less salient.

Reliance on an autonomy-based justification of informed consent as is prevalent in biomedical settings in the west is distorted, as Manson and O'Neill
(2007) suggest. They argue instead for a model of consent to be relational, in
other words set in the context of the relationship between those who seek and
those who give consent in the clinical context. Their approach is instructive,
based on the idea of consent as a product of 'communicative transactions' and
the quality of information flow between the parties involved in giving and
getting consent. Thus, it is not so much the specific detail of the consent instruments and procedures per se which make it ethically better, but rather a focus on

what information is conveyed, by whom, about what and how (the communicative transaction), which makes consent ethically salient.

Manson and O'Neill's point about the quality of communication in relation to consent is critical when applied to the case of the Indian surrogates. In a context where women's childbearing is appropriated by the family as well as the state and their sexual and reproductive consent is taken for granted, it is imperative that the regulations ensure detailed and explicit communication of information about surrogacy procedures. The ART bills did not take adequate measures beyond the standard protocols to ensure that the potential surrogate has full knowledge of the implications of her consent, leading some, such as Palattiyil *et al.* (2010, p. 691), to suggest there is little evidence that Indian surrogates' human rights and physical or psychological health were adequately protected. Others such as Tanderup *et al.* suggest that informed consent is never realised in practice because the surrogates who are invariably of a lower socio-economic status compared to the doctors remain diffident in asking questions and thus remain uninformed about the issues and processes involved (2015, p. 4). This is an issue which remains of critical consideration in the context of the new Surrogacy Bill, 2016.

In enabling payments to be received and in legalising commercial surrogacy, on the other hand, the ART bills contributed to challenging the ideological devaluation of women's childbearing (as 'natural', taken for granted and not being valued in monetary terms). Commercial surrogacy complicates practices of consent further, as it is suggested that a high payment to a surrogate is likely to compromise her capacity to give informed consent by encouraging her to minimise the risks involved in the procedures (Palattiyil *et al.*, 2010).[36]

Until the legislation has the means to redress the pressures which propel women to undertake surrogacy as a 'compulsion' (lack of choice), it is unlikely that the instrument of consent alone, however comprehensively formulated, will ensure surrogate welfare. Like Sunder Rajan (2007), I suggest that the ethical formulations that accompany global biocapital in the south will always be violatory however much attention is paid to the ethical instruments themselves. I have looked indirectly at how these processes impact not only on the subjects (patients of clinical trials or surrogates) of the legislation but also more directly at how the lives of people who share their local moral worlds are profoundly affected. Following Manson and O'Neill (2007) I suggest that it is not so much the detail of the instrument of consent itself that is important but, equally, the context in which it is applied and made relevant that should be of concern.[37] The ART bills urged the need to regulate private fertility clinics, but did not go far enough as it had to encourage these clinics to provide services for a global market at the same time. State legislation, we saw, did not go far enough in enforcing checks on clinics, for instance in examining their recruitment and selection procedures, the kinds of consent and counselling provided and the quality of medical procedures carried out.[38] Amendments to the guidelines between 2008 and 2010, for example, mainly focused on ensuring commissioning couples have more documentation (e.g. proof of citizenship for the intended child) which, though necessary, did not address the ethical issues or exploitation.

The issue of payment is an arena of contestation between those who see the need for reproductive labour to be monetarily rewarded and valued in a capitalistic society and others who believe decisions about childbearing should remain in the domain of maternal altruism. It is also an issue of disagreement between feminists and surrogates across the globe.[39] As Rudrappa (2012) documents in her study of surrogates in Bangalore, surrogacy work and payment is more meaningful to women compared to their work in the garment industry. Comparing these two contexts of 'work', they find their surrogacy work more 'creative' (as in creating life) and financially rewarding compared with their factory work, which is more physically exhausting and debasing in terms of the abuse they face from male co-workers. As garment workers these are not the poorest of women, as Rudrappa points out, but the financially unstable environment in which they work (being laid off when an assignment is completed) drives them to the surrogacy industry to maintain their value as workers. The good care, food, rest and medical treatment they receive while undergoing surrogacy, especially, make this kind of work attractive. These surrogate experiences suggest why payment and commodification are preferred compared to altruistic surrogacy and also reinforce for them the inequalities of maternal care which they receive when they are surrogates compared to when they are not.

Some final reflections ...

The Indian bills, until 2016, have only permitted gestational surrogacy arrangements, following the same model of relatedness prevalent in northern Europe and America, with the intent to sever the possibilities of any long-term claims and relationships developing between the surrogate and the child she carries. But, as gestation in Rajasthan establishes, maternal connections are made through substances other than blood. It is through their 'womb vessels' that women establish ties of maternity with their offspring; kinship ties which the law is unable to disrupt.

Attention to notions of relationality and morally appropriate processes (ritual gifting, for example), through which people marry and become parents in western India, is central to an understanding of how contextually disconnected or 'regulatory' the surrogacy legislation is in reality. Even the process of 'giving away' offspring, as a surrogate does, is not alien to indigenous caste-based conceptions of appropriate parenting. Children may be given away for adoption among close kin (such as the *bua* (FZ), *mausi* (MZ), *nana-mama* (mother's brothers')) if the close relatives are infertile.[40] Daughters are given away at marriage through economic prestations (dowry or *dahej*) and ritual gifting (*kanya dan*) to people who become kin. Like daughters born to be 'given away' at marriage, surrogate babies are also given away.[41] In this context gestational surrogacy can be regarded as an expression of a more familiar form prevalent in existing kinship practice: surrogacy is appropriated into local kinship worlds at the same time that it is derided as an adulterous relationship, or undertaken 'without choice'.

The ART bills have reproduced cultural ideas of reproduction as well as challenged them. They sanctioned the appropriation of surrogate women's fertility for national purposes in line with the patriarchal idea that women's reproductive bodies serve collective interests (of the family, community, caste). Living in such contexts, Indian surrogates are in a similar position, as Teman has described in Israel, wherein surrogates have to reconcile their personal ideas regarding maternity within a wider context where, 'reproduction is celebrated as the (Jewish-Israeli) women's 'national mission' ... a product of both social pressure and explicit government encouragement' (Teman, 2003, p. 80). In the Indian surrogacy bills as with the JSY national programme on safe motherhood (Chapters 2 and 5) we see for the first time an alignment taking place between a state encouraging childbirth (in contrast to its anti-natalist family planning programmes) and the strongly natalist patrilineal ideologies still in place in much of Northern India, where human fertility continues to be widely celebrated in the religious festivals such as Teej and Gangaur and in an everyday contexts of the fasting married women undertake. Though intended to minimise health inequities for surrogates, the 2010 Bill I suggest promoted inequality between women of different child-bearing capacities based on their ability to pay for and access quality health services.[42] With regard to the recent Surrogacy Bill, we find that, although it is responsive to the allegations of exploitation of women, it has created and reinforced other kinds of *social and gender* inequalities in its wake. Of particular significance is the use of 'altruism' as a key trope in its promulgation.

In conclusion, whatever the legal arrangements, the global availability and movement of reproductive technologies which assist procreation has ensured that surrogacy arrangements will continue to take place, bypassing the state, if necessary.[43] Arrangements between clinicians and surrogates were already in place several years before the ART Bill in India was formulated – showing how the legislation is in response to, rather than pre-emptive of, transnational surrogacy (as is the case elsewhere in UK and in Europe, for example). The state needs to do more 'work' in regaining the trust of the people, that it will uphold their welfare and move beyond the provision of informed consent which is inadequate given the compulsions and complexities of decision-making accompanying reproduction in India. To ban surrogacy in India runs the fear of pushing this practice 'underground' and further removed from any kind of legislation ensuring the welfare of those most vulnerable.[44] The Eighteenth Law Commission set up in 2009 to review the ART Bill in respect to surrogacy stated clearly that the prohibition of surrogacy is undesirable. Recognising surrogacy as a 'supreme saviour' of the distresses faced by infertile couples, it advocated active legislative intervention to facilitate the correct use of new technologies (2009, p. 6).[45]

The new legislation of 2016, with its limited and unconstitutional framework (Parthasarthy, 2016), has yet to fully promote procreative freedom, autonomy and equality. For the new legislation to fully act 'as defender of human liberty and an instrument of the distribution of positive entitlements' (Eighteenth Law Commission Review 2009) the focus has to move beyond heteronormative framings and popular notions of altruism which equate motherhood with a sense of preordained 'natural' behaviour (of altruism and sacrifice). Instead, standard bioethical instruments need to be reconstituted to consider the languages, economies, kinship and moralities which frame issues of reproductive choice and consent on the ground. Any bill which regulates access to ARTs must give due consideration to the complex, relational and highly stratified contexts in which women undertake childbearing in India to understand why legally comprehensive consent procedures can co-exist with violations of personhood in practice. Without such consideration, injustice toward poor, infertile women who have neither the economic means nor political voice to access fertility services becomes enshrined within state structures and legal processes which only selectively recognise the need to redress infertility as a right.

Notes

1 See Smerdon (2008) for a history of the formulation of the guidelines between 2000 when the first deliberations took place, 2002 when the draft guidelines were released, 2005 when the national guidelines to regulate ART clinics came into force, to the more comprehensive rules and regulations of the 2008 Bill, further slightly modified in the 2010 version. Sections of this chapter draw on my article (Unnithan-Kumar, 2013) and on my contributions to the Encyclopedia of Anthropology (2018).

2 Even though conditions of secondary sterility are easily treatable through the existing public health infrastructure, these services are virtually non-existent in the public health sector in India (Qadeer, 2009) where the focus has historically been on controlling the fertility of poor women rather than on fertility promotion.

3 Wider issues linked to the commodification of reproduction warrant a discussion beyond the scope of the present article.

4 Two national organisations based in Delhi, SAMA and the Centre for Health and Social Justice, provided key material and insights, as did the centre for Medical Ethics in Mumbai. In Rajasthan, members of the PUCL and legal aid organisations, as well as members of two health based NGOs shared insights and access to up to date legislative responses (for example on the Baby Manji case).

5 At Sussex, along with the law department, we organised a workshop on 'framing international surrogacy' which considered the issues arising from British legislation and practices in a comparative context: July 2016.

6 Bailey (2011), for example, makes a similar point although not directly in relation to the bill. Such processes point to the ways in which 'new legislation can be oppressive for a significant population depending on the politics of its drafters' (Qadeer, 2010, p. 209).

7 Collier and Ong define global assemblages as the abstract, mobile and dynamic circulation of particular forms of governance, technoscience, ethics, for example, that circulate across countries, people and cultures taking on specific forms as local ensembles, and which define new material, collective and discursive relationships … encouraging ethical reflection. (2005, p. 4).

8 A legally enshrined and contractually enforced code of ethics, Sunder Rajan argues, stems from the desire of state and corporations to 'build up capacity', to become global experimental sites, wherein populations are used primarily as (clinical) experimental subjects with little attention to their own therapeutic needs … the form this ethics takes, quite literally the informed consent that volunteers sign, does not mitigate the fundamental structural violence of clinical trials conducted in the third world (2007, p. 75).

9 Another way of putting it would be to think of surrogacy legislation in terms of the limits of the state to exercise biopower as witnessed in the recent challenges it has faced to regulate sex selective abortion despite a history of legislation to do with the Pre-Conception and Prenatal Diagnostic Testing Acts (PNDT Act, 1994, PC-PNDT Act, 2002) which were promulgated to deter sex determination and related abortion.

10 Edwards *et al.*, 1993; Ragoné, 1994; among others.

11 Further media reports (on the cases of DG, GB, as reported in the Hindustan Times 2011, with my anonymisation) reveal similar trajectories: DG started out as an egg donor, donating six times which earned her £4,400. Her first surrogacy paid for her husband's kidney operation and enabled her to buy a small flat in Ahmedabad. She is a surrogate for the second time; now for a Japanese couple. She gets £4,750 to be a surrogate, £2,000 for childcare for two months and gifts. Her sister GB, twenty-three years old, is also a surrogate mother, earning money enabling her to go home to Nepal. These surrogate accounts point both to the fact of an increasing market in reproduction and also the need to investigate how parenthood is caught up in market values and processes (Spar, 2006) in order to regulate it.

12 What Meyers (2001) calls 'matrigynist ideology'.

13 A third important site, beyond the scope of this chapter, is the clinical context where class and caste distinctions as well as medical authority determine the boundaries of autonomy (see especially Ram, 2010; SAMA, 2010; Burke, 2010).

14 Zahida's expenses, for example, came out of existing household resources which were sold (a goat and a TV).

15 Key causes for secondary infertility similar to those identified in the public health literature (Oomen, 2001; Mukherjee and Nadimpally, 2006).

16 In Israel too, as Kahn documents (2000), the stress on the surrogate being unmarried is to prevent an illicit sexual union taking place, as intercourse is regarded as bringing about the union between the husband's sperm and the womb of the carrying mother.

17 Pande (2009b), and as implied in D. Gurung's newspaper interview as quoted above.

18 Surrogate women in Pande's study talk of the value they derive from the fact that 'foreigners' who came to them for procreative assistance.

19 Raveena, carrying a baby for a South Korean couple residing in California, is quoted as saying 'After all, they just give the eggs, but the blood, all the sweat, all the effort is mine. Of course it is going after me' (Pande, 2009b, p. 384). Likening surrogates to their own daughters being given away at marriage and therefore *paraya dhan* (someone else's property), Hetal is quoted as saying

> right from the day she is born we start preparing to give her away. We think she was never ours but still we care for her when she is with us. It will be exactly the same. We know the baby is not ours; they are investing so much money … it is their property. But I will love her like my own….

(Pande, 2009b, p. 387)

20 In 2010, infertile couples travelling to India typically expected to pay £8–13,000 per birth inclusive (Bromfield, 2010). Of this amount, approximately £4,000–5,000 went to the surrogate.

21 There has, nevertheless, been an increasing problem noted with the provision of ART services to gay couples and single men with some providers openly denying them services (Smerdon, 2008).

22 Part I of the 2008 Bill (pp. 1–38) sets out the definitions and provisions in nine chapters on subjects ranging from the registration and duties of clinics to the regulation of research, offences and penalties. Chapter 7 is devoted to 'the rights and duties of patients, donors, surrogates and children' and will be the main section from which this present paper draws. In addition, Part 2 (pp. 39–43) of the bill describes in greater detail the rules as set out in Part 1, and Part 3 (pp. 44–135) provides samples of the schedules, forms and contracts pertaining to the parties involved in the processes of

assisted reproduction, including forms for the agreement for surrogacy (p. 91), consent for donor eggs (p. 95) and information on the surrogate (p. 104). The ART Regulation Bill of 2010 covers only Part I of the 2008 Bill.

23 It defines a *surrogate mother* as,

> a woman who agrees to have an embryo generated from the sperm of a man who is not her husband and the oocyte of another woman, implanted in her to carry the pregnancy to full term and deliver the child to its biological parent(s).
>
> (pp. 4–5, Chapter 1, Preliminaries)

24 In the 2010 version of the bill, this has been changed to 5 live births, to include those of the surrogate.

25 The ART Bill is progressive, especially when perceived in the context of the ban on surrogacy operative in a number of countries such as Australia, China, France, Italy, Germany, Denmark, Mexico, Spain, Switzerland and some states in the USA (Pande, 2009b). By contrast, Israel was the first country where surrogacy was publicly regulated in 1996 (Kahn, 2000; Teman, 2003) and as such provides an interesting comparison to India, as discussed in the paper.

26 The 2010 version of the bill stipulates that the payment to the surrogate be made in five instalments rather than three (2008 version) with the bulk of the payment in the final transaction following the delivery of the child, further disabling the poor household and devaluing the labour of the surrogate (SAMA, 2011).

27 As evidenced by Pande during her fieldwork in Gujarat (2010b).

28 As acknowledged by clinicians to be an indicator of their care (e.g. Smerdon, 2008).

29 According to the Eighteenth Law Commission Review, in the absence of any law to govern surrogacy the 2005 guidelines applied at the time (2009, p. 21).

30 I use the term 'commissioning couples' when referring to couples who seek to undergo surrogacy for a child as documented in reports and articles, but otherwise prefer the term 'intended couples' because it is transaction free, as suggested to me by the surrogates I met in the UK.

31 A concept subject to substantive critique by feminist scholars and anthropologists (for non-western perspectives see, for example, SAMA, 2010; Menon, 2006; Madhok, 2004; Petchesky, 1998).

32 Some critics such as Mohan Rao for example, arguing from an ethical stance point, advocated a complete ban on commercial surrogacy (Rao, 2012).

33 This is in contrast to Israel where the law specifically demands that surrogates are single and unmarried women except under 'severe circumstances' (Kahn, 2000, p. 143).

34 Gestational surrogacy refers to the context where the surrogate does not provide reproductive tissue (her own eggs) and where emphasis is placed on her role in gestating the embryo.

35 Helena Ragoné charts a similar shift in surrogacy practices in the USA, where the moral anxieties to develop kinship ties based in genetics combine with insurance claim anxieties to distance surrogates from the possibilities of 'bonding' (e.g. emotionally and financially) with the children they carry to term (1998).

36 That is one of the main reasons why, according to Palattiyil *et al.* (2010) Indian legislation has so far fallen short of the ethical standards set by the International Federation of Social Work (IFSW).

37 The commodification of surrogacy, while of benefit to the surrogate, has also opened channels for their monetary exploitation and corruption. There has arisen a whole set of people – clinicians, nurses, middlemen, brokers, family members – who view the legalisation of surrogacy as a further opportunity to make money, an issue which is beyond the scope of this chapter. The power of clinics is especially palpable in the Indian context, where the private health sector is largely unregulated and associated with major financial turnovers. The access to funds has enabled the private sector

clinics to equip themselves with the latest cutting-edge technologies, making them far more competitive in the global context compared to the Indian public health provision.

38 For instance, it has especially failed to have any specific clauses that control middlemen in the trade.

39 Jill Hawkins, Britain's most prolific surrogate mother, who has given birth to eight surrogate children in nineteen years, captures this feeling when she says, 'it is not a shameful thing to desperately want a child and pay someone to help' (Burke, 2010).

40 Adoption from outside this context, as entailed in IVF procedures for example, have to be carried out 'in secret' as Bharadwaj (2003) observes.

41 Pande's ethnography on Gujarati surrogate perspectives demonstrates this clearly (1998).

42 The automatic access to healthcare for surrogates is qualified in the 2010 draft bill where quality medical care is contingent on their proving that their symptoms stem from their surrogacy.

43 As indeed other alliances between clinicians and their clients, such as in sex selective abortion, has shown.

44 Here I differ from Smerdon's (2008) analysis which suggests that a ban on surrogacy practices is the only viable option.

45 The review led to modifications in the 2008 Bill, as stipulated in the 2010 Bill. Accepting the complexity of surrogacy legislation, the bill advocated for life insurance for surrogates and the provision of financial support for the baby in the event of the death of the commissioning couple. It also stressed that the husband and the family of the surrogate be involved in the consent procedures. These additions, as they appear in the 2010 Bill, are further contested by feminist and health scholars and activists (e.g. SAMA, 2011).

Bibliography

Almeling, R., 2011. *Sex Cells: The Medical Market for Eggs and Sperm.* Berkeley: University of California Press

Anchayil, A. and Raheem, S., 2009. Commercialisation of the womb: it is left to our legislators to decide whether the pricing of a womb is tolerable or not. *The Hindu,* 1 November, p. 16. Delhi

Bailey, A. Reconceiving Surrogacy: Toward a Reproductive Justice Account of Indian Surrogacy. *Hypatia* 26, no. 4 (2011): 715–41

Bharadwaj, A. Why adoption is not an option in India: the visibility of infertility, the secrecy of donor insemination and other cultural complexities. *Social Science and Medicine* 56, no. 9 (2003): 1867–80

Bromfield. N., 2010. *Global Surrogacy in India: Legal. Ethical and Human Rights Implications of a Growing 'Industry'.* Accessed at www.rhrealitycheck.org/blog/2010/06/10/stateless-babies-legal-ethical-human-rights-issues-raised-growth-global-surrogacy-india

Browner, C.H. and Sargeant, C., 2011. *Reproduction, Globalization and the State: new theoretical and ethnographic perspectives.* Durham: Duke University Press

Burke, J., 2010. India's surrogate mothers face new rules to restrict 'pot of gold'. *Guardian,* 30 July, p. 10

Colen, S., 1995. 'Like a Mother to them': Stratified reproduction and West Indian Childcare workers and Employers. In Ginsburg, F. and Rapp, R., eds., *Conceiving the new world order: the global politics of reproduction.* Berkeley: University of California Press, 78–103

Collier, S. and Ong, A., 2005. Global assemblages, anthropological problems. In Ong, A. and Collier, S., eds., *Global assemblages: Technology, politics and ethics as anthropological problems*. Oxford: Blackwell, 3–22

Edwards, J., Franklin, S., Hirsch, E., Price, F., and Strathern, M., eds., 1993. *Technologies of procreation: Kinship in the age of assisted conception*. London: Routledge

Farmer, P., 1997. On Suffering and Structural Violence: A view from below. In Kleinman, A., Das, V., and Lock, M., eds. *Social Suffering*. Berkeley: University of California Press, 261–85

Franklin, S., 2005. Stem Cells R Us: Emergent Life Forms and the Global Biological. In Ong, A. and Collier, S. eds., *Global Assemblages: Technology, Politics and Ethics as Anthropological Problems*. Wiley-Blackwell, 59–78

Ginsburg, F. and Rapp, R., 1995. *Conceiving the New World Order: The Global Politics of Reproduction*. Berkeley: University of California Press

Goody, J., 1990. *The Oriental, the Ancient and the Primitive: Systems of Marriage and Family in the Pre-industrial Societies of Eurasia*. Cambridge University Press

Government of India (GOI), 2009. Eighteenth Law Commission of India Review: Need for Legislation to Regulate ART Clinics as well as Rights and Obligations to Partis of a Surrogacy. Report no. 228. http://lawcommission of India.nic.in/reports/report228.pdf (accessed on 31 July 2011)

Government of India (GOI), Indian Council for Medical Research, 2005. Draft Guidelines on Assisted Reproductive Technologies. From www.icmr.nic.in

Government of India (GOI), Ministry of Health and Family Welfare, Indian Council of Medical Research, 2010. *The Assisted Reproduction Technologies (Regulation) Bill – 2010 (Draft)*. New Delhi. From http://icmr.nic.in/guide/ART%20REGULATION%20Draft%20Bill1.pdf

Government of India (GOI), Ministry of Health and Family Welfare, Indian Council of Medical Research. 2008. *The ART Bill and Rules 2008* (Draft). New Delhi. From http://icmr.nic.in/art

Government of India (GOI), National Population Policy, 2000. Accessed at www.nhp.gov.in/national-population-policy-2000_pg

Gupta, J.A. Reproductive Biocrossings: Indian Egg Donors and Surrogates in the Globalized Fertility Market. *International Journal of Feminist Approaches to Bioethics* 5, no. 1 (2012): 25–51

Haker, H., 2006. *Reproductive autonomy in light of responsible parenthood: with new science comes the need for a new ethical discourse*. Retrieved May 14, 2011, from www.hds.harvard.edu/news/bulletin_mag/articles/34-1_haker.html

Inhorn, M., 1994. *Quest for Conception: Gender, Infertility and Egyptian Medical Traditions*. Philadelphia: University of Pennsylvania Press

Inhorn, M. Globalisation and Gametes: reproductive 'tourism', Islamic bioethics and Middle Eastern modernity, *Anthropology and Medicine*, 18, no. 1 (2011): 87–103. doi: 10.1080/13648.2010.525876

Kahn, S., 2000. Multiple mothers: Surrogacy and the location of maternity. Chapter 5. In Kahn, S., *Reproducing Jews: A cultural account of assisted conception in Israel*. Durham: Duke University Press, 140–59

Mackenzie, C. and Stoljar, N., 2000. *Relational Autonomy: Feminist Perspectives on Autonomy, Agency and Social Self*. Oxford University Press

Madhok, S., 2004. Heteronomous Women? Hidden Assumptions in the Demography of Women. In Unnithan-Kumar, M. *Reproductive Agency, Medicine and the State: Cultural Transformations in Childbearing*. Oxford: Berghahn, 223–45

Manson, N. and O'Neill, O., 2007. *Rethinking informed consent in bioethics*. Cambridge University Press

Menon, N. 2006. *Recovering Subversion: Feminist Politics beyond the Law*. Springfield: University oif Illinois Press

Meyers, D.T., 2001. The Rush to Motherhood – Pronatalist Discourse and Women's Autonomy. *Signs: Journal of Women in Culture and Society* 26, no. 3 (2001): 735–73

Mukherjee, M. and Nadimpally, S. Local global encounters: Assisted reproductive technologies in India. *Development* 49, no. 4 (2006): 128–34. doi: 10.1057/palgrave. development1100303

Nadimpally, S., Marwah, V. and Shenoi, A. Globalisation of birth markets: a case study of assisted reproductive technologies in India. *Global Health* 7, no. 27 (2011) Accessed at doi: 10.1186/1744-8603-7-27 PMCID: PMC3169454

Oomen, N., 2001. A decade of research on reproductive tract infections and gynaecological morbidity in India. In Ramasubban, R. and Jejeebhoy, S., eds., *Women's Reproductive Health in India*. Jaipur: Rawat

Palattiyil, G., Blyth, E., Sidhva, D., Balakrishnan, G. Globalisation and Cross Border Reproductive Services: Ethical Implications of Surrogacy in India for Social Work. *Journal of International Social Work*, 53, no. 5 (2010): 686–700

Pande, A. 'It may be her eggs but it is my blood': Surrogates and everyday forms of kinship in India. *Journal of Qualitative Sociology* 32, no. 4 (2009a): 379–97

Pande, A. Not an Angel, not a whore: Surrogates as 'dirty workers' in India. *Indian Journal of Gender Studies* 16, no. 2 (2009b): 141–73

Pande, A. Commercial surrogacy in India: Manufacturing a perfect mother-worker. *Signs: Journal of Women in Culture and Society* 35, no. 4 (2010a): 969–92

Pande, A. Transnational Commercial Surrogacy in India: Gifts for Global Sisters? *Reproductive Biomedicine Online* 23, no. 5 (2010b): 618–25

Pande, A. *Reproductive Biomedicine Online* 23, no. 5 (2011): 618–25. 'Transnational Commercial Surrogacy in India: Gifts for global sisters?' Special Issue Cross Border Reproductive Care: Travelling for Conception and the Global ART Market *Reproductive Biomedicine Online* 23, no. 5 (2011): 618–25

Pande, A., 2014. *Wombs in Labor: transnational commercial surrogacy in India*. New York: Columbia University Press

Parthasarthy, S. 2016. Republic of Unreason. *The Hindu*, 1 September 2016, Delhi

Patel, T., 1994. *Fertility Behaviour: Population and Society in Rajasthan*. Oxford University Press

Patel, T., 2007. *Sex Selective Abortion in India*. New Delhi: Sage

People's Union for Civil Society (PUCL), 2008. Files on Surrogacy Legislation

Petchesky, R. (1998), Negotiating Reproductive Rights. In Petchesky, R. and Judd, K. eds. *Negotiating Reproductive Rights*. London and New York: Zed Books, 1–30

Qadeer, I. Social and ethical basis of legislation on surrogacy: Need for debate. *Indian Journal of Medical Ethics* 6, no. 1 (2009): 28–32

Qadeer, I. The ART of marketing babies. *Indian Journal of Medial Ethics* 6, no. 4 October–December (2010): 209–15

Ragoné, H., 1994. *Surrogate motherhood: Conception in the heart*. Boulder: Westview Press

Ragoné, H., 1998. Incontestable Motivations. (Chapter 5) In Franklin, S., and Ragone, H., eds., *Reproducing Reproduction: Kinship, Power and Technological Innovation*. University of Pennsylvania Press, 118–31

Ragoné, H., 1999. The Gift of Life: Surrogate motherhood, gamete donation and the construction of altruism. In Layne. L, ed., *Transformative motherhood: On giving and getting in consumer culture*. New York University Press, 65–89

Raheja, G.G., 1988. *The Poison in the Gift: Ritual, Prestation and the Dominant Caste in a North Indian Village*. University of Chicago Press

Ram, K. Class and the Clinic: the subject of medical pluralism and the transmission of inequality. *Journal of South Asian History and Culture* 1, no. 2 (2010): 199–213

Rao, M. Why all non-altruistic surrogacy should be banned. *Economic and Political Weekly.* 47, no. 21 (2012): 15–17

Rapp, R., 1999. *Testing Women, Testing the Fetus: The social implications of amniocentesis in America*. New York: Routledge

Reddy, S. and Qadeer, I. Medical Tourism in India: Progress or predicament? *Economic and Political Weekly*, 45, no. 20 (2010): 69–75

Rudrappa, S. India's Reproductive Assembly Line. *Contexts* 11, no. 2 (2012): 22–7

SAMA Resource Group for Women and Health, 2010. *Unravelling the fertility industry: Challenges and strategies for movement building*. Report of International Consultation. Delhi: SAMA

SAMA Resource Group for Women and Health, 2011. *The Regulation of Surrogacy in India*. From http://samawomenshealth.wordpress.com/2011/04/23/the-regulation-of-surrogacy-in-india-questions-and-complexities/

Sarojini N.B. and Sharma, A., 2009. The draft ART (Regulation) Bill: in whose interest? *Indian Journal of Medical Ethics* 6, no. 1 (January–March 2009): 36–8. Mumbai: Forum for Medical Ethics Society

Scheper-Hughes, N. 'The Global Traffic in Human Organs' *Current Anthropology* 41, no. 2 (2000):191–224

Shah, C., 2009. Regulate technology, not lives: A critique of the draft ART (Regulation) Bill. *Indian Journal of Medical Ethics, VI* (1), January–March, 32–6. Mumbai: Forum for Medical Ethics Society

Sharma, U., 1984. Dowry in India. In Hirschon, R., ed. *Women and Property – Women as Property*. London: Croom Helm

Sharp, Lesley. 'The Commodification of Body Parts' *Annual Review of Anthropology* 29 (2000): 287–328

Sherwin, S., 1998. A Relational Approach to Autonomy in Healthcare. In Sherwin, S. ed., *The Politics of Women's Health: Exploring Agency and Autonomy*. Philadelphia: Temple University Press

Smerdon, U.R. Crossing Bodies, Crossing Borders: International Surrogacy between the US and India. *Cumberland Law Review* 39, no. 1 (2008): 15–86

Spar, D., 2006. *The Baby Business: How Money, Science, Politics, Drive the Commerce of Conception*. Boston: Harvard Business School

Strathern, M., 1992. *Reproducing the future: anthropology, kinship and the new reproductive technologies*. Manchester University Press

Strathern, M., 2003. Still giving nature a helping hand? Surrogacy: a debate about technology and society. In Cook, R., Sclater, S. and Kaganas, F. eds., *Surrogate motherhood: an international perspective*. Oxford: Hart

Strathern, M., 2011. *Gifts and Commodities Yet Again: When body parts literally circulate*. Presentation at the Anthropology Spring Term Seminar series, University of Sussex, February

Sunder Rajan, K. Experimental Values: Indian Clinical Trials and Surplus Health. *New Left Review* 45 (2007): 67–88

Surrogacy UK. 2015. Surrogacy in the UK: Myth busting and reform. Report of the Surrogacy UK Working Group on Surrogacy Law Reform November 2015, University of Kent

Tanderup, M., Reddy, S., Patel, T. and Nielsen, B. Reproductive ethics in commercial surrogacy: decision-making in IVF clinics in New Delhi. India. *Journal of Bioethical Inquiry* 12, no. 3 (2015): 491–501

Teman, E. The medicalisation of 'nature' in the 'artificial body': Surrogate motherhood in Israel. *Medical Anthropology Quarterly,* 17, no. 1 (2003): 78–99

Teman, E., 2010. *Birthing a Mother: The Surrogate Body and the Pregnant Self.* Berkeley: University of California Press

Thachuk, A.K., 2004. *Midwifery, informed choice and reproductive autonomy: A relational approach.* MA thesis in Women's Studies, Simon Fraser University, Canada

Thomas, M., 2009. Outsourcing surrogacy. Open page, *The Hindu,* 1 November 2009, p. 16, Delhi

Twine, F.W., 2011. *Outsourcing the Womb: Race, Class and Gestational Surrogacy in a Global Market.* London: Routledge

Unnithan-Kumar, M., 2001. Emotion, Agency and Access to Healthcare: women's experiences of reproduction in Jaipur. In Tremayne, S. ed. *Managing Reproductive Life: Cross cultural themes in sexuality and fertility* Oxford: Berghahn

Unnithan-Kumar, M., 1997. *Identity, Gender and Poverty: new perspectives on caste and tribe in Rajasthan.* Oxford: Berghahn

Yasin, F., 2011. *Booming surrogacy industry in India raises legal, social concerns.* Accessed at www.globalpressinstitute.org/global-news/asia/india/booming-surrogacy-industry-india-raises-legal-social-concerns

Zelizer, V. The Purchase of Intimacy. *Law and Social Inquiry* 25, no. 3 (2000): 817–48

7 Making rights real

Legal activism and social accountability

Introduction

In this chapter I focus on the everyday rights-based work of legal civil society organisations in Rajasthan from 2005 onwards to understand how legal aid groups use the language of universal human rights to support diverse forms of claim- making to do with the reproductive body and childbearing. I also reflect on the relationship between feminism and legal activism in India where reproductive rights are popularly invoked in terms of the right *to* childbearing and *against* forced sterilisation. *Prajanani adhikar*, the official legal term for reproductive rights in the Hindi speaking states of North India, literally means the right (*adhikar*) to be a (female) bearer of children (*prajanani*). This terminology and practice of reproductive rights is in contrast to the popular language and related activism in Euro-American, northern as well as southern, feminist contexts which have focused on women's rights to limit their fertility and is centred on contraception and (with varying intensity) on abortion (Unnithan and Dubuc, 2017; Heitmeyer and Unnithan, 2015). At the outset these framings point to very different contexts of politics vis-à-vis the state and to diverse conceptualisations of selfhood and bodily autonomy (as referred to in chapter 6 on surrogacy). But in both settings human rights frameworks have strengthened mobilisation for greater accountability on maternal health from the state. Human rights framing has enabled health activists, including feminists in India, to recast maternal mortality as a human rights violation and thereby as a means to seek better quality public health services (Chapter 2 and Unnithan, 2003).[1] At the same time, Indian feminists, like their western counterparts, have influenced legal activism away from a focus on childbearing (as have feminist mobilisations elsewhere in the south (for example: Cornwall and Molyneux, 2008; Morgan, 2014; Unnithan and De Zordo, 2018) toward broader everyday issues of gender violence. Legal activist work in India has been especially successful when it has drawn on feminist inspired notions of reproductive rights to address domestic violations, but as previous work has shown this has equally been limited by the narrowness of such framing (Madhok, Unnithan, Heimeyer, 2014). In this chapter and the next I reflect on the range and cultural implications of such rights work undertaken by legal activists in terms of anthropological, legal and development scholarship on the 'culture of rights' (Cowan, Dembour and Wilson, 2001; Cowan, 2009), the 'translation' and 'power of rights' (Merry, 2011, 2009, 2006; Goodale, 2007; Yamin and Lander, 2015) and rights as mechanisms of social accountability (Yamin and Lander, 2015; Storeng and Behague, 2017; Joshi and Houtzager, 2012). I use social accountability in Joshi and Houtzager's political sense of the term to mean an 'ongoing engagement of collective actors in civil society to hold the state to account for failures to provide public goods' (Joshi and Houtzager, 2012, p. 150) but I also refer to the gendered notions of responsibility, duty and moral obligation as more informal mechanisms of accountability at work in everyday institutional practices of reproductive rights and claim-making.

In this chapter I show how legal interventions of CSOs both help establish collective, community-based claims over public health services (Heitmeyer and Unnithan, 2015) and, equally, enable women to exercise individual rights to resist collective claims (of the family and community) on their sexual and reproductive bodies. The legal work enabling women to be recognised as members of collectives *and* as individual rights bearers is especially critical in cases where collective claims on their bodies involve reproductive and sexual appropriation and abuse (as seen for example in the feminist, legal discourse in India on protection against domestic violence: Jaisingh, 1992). I draw on fieldwork conducted along with the research team in Rajasthan (as set out in Chapter 2) from July 2009 to June 2010, which included working with local legal aid organisations; a national legal aid organisation; networks of lawyers, judges, advocates, family counsellors and members of family and district courts; the Rajasthan high court as well as at the state Human Rights Commission. The interviews and discussions enabled insights into how legal activists understood and drew together popular and universal notions of reproductive rights and entitlements, navigating through constitutional, indigenous and international frame-works of legal redress and justice. The arguments in this chapter also draw on joint publications[2] (and fieldwork quotes used in these publications) as well as years of discussion with members of the Rajasthan section of the People's Union of Civil Liberties (PUCL) and legal academics from the Rajasthan University Women's Association (RUWA). These multiple meetings demonstrated that legal activism, even at the 'grassroots',[3] could be limited by its defence of 'duties' among civil society organisations (Madhok, Unnithan and Heitmeyer, 2014; Unnithan and Heitmeyer, 2015) as articulated within indigenous reproductive and sexual claims making practices (illustrated in Chapters 3 and 4). Anchored in 'thick' ethnographic approaches to the diverse forms of rights work, project team findings suggested that *beyond* the social science critiques of human rights (notably Brown, 2004; Žižek, 2005; Wilson, 2001; Ferguson, 1990; Englund, 2006), which have demonstrated that human rights paradigms invoked in countries of the global south serve to reinforce existing power hierarchies, human rights frameworks in India have also been instrumental in challenging the economic and political status quo (Unnithan and Heitmeyer, 2014; Heitmeyer and Unnithan, 2015).

In this chapter I extend this previous work to examine the idea of CSOs as a field of reproductive power, as discussed in Chapter 2. In support of the observations of Bernal and Grewal (2014) that NGOs do not represent a *unified* field of power, I consider how feminist ideas may drive the operation of reproductive rights work in the legal aid CSOs in Rajasthan, but often remain submerged (also see Povinelli, 2006; Dave, 2012; Bernal and Grewal, 2014) within a socialist yet patriarchal ideology such as an ethic of service, on the one hand, and a commitment to a secular, liberal politics, on the other. While ideas of gender equality and social justice are embedded in the work of feminist influenced legal aid work, how, exactly, rights are linked to wider, systems-based gender justice remains elusive. As Agnes (1999) has so powerfully argued in the case of the history of family law reform in India, women's rights issues in particular fall through the diverse political forces driving change. As noted in previous work on the issue, as argued by feminist scholars such as Menon (2004) it is clear that feminist ideas which have been most effectively mobilised in legal contexts are the ones which coalesce around tropes of violence and disembodied forms of subjecthood to the exclusion of other ways of claiming gender equality (Madhok, Unnithan and Heitmeyer, 2014). While such a framing opens up certain avenues for claim-making they foreclose others, as demonstrated in the work of 'grassroots' (often globally linked) CSOs whose support for 'universal' feminist rights may be weaker.

The anthropological approach to human rights in this chapter, following Goodale,

> takes human rights normativity itself as a key category of analysis and ... (is discursive in that) it assumes that social practice is in part constitutive of the idea of human rights itself, rather than simply the testing ground on which the idea of universal human encounters actual ethical or legal systems.
>
> (Goodale, 2007, p. 8)

It entails a focus on 'human rights talk' as being not only about 'how people speak about the postivised rules in national or international law or aspire to expand and interpret them in new ways' (Wilson, 2007, p. 350) but also, as fieldwork in Rajasthan suggested, in how they speak about, combine and expand on long rooted indigenous traditions of rights and justice (denoted by concepts such as *adhikar, huq* and *nyaya*). The ethnography in this chapter reinforces anthropological critiques of the legal understanding of 'culture' as a problem (a barrier to be overcome) for the realisation of human rights (Cowan *et al.*, 2001; Merry, 2001). When simplistic notions of culture are invoked in legal discourse through selective representations of sex, gender, class and ethnicity it functions to widen the gap between the law and lived experiences of violation.

Ethnographic material in this chapter also reminds us that rights work can put further distance between the benefits of rights legislation and those subjects who find it difficult to claim access to legal rights. The fact that being poor can inhibit one's access to rights, as in the case of a number of families interviewed, points to the significance of a political economy critique of rights (Englund's work for example). At the same time, the gains made by human rights activism in the Indian context suggests that a legal rights framework provides for now, in Petchesky's terms, the 'most *viable rhetorical structure* available to civil society groups for making social and erotic justice claims, seeking redress or accountability'.[4]

In the following sections I focus on the work of four legal aid organisations offering a spectrum of legal aid support to explore the different types of legal aid cultures and particularised framings of rights. As in chapter 2 on health related CSOs, field research revealed that within the legal CSO community, rights were invoked in a selective and instrumental, but also a morally invested, discourse (Madhok, Unnithan and Heitmeyer, 2014; Heitmeyer and Unnithan, 2015) including to do with social accountability by members of the legal aid CSOs. The differing modes of 'making human rights in the vernacular' (Merry, 2006, p. 219) across these organisations suggests that the transformatory impact of human rights-based activism may be very limited. Nevertheless, new spaces (physical, conceptual, deliberative) have emerged where the discourse of reproductive violence as 'natural' is challenged even as popular critiques of human rights as against reproductive rights become entrenched (for example, Morgan, 2014).

Responsible reproduction: the power of duties over rights

The implicit submission of individual sexual and reproductive desires to collective (caste/kin) norms is a recurring theme in the everyday talk about women's duties and responsibilities to do with childbearing in Rajasthan. The moral force of the expectation that women engage in childbearing is most clearly enunciated in the (patri-focused) language of 'duties' where women's bodies are seen to exist primarily to fulfil the requirements of social reproduction.[5] These ideas have a long tradition anchored as they are in indigenous legal discourse on marriage, family and property ownership. Notions of duty (referred to by the Hindi term *dharma*, or by the equally popular Urdu term of *farz*) foreground kinship obligations between spouses, siblings and parents form the legal basis of thinking about institutional obligations of family, caste, community and village. Notions of rights in terms of entitlements (popularly conceptualised as *huq*) flow from the sense of having fulfilled one's duties.

The roots of these ideas of duty lie in the plural codified laws and customs governing Hindu marriage and family relationships operating in ancient and pre-colonial India and especially in the *nibhandhas* (commentaries) and *smritis*, (memorised words which comprised the *dharmasutras* and *dharmashsatras*; Agnes, 1999, p. 12).[6] They also formed the basis of the two main schools of Hindu law in the eleventh and twelfth centuries: the *Mitakshara* and the *Dayabhaga*, respectively validated in colonial Anglo-Hindu law and informing laws in post-independent India (Agnes, 1999, p. 13). In the more popular *Mitakshara* legal tradition (widespread in British India including Rajasthan; also see

Unnithan-Kumar, 1997), it was the Hindu joint family and its basis in the male coparcenary unit which was extolled. Women were not regarded as members of the joint family and therefore had no property rights. As Agnes (1999, p. 11) notes, the Hindu joint family asserted sexual control over women by denying them the right to control property. The notion that the (male) head of the family owned the property for all members of the family, including its female members, also meant that women had the right to maintenance, including the right to residence. The right to maintenance has played a significant role in the activism around women's rights in independent India, as discussed further in this chapter. *Adhikar*, the term commonly referred to as 'rights' in legal contexts, emerged in the nineteenth century where it appeared in more legislative contexts and designated power or office (i.e. the rights or privileges due to a particular title or rank) (Madhok, 2009, p. 16). In her analysis of these terms as used in Rajasthan, Madhok suggests that despite some overlap between these indigenous notions of rights and the rights of mainstream liberal theory, the former is generally broader in scope in that it incorporates individual *and* collective rights as well as both positive and negative rights (Madhok, Unnithan and Heitmeyer, 2014).

For legal activists who worked closely with members of low- and middle-class families in Rajasthan, the idea of actively claiming rights from the state was a foreign concept as the state (*sarkar*), like the family, was regarded as a 'natural' (parental) caretaker of its members' well-being. The role of the state as a benevolent guardian was invoked in references to the state as *mai-baap* (Hindi term for 'our mother-father') in Rajasthan, implying that rights would flow spontaneously and automatically from the state as they did in the family. There is an implicit notion of 'natural' responsibility and 'duty' attributed to the state, as in customary law to the male head of household, who is presumed to uphold rights of individual members, making the actual staking of claims by individual members out of place and morally unacceptable. In turn, for family members it was not considered appropriate to think about their individual rights but, instead, concentrate on their obligations and duties as members of the family. These paternalistic notions of rights were not just restricted to local non-feminist activists, but also found among top lawyers and advocates in Rajasthan. The idea of human rights as well was found wanting precisely because it did not emphasise duties enough, as was made clear in interviews with Jain-ji (pseudonym) a retired leading lawyer as well as with the head of the State Human Rights Commission at the time. Even legal activists working with Dalits[7] and against caste-based discrimination strongly voiced their support for an emphasis on duties within human rights frameworks. As SK, the head of the regional Dalit-based legal CSO pointed out, 'The weakness (with the universal rights-based approach) is that people are not fulfilling their duties. Everyone talks about rights but not their duties (*rights ki baat sab karte hain par duties ki nahi*)' (SK, fieldwork interview, 2010; Unnithan and Heitmeyer, 2014, p. 1371).

In contrast to the paternalistic focus on duties by members of the legal community, for feminist activists in the health and legal fields such as Sheela, Dheera and Bhavna, who belonged to middle- and upper-class backgrounds, drawing on (universal) rights language has been especially important precisely as a *counter* to the notion that 'rights-imply-duties' (Unnithan and Heitmeyer, 2014, p. 1368) appropriated by those such as SK above, who insist on women's familial responsibilities rather than their rights as household members. Where the feminist activists have succeeded in joint mobilisations with grassroots activists, making the boundaries between grassroots feminist and more elite feminist activism more permeable, their critical thinking has been around the need to raise awareness of women's rights in terms of their own entitlements rather than in meeting the entitlements of others regarded as 'one's duty' (Indira, Women's Public Rights Forum, personal communication, March 2009; Unnithan and Heitmeyer, 2014). In the next section I examine more closely what such notions of duty and social accountability imply for the practice of human rights by legal aid organisations who work with lower class families.

Notwithstanding the view of the state as a benefactor, the need for institutional accountability from the state was raised by many CSO workers at the grassroots, who were working more generally to raise the profile of a rights-based approach. Here, human rights language was deployed to wrest benefits from the state in a context viewed in the sense of a Marxist class struggle and related confrontation (*sangharsh*) to gain rights from the state. As one respondent suggested, 'Human rights enables us to work towards achieving human needs (like employment [*rozgar*]) through struggle [*sangharsh*].' [Human rights mean] achieving human needs through struggle' (fieldwork interview, 2009; Unnithan and Heitmeyer, 2014, p. 1371). Another community-based member and grassroots rights activist from western Rajasthan echoed Petchesky's idea that the rights discourse was an important rhetoric to gain benefits from the state when he suggested that, 'In the end, it is the government's responsibility to provide these services' and that it was their work as a CSO) to raise awareness (*jaagruk*) in the community about their rights to these services' (excerpt from fieldwork interview, western Rajasthan, 2009; Unnithan and Heitmeyer, 2014, p. 1273). The notion of rights-based approaches as inculcating a sense of institutional accountability also emerged in local offices of transnational organisations such as UNICEF. The Indian director of the development programmes in the state at the time was clear in her belief that: 'Rights work as a spotlight and as a search-light to highlight violations. As such, working with a rights-based approach means that processes are just as important as results.' (Fieldwork interview, 2009; Unnithan and Heitmeyer, 2014, p. 1372).

I now turn to examine more closely how rights emerge 'as culture' in the rights work undertaken by legal activists following Cowan, Dembour and Wilson's (2011, p. 14) sense of the culture of law where 'law is conceived as a worldview or structuring discourse which shapes how the world is apprehended'. It is in this sense that the contestation over what constitutes a rights-based approach among legal activists themselves, as well as an understanding of which ideas of rights are actually drawn upon and how they are put into practice, become salient, as discussed in the following sections.

Translation, mediation and the practice of rights

Notions to do with the 'translation' of human rights, such as Merry's concept of the 'vernacularisation' of human rights (Merry, 2006, 2009; Goodale and Merry, 2007), have been central to anthropological analysis of rights work undertaken by civil society groups, including work of the research team in India discussed in this chapter. 'Vernacularisation' refers to the processes adopted by advocates and activists in local organisations in framing the legal grievances of their petitioners into human rights language through an 'appropriation and translation of human rights' (Merry, 2006, p. 219). Through the notion of 'translation' Merry foregrounds the work of national elites and middle level social activists in making universal rights understandable and accessible through processes of mediation undertaken between universal and more local notions of rights. The translation of rights undertaken by legal aid organisations is especially significant in a country such as India, which has its own distinctive constitution based law, a whole realm of religiously sanctioned rights (personal laws) and a set of rights as ratified by international treaties. Legal aid CSOs become important educators and mediators of rights as they translate ideas of rights not just 'downwards' (providing accessible explanations of universal rights) but also 'upwards' (making indigenous rights knowable to law policymakers). But how exactly do they understand, 'assemble', in Ong and Collier's sense (2005), and mobilise rights?

Work carried out in Rajasthan from 2009 has suggested that the 'translation' of human rights by CSOs is nested at various levels stemming from the different legal registers (the Indian constitution, international law, indigenous frameworks) in which mediation is undertaken (Unnithan and Heitmeyer, 2014). Legal, feminist, grassroots, national and region-based activists approached human rights from very diverse ethical and moral standpoints and critically differed in their translation of such ideas into their work, as we see below. At the outset it is, as Goodale (2007, p. 8) suggests, in the visionary or aspirational and not just normative capacity that activists are led to embrace human rights and enact their sense of moral responsibility. In this section I draw on a year's ethnographic fieldwork which included research on legal aid organisations and networks in Jaipur and Delhi with a research team, and further independent fieldwork over shorter periods in 2015, 2017 and 2018 to describe different institutional and personal approaches that legal activists employed in framing and realising reproductive rights.

Seva,[8] a legal aid organisation formally founded in 1995, is deeply embedded in local activist networks in Rajasthan. PKS, its founder director and a specialist in labour law, has championed issues of poverty and economic rights within local movements of social activism in Rajasthan. He regards himself as a Gandhian and described his legal work and that of the organisation as following in the Gandhian tradition of voluntary social service (*seva*). As a leading lawyer in the Right to Information (RTI) movement, I first met PKS shortly before 2005 when the RTI Act was promulgated, a process in which he played a key role.

The issue of holding the state accountable for the development funds it received formed the crux of the long campaign carried out by a network of RTI activists until it became law in 2005. PKS was at the centre of this group, also serving as the main lawyer for the Rajasthan branch of the People's Union of Civil Liberties (PUCL) and working in close association with other feminist activists in the state with whom he has shared a long history in women's activism. From 1995, he was supported in his work by a small group of legally trained personnel, including members of his family, who also undertook to provide voluntary services to those who could not afford to pay the fees for legal representation.

At the time of field research, with the project team in 2010, PKS was very involved in instituting legal reform to combat corruption in the Indian legal system. This included the idea of devolving legal procedures to the village and block levels (through the *gram nyayalaya*) as a means of enhancing judicial accountability and local people's access to the law and working along with the state and other like-minded lawyers. In this work, as in past work on the RTI Act and with the PUCL, PKS and the lawyers working with him at Seva, largely drew on the Indian constitutional framework (on Fundamental Rights guaranteeing civil liberties, part III of the Indian Constitution and on the non-justiciable Directives of State Policy, part IV of the Constitution) rather than from specific international laws. While Seva lawyers did not work on reproductive rights issues per se, a significant part of their work in family and district courts was on cases of domestic violence, which brought their interest in family and property law together with sexual and reproductive health and rights in the Indian context. In Rajasthan it was common legal activist practice to invoke the Protection of Women from Domestic Violence Act (PWDVA 2005) rather than international women's rights law such as the Convention for the Elimination of All Forms of Discrimination Against Women (CEDAW). In its selection of 'domestic violence' as the dominant trope through which a range of intimate, social and economic gender-based violations could be addressed, Seva was influenced by a number of feminist activists, Sharada, Kavita, Aruna, Indira to name a few, who deployed the paradigm of violence as a strategic means to facilitate recourse to legal redress in contexts (family and household) where it has historically been difficult for those less powerful (women, children, dependents) to negotiate for their entitlements (Jaisingh, 1992; Suneetha and Nagraj, 2005).

Seva was known in the state for its legal expertise in assisting claimants who sought protection from domestic abuse. They had worked in the RTI with a network of feminist activists who were at the same time seeking to promote the enactment of the Protection of Women from Domestic Violence (PWDV) Bill, which subsequently also became an Act in 2005. The PWDV Act has, since its promulgation, been especially popular among lawyers who have drawn on it to address a whole set of family and household (private domain) related bodily harms on women, notably stemming from related dowry demands from the husband's family. The anti-dowry legislation (Dowry prohibition Act 1961 and Indian Penal Code Sections 304B and 498A as well as 198A of the Criminal Procedure Code of 1983), in which the practice of dowry is regarded as unlawful and a criminal offence (with imprisonment clauses for demanding, soliciting, giving and harassment for dowry), was the only legislation available to challenge the violence (physical, material, mental) faced by women in their affinal homes (Mathur, 2005; Jaisingh, 1992; Madhok, Unnithan and Heitmeyer, 2014). The PWDVA provided a civil law remedy to prevent the abuse of power within the 'domestic' arena, including that of dowry-related harm or injury.

According to Shruti, a Seva lawyer specialising in domestic violence cases, the Protection of Women from Domestic Violence Act (PWDVA 2005) was distinctive because it captured a number of inter-related violations encountered by the women who sought legal counsel from Seva, all of which were directly related to what she considered 'reproductive rights':

> Often, when a woman files a case under the Domestic Violence (DV) Act, she comes to us with a number of problems: for example, that (her in-laws) are making dowry demands, that they are putting pressure on her for having a male child (*beta janam dena*), that her husband uses bad language with her (*galiyan deta hai*), she is being tortured by her in-laws who don't provide her with food or medicine when she is ill'.
> (Fieldwork interview 2010; Heitmeyer and Unnithan, 2015, p. 384
> (Abbreviated by me.))

What is evident from Shruti's account is the way that reproductive violence (against infertility or producing male children) is connected with a whole set of material issues which coalesce around dowry-related threats and related economic anxieties and desires. It is the mobilisation by legal activists for legal interventions in the 'private' domain of the household which has enabled women's political, economic and reproductive rights to be addressed, precisely because reproductive rights, control over one's body and choices to do with sex, pregnancy and childbearing are connected with rights over property, entitlement to residence and flows of moveable wealth in the form of dowry (Madhok, Unnithan and Heitmeyer, 2014). Family courts in particular are set up to deal with issues arising from the application of 'personal law', where marriage, succession, inheritance and property matters are framed through religious or customary law.

To understand the process entailed in bringing such violations from the home to the court, I ask Seva lawyer VS on a visit to the residence of PKS where Seva has its office how, exactly, their expertise is sought out in such cases.

MU: How do women approach you ... what do they ask for?
VS (lawyer): Mostly women come to us and say *mein kya karun* (what should I do?), *inhe samjhado* (make him understand) and *nyay dilwa do* (give us justice).
MU: Does this mean there is an awareness of injustice.... What do they feel will be possible?
VS: No, not really. These women who come to us just want their minimum needs taken care of (*ki mera gujara chal jaye*) so that they can survive.

DS (lawyer): We say *gharelu hinsa kanun* (domestic violence law) has given you the right (*adhikar*) to reside in their own home – we tell them these things

(Fieldwork interview 2010; Madhok, Unnithan and Heitmeyer, 2014, p. 1235)

The excerpt is revealing of how processes of translation take place: the procedure commences with women's requests for Seva lawyers to intervene on their behalf to procure the minimum amount required to meet their material survival needs. While women make these requests couched in the language of seeking justice (*nyaya*), the lawyers convert this into the language of rights (*adhikar*) offering specific legislative means (court action through invoking the PWDVA 2005) as a resolution. The passage recounted by VS is also indicative of how he equates rights with not just material needs but also a broader set of entitlements such as the right to residence (as enshrined in the *Mitakshara* legal tradition; Agnes in section above). His statements also reflect a wider understanding of human rights prominent in a number of community-led grassroots organisations for whom human rights was a fight against poverty and marginality: '(Human rights mean that) the poor, marginalised, women, dalit and helpless people have the right to live comfortably': CR, from a village and lower caste background, Director, UJ Sansthan. (Unnithan and Heitmeyer, 2014, p. 1371).

Although Seva lawyers such as VS and Shruti worked on a number of domestic violence cases in the family and district courts, where these were adjudicated upon, rarely did these proceed further to the Rajasthan High Court. In reality litigation, even in cases filed by women in the family courts, rarely went further than the initial hearings. Most of these were settled through 'mediation', which took place with counsellors and with activists working with Seva. As feminist support groups such as Salah and Shakti – who provided voluntary counselling services at female police stations and shelters for women affected by domestic violence – stressed, a majority (over two-thirds) of the cases are settled through mediation between the parties in conflict and long before they ever reach the courts. *Shakti* counsellors revealed from their records of cases that that only 21 per cent of the total number of cases handled by the centre were eventually referred to the police while the remaining 79 per cent were resolved through 'negotiations, emotional support, economic rehabilitation and legal aid' (MSSK, 2002; Heitmeyer and Unnithan, 2015).

The emphasis placed on mediation rather than litigation stems from two important social and moral realities of women's lives: first, that few women have the economic and social resources to live independently as single or divorced woman without the support of their husband and affinal family; and, second, there was a strong belief among most of the mediators that the 'integrity' of the family should be maintained at all costs. A long-time women's activist in Rajasthan involved in setting up Salah and in campaigning for women-only police stations reinforced this as she explained: '*ghar ko jodna hai, hinsa ko rokna hai*' (we must stop the violence to unite the house.) (Statement made by

RP, founder activist of Salah in an interview during field research in 2010; Madhok, Unnithan and Heitmeyer, 2014, p. 1236).

Even PKS, founder director of Seva believed that women should be wary of the court procedures and that pragmatically speaking there were few avenues for emotional and material redress in situations of domestic violence. I tell them, he says:

> There is suffering in the process of moving the courts ... you will feel you are again being raped. This is why at Seva we first send cases for mediation (to Salah) and only after that has failed do we get involved to directly start the legal process. I prefer reconciliation. We don't want to be house break-ers, we advise adjustment and tolerance on the part of both parties.
>
> (Field research interview, 2010)

If cases proceeded to the family court, it was the PWDVA which was seen by PKS and members of the feminist support groups to bestow the best (material) benefits for women as claimants. For feminist legal activists and practitioners (at a national level, such as in the PUCL and the *Samjhota* national, legal group) the right of a women to reside in the familial residence in the event of being subject to domestic violence by other residents of the household was protected by her right to residence in the marital home even after a complaint had been filed, and was a victory for their campaign (Madhok, Unnithan and Heitmeyer, 2014, p. 1235). The conflict between seeing the family as both the primary site of reproductive and other violations faced by women, as well as the institution through which women gain social value and from where access to economic and political resources are gained, lies at the crux of activist support for mediation through counselling, who advise against litigation. For Seva and grassroots fem-inist activists such as Mamta and Nirja, the main source of oppression against women is the *family*, not the state, even though the state is constitutionally bound to guarantee the protection of women. And yet, the family is also the main insti-tution to which women are duty bound and herein lies a schism between Seva's approach along with the majority of feminists supporting the PWDVA and more universal feminist values (which prioritise rights). The primacy of the notion of duties rather than rights aligns Seva philosophy with the wider attitudes of the legal community in Rajasthan, which are patriarchal and caste-based. This is symbolised by the remarks of Jain-ji and for SK, the head of the regional dalit-based legal CSO who both suggested that the weakness of the universal rights-based approach lay in the fact that it did not put enough emphasis on the fulfilment of duties. Rights-based frameworks which set out entitlements *owed* to the individual by the state conflict with local notions of the responsibilities of the individual towards other social collectives and to the gendering of rights, which are deeply entrenched among legal actors themselves.

Locally grounded legal activists working in organisations such as Seva, Salah and Shakti, and even local branches of the PUCL, used the law as a means to improve women's status and negotiate power within the family to enable them greater control over their bodies, fertility, childbearing and access to maternal healthcare. The legal and counselling strategies they drew upon, however, lent themselves to *reproducing* those very same normative ideas that relegate women's identities to their roles as mother, wife or daughter-in-law in the family which is deeply patriarchal and hierarchical in rural Rajasthan (Madhok, Unnithan and Heitmeyer, 2014). By forcing women to go back to live with their oppressors, i.e. in its insistence that their right is only in terms of their marital home and not for the state to provide them with alternative secure housing, is where the law fails the cause of women at the same time as it absolves the state from being accountable.

Human rights and social accountability

Within the legal aid community, fieldwork also revealed an organisation of lawyers who worked explicitly to engage the language and practice of human rights to bring the state to account in its failure to guarantee safe and quality maternal health services. In contrast with Seva and Salah, who focused primarily on the power dynamics within the family through counselling and mediation, activists from 'Kanun', a larger, national, Delhi-based organisation, prioritised making the state accountable in its role as a duty-bearer of rights. A large, national legal activist organization in India, set up in 1989 by lawyer CG, Kanun's specific aim was to advance the *human rights* of the poor. It drew upon multiple legal strategies to bring about social change, notable among them was its creative use of public interest litigation (PIL) which are primarily social action litigations filed in recognition that sections of the population (those who are marginalised, vulnerable, poor) may not be in a position to put forward their own claims (Epp, 1998).

Discussing Kanun's explicitly rights-based approach, an intern working on reproductive rights within the organisation explained:

> Because when you use the language of rights, you make [the state] account-able. If you talk about it in terms of targets or commitments it becomes an airy-fairy promise that governments can take up or opt out of when it's con-venient to them and it's not urgent. When you talk about rights there's a sense of immediacy and they're legally binding. We (at Kanun) never asked for anything that India hadn't already signed up to (i.e. international human rights conventions).
>
> (Fieldwork interview in 2010; Heitmeyer and Unnithan, 2015, p. 381)

In 2008, Kanun set up its Reproductive Rights Unit to focus entirely on pro-moting and protecting reproductive rights. By 2018 the lawyers in the group had grown from two to over sixteen as Kanun lawyers successfully litigated against systemic discrimination faced by pregnant women in public hospitals in 2010, discussed further below. Kanun has transnational links in the area of reproduc-tive rights, working with global groups on legal redress for reproductive rights.

In particular, it maintains close links with a key reproductive rights global activist and research group based in Washington, D.C., which provided both research as well as funding to support grass roots advocacy at the time of fieldwork. Kanun is also well-connected with other nationally constituted groups working on health issues from a rights-based perspective, such as the *Jan Swasthya Abhiyan* (People's Health Movement) and organisations such as the PUCL and national law organisations such as *Samjhota*. Although it has offices in eighteen different states, these are not very active in terms of their relationship with more grassroots legal aid organisations such as Seva.

One of the most important cases for reproductive rights, argued by Kanun lawyers and a prominent instance in which the judgement explicitly used the language of reproductive rights in a court decision,[9] was that of Shanti Devi (*Laxmi Mandal & Ors* v. *Deen Dayal Hari Nager Hospital & Ors W.P.* (C) 8853/2008). Shanti Devi was a woman in labour who had been repeatedly denied access to emergency obstetric care and subsequently died after giving birth to her premature daughter on 20 January 2010. The Delhi High Court judgment for this case (delivered in June 2010) ruled in favour of the petitioners and the case drew global and national attention to the issue of reproductive rights in India. Ruling on a Public Interest Litigation (PIL) case filed by Kanun on the death of two pregnant women, Shanti Devi and Jaitun, as a result of being denied emergency and systematic obstetric care, the court decreed that obstetric and ante-natal care of women and their new-born infants constituted a *fundamental right* and its provision was the *responsibility of the State* (Madhok, Unnithan and Heitmeyer, 2014; Unnithan and Heitmeyer, 2015).

In declaring reproductive rights to be constitutionally guaranteed rights, the court made a historic decision given the lack of explicit legislative recognition of reproductive rights within Indian statutes. It chose, instead, to situate 'reproductive rights' within a broad interpretation of the constitutionally guaranteed right to life enshrined in the Indian Constitution (Article 21) as well as various international covenants on reproductive rights.[10] The judgement was historic as, following on from the Ramakant Rai case, 'reproductive rights' were cited as a right enunciated in the Indian Constitution (specifically Article 21 on the right to life) as well as international human rights covenants ratified by India (ibid., 12–19). Reproductive rights were referred to in terms of 'the right to reproductive health of the mother and the right to health of the infant child' (*Laxmi Mandal & Ors* v. *Deen Dayal Hari Nager Hospital & Ors W.P.(C)* 8853/2008, p. 12.)[11]

Here we see that it is litigation which has been the primary strategy in enacting social change and pressuring the state to take action, rather than mediation or family counselling. And like the interpretation of reproductive rights cases in more northern contexts, Kanun lawyers had focused on an instance in which the state had not, in the words of Corrêa and Petchesky (1994), fulfilled the *enabling conditions* for the realisation of reproductive rights for all women. A significant difference between the work of Kanun and organisations such as Seva and Salah is the focus on the state, rather than the family, as the primary duty-bearer responsible for the oppression as well as the protection of women.

Discussion

A focus on the rights and practices of legal aid CSOs above has shown that although these organisations all engage in exercises of translation and account-ability making, they do so in a diversity of ways, drawing on different combinations of indigenous, constitutional and transnational ideas of rights. As the feminist influenced legal activist work in India demonstrates, human rights as a transnational language need not always be experienced as hegemonic in the sense that other idioms of claim-making are displaced or rendered ineffective. But vernacular interpretations of human rights may not simply form additional 'layers' as Merry (2006, p. 220) suggests, but rather form meaningful discursive ensembles relevant to particular historically situated practices of rights in 'actual spaces that are law-like' (Goodale, 2007, p. 8). In their engagement with human rights in India, civil society members have had some success in reframing universal concepts of rights,[12] as is clear from the successful mobilisations to do with right to information (RTI, 1994–2005) and the prevention of domestic violence (PWDVA, 1992–2005). In both these instances rights activists have engaged in 'translating' *across* civil and political rights, *combining* basic economic and social rights.[13] This kind of mobilisation is important in considering the emerging discourse on the diverse ways in which rights over the body (individual and collective) are expressed and claimed.

Seva's politics of rights is one that foregrounds class rather than gender. Rights require not only clear articulation within legal structures but also new possibilities for opening up the ways in which rights claims can be realised by those who have little by way of social capital (Suneetha and Nagaraj, 2005). Seva members were acutely conscious of the poor economic conditions which their claimants came from but, in their emphasis on mediation which focused on preserving the sanctity of the family, women claimants were forced to find sanctuary in those very contexts which lay collective claim to their bodies and oppressed them in the first place. In returning women to the very depths of oppressive patriarchal household and family conditions, legal work by Seva could be seen as upholding the gender status quo.

Although women are ostensibly the focus of the domestic violence legislation central to Seva lawyers work on reproductive rights, ultimately there is no radical break from those very gender norms (symbolised by the power of duties and the process of mediation) that circumscribe the reproductive choice and bodily autonomy of the women they are seeking to empower. Feminist activists supporting Seva have been creative in reframing the law to recognise women's rights to marital residence, thereby gaining for them basic economic rights. But they have been unable to secure women's rights to bodily (and mental) safety rights and, indeed, have been critiqued for enhancing women's vulnerabilities by sending them back into close proximity with their aggressors (Agnes, 1999). As Madhok wrote in our joint article, 'while the discourse on violence allows for women's experiences of violation to be spoken for more easily than through a frame of reproductive rights',[14] it nevertheless 'installs women as victims', a frame which lends itself to victimising the very women the PWDV Act seeks to protect (Madhok, Unnithan and Heitmeyer, 2014, p. 1237). Feminist activists Agnes, Suneetha and Nagaraj similarly suggest that 'violence' is inadequate in capturing the kinds of battles women face in the household and family which are located in the wider networks of caste, kinship and the community of elders – and this requires relief beyond what the courts and police provide.

The practice and politics of rights of Kanun members appear much more gender radical in that reproductive rights are invoked in a denotative manner (i.e. specific human rights clauses are invoked (Goodale, 2007, p. 132; Wilson, 2007, p. 359). Their successful intervention for greater state accountability with regard to safeguarding against maternal mortality can be seen as an example of what Petchesky (2003) refers to as the 'gendering of health and human rights' where feminist activism has led to a radical shift in legal framing and a novel form of reproductive politics. In its framing of maternal mortality as a human rights issue, the explicit rights work of Kanun was able to address the larger issue of structural discrimination and violence. Framing maternal mortality as a human rights issue served to change the frame of reference from viewing it primarily as a failure of public health systems to exposing the structural questions of discrimination which have led to such high rates of mortality in the first place.

Kanun's work is an example of how a 'culture of rights' works, as Cowan *et al.* (2001, p. 14) suggest, both as a set of ideas and in the realm of practices. It is individualistic in conception, it addresses suffering through a legal rather than an ethical framework and it emphasises individual rights over duties and needs. Law is conceived as a structuring discourse and facts are socially constructed through legal conventions, rules of evidence and the rhetoric of legal actors. However, as Indian feminist scholarship suggests, while the rights framework used explicitly by Kanun confers subjecthood on persons, its realisation depends upon their ability to speak in its own terms' (Menon, 2004). Kanun recognises the individual rights of women but fails to recognise the inequitable context of the 'private' which denies women the ability to be that free choosing individual (Madhok in Madhok, Unnithan, Heitmeyer, 2014).

While Kanun, more than Seva, has held the state responsible for creating 'conditions of life in line with the modernist vision of the good and just society which emphasises autonomy, choice, equality, secularism, and protection of the body' (Merry, 2006, p. 220), Kanun rights work has had less resonance on the ground in terms of women's everyday lives and less traction with grassroots gender activism. The emphasis placed on litigation by Kanun, which brings the individual in direct relation with the state, is not one which addresses political and economic rights for women in the household as in the case of Seva.[15] But rather than viewing the different approaches adopted by the two organisations discussed in this chapter in a binary sense, with Kanun explicitly drawing on international human rights frameworks and Seva using the Indian constitutional and local frameworks, ethnographic work suggests that the legal aid processes in India are not mutually exclusive but, rather, speak to diverse modes of claims-making which together form a spectrum of legal reproductive rights work in the country.

190   *Making rights real*

As Menon suggests, the experience of feminist politics in the arena of law

> not only raises questions about the capacity of the law to act as a trans-
> formative instrument but more fundamentally points to the possibility that
> functioning in a manner compatible with legal discourse can radically
> refract the ethical and emancipatory impact of feminism itself.
>
> (Menon, 2004, p. 3)

Indeed, the question has been raised whether legally situated interventions can adequately empower women in the broader context of their struggles. The frame of social justice, as I argue in the next chapter, is important precisely as it enables an engagement with morality in a broader socio-cultural sense, and not only with rights in terms of the law (Bailey, 2011; Unnithan and Pigg, 2014).

Notes

1 The global health and human rights community which includes northern and southern feminist activists has especially driven this recasting of maternal mortality as a human rights issue (see WHO and UNFPA material on maternal mortality from 2008 onwards).
2 Some of the material in this chapter has appeared in other reports and papers, includ-ing those I have co-authored with members of the research team: Unnithan, Heitmeyer and Kacchawa (report 2010), Unnithan and Heitmeyer, 2014; Madhok, Unnithan and Heitmeyer, 2014; Heitmeyer and Unnithan, 2015.
3 I use the single quotation marks to signify that the term grassroots is used in a way which does not assume a disconnection from the global.
4 Correa, Petchesky and Parker, 2008, p. 152. A similar argument has been made about rights based development frameworks which have enabled the reframing of the meaning of 'participation' in health programmes (Cornwall and Nyamu Musembi, 2004; Cornwall and Welbourn, 2003; Unnithan and Heitmeyer, 2012).
5 These ideas have been discussed in greater detail in Unnithan 2001 and 2004 where I suggest that ideas of social obligation and experiences of spousal intimacy are important influences guiding women in their decision-making in childbearing and health-seeking.
6 Formulated between the eighth century BC and fifth century AD by diverse social thinkers, the *smritis* and commentaries set out a *dharma* or code of conduct (covering law, ethics and morality) which upheld a patriarchal family and focused on the social obligations and duties of caste, individuals and family members (Agnes, ibid.).
7 The term 'dalit' is a name adopted by more politicised members of the Scheduled Castes ('ex-untouchables').
8 I have kept the same pseudonyms as in previous joint publications but the analysis in this chapter and the next extends to periods beyond the joint fieldwork.
9 For example, as Kaur has noted, while the decision in the case of *State of Haryana* v. *Smt. Santra* (2000) was favourable to the petitioner for medical negligence during a sterilisation procedure, the judgement issued by the court was not based on the recognition of a violation of reproductive rights. Rather, the judgement was premised on the importance of population control given that 'in order that [the Indian nation may enter] into an era of prosperity, progress and complete self-dependence, it is necessary that population is arrested' (cited in Unnithan, Heitmeyer and Kachhawa, 2010, p. 60).

10 Here the Court was in line with a series of recent Supreme Court judgments to invoke international covenants, the most famous among them being *Vishakha* v. *State of Rajasthan* (1997) where CEDAW was used to lay down guidelines on sexual harassment at the workplace.
11 Specifically, the judgment cites the Universal Declaration of Human Rights, the International Covenant on Civil and Political Rights (ICCPR), the International Covenant on Economic, Social and Cultural Rights (ICESCR), the Convention on the Elimination of All Forms of Discrimination against Women (CEDAW), the Convention on the Rights of the Child (CRC) and General Comment No. 14 of 2000 by the Committee on Economic Social and Cultural Rights on the right to health under the ICESCR.
12 Than in, say, southern Africa (Wilson, 2001; Englund, 2006).
13 The success of the RTI activists (members of the Mazdoor Kisan Shakti Sangathan, MKSS) in central Rajasthan in ensuring that poor rural labourers received the minimum wages owed to them for their work on state organised drought relief works, (and that they received the essential commodities they were entitled to through the public distribution system) lay in resituating 'information' within the framework of rights guaranteed by the Indian constitution: from its juxtaposition with the right to freedom of expression, and locating it instead within the constituent provisions guaranteeing the right to life and livelihood (Jenkins and Goetz, 1999).
14 Scholars such as Bernal and Grewal, 2014; Spivak, 1999; and Menon, 2004 have noted the ease with which political mobilisations centred on women gather momentum and political support and the ways in which they fix upon third world women who require saving from political violence.
15 The majority of cases handled by the Reproductive Rights Unit are tracked down through the local media or fact-finding missions, this lies in contrast to Seva, whom women and families approach directly, or through referral from local women's groups and police stations (*thana*s) for women.

Bibliography

Agnes, F., 1999. *Law and Gender Inequality: The Politics of Women's Rights in India.* New Delhi: Oxford University Press
Bailey, A. Reconceiving Surrogacy: Toward a Reproductive Justice Account of Indian Surrogacy. *Hypatia* 26, no. 4 (2011): 715–41
Bernal, V. and Grewal, I., eds. 2014. *Theorising NGOs: States, Feminisms and Neoliberalism.* Durham: Duke University Press
Brown, W. 'The Most We Can Hope For …': Human Rights and the Politics of Fatalism. *The South Atlantic Quarterly* 103, no. 2/3 (2004): 451–63
Cornwall, A. and Molyneux, M., 2008. *The Politics of Rights: Dilemmas for Feminist Praxis.* Routledge: London
Cornwall, A. and Nyamu-Musembi, C. Putting the 'Rights-based Approach' to Development into Perspective, *Third World Quarterly* 25, no. 8 (2004): 1415–37
Cornwall, A. and Welbourn, A., 2003. Introduction. In *Realising Rights: Transforming Approaches to Sexual and Reproductive Well-being.* London and New York: Zed Books.
Corrêa, S. and Petchesky, R., 1994. Reproductive and sexual rights: a feminist perspective. In Sen, G., Germain, A. and Chen, L.C., eds. *Population policies reconsidered: health, empowerment, and rights.* Boston MA: Harvard University Press, 107–23. (Harvard Series on Population and International Health)
Correa, S., Petchesky, R. and Parker, R., 2008. *Sexuality, Health and Human Rights.* London and New York: Routledge

Cowan, J., 2009. Culture and Rights after Culture and Rights. In Goodale, M., ed. *Human Rights: an anthropological reader.* Wiley-Blackwell, 305–32

Cowan, J., Dembour, M. and Wilson, R., 2001. *Culture and Rights.* Cambridge University Press

Csordas, T., ed. 1994. *Embodiment and Experience: The existential ground of culture and self.* Cambridge University Press

Dave, N., 2012. *Queer Activism in India: A Story in the Anthropology of Ethics.* Durham: Duke University Press

Englund, H., 2006. *Prisoners of freedom: Human rights and the African poor.* Berkeley: University of California Press

Epp, C., 1998. *The Rights Revolution: Lawyers, Activists and Supreme Courts in Comparative Perspective.* University of Chicago Press

Ferguson, J., 1990. *The anti-politics machine: 'Development', depoliticization, and bureaucratic power in Lesotho.* Cambridge University Press

Goodale, M., 2007. Introduction: Locating rights, envisioning law between the global and the local. In Goodale, M. and Merry, S., eds., *The Practice of Human Rights: Tracking Law between the Global and the Local.* Cambridge University Press

Goodale, M., 2007. The power of right(s): tracking empires of law and new modes of social resistance in Bolivia (and elsewhere). In Goodale, M. and Merry, S., eds., 2007. *The Practice of Human Rights: Tracking Law between the Global and the Local.* Cambridge University Press

Goodale, M., 2009. Introduction: Anthropology and Human Rights. In Goodale, M. ed., *Human Rights: an anthropological reader.* Oxford: Wiley-Blackwell, 1–20

Goodale, M. and Merry, S., eds., 2007. *The Practice of Human Rights: Tracking Law between the Global and the Local.* Cambridge University Press

Heitmeyer, C. and Unnithan, M. Bodily rights and collective claims: the work of legal activists in interpreting reproductive and maternal rights in India. *Journal of the Royal Anthropological Institute* 21, no. 2 (2015): 374–91

Jaisingh, I. Lawyer's Collective. 1992. *Legal Aid Handbook. 1: Domestic Violence.* Delhi: Kali for Women

Jenkins, R. and Goetz, A.M. Accounts and accountability: theoretical implications of the right-to-information movement in India. *Third World Quarterly* 20, no. 3 (1999): 603–22

Joshi, A. and Houtzager, P. Widgets or Watchdogs? Conceptual explorations in social accountability. *Public Management Review* 14, no. 2 (2012): 145–62

Lim, S.S., Dandona, L., Hoisington, J.A., James, S.L., Hogan, M.C. and Gakidou, E. India's Janani Suraksha Yojana, a conditional cash transfer programme to increase births in health facilities: an impact evaluation. *The Lancet* 375, no. 9730 (2010): 2009–23

Madhok, S., 2009. Five Notions of Haq: gender rights and citizenship in north-western India. Working Paper Series, Gender Institute, London School of Economics.

Madhok, S., Unnithan, M. and Heitmeyer, C. On Reproductive Justice: 'Domestic Violence', Rights and the Law in India. *Culture, Health and Sexuality* 16, no. 10 (2014): 1231–44. http://dx.doi.org/10.1080/13691058.2

Mathur, K., 2004. *Countering gender violence: initiatives towards collective action in Rajasthan.* New Delhi: Sage

Menon, N., 2004. *Recovering Subversion: Feminist Politics Beyond the Law.* Springfield: University of Illinois Press

Menon, N. Sexuality, caste, governmentality: contests over 'gender' in India. *Feminist Review* 91, no. 1 (2009): 94–112

Merry, S., 2001. Changing Rights, Changing Culture. In Cowan, J., Dembour, M. and Wilson, R., 2001. *Culture and Rights*. Cambridge University Press, 31–55

Merry, S., 2006. *Human Rights and Gender Violence: Translating International Law into Local Justice*. University of Chicago Press

Merry, S., 2009. Legal Transplants and Cultural Translation: Making Human rights in the vernacular. In Goodale, M., ed. *Human Rights: an anthropological reader*. Wiley-Blackwell, 305–32

Merry, S.E. Measuring the World: Indicators. Human Rights and Global Governance. Current Anthropology 52, no. 52 (S3) (2011): 83–95

Morgan, L. Claiming Rosa Parks: conservative Catholic bids for 'rights' in contemporary Latin America. *Culture Health and Sexuality* 16, no. 10 (October–November 2014): 1245–58

MSSK, 2002. Mahila Suraksha Salah Kendra in-house publication

Ong, A. and Collier, S., 2005. *Global Assemblages: Technology, Politics and Ethics as Anthropological Problems*. Blackwell Publishing: Wiley-Blackwell

Petchesky, R., 2003. *Global Prescriptions: Gendering health and human rights*. New York: Zed

Povinelli, E., 2006. *The empire of love: toward a theory of intimacy, genealogy and carnality*. Durham and London: Duke University Press

Spivak, G. 1999. *A Critique of Postcolonial Reason*. Boston, MA: Harvard University Press.

Storeng, K., Behague, D. 'Guilty until proven innocent': The Contested Use of Maternal Mortality Indicators in Global Health'. *Critical Public Heath* 27, no. 2 (2017): 163–76

Suneetha, A. and Nagaraj, V. Adjudicating (Un)domestic Battles. *EPW* 40, no. 38 (17 September 2005): 4101–3

Tarantola, D., Unnithan, M., McGoey, L., Kuruvilla, S., Franz-Vasdeki, J. and Hunt, P., 2013. Emerging themes: the features of an enabling environment and the scarcity of research and evaluation. In Monograph. *Women and Children's Health: evidence of impact of Human Rights*. Geneva: WHO

Unnithan, M. and de Zordo, S. Re-situating abortion: Bio-politics, global health and rights in neo-liberal times. *Global Public Health* [Special Issue] 13, no. 6 (2018). https://doi.org/10.1080/17441692.2018.1445271

Unnithan, M., Dubuc, S. 2017. Reflections on the recent controversy around gender selective abortion in the UK. Published online in *Global Public Health*, at: www.tandfonline.com/doi/full/10.1080/17441692.2017.1346694 and in Unnithan, M. and S. de Zordo, Re-situating Abortion: Bio-politics, Global Health and Rights in Neo-liberal Times. *Global Public Health* 13, no. 6 (2013)

Unnithan, M. and Heitmeyer, C. Global Rights and State Activism: Reflections on Civil Society-State partnerships in Health in NW India. *Contributions to Indian Sociology* 46, no. 3 (2012): 283–30

Unnithan, M. and Heitmeyer, C. Challenges in 'translating' human rights: Perceptions and practices of civil society actors in Western India. *Development and Change* 45, no. 6 (2014): 1361–84

Unnithan, M. and Pigg, S.L., eds. Justice, Sexual and Reproductive Health Rights – Tracking the Relationship. *Special Symposium of the journal Culture, Health and Sexuality* 16, no. 10 (2014): 1181–8

Unnithan, M., Heitmeyer, C. and Kacchawa, P., 2010. *Thinking through rights-based development and health: institutional approaches to social inequality and gender violence in reproductive, maternal and sexual health*. Workshop Report. Jaipur: TTC Centre

Unnithan-Kumar, M., 1997. *Identity, Gender and Poverty: new perspectives on caste and tribe in Rajasthan.* Oxford: Berghahn

Unnithan-Kumar, M., 2001. Emotion, Agency and Access to Healthcare: women's experiences of reproduction in Jaipur. In S. Tremayne ed., *Managing Reproductive Life: Cross-cultural themes in fertility and sexuality.* Oxford series in Fertility, Reproduction and Sexuality, general editors: D. Parkin and S. Tremayne. Oxford: Berghahn, 27–51

Unnithan-Kumar, M., 2003. Reproduction, Heath, Rights: Connections and Disconnections. In Wilson, R. and Mitchell, J. eds., *Human Rights in Global Perspective.* London: Routledge

Unnithan-Kumar, M., 2004. Conception Technologies, Local Healers and Negotiations around Childbearing in Rajasthan. In M. Unnithan-Kumar ed., *Reproductive Agency, Medicine and the State.* Oxford: Berghahn, 59–82

Wilson, R., 2007. Tyrannosaurus Lex: The anthropology of human rights and transnational law. Goodale, M., and Merry, S. eds. *The Practice of Human Rights: Tracking law between the global and the local.* Cambridge: Cambridge University Press, 342–70

Wilson, R.A., 2001. *The Politics of Truth and Reconciliation in South Africa: Legitimizing the Post-Apartheid State.* Cambridge University Press

Yamin, A. and Lander, F. Implementing a Circle of Accountability: A Proposed Framework for Judiciaries and other Actors in Enforcing Health-Related Rights. *Journal of Human Rights*, 14, no. 3 (2015): 312–31

Žižek, S. 'Against Human Rights', *New Left Review* 34 (2005): 115–31

8 Re-imagining rights and the quest for reproductive justice

Rights (*adhikar*) have arrived but justice (*nyaya*) has not followed.
(Fieldwork respondent, Jaipur 2010)

In this book I have developed the notion of reproductive politics as being about gendered struggles over the reproductive body as a physical, social and discursive entity. I suggest that as a concept reproductive politics provides an analytic lens to understand the diffusion of global norms such as reproductive rights – how they circulate, get rooted and what they come to mean for the poor in their relation to the state and for how development is practised by state, professional and civil society actors. A key concern has been to analyse the implications that sexual reproductive health rights discourse has for development practice and equally for longer established indigenous reproductive claims-making processes. As a politically informed process based on both discourse and lived experience, the focus on fertility and reproduction in this book goes beyond an apolitical rendering of these topics within demographic and population literature (Zaidi and Morgan, 2017). In so doing I have attempted to provide critical insight into the ways in which citizenship is made meaningful in everyday contexts where social reproduction is negotiated at the intersection of family, community, and state and civil society interests and concerns.

In this concluding chapter of the book[1] I reflect on the overall complex meanings and interdependencies between sexual, reproductive and health rights that have emerged in the findings of the fieldwork. I draw on recent (predominantly feminist) scholarship on justice, including the moral basis of justice (Sen, 2009), to suggest new ways of imagining rights which capture on the ground complexities in an inclusive frame of reproductive justice. Following Ross among others, I see reproductive justice as primarily a framework about power which 'encompasses both reproductive health and rights but includes these in such a way as to advance gender, social and economic equality' (Madhok, Unnithan, Heitmeyer, 2013). I suggest that a more explicitly plural, justice-based approach as evidenced within recent legal aid mobilisation in India extends socio-legal analyses beyond ideas on the 'rights-revolution' as discussed by Epp (1998). Finally, in the Epilogue which follows on from this chapter I reflect on how current global policy discourse on reproductive health rights is engaged in designing methodologies which capture the complexities of plurality and power to evidence the impact of the lived experience of rights. Drawing on recent WHO work on evaluating the impact of evidence of rights-based health interventions on women and children's health (Bustreo, 2013), I consider the methodological opportunities and challenges that arise for researchers and policymakers of using lived experience to inform evidence on reproductive health rights.

As international organisations and national governments are working to promote a rights-based approach to health as a means of bringing about positive transformations in health outcomes,[2] and veer to adopt rights-based approaches in the face of unmet Millenium and Sustainable goals (MDG and SDG respectively), in the process they give rise to new languages, registers (of safety, risk and responsibility) and forms of subjectivity. As the observations in the preceding chapters demonstrate, there is a significant need to critically examine the unqualified application of human rights to health (Yamin, 2016). In the face of the Cairo consensus on reproductive health rights, where to invoke 'rights' is to redress the shortcomings of sexual and reproductive health policies, there has emerged a sense of the (limited) application of human rights-based frameworks in the face of entrenched unequal distributions of power and privilege in society.

Overall, the work in the book is written in the realisation that while rights-based protocols are themselves increasingly powerful instruments which promote and reinforce autonomy and self-determination of individuals, they are limited precisely in that they obscure other modes of being, belonging, connections, obligations and affiliations generated by overlapping collectivities (Hodgson, 2011, p. 11). The disconnect between bodily rights as imagined by the state in India and by individuals and community members whose accounts populate this book suggests a lack of commitment by policymakers to understand alternative imaginings, languages, ideas and practices of rights outside the framework of universal rights (although recent legal activism in India has moved some way against this tide as I discuss below). The notion that 'rights' are conceptualised as a *combination* of individual and collective desires and interests (as morally and contextually constituted) stands in contrast to the idea of the primacy of individual rights (and notions of self, based on this) which lie at the heart of universal notions of rights (UDHR, 1948).

Ethnographic studies of rights (Wilson and Mitchell, 2003; Wilson, 1997; Merry, 2006; Goodale and Merry, 2007; Cowan *et al.*, 2001; Unnithan-Kumar, 2003; Ram, 2013; and others) which have tracked 'local' responses, including to reproductive and sexual health rights, have importantly shown there to be a complex con(dis)junction between ideas of rights as lived, embodied, articulated and claimed, from more universal understandings of rights as they are situated within legal and international discourse and practice.[3] As we have seen in the various chapters of this book, critiques to the universal narrative of reproductive health rights emerge in the form of ground-up challenges wherein such rights are conceptualised differently. In Chapter 4, for example, it was clear that women's embrace of selective reproductive technologies and their preference for aborting girls was motivated by the combined interest of their own sense of entitlement (to status, dignity and economic security for themselves and their unborn daughters) and wider, familial and class-based expectations for a better social and economic future of the family following the birth of sons. The fact that many private local doctors supported this 'choice', ironically by drawing on the language of universal rights, also revealed the complex interplay of rights and 'choice' with market forces (in the access to reproductive technologies).

Human rights-based frameworks of health provision have, on the one hand, provided an alternative to market models in their treatment of citizens as rights-bearers rather than as consumers or users subject to market forces. Such frameworks for claiming health rights and entitlements have enabled new forms of citizen participation, referred to as biological and therapeutic citizenship, to emerge in many parts of the world (Petryna, 2002; Nguyen, 2005). When such opportunities have been created by those who are poor and marginalised themselves, often in conjunction with civil society groups, they have opened up 'new interfaces between marginalised people and the institutions that affect their lives' as Robins and von Lieres (2004, p. 576) describe for the rights-based, anti-apartheid strategies used by the Treatment Action Campaign (TAC) in South Africa. Such instances also emerge as sustained individual struggles with the state as Petryna suggests in her ethnography of those affected by the Chernobyl nuclear disaster in Soviet Russia. Both kinds of rights-based mobilisations have been undertaken in India, as described in this book.

But equally, as some human rights scholars and the ethnography in the book underscores, these very rights processes have also reinforced neo-liberal market tendencies, the maintenance of the status quo and suffering related to marginalisation (Biehl, 2007; Das, 2015). The JSY safe motherhood programme with cash incentives (Chapters 2 and 5) has engendered a sense of entitlement among women and their families but equally in its use of cash incentives has strengthened faith in market models of health and made rights measurable by cash.[4] The array of contraceptive options in India's family planning programme speaks simultaneously to the concept and language of rights as it does to the logic of the market as we saw with regard to the 'cafeteria' of contraceptive choices offered by the state in Chapter 2.

Wider structural inequalities which underpin poverty and economic exploitation are difficult to address through a rights paradigm which focuses on the individual alone. As Aggleton and Parker suggest with reference to sexual rights, the darker, oppressive and discriminating forms associated with rights have their origins in deeper structures of violence which necessitate wider struggles of justice (2010).[5] In linking reproductive rights and health to social justice, reproductive justice shifts the emphasis from individual choice talk to issues of systemic inequities (Bailey, 2011; Madhok, Unnithan and Heitmeyer, 2013), further explored below.[6]

Rights and justice: the (dis)connections

As human rights frameworks have come to influence health development policy, planning and programmes in India and globally, there is a strong sense among the women and men whose lives I document in this book that 'rights (*adhikar*) have arrived but justice (*nyaya*) has not followed' (quote from the fieldwork respondent appearing at the start of this chapter) . As documented in the preceding chapters, a swell of opinion has arisen from the ground up, challenging and interrogating the meanings, use and language of rights by those who are weak, poor, ill, politically vulnerable and marginal subjects before the law. The sentiment that rights have failed to deliver justice is also widespread among the health workers, activists and development actors in Rajasthan who have devoted their lives to promoting gender equality, reproductive sexual health and well-being as we saw in Chapters 2, 5 and 7. The disconnect between rights and justice finds resonance in the conceptual work of social scientists highly critical of the moralising, neo-colonial and neo-liberal tendencies implicit in international human rights frameworks (Brown, 2004; Zizek, 2005; for example). At the same time, it is important to note that, while important, the criticism of rights discourse in its general form does not fully account for what actually occurs when human rights frameworks become local social facts, embodied within people's experiences of health programmes and policies and in the everyday practices of development actors and local struggles for justice. These experiences underscore the need to closely examine not only what rights and justice have come to mean but how they are combined discursively and in practice when it comes to reproductive and sexual subjectivities, subjecthood and sexual and reproductive health.

Notions of justice, as we know, have underpinned and moved rights forward in terms of a global health policy agenda, of which the concept of Reproductive Health formulated at the Cairo International conference on Population and Development (ICPD) in 1994 is a dramatic example. However, the need for a more comprehensive understanding of how to theorise structural injustices which underlie women and men's sexual and reproductive lives is only now emerging.[7] Even among public health and legal scholars who regard the application of a human rights framework to health as key to redressing social injustices (Gruskin and Tarantola, 2008; Yamin, 2016) there is concern that such frameworks be made more contextually relevant and practiced. As Gruskin and Tarantola suggest, a human rights focus in public health puts the spotlight not only on who is disadvantaged and who is not but, importantly, on whether a disparity in health outcomes results from an injustice (2008, p. 140). These new frameworks for human rights draw the attention of public health planners and policymakers toward *process* as much as outcome, and to the workings of *power* (wherein human rights violations represent 'pathologies of power' in Farmer's sense (Farmer, 2005). The value that is added by such a human rights-based approach (HRBA) to health is, as Gruskin and Tarantola suggest, in *systematising* attention to the issues of availability, accessibility and acceptability of services, facilities and goods in terms of cultural and other forms of appropriateness, and providing medically sound services of the highest quality (the 3AQ approach to health facilities, goods, services and programmes (Bustreo *et al.*, 2013).

The HRBA framework provides a significant instrument with which to conceptualise and advance change in systems where inequality and injustice permeate, however, as the ethnography in the book suggests, it is not sufficient for enabling social transformation without a consideration of the different ways in which power, rights and justice are framed, evoked, embodied, practised and made meaningful on the ground. What kinds of accountability underlie gender-just transformation and how might these be better framed through inclusive and empathic understandings of the moral world of suffering as an everyday experience (Kleinman, 1995; Kleinman, Das and Lock, 1997). I have found it useful to approach such questions through understandings of justice in a broader sense. This is a sentiment I find echoed in Sen's understanding of justice where, as he suggests, 'the focus on actual lives has far-reaching implications for the nature and reach of the idea of justice' (Amartya Sen, *The Idea of Justice*, 2009, p. 3).

As a concept, the notion of justice is important as it takes us beyond the legal domain where rights are salient, to engage individuals and community in a moral sense (or in Sen's words, 'a sense of wrongdoing or clearly remedial injustice which moves us' (2009, p. viii).[8] Reproductive justice has similarly been distinguished from rights in its function as a 'moral indicator' (Bailey, 2011). The notion of reproductive justice, Bailey elaborates, cannot account for an independent moral theory until it accounts for why reproductive oppression is morally wrong or *how* reproductive goods and services *ought* to be fairly distributed (2011, p. 728); for example, in the case of surrogacy arrangements as discussed in Chapter 6.

Beyond rights, justice speaks truth to power in ways that pose a direct challenge to systemic reproductive and health inequalities (Farmer, 2005; Yamin, 2016). Reproductive justice, as Luna and Luker highlight, is predicated on notions of social justice which emphasise intersectional social identities as well as community development solutions to structural inequalities. As a concept it goes beyond a focus on marginalised populations because, as they suggest, 'examining the reproductive disciplining of some groups' experience also highlights the reproductive privileging of others' (Luna and Luker, 2013, p. 328, and in the preceding Chapters 3 and 6 on infertility and surrogacy respectively).

Drawing together empirical material from activists working in health in Tamil Nadu and women's accounts of spirit possession in the region, Ram (2013) suggests that in India the framework of social justice has come to *encompass* the discourse of rights, particularly in the area of health. Discourses of justice encompass discourses of rights, she argues, ultimately because experiences of injustice are more primordially related to certain features of human embodiment. Through sensory modes of perception and movement, our bodies affect a synthesis with the world around us, its people and its places. Any sharp break or rupture in that synthesis may be experienced in certain moods as injustice. Injustice, and its corollary the need for justice, are thus, Ram suggests, more basic to experience than rights. It also means discourses of justice will necessarily be more varied than those on rights since they emerge, she goes on to note, from very different kinds of human syntheses between body and world.

It is in the mobilisation of individuals and communities to create structural change that notions of justice emerge as moral indicators (Bailey, 2011). Activist and other kinds of political traditions are active ingredients in bringing about the kind of syntheses (between body and world) that Ram discusses, integrating past and present to constitute embodied notions of justice.[9] In the reframing of rights claims through narratives of securing justice, women and activists in Rajasthan develop expansive responses to legislation which are in tune with the varying conditions under which women experience a lack of power and entitlement. It is in such kinds of legal activist mobilisation for social justice, as I describe for Rajasthan below, that rights are being reimagined (and it is in the diverse voices of the actors engaged in such mobilisation that we are likely to see the emergence of a theory of justice which is people rather than institution focused, as Sen (2009) proposes).

Justice work among health activists is taking a distinctive turn in the form of legal activism around sexual and reproductive rights in India, engendering a stronger connection between the law and social movements than previously imagined in the work of Epp (1998), or Luna and Luker. This kind of justice work is distinct from the mobilisation around rights referred to in previous chapters, which occurred in the absence of any overarching legislative framework safeguarding rights against reproductive violations. There, the project team found progressive legal advocacy and feminist groups invoking specific clauses within existing laws, such as the right to residence in cases of domestic abuse to safeguard reproductive rights. Though creative, these stand-alone strategies have failed to address the structural injustices that underpin the recurring of reproductive violations (Madhok, Unnithan and Heitmeyer, 2013).

Mobilising for reproductive justice: legal activism, 'lawfare' and bodily integrity

> There has been a sea change in the language of the courts … we talk about bodily integrity and not about population control.
>
> (SB, Kanun, fieldwork notes, March 2018)

As the writing of this book comes to an end I make more trips to India (in August 2017 and March 2018) to meet with legal rights activists.[10] I am struck by the number of bills and petitions that have been through the courts involving gender and bodily rights over the past two years: on forced sterilisation, child marriage, the triple *talaq* (against the legitimacy of the annulment of marriage within Muslim personal law), dowry and rape (including the complex entanglement of marital rape and rape in child marriage) and by the increasing legal activism that has made these issues visible in the courts. On a revisit with CG of Kanun, he talks about how they have been experiencing 'a tsunami of rights legislation' over the past two years. I am especially struck by the increasingly activist social justice approach adopted by the Kanun lawyers compared to eight years ago.[11]

The Reproductive Rights Unit of Kanun has expanded over the past eight years to include a group of sixteen lawyers and ten social activists working across sixteen states. SB, who now heads the unit, recounts that over the past two to three years they have filed 688 petitions on reproductive health and rights issues alone. This works out to over 200 cases a year, which seems phenomenal to me. I query the extent to which these cases draw on the language of reproductive rights. SB suggests that the use is explicit, and a turning point in the legal invocation of reproductive rights language in the courts. According to her, there has been 'a sea change in the language of the courts ... we talk about bodily integrity and not about population control'. The language of bodily integrity deployed by SB and her team has been to argue cases of abortion rights, against forced sterilisation in health camps (the Bihar incident in 2012 brought forward by health activist Devika Biswas) and more recently against both marital rape and the anomaly of child marriage (with regard to the age of consent).

The other area of growth has been with regard to Public Interest Litigation (PIL) petitions where individuals can bring cases on behalf of others, which is a key trope through which the reproductive rights cases have been presented in courts. The rise of the PIL has been distinctive to the Indian Supreme court's efforts to democratise access to the courts, as Epp among others noted already in 1998. Developed in India in the years after the Emergency, the PIL lawsuits were actively encouraged by Chief Justice Bhagwati in the 1980s (Epp, 1998, p. 86). The PIL petition in 2013, argued by Kanun lawyers, related to forced sterilisation brought by health activist Devika Biswas against Bihar State for carrying out unlawful sterilisations on fifty-two women (*Devika Biswas* v. *Union of India and others, petition* no. 95). The sterilisations were carried out without any prior consent in unhygienic and unsafe conditions where women were operated upon on school tables (as opposed to in the hospital), under torchlight and without running water or sanitary gloves. On 14 September 2016, the Supreme Court upheld the charges brought by Biswas and found the state health department in violation of women's reproductive rights and right to health, the two key components of the right to life under the Indian Constitution (ESCR net case law database accessed 4/4/2018). Kanun lawyers played a major role in representing Biswas along with the support of health and human rights NGOs.[12] The significance of the Supreme Court ruling was that it made sterilisation carried out without consent by any state government unlawful and specifically linked the practice of sterilisation to processes which meet human rights standards.[13] The process was made easier, Kanun lawyers pointed out, as it followed on from a preceding case (*Ramakant Rai* v. *Union of India*) argued by them (and supported by NGOs Health Watch and Centre for Reproductive Rights) in 2007 against the violation of sterilisation procedures (as laid out in the Ministry of Health Guidelines of 1999).

The recent cases point to two main trends which suggest that rights work at a legal level in India is increasingly encompassed within a more expansive social justice approach. First, as described above, the cases were filed in terms of PILs which, as legal scholars such as Epp have noted, are primarily *social action* litigations filed in recognition of the rights of others unable to assert their own claims (Epp 1998, p. 87; my emphasis). Second, it was CSO members who provided the data from the field (having carried out their own investigations and fact finding) to support Kanun lawyers, pointing toward a broader social justice base as the starting point for the litigation itself. This imbrication of social justice action within the law has its roots not only in the legal response to the excesses of the Emergency (as legal scholars would argue) but, equally, in the justice consciousness inspired through feminist social campaigning from the 1990s around socio-economic rights in Rajasthan and elsewhere in India.

In his seminal work on legal activism in India, Charles Epp predicted a palpable, if weak, trend in terms of a 'rights revolution' in the Indian judiciary in the 1990s. In his examination of the role of lawyers, activists and supreme courts in the expansion of new constitutional rights in the US, Canada, India and Britain, Epp importantly notes that sustained judicial attention and approval for individual rights in these countries grew mainly from the pressure from below (legal activism) rather than leadership of the judiciary from above (1998, p. 2). His key argument is that in each country the growth of support structures for legal mobilisation democratised access to supreme courts during the period of the study (1960 to 1990) and provided a principal condition for the *judicial rights revolution* (my emphasis). The rights revolution, which he defines as a 'sustained developmental process that produced or expanded the *new* civil liberties and rights[14] ... was marked by a constitutional guarantee of individual rights, judicial independence, leadership from activist judges and a rise of rights consciousness in popular cultures' (1998, p. 7). Epp argues that such a revolutionary, democratised access to the Supreme Court was only possible through the widespread support for legal mobilisation and deliberate strategic organising by legal advocacy groups, lawyers and funding. While the greatest growth in sustained development of rights has been in the US and Canada, the weakest was in India, primarily due to the weak development of the support infrastructure for legal mobilisation.

India may not have had the necessary conditions for a rights revolution in the 1990s, but the insights from some of the recent 'tsunami' of cases undertaken by Kanun's reproductive rights unit, as indeed by other legal aid organisations elsewhere in India,[15] suggests legal aid organisations have grown both in strength and mobilisation capacity through their links with and support of civil society institutions. I suggest that this has facilitated a stronger and more sustained rights agenda in India than initially predicted by Epp. Much of this rights mobilisation is also more manifestly gender oriented.

Activists use of rights and the law as strategies to advance contested political goals have also been referred to as a form of 'lawfare'. While the use of law and litigation has been linked to the growth of neoliberalism (Comaroff, 2001;

Morgan, 2014), others working in the domain of sexual reproductive rights see in it a particularly useful ideological contestation against gender discrimination (Gloppen, forthcoming). According to Gloppen the concept of lawfare overlaps with legal mobilisation in the sense that both refer to civil society actors using intentional strategies that engage rights or legal institutions as part of a broader socio-political struggle. But, as she points out, not all forms of legal mobilisation constitute lawfare. Only if the legal mobilisation it forms part of is 'an ongoing, contentious struggle between organised social interests for (or against) social transformation and if litigation forms part of it' then the mobilisation constitutes lawfare (ibid.). In other words, litigation only becomes lawfare if it forms part of a broader strategy. Following Gloppen, I would suggest that what is emerging in the context of an increasingly strategic and expansive sexual and reproductive rights work undertaken by legal aid organisations in India is a form of gender and justice oriented lawfare. These mechanisms of lawfare will, hopefully, not just democratise access to the courts but will also make the attainment of justice more imaginable, where women are able to experience *nyaya milgaya* (the receipt of justice).

I want to conclude this section by returning to the notion of bodily integrity, alluded to earlier by SB, to suggest that with certain modifications this may be an important new trope to consider within emerging forms of sexual reproductive lawfare. I draw on a selection of legal and feminist literature on the subject (Neff, 1990; Miller, 2007; Fox and Thomson, 2017) to elaborate further on a gendered perspective to lawfare.

As Neff observes in her work on pregnancy terminations within American jurisprudence, US courts have, outside of the abortion debates, long recognised the central importance of a person's rights to bodily integrity. Defined as the right of every individual to the possession and control of his own person, free from restraint or interference of others (1990, p. 337), the right to bodily integrity, Neff suggests, has been recognised as a sacred, inviolable, inalienable and fundamental right. And yet, as a notion guaranteeing one's security or physical liberty, including from governmental violation, bodily integrity has not been applied by courts in their analysis of reproductive rights (at the time of her writing in the 1990s). Discussions on the subject with lawyers working on abortion rights in the UK have also suggested the same. Given this context, the allusion by Kanun lawyers to the use of bodily rights as a concept framing their reproductive rights court cases seems intriguing.

In the US, the court cases on abortion have instead relied on the right to privacy principle, Neff suggests; a concept which she argues lacks meaning in that it fails to reflect the *physical* reality of women's condition. The unique physical intrusion (and invasion of bodily boundaries) of an unwanted pregnancy on a woman (as recognised in the bodily integrity doctrine), Neff proposes, is not captured in the right to privacy which is socially based and about privacy in terms of the family, marriage and the doctor-patient relation. And further, she suggests that a focus on the principle of privacy establishes a barrier to viewing women's bodies in a holistic way, enabling the state to 'conceptually enter the (pregnant women's) body, seize control and establish an adversarial relation between her and her womb' (1990, p. 350). Neff's ideas resonate with the ways in which reproductive rights are imagined in indigenous discourse in Rajasthan as about rights to bear children (as we saw in Chapters 3 and 7 earlier, for example). It also raises the important issue, as seen in the debates at the intersection of universal and indigenous rights, of how women can have rights in and over their bodies if their wombs are 'owned' by others (the state, community, family).

The unqualified application of the concept of bodily integrity to reproductive autonomy has been challenged by feminist theorists. Miller (2007), for example, suggests that the rise of notions such as consent and the right to bodily integrity have led to a greater and more relentless regulation of women's bodies with the rise of rights paradigms (and juridically defined citizenship) in the late twentieth and early twenty-first centuries.[16] Instead, like Foucault and Agamben[17] she is interested in a biopolitical rather than juridical model of citizenship, and taking their position further, it is the womb that she sees as the setting for political subject formation.

Fox and Thomson (2017) also challenge the idea of 'traditional bodily integrity' as a core legal value because of its grounding within the physical basis of the body, which they suggest leads courts and legislators toward punitive sanctions. A focus on the physical also ignores the mental effects of such violations, reinforcing a mind/body dualism within legal discourse. Instead, they suggest the notion of 'embodied integrity' as a concept which brings together physical and mental aspects of bodies, which enables theorising from lived experience and incorporates an ontological perspective (in the sense of 'our bodies are who we are'). Through supplementing the notion of bodily integrity in this way they suggest it is possible to overcome 'the indeterminacy and cultural contingency as well as the gendered and racialised ways it (the traditional notion of bodily integrity) operates in practice' (2017, pp. 502, 515).

Their ideas have been developed through work on parental decisions to do with non-therapeutic interventions on children in the UK (and with regard to decisions on genital cutting in particular) showing how the use of bodily integrity, per se, in legal arguments opposing Female Genital Cutting (FGC) does not enable diverse positions to be heard and results in an 'unusually sweeping and punitive response' (2017, p. 507). The concept of bodily integrity is especially invoked in cases of FGC, but I would suggest that could hold equally for 'third world' women's sexual reproductive health rights violations, including those of maternal mortality (found in the discourse on human rights violations of international bodies such as the UN and WHO) where harm, violence and mutilation are foregrounded, effectively shutting down any other positions that may exist. It is in this sense that, as Fox and Thomson suggest, bodily integrity in its unqualified guise (based on a simplistic notion of ownership of the body) may not address the need for reproductive justice in the context in which legal aid organisations such as Kanun operate.

Overall, following the argument made in the lines above I suggest that until reproductive rights are revisioned legally, and in policy terms in a way that tackles the systemic injustices and the embodied power inequities accompanying sexual reproductive health violations, it is unlikely that reproductive justice will be achieved. This is particularly the case where the indivisibility of reproductive rights from other economic and social rights is not given due regard.

In conclusion

Drawing on ethnographic work of individual and community responses to rights-based maternal and reproductive health interventions presented in the preceding chapters, I suggest that the substitution of a biopolitics of population with a politics of individual rights and autonomy (as 'people-centred development') has been neither smooth nor seamless, complete or certain, as imagined. Institutional versions of reproduction, health and rights have been challenged in this book from the perspective of those who are infertile and unable to gain personhood (as we discussed in Chapter 3) and others who provide and choose to undertake sex selective abortion (Chapter 4). Equally significant have been the perspectives of health workers and activists (Chapters 5, 6 and 7), including legal aid organisations who have worked to promote and translate, but also challenge, the very institutional processes informing health and rights of which they are a part.

The notion of reproductive politics as developed in this book can be regarded as a connective tissue drawn across this broad spectrum of embodied and contested reproductive sites, spaces and experiences: social, physical, institutional and discursive. It can be described as a politics where ideas of 'reproductive health as about women as mothers' and 'reproductive rights as about childbearing' collide and endure alongside notions of 'individual bodily rights' and 'universal' rights-based approaches. In Rajasthan, it is the politics situated at the junction where familial obligation and expectation to produce children (often referred to as a woman's 'duty') *overrides* her 'right' *not* to undertake childbearing. In such a context, where childbearing is intrinsic to the construction of personhood of all women (in a structural sense) and their attainment of full adult social status as mothers and wives, the idea of *individual* choice is complex and difficult to isolate.

Assertions of universal rights to maternal, sexual reproductive health become mediated by civil society actors working from within these local, moral contexts. The activism centred on women's maternal subjectivity has produced intended and unintended material and discursive consequences. Situated within global flows of techniques, technologies and ideas of ethics and governance, civil society engagement with rights in India has been dynamic, creative and, whatever its limitations, has engendered a process of critical reflection on individual autonomy and self-actualisation as being neither gender nor context (historical and social) or even power neutral concepts in the times we live in.

In sum, the broad range of what constitutes human rights-based work (legal, medical, social, political) means it is necessary to move across a number of settings to reflect on how discrimination is built into state and non-state institutional structures and global systemic processes. I have found more recent forms of ethnographic method, such as ethnographies of globalisation with their focus on capturing flows of ideas and information across different discursive levels, pertinent to assembling human rights related evidence (especially Merry 2006, 2011), as I reflect on in the Epilogue. The new 'de-territorialised ethnography' which Merry undertakes in her study of gender violence and human rights is able to examine 'place-less phenomena in a place, small interstices in global processes where decisions are made, track global information flows and mark the points at which competing discourses intersect in the myriad links between global and local conceptions and institutions' (Merry, 2006, p. 29). Following her work, I have collected information on and examined the rights work of different groups of local and national legal activists working across domestic and international frameworks as they invoke a variety of legal instruments (universal human rights conventions; Indian constitutional law) to hold the state accountable (in cases of preventing maternal death; guaranteeing rights in the marital residence; and ensuring freedom from abuse of reproductive rights, for example).

Other methods, such as 'deliberative methods' originating within the political sciences, have also been of particular significance in gathering plural forms of data (Abelson, 2013). As Abelson suggests, these methods are more specifically focused on the element of deliberation (the act of considering different points of view and coming to a reasoned decision) in terms of problem solving, compared to other group and participatory methods. Deliberative methods represent an approach which enable individuals from different backgrounds, interests and values to 'listen, understand, potentially persuade and ultimately come to more reasoned, informed and public-spirited decisions' (2013, p. 609). As a collective means of involving the public and patients in decisions that affect them rather than existing participation methods, deliberative methods are emerging as practical aids for decision makers to tackle challenging public policy issues that require a range of evidentiary inputs. An example of this would be the *nari adalats* (women's courts) which emerged from earlier models of *nyay panchayat* (justice tribunals; Iyengar, 2007) as a means of directly accessing the voices of victims of caste and gender abuse. The strength of the *nari adalats*, which arose in the late 1980s as part of the Mahila Samkhya joint Government-NGO programme in Gujarat, was based on its knowledge of local practices, customs and social networks to gather evidence and negotiate agreements especially around cases of domestic violence. Informed, like the Women's Development Programme in Rajasthan, by perspectives within the Indian women's movement at the time (Unnithan and Srivastava, 1997), the courts focused on strengthening notions of self and building social relationships. This involved a contradictory approach of reconciliation with the violators in cases of domestic violence, which undermined the effectiveness of the law in redressing women's rights in the long run (Chapter 7).[18] Another more widespread practice was that of the *Jan Sunwai* (an RTI related public hearing in India) which is a deliberative process used by the state to gain evidence of the experience of rights to health, employment and information. The idea of conducting a *sunwai* (a public hearing) has since become a popular demand when an injustice is perceived to have taken place (see for example, Mathur, 2004). It is also an example of how contextually situated practices of justice help shape more global processes of rights.

Overall, this has been a journey of research from which I have learnt about other worlds and lives and of the exciting and frustrating processes of theorising reproductive politics from the ground up. I am left reflecting on how much more needs to be done in connecting everyday aspirations and imaginations of health, rights and justice with development practice.

Notes

1 Parts of this chapter draw on the special issue co-edited with S.L. Pigg on *Justice, Sexual and Reproductive Health Rights: Tracking the Relationship* (2014), a conference on global flows, human rights, sexual and reproductive health: ethnographies of institutional change in the south, held by the first author at the University of Sussex, UK, in July 2011 and a subsequent panel on 'Global flows, sexual and reproductive health and rights: ethnographies of crossing and 'translation' in the global South' which was organised by both the authors at the American Anthropological Association meeting in San Francisco in November 2012. The chapter also draws on published research with Madhok and Heitmeyer (2013) and on what constitutes evidence of human rights related interventions (Unnithan, 2015; Bustreo, 2013).

2 See UNFPA reports such as State of the World's population, Bustreo *et al.* (2013) monograph on evaluating the impact of rights, and the proposed bill on Universal Health coverage in India, for example.

3 Standing *et al.*, 2011; Aggleton and Parker, 2010; Correa, Petchesky and Parker, 2008; Pigg, 2005; Unnithan-Kumar, 2003; Cornwall and Wellbourne, 2001; Petchesky and Judd, 1998. Situating these concerns in the context of lived experience and in field based ethnography enables us to 'see' the social and cultural effects of work done in the name of human rights. As recent studies investigating sexual and reproductive health rights (SRHR) in terms of lived experience point out, such a perspective is important as it enables an identification of the bottlenecks in 'mainstreaming' rights-based programmes, and the gaps in the understanding of policymakers (especially see Standing *et al.*, 2011). Such works are important in taking rights beyond the abstract policy and legal formulations, but remain limited in that their focus is in operationalising rather than contesting the very frames of SRHR in the first place.

4 The fact that health is a commodity which you can buy (health commodification) is not a new idea as Nichter (2008) attributed to the pervasive market in tonics in India in the 1980s, which he described as India's 'tonic culture'.

5 As tropes, sex and sexuality, according to Aggleton and Parker (2010, p. 5), hold out the possibilities of both empowerment and destruction wherein 'so much of sex ties not to autonomy, reciprocity and mutuality but to the expression of power and control'.

6 The negative sides to the competition over rights emerge precisely around issues of power and control in ways in which, for example, new 'victims' are installed (e.g. through the prevention of domestic violence legislation, as we saw in Chapter 7), or how new kinds of responsibility are defined which are unjust, such as in increasing the care burdens of women already entrusted with major responsibilities in the household and family (as in South Africa; Macgregor and Mills, 2011), or in reinforcing long-standing essentialisms (as in the rights of 'indigenous' and minority groups including women, Morgan, 2014). The fact that sexual reproductive health rights only become articulated as part of a broader language of social (in)justice, rather than as

clearly defined rights in themselves, might also point to a particular 'culture' of rights articulation specific to southern countries (Cornwall and Nyamu-Musembi, 2004).

7 Bailey, 2011; Aggleton and Parker, 2010; Ross, 2009; Correa *et al.*, 2008; Yamin, 2016; Farmer, 2005.

8 The identification of a redressable injustice, according to Sen, stimulates reflection on the nature of justice/injustice and is central to a theory or 'reasoned scrutiny' of justice.

9 This is the result, she argues, of a much longer history going back to the interaction between colonialism and nationalism. She traces this history as an ongoing tradition that can be concretely and empirically tracked to demonstrate how a framework of social justice has transformed the invocation of rights in the area of health activism. Through ethnographic research she shows how a tradition such as this is both transmitted and renewed afresh by individuals, organisations and generations.

10 The trips are to carry out fieldwork with legal aid organisations on a new project on sexual and reproductive lawfare in India with colleagues Siri Gloppen and Alicia Yami. I thank Siri for facilitating the visit.

11 As a legal organisation involved with NGOs as well as individual petitioners, CG explains 'our advocacy work starts when we have a win in the courts. With each win we feel invigorated. We can influence (policy decisions) as we have a court order behind us.' He urges that more NGOs should have a legal wing.

12 Kanun had the support of the National Alliance for Maternal Mortality and Human Rights, Health Watch Forum and the Population Foundation of India; ESCR case law data base accessed on 4 April 2018.

13 The ruling firmly stated that sterilisation practices should be available, accessible, acceptable, of good quality and free from discrimination, violence, coercion and based on full, free and informed decision-making: www. ECSR-net.org (accessed on 4 April 2018).

14 The new rights that Epp refers to are those which emerged in the judicial interpretation of US constitutional law and statues in this century (1998, p. 7) and those which encompass rights such as the freedom of the exercise of religion, right of privacy, against discrimination, right to due process and women's rights.

15 Current fieldwork with legal aid organisations in Bangalore with colleagues Siri Gloppen and Alicia Yamin suggests a similar pattern of rights work and creative, alternative justice based language emerging to promote gendered sexual and reproductive rights.

16 According to Miller, the origins of reproductive legislation and rights lay in the nineteenth century fear of what she terms as 'race suicide' (the fear that declining birth rates would lead to the annihilation of emerging ethnically constituted political collective) legitimising strict controls over reproduction and a criminalisation of abortion.

17 Miller, 2007, p. 5

18 These have had very little traction on the ground despite keen interest in development and legal circles (Iyengar, 2007). The *sunwai* have been a more effective way of gathering evidence especially on gender-based violence (Mathur, 2004).

Bibliography

Abelson, J. (2013). Using qualitative research methods to inform health policy: the case of public deliberation. In Bourgeault, I., Dingwall, R. and de-Vries, R., eds. *Sage Handbook of Qualitative Methods in Health Research*. London: Sage, 608–21

Aggleton, P. and Parker, R., eds. 2010. Introduction. In *Routledge Handbook of Sexuality, Health and Rights*. London and New York: Routledge, 1–8

Bailey, A. Reconceiving Surrogacy: Toward a Reproductive Justice Account of Indian Surrogacy. *Hypatia* 26, no. 4 (2011): 715–41

Barry, C.A. The role of evidence in alternative medicine: Contrasting biomedical and anthropological approaches. *Social Science and Medicine* 62, no. 11 (2006): 2653

Biehl, J., 2007. *Will to live: AIDS therapies and the politics of survival.* Princeton University Press

Brown, W. 'The Most We Can Hope For …': Human Rights and the Politics of Fatalism. *The South Atlantic Quarterly* 103, no. 2/3 (2004): 451–63

Bustreo, F. and Hunt, P. *et al.*, 2013. Women and Children's Health: Evidence of Impact of Human Rights. Geneva: World Health Organisation. Accessed at: www.who.int/iris/bitstream/10665/84203/1/9789241505420_eng.pdf

Comaroff, J. Colonialism, Culture and the Law. *Law and Social Enquiry.* 26, no. 2 (2001): 305–14

Cornwall, A. and Nyamu-Musembi, C. Putting the 'Rights-based Approach' to Development into Perspective. *Third World Quarterly.* 25, no. 8 (2004): 1415–37

Cornwall, A. and Welbourn, A., 2001. Introduction. In Cornwall, A. and Welbourn, A., eds. *Realising Rights: Transforming Approaches to Sexual and Reproductive Well-Being.* London and New York: Zed Books, 1–20

Correa, S., Petchesky, R. and Parker, R., 2008. *Sexuality, Health and Human Rights.* London and New York: Routledge

Cowan, J., Dembour, M. and Wilson, R., 2001. *Culture and Rights.* Cambridge University Press

Das, V., 2015. *Affliction: Health, Disease and Poverty.* Fordham. NY: Fordham University Press

Dasgupta, J., 2014. *A Framework for applying human rights-based approaches to prevent maternal mortality and morbidity.* Lucknow: Sahayog

Epp, C., 1998. *The Rights Revolution: Lawyers, Activists and Supreme Courts in Comparative Perspective.* University of Chicago Press

ESCR case law database *Ramakant Rai* v. *Union of India WP* © no. 209 of 2003. International Network for Economic, Social and Cultural Rights. www.escr-net.org/caselaw database accessed on 11 April 2018

ESCR- Net. Case law data base. *Devika Biswas* v. *Union of India and others*, Petition no. 95 of 2012. International Network for Economic, Social and Cultural Rights. www.escr-net.org/caselaw (accessed on 11 April 2018)

Farmer, P., 1998. *Infections and Inequalities.* Berkeley: University of California Press

Farmer, P., 2005. *Pathologies of Power: Health, Human Rights and the New War on the Poor.* Berkeley: University of California Press

Fox, M. and Thomson, M. Bodily integrity, embodiment and the regulation of parental choice. *Journal of Law and Society* 44, no. 4 (2017): 501–31

Gloppen, S., forthcoming: Conceptualising lawfare: A typology and theoretical framework. In Gloppen, S. and Langford, M., eds. *International Sexual and Reproductive Rights Lawfare*

Goodale, M. and Merry, S., eds., 2007. *The Practice of Human Rights: Tracking Law between the Global and the Local.* Cambridge University Press

Gruskin, S. and Tarantola, D., 2008. Health and Human Rights: Overview. In Heggenhougen, K. and Quah, S., eds. *International Encyclopedia of Public Health* (Vol. 3) San Diego: Academic Press, 137–46

Hodgson, D.L., 2011. Introduction: Gender and Culture at the Limit of Rights. In *Gender and Culture at the Limit of Rights*. Philadelphia: University of Pennsylvania Press

Iyengar, S., 2007. *A Study of Nari Adalats (Women's Courts) and Caste Panchayats in Gujarat.* Report for UNDP: Gender mainstreaming in the Asia-Pacific region. Accessed on 8 December 2016. file://Nari%20adalat%20UNDP%20CaseStudy-05-India.pdf

Kleinman, A. 1995. *Writing at the Margin: Discourse between anthropology and medicine.* Berkeley: California University Press

Kleinman, A., Das, V. and Lock, M., eds. 1997. *Social Suffering.* Berkeley: University of California Press

Luna, Z. and Luker, K. Reproductive Justice. *Annual Review of Law and Social Sciences* 9 (2013): 327–52

Macgregor, H. and Mills, E., 2011. Framing rights and responsibilities: accounts of women with a history of AIDS activism. *BMC International Health and Human Rights* 11 (Suppl 3): S7.

Madhok, S., Unnithan, M. and Heitmeyer, C., 2013. On Reproductive Justice: 'Domestic Violence', Rights and the Law in India. *Culture, Health and Sexuality.* Accessed at http://dx.doi.org/10.1080/13691058.2

Marmot, M. The Social Determinants of Health. *The Lancet* 365, no. 9464 (2005): 1099–104

Mathur, K., 2004. *Countering gender violence: initiatives towards collective action in Rajasthan.* New Delhi: Sage

Merry, S. Measuring the World: Indicators, Human rights and Global governance. *Current Anthropology* 52, no. 3 (2011): 83–95

Merry, S.E., 2006. H*uman Rights and Gender Violence: Translating international law into local justice.* Chicago University Press

Miller, R., 2007. *The Limits of Bodily Integrity: Abortion, Adultery and Rape Legislation in Comparative Perspective.* Aldershot: Ashgate

Morgan, L. Claiming Rosa Parks: conservative Catholic bids for 'rights' in contemporary Latin America. In Culture, Health and Sexuality. Special Symposium. Sexual and reproductive health rights and justice – tracking the relationship. Guest Editors Unnithan, M. and Pigg, S.L. *Culture, Health and Sexuality* 16, no. 10: (2014): 1245–59

Neff, C. Woman, Womb and Bodily Integrity. *Yale Journal of Law and Feminism* 3, no. 2 (1990): 327–53. Accessed April 2018 at http//digitalcommons.law.edu

Nguyen, V.K., 2005. Antiretroviral globalism, biopolitics and therapeutic citizenship. In Ong, A. and Collier, S., eds. *Global Assemblages: Technology, Politics and Ethics as Anthropological Problems.* Malden: Blackwell Publishing

Nichter, M., 2008. *Global Health: why cultural perceptions, social representations, and biopolitics matter.* Tucson: University of Arizona Press

Ong, A. and Collier, S., eds. 2005. *Global Assemblages: Technology, Politics and Ethics as Anthropological Problems.* Malden: Blackwell Publishing

Petchesky, R. and Judd, K., eds. 1998. *Negotiating Reproductive Rights: Women's Perspectives across Countries and Cultures.* London and New York: Zed Books

Petryna, A., 2002. *Life Exposed: Biological Citizens After Chernobyl.* Princeton University Press

Pigg, S.L., 2005. Globalising the Facts of Life. In *Sex in Development: Science, Sexuality and Morality in Global Perspective.* Durham and London: Duke University Press, 39–66

Ram, K. Class and the clinic: the subject of medical pluralism and the transmission of inequality. *South Asian History and Culture* 1, no. 2 (2010): 199–213

Ram, K., 2013. *Fertile Disorder: Spirit Possession and its Provocation of the Modern.* Hawaii University Press

Ravindaran, T.K.S., 2009. *Equity in maternal health policies.* Presentation at Wellcome School of Bioethics, Mumbai, November.

Robins, S. and von Lieres, B. Remaking Citizenship, Unmaking Marginalisation: the Treatment Action Campaign in Post-Apartheid South Africa. *Canadian Journal of African Studies* 38, no. 3 (2004): 575–86

Ross, L. J., 2009. The Movement for Reproductive Justice. *Collective Voices* 4, no. 10: 8–9

Sen, A., 2009. *The Idea of Justice.* Harvard University Press

Standing, H, Oronje, R. and Hawkins, K., eds. Contextualising rights: the lived experience of sexual and reproductive health rights. *BMC International Health and Human Rights* 11, no. 3 (2009). Available at: www.biomedcentral.com/bmcinthealthhumrights/supplements/11/S3

Standing, H., Hawkins, K., Mills, E., Theobald, S. and Undie, C. Introduction: Contextualising Rights in Sexual Reproductive Health. *BMC International Health and Human Rights* 11, Suppl 3 (2011): S1

Tarantola, D., Unnithan, M. and McGoey, L., *et al.* 2013. Chapter 4. Emerging Themes: the features of an enabling environment and the scarcity of research and evaluation. In Bustreo, F., Hunt, P. *et al.*, *Women and Children's Health: Evidence of Impact of Human Rights* Geneva: World Health Organisation. Accessed at: www.who.int/iris/bitstream/10665/84203/1/9789241505420_eng.pdf

Unnithan-Kumar, M. and Srivastava, K., 1997. Gender Politics, Development and Women's Agency in Rajasthan. In: Grillo, R. and Stirrat, R. eds., *Discourses of Development: Anthropological Perspectives.* Oxford: Berg, 157–83

Unnithan, M. Learning from Infertility: gender, health inequities and faith healers in women's experiences of disrupted reproduction in Rajasthan. *South Asian History and Culture* 1, no. 2 (2010): 315–28

Unnithan-Kumar, M., 2001. Emotion, Agency and Access to Healthcare: women's experiences of reproduction in Jaipur. In Tremayne, S. ed., *Managing Reproductive Life: Cross-cultural themes in fertility and sexuality.* Oxford: Berghahn, 27–52

Unnithan-Kumar, M., 2003. Reproduction, Health, Rights: Connections and Disconnections. In Mitchell, J. and Wilson, R., eds. 2003. *Human Rights in Global Perspective: Anthropology of Rights, Claims and Entitlements.* London: Routledge, 183–209

van der Geest, S. and Finkler, K. Hospital Ethnography: Introduction. *Social Science and Medicine* 59, no. 10 (2004): 1995–2001

Vora, K.D., Mavalankar, D.V., Ramani, K.V., *et al.* Maternal Health Situation in India: A Case Study. *Journal of Health, Population and Nutrition* 27, no. 2 (2009): 184–201

Wilson, R. and Mitchell, J., eds. 2003. *Human Rights in Global Perspective: Anthropology of Rights, Claims and Entitlements.* London: Routledge

Wilson, R., ed. 1997. *Human Rights, Culture and Context: anthropological perspectives.* Chicago: Pluto Press

World Health Organization, 2007. *Task shifting to tackle health worker shortages.* Geneva: World Health Organization

Yamin, A. Will we take suffering seriously? Reflections on what applying a human rights framework to health means and why should we care. *Health and Human Rights* 10, no. 1 (2008): 45–63

Yamin, A., 2016. *Power, Suffering and the Struggle for Dignity: human rights frameworks for health and why they matter.* Philadelphia: University of Pennsylvania Press

Zaidi, B. and Morgan, S.P. The Second Demographic Transition Theory: A review and appraisal. *Annual Review of Sociology* 43 (2017): 473–92

Žižek, S. Against Human Rights. *New Left Review* 34, no. 34 (2005): 115–31

Epilogue
The politics of measurement and the meaning of evidence

In the emphasis on the discursive and lived experience of reproduction, health and rights in this book I depart from the more routine, standardised and statistical ways in which reproductive health is presented in public health discourse in India and globally. Instead, I take a more subjective and interpretive approach to include data on the diverse ways in which the people I met talked about, imagined, discussed, practised and evaluated sexual reproductive health and rights (SRHR) in Rajasthan.[1] In this closing section of the book I reflect on the value that a ground up perspective on SRHR issues has in a context where policy-making in development as well as in public health is turning more consciously toward human rights-based framings (Yamin and Boulanger, 2013; Fukuda-Parr, 2016). At the same time, however, maternal and reproductive health are being reconstituted through ever more narrowly defined indicators[2] and bases of evidence which have their own 'disciplining' effects (Foucault, 1976; Merry, 2011; Lock and Nguyen, 2010; Wendland, 2007; Lambert, 2006; Erikson, 2011; Adams, 2013).[3] Indicators themselves, such as the maternal mortality rates, gain authority beyond their remit when they are interpreted as measures not simply of the population level risk of maternal death but as indicators of health system functioning and an index of the progress toward the global development goals such as the Millennial and Sustainable Development Goals (Storeng and Behague, 2017, p. 163).[4] What are the implications for anthropological research of such a politics of measurement and evidence at the intersections of reproduction, health and rights?

The shift in global health from the 1990s, as Das (2015) notes, toward increasingly sophisticated statistical models and precise calculations which frame expert discourse on health has notably lacked a focus on health subjectivities. Framed as a 'new consensus on health as a global public good' it has erased the actual health circumstances and experiences of the poor and obscured the means of capturing 'the multiplicity of ways in which vital norms and social norms intersect in the lives of the poor' (Das, 2015, p. 185). It is to the question of how critical anthropological perspectives might enable current global sexual reproductive health policy to speak to the experiences of poor women and men, living in contexts of vulnerability, discrimination and uncertainty, and how these can be included in the framing of what counts as evidence that I offer the following reflections.[5]

Global policy and the lived experience of reproductive health and rights

Toward the end of my funded research on rights in 2012, I was invited to join a small steering group at the World Health Organisation (WHO) in Geneva working on the 'evidence of the beneficial impact of human rights-based approaches on women's and children's health'. The initiative had come from those working within the WHO unit on family, women and children's health, which was seeking to mainstream a human rights-based approach in global maternal and child health policy. I was invited to contribute to a section on methodology, based on my recent ethnographic research on reproductive and maternal health rights. I welcomed the opportunity to engage with policymakers to open out the discussion on reproductive health from the perspective of the women from the field area as well as other anthropological writing on the subject. Given that the causal forces driving human rights-based health outcomes were multiple and difficult to map in a conventional sense (of cause and effect), I hoped to challenge the existing global health framing of evidence.

As fieldwork on the lived experience of rights had shown, and as I have argued throughout the chapters in this book, human rights and reproductive rights are difficult to quantify, nor can they be addressed through the application of discrete legal instruments alone as we saw in Chapters 7 and 8. Being relational and lived, socially constituted, historically shaped and culturally made meaningful, reproductive rights require interpretive modes of analysis to be fully comprehended.

It was vital, given the abundance of the non-experimental forms of interpretive evidence that emerged from the field-research on rights, to ensure that health subjectivities and epistemological diversity were not erased in the WHO search for what was considered 'most robust' by the standards of evidence-based medicine or EBM (Lambert, 2006, 2013; Unnithan, 2015). In her study, Wendland, for example, demonstrates how by ignoring maternal subjectivities evidence-based obstetrics in the US has been increasingly used to justify the routinisation of caesarean sections even in those cases where there is no medical imperative for such an intervention (2007, p. 220). Similarly, ethnographic studies, which capture experiential knowledge through illness narratives, health worker biographies, accounts and mapping of health-seeking, birth histories and, in their more recent focus on institutional biographies hospital ethnography (van der Geest and Finkler, 2001; Zaman, 2005; Street, 2014; Livingston, 2012), are critical to building evidence for health planning and delivery from the ground up.

In the WHO meeting along with other social scientists[6] we made clear that the evidence of the impact of human rights-based interventions on health would require more than the standard, experimental paradigms of evaluation. An approach was needed which enabled plural epistemological interpretations of evidence and methodological diversity. A majority of the WHO steering committee members were open to recognising the plurality of approaches in determining *plausible* evidence of the impact of rights-based health interventions (WHO, 2013), even though plural forms of evidence, such as observational studies, lay people's perceptions and accounts, users or patients' individual narratives, collective assessments, and historical and ethnographic case studies are often perceived as less reliable (Adams, 2013; Wendland, 2007).[7] Plausibility was understood to result from assessing a range of sources of evidence which are non-random and context-determined (including in a historical and geographical sense; Tarantola, Unnithan and McGoey, 2013). As Kachur suggests, plausibility-related evidence is 'assembled from multiple additional indicators … to support the credible conclusion that the intervention was *delivered sufficiently* and could *reasonably* be interpreted to have caused or contributed to the observed impact' (Kachur 2011, p. 203, emphasis added; Unnithan, 2015, p. 48).

As a distinctive kind of qualitative approach (a point that needed emphasis in the WHO deliberations) ethnographic research which entailed the collection of evidence through personal and individual ways of knowing (rather than through standardisation and randomisation), and where knowledge is co-constructed in the interaction between the researcher and respondent,[8] was especially suited to the task of collecting plausible forms of evidence.[9] The fact that ethnographic research is 'partial' should be regarded as its strength rather than its weakness in evaluating the effects (positive and negative) of rights-based interventions. It is 'partial' in the sense that it recognises that knowledge created is subjective as well as situated and therefore only knowable in parts (Haraway, 1991) and evolved in a space where the researcher's emotions, intuitions, relations with others, bodily ways of knowing and self-reflection on these intersect with those of the respondent ('body-world relations'; Csordas, 2015, p. 50).

The resulting WHO monograph produced from the proceedings emphasised the importance of developing research using qualitative and ethnographic methods as a priority area for policymakers. The shift from a singular focus on *probable* (statistical, experimental) conclusions toward a *plausible* approach (Tarantola, Unnithan and McGoey, 2013) was a significant step given the continuing focus on probability as central to EBM.

Although I came away from the experience with the WHO feeling positive that a plausibility approach which gave due regard to context and the co-effects of multiple factors was deemed appropriate for evaluating human rights-based interventions, I was nevertheless concerned whether this was a sufficient intervention given the increasing power of human rights indicators to produce convenient forms of knowledge and as an instrument of global disciplining and governance. As Merry has so pertinently observed, indicators are not only 'rapidly multiplying as tools for assessing and promoting a variety of social justice and reform strategies around the world' but they also powerfully inspire (or discipline, in a Foucauldian sense) those who are measured to perform better (2011, p. 89). To stem the disciplinary power (of blame) associated with the practice of invoking indicators requires a shift away from a focus on numbers back to the person and relational experiences of receiving and delivering health care (as I argued in Chapter 5 on health care workers). A good example of the failure to apprehend the effects of power in the domain of health care delivery can be understood in relation to the notion of 'task shifting' (Cataldo and Kielman, 2015).

The concept of 'task shifting' has emerged as an important policy strategy in global health to maximise 'relations of care' at the same time as addressing health worker shortages through redistributing specialist knowledge and activities among health sector workers (WHO, 2008). The policy decision of the Indian State in its NRHM programme was to 'shift' the burden of care from the ANM to the ASHA health worker (Chapter 5) showing an unrealistic expectation from health planners that the ASHA would be able to manage maternal health care issues at the village level without due attention to her weak social status. As Cataldo and Kielman (2015) have observed with regard to 'task shifting' processes in HIV and Aids health work, the intrinsically hierarchic nature of social division in diverse, real life health systems and the impact of these on staff relations and patient provider interaction has challenged the success of the task shifting strategies and the quality of patient care provided.[10] The indignity of her marginal position (as poor and low skilled) experienced by the ASHA within government hospitals and within the very programmes set up to deliver women's health rights underlies the failure of her health rights-based work. It is precisely at such junctures of the struggle for respect, alongside the quest for better livelihoods and the freedom from illness and social suffering, that, as Farmer and Yamin note, the interrelationship between health, the (perpetuation of) structural violence and the (lack of) human rights become visible (Farmer, 2005; Yamin, 2008).[11] Caste and class discrimination of women and female health workers continues to permeate healthcare settings not only in Rajasthan but equally in other states such as Uttar Pradesh (Dasgupta, 2011; Jeffery and Jeffery, 2010). Even in Tamil Nadu, the Indian state with the best maternal health indicators poor women, as Ram has documented in her ethnographic work in Tamil Nadu, continue to be mistreated, abused, given less quality time, attention and medication, and rendered 'bioavailable' for state family planning programmes (Ram, 2010).

Civil society and feminist health and legal scholar activists in India continue to work at these critical junctures of structural violence and individual suffering. Their diverse engagement with rights-based development ideas and practices as I show in this book, contribute to understanding how CSOs operate within global fields of power, progressing but also re-framing gender-just development on the ground. While bringing human rights paradigms within development thinking and practice has created a new class and culture of CSO rights appropriation, it has also brought in much more recognition of the values of respect and dignity in a formal, legal sense (Fredman, 2018) for those who are subjects of state fertility interventions. It has also shown me how transnational feminist activism, to which southern feminists in India have powerfully contributed, has pioneered paradigms of substantive gender equality[12] from the 1990s onwards, which are only now being acknowledged in the worlds of health policy. As these early advocates suggest, while human rights paradigms may enhance accountability within development practice we cannot as yet assume they will produce the empathy and passion required for gender-just transformation.

Moving on: taking the 'body-person' into account

As we learn in the context of non-biomedical therapeutic interventions in the chapter on infertility in this book, what counts as evidence of good healing practice on the ground is not only relief from physical symptoms but a sense of gaining relief from stigma, and of ways in which the body-self connection and social and individual identity is often reconstituted through the therapy.[13] Local healers are considered efficacious, as emerged in the research relating to infertility in Rajasthan, because they are perceived to be able to alleviate conditions of 'social death' or stigma associated with the disruption of social relations and the ruptured moral sense of self that accompanies infertility (Chapter 3 and Unnithan, 2010). Local healers deliver care that is embodied, taking the body-person into account in the sense that healing is framed in terms of a contextual understanding of the body as a lived entity, constituted intersubjectively (as the 'mindful' body; following the use of the term by Scheper-Hughes and Lock, 1987 and Csordas, 1994. Healthcare provision in Rajasthan, we have learned, is evaluated by users in the context of *previous* bodily experiences of healthcare. The experience for rural and poor women targeted by the state's family planning programmes in the 1980s was one of overwhelming coercion, where women were forcibly sterilised. This was followed in the 1990s by the rights-based contraceptive 'choice', the 'cafeteria' approach where a variety of options such as pills, condoms and intrauterine devices were provided (Chapter 2). Ironically, as we saw in Chapters 2 and 5, despite the cafeteria of contraceptive choices sterilisation has remained the preferred method of contraception. The insidious dominance of the fertility control approach, especially works against those couples who wish for services redressing infertility (and the continuing neglect of widespread reproductive tract infections which underlie secondary sterility).

The picture of contraceptive 'behaviour' is becoming more complex in the younger generation. Zahida informs me, as I complete this book, that younger Muslim couples in her community, including her four married sons and daughter, all now use the Mala-D *goli* (contraceptive pill) as they only want two children.

> It is Rs5/- per strip. Although the Saheli *goli* is better as you have to take it only once a week, it is more expensive. The Nirodh (condom) may be used but no one is going in for the Copper T (intra-uterine device) anymore.

I ask whether this is accompanied by a stated gender preference to which she answers, 'everyone is getting an ultrasound scan to have at least one boy; even when the whole procedure takes Rs10–15 lakhs'. Zahida continues, 'Once you have conceived (*baccha lag gaya*) and if you don't want a child you can get a goli from Maulana for around Rs500/-, which has much more force and will clear it.' She warns that it is a process fraught with danger (*khatra*), 'Chand bibi's daughter who took this recently bled so much she nearly died. They ended up removing her *bacchadani* (uterus) and she survived.' Zahida's account reinforces the observations made in Chapter 4 on the 'routinisation' of sex selective abortion and the negligible effects of the state policy to do with the criminalisation of sex selective abortion. But it is worth noting that such fertility behaviour is not necessarily universal across all families and communities. According to Vimlesh,

> At the time of the pregnancy with Anjali (her youngest granddaughter who is eighteen months), there was talk of *safai* (literally cleaning; abortion) but we did not get it done. No, we did not know the baby was a girl – we decided to have it. Whatever the sex, *safai* is a *paap* (sin), especially at two to three months.

Over the twenty years since I started this work, which has spanned the period of the Millennial Development Goals and into the era of the Sustainable Development Goals (2005 to 2015 and 2015 to 2030 respectively) there have been great shifts in thinking about childbearing, which reflect the complex intersection of a globalisation of human rights paradigms[14] with situated reproductive politics. Tracking the journey of ideas and meanings of reproductive rights through diverse fields of power and through the experiences of differently located people and groups within these fields has provided an invaluable lens on the social, cultural, material and political transformation in this part of India.

As this book goes to press, I ask my close collaborators what the future looks like for them. Zahida assures me she will continue to live in the peri-urban 'village' where I first met her. It is a context which has experienced rapid urbanisation and is now part of the city 'proper'. Members of her community have sold their land to housing associations and their farms have given way to tower block apartments and offices. Zahida and the women and men of her age have all left behind the worries of financial insecurity. Yet her four sons have not landed good jobs and Sharaz whose birth I documented in 2001 (the baby that fitted in Zahida's hand; Unnithan-Kumar, 2001) and who is thirty-four years old now is intermittently working as a *beldar* (daily wage labour). Vimlesh, on the other hand, tells me proudly that her son Sundar will be completing his twelfth class soon (there is large age gap between his birth nineteen years ago and that of his sister Sunila (one of the twins), aged thirty, whose eldest son is now aged nine). Sundar is doing well at school and Vimlesh is hopeful he will go to college, study computing, get married and get a job in Jaipur city. Her own plans are to return to her husband's village near Deoli 'in the next ten years or so when I cannot work anymore'. They have built two rooms there, taking loans (*kurza*), but farming will be sporadic because there is no water. She will be close to her daughter Sunila who now has three children and helps her husband with farming (even though I know she had done well at school). After the birth of Anjali, which took place in the private village hospital, they received money along with free drugs and vaccinations worth up to Rs7,000/-. This money has been deposited in the bank for Anjali's education, and for her marriage.

Notes

1 I do not suggest that numerical and quantitative data collection is not of use but rather how this can be framed by qualitative insights.

2 See for example interesting discussion on the 'narrowing down' of MDG 5 to maternal health (Yamin and Boulanger, 2013).

3 As these authors note, the overwhelming propensity for interventions to be 'evidence-based' is driven by the notion that the best medical decisions are informed by results of randomised controlled trials and other forms of statistical data, which in turn obscures the value of qualitative data. Lock and Nguyen demonstrate how it is through assigning a probability value that the uncertainty presented by chance factors comes to be controlled enabling Random Control Trials or RCTs to be rigorous (2010, p. 183).

4 Charting the growth of maternal mortality as a powerful global development indicator, Storeng and Behague suggest that such measures are produced primarily to secure political attention in an increasingly competitive policy space, beyond the need for data driven by grant-giving and receiving bodies to procure and sustain funding (and where the production of figures justify investment flows; 2017, p. 165).

5 Following Lambert (2006), it is also worth keeping in mind the ends which the data on evidence serves, making for a distinction between an *evidence for* (use in clinical interventions) versus an *evidence of* the impact of rights.

6 The committee of ten people was made up of a sociologist, an anthropologist and human rights experts including lawyers, civil servants and public health specialists.

7 A common critique of experientially informed data is that it is dependent on reliability of the informants. Cognisant of the fact that some respondents are likely to be more reliable than others and some more willing to share their experience compared to others, ethnographers talk to a whole range of people across class, gender and sexual orientation, age groups, political affiliation and regional and religious groups to capture the required information in a systematic, triaged way. In addition, time-based variations are accounted for through the observation of processes such as life-course events and ritual, which are occasions when the social aspects of rights become materially tangible.

8 Unlike other qualitative approaches, ethnographic research generates information on meaning and intention as well as with regard to practice, recognising that there can be a difference between what people say or think they ought to do, and what they actually do, or think they do.

9 Rather than the production of an overarching singular form of evidence, the premise is that a different piece of evidence is produced each time (Barry, 2006).

10 Especially in the context of HIV care, formal task shifting initiatives have seen the delegation of testing and counselling services to lay health workers and ART services to nurses, as well as in the move to enable PLWHA 'expert patients' to undertake clinic-based tasks in homes (Cataldo, Kielman and Kielman, 2015).

11 As Farmer's political economy perspective on health suggests, that it is the poor who are most likely to bear the burden of illness, poverty predisposes the poor to fall ill (as he observed in his work on the social patterns through which HIV and Aids spread in Haiti in the late 1980s and 1990s). This systemic, social and economic propensity, which leads certain people to fall ill compared to others, is what he terms 'structural violence' (Farmer 2005, p. 198). Farmer's work is important as it focuses on the pervasive, structural nature of health abuses. In this perspective, health issues, rather than viewed as separate from rights, are in fact inextricably intertwined with rights conceived as social and economic rights (Farmer, 2005, p. 217).

12 Fredman, 2018.

13 Non-biomedical systems of healing evoke a relational sense of context in their premise that the remedial therapeutic effect resides 'inside an energetic system that

comprises the patient, the remedy, the healer and the setting' (Barry, 2006, p. 2647; Unnithan, 2015).

14 The relevance of human rights as going beyond economic interests is envisioned in the case of the SDGs as suggested by Fukuda-Parr, 2016 for example.

Bibliography

Adams, V. 2013. Evidence-based global health: Subjects, profits, erasures. In Biehl, J., and Petryna, A. eds. *When People come first: Critical studies in global health.* Princeton University Press, 54–90

Barry, C.A. The role of evidence in alternative medicine: Contrasting biomedical and anthropological approaches. *Social Science and Medicine* 62 (2006): 2653

Cataldo, F., Kielmann, K., Kielmann, T. *et al.* Deep down in their heart they wish they could be given some incentives: a qualitative study on the changing roles and relations of care among home-based caregivers in Zambia. *BMC Health Services Research* 15, no. 36 (2015): 1–10

Csordas, T., 2015. Toward a Cultural Phenomenology of Body-World Relations. In Ram, K. and Houston, C., eds. *Phenomenology in Anthropology: A Sense of Perspective.* Bloomington: Indiana University Press, 50–67

Csordas, T., ed. 1994. *Embodiment and Experience: The existential ground of culture and self.* Cambridge University Press

Das, V., 2015. *Affliction: Health, Disease and Poverty.* New York: Fordham University Press

Erikson, S. 2011 Global Ethnography: Problems of Theory and Method, Browner, C. and Sargeant, C. eds, *Reproduction*

Farmer, P., 2005. *Pathologies of Power: Health, Human Rights and the New War on the Poor.* Berkeley: University of California Press

Dasgupta, J. Ten years of negotiating rights round maternal health in Uttar Pradesh, India. BMC International Health and Human Rights 2011: Suppl 3, S4 https://doi.org/10.1186/1472-698X-11-S3-S4

Foucault, M., 1976. *History of Sexuality.* Paris: Hachette

Fredman, S. 2018. Working Together: Human Rights, Sustainable Development Goals and Gender Equality. Report of the British Academy, November 2018, 1–49

Fukuda-Parr, S. From the MDG to the SDG: shifts in purpose, concept and politics of global goal setting for development. In *Gender and Development* 24, no. 1 (2016): 43–52

Haraway, D., 1991. *Simian, Cyborgs and Women: The reinvention of nature.* London: Routledge

Iyengar, S., Iyengar K. and Gupta, V. Maternal Health: A Case Study of Rajasthan. *Journal of Health, Population and Nutrition* 27, no. 2 (2009): 271–92

Jeffery, P., and Jeffery, R., 2010.Only when the boat has started sinking: a maternal death in rural north India. *Social Science and Medicine* 71 (2010): 1711–18

Kachur, P. 2011. The plausibility design, quasi-experiments and real-world research: a case study of anti-malarial combination treatment in Tanzania. In W. Geissler and C. Molyneux eds. *Evidence, ethos and experiment.* Oxford: Berghahn, 203

Lambert, H. Accounting for EBM: Notions of evidence in medicine. *Social Science and Medicine* 62, no. 11 (2006): 2633–45

Lambert, H. Plural forms of evidence in public health: tolerating epistemological and methodological diversity. *Evidence and Policy* 9, no. 1 (2013): 43–8

Lock, M. and Nguyen, V-K., 2010. *An Anthropology of Biomedicine.* Hoboken NJ: Wiley-Blackwell

Merry, S. Measuring the World: Indicators, Human rights and Global governance. *Current Anthropology* 52, no. 3 (2011): 83–95

Ram, K. Class and the clinic: the subject of medical pluralism and the transmission of inequality. *South Asian History and Culture* 1, no. 2 (2010): 199–213

Scheper-Hughes, N. and Lock, M. The Mindful Body: A prolegomenon to future work in medical anthropology. *Medical Anthropology Quarterly* 1, no. 1 (1987): 6–41

Storeng, K. and Behague, D. 'Guilty until proven innocent': the contested use of maternal mortality indicators in global health. *Critical Public Health* 27, no. 2 (2017): 163–76

Street, A., 2014. *Biomedicine in an unstable place: infrastructure and personhood in a Papua New Guinean Hospital.* London and Durham: Duke University Press

Tarantola, D., Unnithan, M. and McGoey, L., *et al.* 2013. Chapter 4. Emerging Themes: the features of an enabling environment and the scarcity of research and evaluation. In Bustreo, F. *et al.*, *Women and Children's Health: Evidence of Impact of Human Rights.* Geneva: World Health Organisation. Accessed at: www.who.int/iris/bitstream/10665/84203/1/9789241505420_eng.pdf

Unnithan, M., 2010. Learning from Infertility: Gender, Health Inequities and Faith Healers in Women's Experiences of Disrupted Reproduction in Rajasthan. In Doron, A. and Broom, A., eds. *South Asian History and Culture, Special Issue on Health, Culture and Religion: Critical Perspectives.* London: Routledge, 315–28

Unnithan, M. What Constitutes Evidence in Human Rights Based Approaches to Health?: Learning from lived experiences of maternal and sexual reproductive health. *Harvard Journal of Health and Human Rights* 17, no. 2 (2015): 45–57

Unnithan-Kumar, M. 2001. Emotion, Agency and Access to Healthcare: women's experiences of reproduction in Jaipur, in S. Tremayne ed., *Managing Reproductive Life: Cross-cultural themes in fertility and sexuality.* Oxford series in Fertility, Reproduction and Sexuality, general editors: D. Parkin and S. Tremayne. Oxford: Berghahn

Unnithan-Kumar, M. 2003. Reproduction, Health, Rights: Connections and Disconnections, In, J. Mitchell and R. Wilson eds., Human Rights in Global Perspective: Anthropology of Rights, Claims and Entitlements, London: Routledge ASA series, 183–209

van der Geest, S. and Finkler, K. Hospital Ethnography: Introduction. *Social Science and Medicine* 59, no. 10 (2004): 1995–2001

Wendland, C. The Vanishing Mother: Cesarian section and 'Evidence-based Obstetrics'. *Medical Anthropology Quarterly* 21, no. 2 (2007): 218–33

World Health Organization. 2008. *Task Shifting: Global recommendations and guidelines.* www.who.int/workforcealliance/knowledge/resources/taskshifting_guidelines/en/

World Health Organisation. 2013. *Women and Children's Health: Evidence of Impact of Human Rights.* Geneva. Accessed at: www.who.int/iris/bitstream/10665/84203/1/9789241505420_eng.pdf

Yamin, A. Will we take suffering seriously? Reflections on what applying a human rights framework to health means and why should we care. *Health and Human Rights* 10, no. 1 (2008): 45–63

Yamin, A., and Boulanger, V., 2013. From Transforming Power to Counting Numbers: The evolution of sexual reproductive health and rights in development and where want to go from here. Harvard School of Public Health: *Working Paper series.*

Zaman, S. 2005. *Broken Limbs, Broken Lives: Ethnography of a Hospital Ward in Bangladesh.* Netherlands: Het Spinhuis

Glossary

adhikar	right(s)
admi	husband
admi ka paani	semen (literally, 'water of the man')
ajaan	blessing of Allah; bestowed in the ear of newly born babies
aouth	family-based healer (Hindu)
angrezi dawai	Biomedicine (literally, 'english medicine')
bachha-dani	womb/uterus (literally, 'baby vessel/basket')
bachha girna	miscarriage (literally, 'baby dropped')
bachha girana	abortion (literally, 'dropping the baby')
bachha kadna	induced abortion (literally, 'removing the baby')
bandh nalli	tied/blocked (fallopian) tubes
banjhpan	infertility
banjhdi	infertile woman
balika janmotsav	celebration on birth of girls
bhanghi	untouchable caste
bhav aana	feeling possessed
bharna	type of healing – feeling the body being 'filled'
bhroon/jeev hatya	abortion (literally, 'killing of the foetus/life')
bori	jute sac
bua-sas	sister(s)-in-law
charpai	rope bed
cheera	incision
chukker	dizziness
daan	gift
dahej	dowry
dai	midwife
dakan	jealous women to whom infant deaths are sometimes attributed
dard	pain
dard vali sui	injection of the pain of labour; oxytocin
dayabhaga	form of property inheritance
dharma/farz	duty (in Hindi/Urdu, as in kinship and relational obligations)

grahak	patient/client
hawa	spirit (literally, 'wind' which causes illness)
hawa ka jor	the force of the wind
himmat rakh	keep courage
huq	right (entitlement)
ilaj	treatment
jaanch	diagnosis
japa	birth
japa ghar	delivery hut
jati pramaan patra	caste registration documents
jhada	type of healing (literally, 'sweeping')
kacchi basti	informal settlement
kanya dan	ritual gift, dowry (literally, gift of the daughter)
kapda-latta	menstruation (literally, 'the cloth')
keda jaapa	difficult birth
khoon	blood
khoon ki kami	a lack of blood
khushi hona	sexual intercourse (literally, 'being happy)
kumzori	feeling of physical/bodily weakness
mahawari	menstruation (monthly flow)
mai-baap	parental benefaction (literally, 'mother-father')
mama	mother's brother
manav adhikar	human rights
mata mai	female faith healer (Hindu)
mausi	mother's sister
mazdoori	labour; work
milna	sexual intercourse (literally, 'to meet')
mitakshara	form of property inheritance
nai	barber caste; performing circumcision for Hindus and Muslims
nahaana	sexual intercourse (literally, 'bathing')
nala	umbilical cord
nalli	tube/fallopian tube
nazar	gaze (ill-intentioned 'evil eye')
olnal	placenta
oonpar ki hawa	divine force (literally, 'ill wind from above')
paap	sin/wrongdoing
pahchan patra	identity card
pair padna	menstruation (literally, blood 'falling on the feet')
pakad	force (literally, 'hold' e.g. of a healer)
panchayat	village-based council
pareshani	suffering
prajanani adhikar	reproductive rights (literally, 'the right to bear children')
safai	cleansing of the uterus ('miscarriage')
safed pani	vaginal discharge

sakti	sacred female power
saman	material goods (as in dowry)
sambhalne-vale	those who care for you; social networks
sathu behna	divine beings (literally, 'seven sisters')
seva	service
shareer nikalna	prolapse of the uterus (literally, the 'body out')
soochna ka adhikar	right to information
swasthya adhikar	health rights
syyed	family-based healer (Muslim)
ulta	'reverse', breech (position of foetus)
ulti	nausea/vomiting
vrat	fasting (denial of food)

Index

Taylor & Francis Group
an **informa** business

Taylor & Francis eBooks

www.taylorfrancis.com

A single destination for eBooks from Taylor & Francis
with increased functionality and an improved user
experience to meet the needs of our customers.

90,000+ eBooks of award-winning academic content in
Humanities, Social Science, Science, Technology, Engineering,
and Medical written by a global network of editors and authors.

TAYLOR & FRANCIS EBOOKS OFFERS:

A streamlined
experience for
our library
customers

A single point
of discovery
for all of our
eBook content

Improved
search and
discovery of
content at both
book and
chapter level

REQUEST A FREE TRIAL
support@taylorfrancis.com

Routledge
Taylor & Francis Group

CRC Press
Taylor & Francis Group